THE FUNDAMENTALS OF POLITICAL SCIENCE RESEARCH
THIRD EDITION

This third edition of the best-selling *The Fundamentals of Political Science Research* provides an introduction to the scientific study of politics. It offers the basic tools necessary for readers to become both critical consumers and beginning producers of scientific research on politics. The authors present an integrated approach to research design and empirical analyses whereby researchers can develop and test causal theories. The authors use examples from political science research that students will find interesting and inspiring, and that will help them understand key concepts. The book makes technical material accessible to students who might otherwise be intimidated by mathematical examples. This revised third edition features new "Your Turn" boxes meant to engage students. The edition also has new sections added throughout the book to enhance the content's clarity and breadth of coverage.

Paul M. Kellstedt is a professor of Political Science at Texas A&M University. He is the author of *The Mass Media and the Dynamics of American Racial Attitudes* (Cambridge University Press, 2003), winner of Harvard University's John F. Kennedy School of Government's 2004 Goldsmith Book Prize. In addition, he has published numerous articles in a variety of leading journals. He is the recently named editor-in-chief of *Political Science Research and Methods*, the flagship journal of the European Political Science Association.

Guy D. Whitten is a professor of Political Science, as well as the Director of the European Union Center, at Texas A&M University. He has published a variety of articles in leading peer-reviewed journals. He is on the editorial boards of the *American Journal of Political Science*, *Electoral Studies*, and *Political Science Research and Methods*.

THE FUNDAMENTALS OF

Political Science Research

Third Edition

Paul M. Kellstedt

Texas A&M University

Guy D. Whitten

Texas A&M University

CAMBRIDGE
UNIVERSITY PRESS

CAMBRIDGE
UNIVERSITY PRESS

University Printing House, Cambridge CB2 8BS, United Kingdom

One Liberty Plaza, 20th Floor, New York, NY 10006, USA

477 Williamstown Road, Port Melbourne, VIC 3207, Australia

314–321, 3rd Floor, Plot 3, Splendor Forum, Jasola District Centre, New Delhi – 110025, India

79 Anson Road, #06–04/06, Singapore 079906

Cambridge University Press is part of the University of Cambridge.

It furthers the University's mission by disseminating knowledge in the pursuit of education, learning, and research at the highest international levels of excellence.

www.cambridge.org
Information on this title: www.cambridge.org/9781316642672
DOI: 10.1017/9781108131704

© Paul M. Kellstedt and Guy D. Whitten 2009, 2013, 2018

First edition published 2009
Second edition published 2013
7th printing 2017
Third edition published 2018

Printed in the United States of America by Sheridan Books, Inc., 2018

A catalogue record for this publication is available from the British Library.

Library of Congress Cataloging-in-Publication Data
Names: Kellstedt, Paul M., 1968– author. | Whitten, Guy D., 1965– author.
Title: The fundamentals of political science research / Paul M. Kellstedt,
    Texas A&M University, Guy D. Whitten, Texas A&M University.
Description: 3rd edition. | New York : Cambridge University Press, [2018]
Identifiers: LCCN 2018001773 | ISBN 9781316642672 (pbk.)
Subjects: LCSH: Political science–Research.
Classification: LCC JA86 .K45 2018 | DDC 320.072–dc23
    LC record available at https://lccn.loc.gov/2018001773

ISBN 978-1-316-64267-2 Paperback

Additional resources for this publication at www.cambridge.org/KellstedtWhitten3ed

Dedicated to

Lyman A. Kellstedt, Charmaine C. Kellstedt,

David G. Whitten, and Jo Wright-Whitten,

the best teachers we ever had

— PMK and GDW

Brief Contents

Contents

Figures

Tables

Preface to the Third Edition

We received a great deal of constructive feedback on the second edition of this book. In crafting a new edition, our challenge was to try to produce a book that incorporated as much of this feedback as possible, coupled with our ideas for changes, without expanding the book by an unreasonable amount. Our general goals for this edition were to continue to strive to make our explanation of the material even more clear, and to keep up with continuously developing trends in the literature.

We continue to update both the general and instructor-only sections of the webpage for our book (http://www.cambridge.org/fpsr). As before, the general section contains data sets available in formats compatible with SPSS, Stata, and R. The instructor-only section contains several additional resources, including PowerPoint and TEX/Beamer slides for each chapter, a test-bank, and answer keys for the exercises.

Perhaps the most visible change we have made comes in the form of new "Your Turn" boxes. In an effort to increase student engagement with the material, we have introduced, throughout the book, short boxes – some with links to outside material, some with questions about implications – in an attempt to get students to apply the lessons of that chapter to a new situation.

As outlined above, we have made broad changes that permeate all of the book, but we have also made major changes to particular chapters as follows:

- We have expanded Chapter 2, "The Art of Theory Building," by adding a new section on "Three Strategies toward Developing an Original Theory." Consistent with the discipline's increasing use of interactive models, this section includes new material on conditional theories about how a Z variable can modify the relationship between X and Y. Also in the chapter, we have a new section on how to build on previous scholarly work.

- We have added a new section to Chapter 4 on how to effectively summarize and critique scholarly work that is in the literature.
- To increase the ease of presentation, we have taken Chapter 5 from the second edition, "Getting to Know Your Data: Evaluating Measurement and Variations," and split it into two (Chapters 5 and 6) in this new edition. The new Chapter 5 is titled "Measuring Concepts of Interest," and the new Chapter 6 is entitled "Getting to Know Your Data."
- We have added a new section to Chapter 7 on the challenges of random sampling in advanced contemporary societies.
- We have updated the data in a very large portion of our examples.
- We have expanded our explication of the logic behind chi-squared tests and tabular analysis in Chapter 8 to make the argument flow more smoothly and the example unfold more naturally.
- We have added a new section to Chapter 10, "Multiple Regression: the Basics," on how to effectively present figures and tables.

Acknowledgments to the Third Edition

We have benefited tremendously from the advice and support of a large variety of individuals in preparing the third edition of this book.

As ever, we are grateful for the constructive criticism we've received since the publication of the second edition. The thoughtful engagement by so many students and faculty from around the world has been instrumental in shaping the changes that we've made to this third edition. We do our best to keep a running tally of people who have contacted us with questions and comments, but we've almost certainly left some people off this list, and we apologize for the omissions. We owe a debt of gratitude to the following people for their feedback: Ryan Bakker, Florian Hollenbach, Doug Kriner, Eric Lawrence, Matt Lebo, Bob Lupton, Joanne Miller, Dave Peterson, Mark Pickup, Nicholas Rivers, and Ammar Shamaileh.

The guidance and encouragement from the professionals at Cambridge University Press have been instrumental in seeing this project through to completion. In particular, we thank our editor, Robert Dreesen, for his continued support of us and our work. Every conversation with him – whether at a conference or on the phone – energized us and kept our focus squarely on the quality of the manuscript. It has surely made the book better, and for that, we are most grateful.

We continue to be sustained by the love and support of our families. We do not have the words that can adequately express how thankful we are for Christine, Anna, Deb, Abigail, and Elizabeth.

Acknowledgments to the Second Edition

We had a tremendous amount of help writing the first edition of this book and even more as we prepared this second edition.

Since the publication of the first edition of this book, we have enjoyed a steady stream of feedback from colleagues around the world. We would like to thank all of the students, faculty members, and others who took time from their busy schedules to offer us their questions, criticism, praise, and general thoughts about the first edition of this book. Although we have inevitably forgotten some names from this list, and we apologize to those who we have forgotten to mention here, we would like to thank the following people for the feedback that they provided on the first edition: Rick Bairett, Lorena Barberia, Neal Beck, Dan Doherty, Sean Gailmard, Steve Haptonstahl, Jude Hays, Karen Long Jusko, Kerem Ozan Kalkan, Eric Lawrence, Suzie Linn, Cherie Maestas, Vince Mahler, Scott Moser, Harvey Palmer, Evan Parker-Stephen, Dave Peterson, John Transue, Jenifer Whitten-Woodring, Cameron Wimpy, and Jason Wittenberg.

As we mentioned in the acknowledgements to the first edition of this book, we would never have written it without Ed Parsons's encouragement and sage advice. As such, we were happy for Ed but very nervous when he told us that he was leaving Cambridge University Press. Our new editor, Robert Dreesen, has been incredibly helpful and incredibly patient with us. We would like to thank Robert for his useful advice and encouragement throughout the preparation of this edition and his emphasis on the quality of the manuscript over considerations about timing.

This project would not have been possible without the love and patience of our families. Christine, Deb, Abigail, and Elizabeth were once again very generous with their patience and highly supportive throughout the process – as was Anna, the newest addition to our support team.

Acknowledgments to the First Edition

An inevitable part of the production of a book like this is an accumulation of massive intellectual debts. We have been overwhelmed by both the quality and quantity of help that we have received from our professional (and even personal) contacts as we have gone through every stage of the preparation of this manuscript.

This book arose out of more than twenty years of combined teaching experience at Brown University; the University of California, Los Angeles; the University of Essex; the University of Minnesota; and Texas A&M University. We tried out most of the examples in this book on numerous classes of students before they were refined into their present state. We thus owe a debt to every student who raised his or her hand or showed us a furrowed brow as we worked our way through these attempts to explain the complicated processes of scientifically studying politics.

More immediately, this project came out of separate and skeptical conversations that each author had with Ed Parsons during his visit to Texas A&M in the spring of 2006. Without Ed's perfect balance of candor and encouragement, this book would not have been started. At every stage in the process he has helped us immensely. He obtained three sets of superbly helpful reviews and seemed always to know the right times to be in and out of touch as we worked our way through them. It has been a tremendous pleasure to work with Ed on the book.

Throughout the process of writing this book, we got a steady stream of support, understanding, and patience from Christine, Deb, Abigail and Elizabeth. We thank them for putting up with our crazy hours and for helping us to keep things in perspective as we worked on this project.

For both authors the lines between family, friends, and professional colleagues are pretty blurry. We relied on our combined networks quite heavily at every stage in the production of this book. Early in the process of putting this manuscript together we received sage advice from Jeff

Gill about textbook writing for social scientists and how to handle early versions of our chapters. Our fathers, Lyman A. ("Bud") Kellstedt and David G. Whitten, provided their own unique and valuable perspectives on early drafts of the book. In separate but related ongoing conversations, John Transue and Alan M. Brookhart engaged us in lengthy debates about the nature of experiments, quasi-experiments, and observational studies. Other colleagues and friends provided input that also improved this book, including: Harold Clarke, Geoffrey Evans, John Jackson, Marisa Kellam, Eric Lawrence, Christine Lipsmeyer, Evan Parker-Stephen, David Peterson, James Rogers, Randy Stevenson, Georg Vanberg, Rilla Whitten, and Jenifer Whitten-Woodring.

Despite all of this help, we remain solely responsible for any deficiencies that persist in the book. We look forward to hearing about them from you so that we can make future editions of this book better.

Throughout the process of writing this book, we have been mindful of how our thinking has been shaped by our teachers at a variety of levels. We are indebted to them in ways that are difficult to express. In particular, Guy Whitten wishes to thank the following, all from his days at the University of Rochester: Larry M. Bartels, Richard Niemi, G. Bingham Powell, Lynda Powell, William H. Riker, and David Weimer. Paul Kellstedt thanks Al Reynolds and Bob Terbog of Calvin College; Michael Lewis-Beck, Vicki Hesli, and Jack Wright at the University of Iowa; and Jim Stimson and John Freeman at the University of Minnesota.

Though we have learned much from the aforementioned professors, we owe our largest debt to our parents: Lyman A. "Bud" Kellstedt, Charmaine C. Kellstedt, David G. Whitten, and Jo Wright-Whitten. We dedicate this book to the four of them – the best teachers we ever had.

1 The Scientific Study of Politics

OVERVIEW

Most political science students are interested in the substance of politics and not in its methodology. We begin with a discussion of the goals of this book and why a scientific approach to the study of politics is more interesting and desirable than a "just-the-facts" approach. In this chapter we provide an overview of what it means to study politics scientifically. We begin with an introduction to how we move from causal theories to scientific knowledge, and how a key part of this process is thinking about the world in terms of *models* in which the concepts of interest become variables that are causally linked together by theories. We then introduce the goals and standards of political science research that will be our rules of the road to keep in mind throughout this book. The chapter concludes with a brief overview of the structure of this book.

Doubt is the beginning, not the end, of wisdom.
　　—Chinese proverb

1.1 POLITICAL *SCIENCE*?

"Which party do you support?" "When are you going to run for office?" These are questions that students often hear after announcing that they are taking courses in political science. Although many political scientists are avid partisans, and some political scientists have even run for elected offices or have advised elected officials, for the most part this is not the focus of modern political science. Instead, political science is about the scientific study of political phenomena. Perhaps like you, a great many of today's political scientists were attracted to this discipline as undergraduates because of intense interests in a particular issue or candidate. Although we are often drawn into political science based on political passions, the most respected political science research today is conducted in a fashion that makes it impossible to tell the personal political views of the writer.

Many people taking their first political science research course are surprised to find out how much science and, in particular, how much math are involved. We would like to encourage the students who find themselves in this position to hang in there with us – even if your answer to this encouragement is "but I'm only taking this class because they require it to graduate, and I'll never use any of this stuff again." Even if you never run a regression model after you graduate, having made your way through these materials should help you in a number of important ways. We have written this book with the following three goals in mind:

- *To help you consume academic political science research in your other courses.* One of the signs that a field of research is becoming scientific is the development of a common technical language. We aim to make the common technical language of political science accessible to you.
- *To help you become a better consumer of information.* In political science and many other areas of scientific and popular communication, claims about causal relationships are frequently made. We want you to be better able to evaluate such claims critically.
- *To start you on the road to becoming a producer of scientific research on politics.* This is obviously the most ambitious of our goals. In our teaching we often have found that once skeptical students get comfortable with the basic tools of political science, their skepticism turns into curiosity and enthusiasm.

To see the value of this approach, consider an alternative way of learning about politics, one in which political science courses would focus on "just the facts" of politics. Under this alternative way, for example, a course offered in 1995 on the politics of the European Union (EU) would have taught students that there were 15 member nations who participated in governing the EU through a particular set of institutional arrangements that had a particular set of rules. An obvious problem with this alternative way is that courses in which lists of facts are the only material would probably be pretty boring. An even bigger problem, though, is that the political world is constantly changing. In 2016 the EU was made up of 28 member nations and had some new governing institutions and rules that were different from what they were in 1995. Students who took a facts-only course on the EU back in 1995 would find themselves lost in trying to understand the EU of 2016. By contrast, a theoretical approach to politics helps us to better understand why changes have come about and their likely impact on EU politics.

In this chapter we provide an overview of what it means to study politics scientifically. We begin this discussion with an introduction to how we move from causal theories to scientific knowledge. A key part of this process is thinking about the world in terms of *models* in which the concepts of interest become **variables**[1] that are causally linked together by theories. We then introduce the goals and standards of political science research that will be our rules of the road to keep in mind throughout this book. We conclude this chapter with a brief overview of the structure of this book.

1.2 APPROACHING POLITICS SCIENTIFICALLY: THE SEARCH FOR CAUSAL EXPLANATIONS

I've said, I don't know whether it's addictive. I'm not a doctor. I'm not a scientist.
        —Bob Dole, in a conversation with Katie Couric about tobacco during the
        1996 US presidential campaign

The question of "how do we know what we know" is, at its heart, a philosophical question. Scientists are lumped into different disciplines that develop standards for evaluating evidence. A core part of being a scientist and taking a scientific approach to studying the phenomena that interest you is always being willing to consider new evidence and, on the basis of that new evidence, change what you thought you *knew* to be true. This willingness to always consider new evidence is counterbalanced by a stern approach to the evaluation of new evidence that permeates the scientific approach. This is certainly true of the way that political scientists approach politics.

So what do political scientists do and what makes them scientists? A basic answer to this question is that, like other scientists, political scientists develop and test theories. A **theory** is a tentative conjecture about the causes of some phenomenon of interest. The development of **causal** theories about the political world requires thinking in new ways about familiar phenomena. As such, theory building is part art and part science. We discuss this in greater detail in Chapter 2, "The Art of Theory Building."

---

[1] When we introduce an important new term in this book, that term appears in boldface type. At the end of each chapter, we will provide short definitions of each bolded term that was introduced in that chapter. We discuss variables at great length later in this and other chapters. For now, a good working definition is that a variable is a definable quantity that can take on two or more values. An example of a variable is voter turnout; researchers usually **measure** it as the percentage of voting-eligible persons in a geographically defined area who cast a vote in a particular election.

Causal theory

Hypothesis

Empirical test

Evaluation of hypothesis

Evaluation of causal theory

Scientific knowledge

Figure 1.1 The road to scientific knowledge

Once a theory has been developed, like all scientists, we turn to the business of testing our theory. The first step in testing a particular theory is to restate it as one or more testable hypotheses. A **hypothesis** is a theory-based statement about a relationship that we expect to observe. For every hypothesis there is a corresponding **null hypothesis**. A null hypothesis is also a theory-based statement but it is about what we would observe if there were no relationship between two variables of interest. **Hypothesis testing** is a process in which scientists evaluate systematically collected evidence to make a judgment of whether the evidence favors their hypothesis or favors the corresponding null hypothesis. The process of setting up hypothesis tests involves both logical reasoning and creative design. In Chapter 3, "Evaluating Causal Relationships," we focus on the logical reason side of this process. In Chapter 4, "Research Design," we focus on the design part of this process. If a hypothesis survives rigorous testing, scientists start to gain confidence in that hypothesis rather than in the null hypothesis, and thus they also gain confidence in the theory from which they generated their hypothesis.

Figure 1.1 presents a stylized schematic view of the path from theories to hypotheses to scientific knowledge.[2] At the top of the figure, we begin with a causal theory to explain our phenomenon of interest. We then derive one or more hypotheses about what our theory leads us to expect when we measure our concepts of interest (which we call variables – as was previously discussed) in the real world. In the third step, we conduct **empirical** tests of our hypotheses.[3] From what we find, we evaluate our hypotheses relative to corresponding null hypotheses. Next, from the results of our hypothesis tests, we evaluate our causal theory. In light of our evaluation of our theory, we then think about how, if at all, we should revise what we consider to be scientific knowledge concerning our phenomenon of interest.

A core part of the scientific process is skepticism. On hearing of a new theory, other scientists will challenge this theory and devise further tests. Although this process can occasionally become quite combative, it is

[2] In practice, the development of scientific knowledge is frequently much messier than this step-by-step diagram. We show more of the complexity of this approach in later chapters.

[3] By "empirical" we simply mean "based on observations of the real world."

a necessary component in the development of scientific knowledge. Indeed, a core component of scientific knowledge is that, as confident as we are in a particular theory, we remain open to the possibility that there is still a test out there that will provide evidence that makes us lose confidence in that theory.

It is important to underscore here the nature of the testing that scientists carry out. One way of explaining this is to say that scientists are *not* like lawyers in the way that they approach evidence. Lawyers work for a particular client, advocate a particular point of view (like "guilt" or "innocence"), and then accumulate evidence with a goal of proving their case to a judge or jury. This goal of *proving* a desired result determines their approach to evidence. When faced with evidence that conflicts with their case, lawyers attempt to ignore or discredit such evidence. When faced with evidence that supports their case, lawyers try to emphasize the applicability and quality of the supportive evidence. In many ways, the scientific and legal approaches to evidence couldn't be further apart. Scientific confidence in a theory is achieved only after hypotheses derived from that theory have run a gantlet of tough tests. At the beginning of a trial, lawyers develop a strategy to *prove* their case. In contrast, at the beginning of a research project, scientists will think long and hard about the most rigorous tests that they can conduct. A scientist's theory is never *proven* beyond the shadow of a doubt because scientists are always willing to consider new evidence.

The process of hypothesis testing reflects how hard scientists are on their own theories. As scientists evaluate systematically collected evidence to make a judgment of whether the evidence favors their hypothesis or favors the corresponding null hypothesis, they *always* favor the null hypothesis. Statistical techniques allow scientists to make probability-based statements about the empirical evidence that they have collected. You might think that, if the evidence was 50–50 between their hypothesis and the corresponding null hypothesis, the scientists would tend to give the nod to the hypothesis (from their theory) over the null hypothesis. In practice, though, this is not the case. Even when the hypothesis has an 80–20 edge over the null hypothesis, most scientists will still favor the null hypothesis. Why? Because scientists are very worried about the possibility of falsely rejecting the null hypothesis and therefore making claims that others ultimately will show to be wrong.

Once a theory has become established as a part of scientific knowledge in a field of study, researchers can build upon the foundation that this theory provides. Thomas Kuhn (1962) wrote about these processes in his famous book *The Structure of Scientific Revolutions*. According to Kuhn, scientific fields go through cycles of accumulating knowledge based on a set of shared assumptions and commonly accepted theories about the way that the world works. Together, these shared assumptions and accepted theories form what we call a **paradigm**. Once researchers in a scientific field have widely accepted a paradigm, they can pursue increasingly technical questions that make sense only because of the work that has come beforehand. This state of research under an accepted paradigm is referred to as **normal science**. When a major problem is found with the accepted theories and assumptions of a scientific field, that field will go through a revolutionary period during which new theories and assumptions replace the old paradigm to establish a new paradigm. One of the more famous of these scientific revolutions occurred during the sixteenth century when the field of astronomy was forced to abandon its assumption that the Earth was the center of the known universe. This was an assumption that had informed theories about planetary movement for thousands of years. In his book *De revolutionibus orbium coelestium* of 1543 (translated 2004 as *On the Revolutions of Heavenly Spheres*), Nicolaus Copernicus presented his theory that the Sun was the center of the known universe. Although this radical theory met many challenges, an increasing body of evidence convinced astronomers that Copernicus had it right. In the aftermath of this **paradigm shift**, researchers developed new assumptions and theories that established a new paradigm, and the affected fields of study entered into new periods of normal scientific research.

It may seem hard to imagine that the field of political science has gone through anything that can compare with the experiences of astronomers in the sixteenth century. Indeed, Kuhn and other scholars who study the evolution of scientific fields of research have a lively and ongoing debate about where the social sciences, like political science, are in terms of their development. The more skeptical participants in this debate argue that political science is not sufficiently mature to have a paradigm, much less a paradigm shift. If we put aside this somewhat esoteric debate about paradigms and paradigm shifts, we can see an important example of the evolution of scientific knowledge about politics from the study of public opinion in the United States.

In the 1940s the study of public opinion through mass surveys was in its infancy. Prior to that time, political scientists and sociologists assumed that US voters were heavily influenced by presidential campaigns – and, in particular, by campaign advertising – as they made up their minds about the candidates. To better understand how these processes worked, a team of researchers from Columbia University set up an in-depth study of public opinion in Erie County, Ohio, during the 1944 presidential election. Their study involved interviewing the same individuals at multiple time periods across the course of the campaign. Much to the researchers' surprise, they found that voters were remarkably consistent from interview to interview in terms of their vote intentions. Instead of being influenced by particular events of the campaign, most of the voters surveyed had made up their minds about how they would cast their ballots long before the campaigning had even begun. The resulting book by Paul Lazarsfeld, Bernard Berelson, and Hazel Gaudet (1948), titled *The People's Choice*, changed the way that scholars thought about public opinion and political behavior in the United States. If political campaigns were not central to vote choice, scholars were forced to ask themselves what *was* critical to determining how people voted.

At first other scholars were skeptical of the findings of the 1944 Erie County study, but as the revised theories of politics of Lazarsfeld et al. were evaluated in other studies, the field of public opinion underwent a change that looks very much like what Thomas Kuhn calls a "paradigm shift." In the aftermath of this finding, new theories were developed to attempt to explain the origins of voters' long-lasting attachments to political parties in the United States. An example of an influential study that was carried out under this shifted paradigm is Richard Niemi and Kent Jennings' seminal book from 1974, *The Political Character of Adolescence: The Influence of Families and Schools*. As the title indicates, Niemi and Jennings studied the attachments of schoolchildren to political parties. Under the pre-Erie County paradigm of public opinion, this study would not have made much sense. But once researchers had found that voters' partisan attachments were quite stable over time, studying them at the early ages at which they form became a reasonable scientific enterprise. You can see evidence of this paradigm at work in current studies of party identification and debates about its stability.

1.3 THINKING ABOUT THE WORLD IN TERMS OF VARIABLES AND CAUSAL EXPLANATIONS

So how do political scientists develop theories about politics? A key element of this is that they order their thoughts about the political world in terms of concepts that scientists call *variables* and causal relationships between variables. This type of mental exercise is just a more rigorous way of expressing ideas about politics that we hear on a daily basis. You should think of each variable in terms of its *label* and its *values*. The **variable label** is a description of what the variable is, and the **variable values** are the denominations in which the variable occurs. So, if we're talking about the variable that reflects an individual's age, we could simply label this variable "Age" and some of the denominations in which this variable occurs would be years, days, or even hours.

It is easier to understand the process of turning concepts into variables by using an example of an entire theory. For instance, if we're thinking about US presidential elections, a commonly expressed idea is that the incumbent president will fare better when the economy is relatively healthy. If we restate this in terms of a political science theory, the state of the economy becomes the **independent variable**, and the outcome of presidential elections becomes the **dependent variable**. One way of keeping the lingo of theories straight is to remember that the value of the "dependent" variable "depends" on the value of the "independent" variable. Recall that a theory is a tentative conjecture about the causes of some phenomenon of interest. In other words, a theory is a conjecture that the independent variable is causally related to the dependent variable; according to our theory, change in the value of the independent variable *causes* change in the value of the dependent variable.

This is a good opportunity to pause and try to come up with your own causal statement in terms of an independent and dependent variable.[4]

YOUR TURN: Come up with your own causal statement

Try filling in the following blanks with some political variables:

_____ causes _____

Sometimes it's easier to phrase causal propositions more specifically in terms of the values of the variables that you have in mind. For instance,

higher _____ causes lower _____

or, as the case may be,

higher _____ causes higher _____

Once you learn to think about the world in terms of variables, you will be able to produce an almost endless slew of causal theories. In Chapter 4 we will discuss at length how we design research to evaluate the causal claims in theories, but one way to initially evaluate a particular theory is to think

---

[4] Periodically in this book, you will find "Your Turn" boxes which ask you a question or ask you to try something. These boxes are designed to help you see if you are understanding the material that we have covered up to the point where they appear.

about the causal explanation behind it. The causal explanation behind a theory is the answer to the question: "Why do you think that this independent variable is causally related to this dependent variable?" If the answer is reasonable, then the theory has possibilities. In addition, if the answer is original and thought provoking, then you may really be on to something. Let's return now to our working example in which the state of the economy is the independent variable and the outcome of presidential elections is our dependent variable. The causal explanation for this theory is that we believe that the state of the economy is *causally related* to the outcome of presidential elections *because* voters hold the president responsible for management of the national economy. As a result, when the economy has been performing well, more voters will vote for the incumbent. When the economy is performing poorly, fewer voters will support the incumbent candidate. If we put this in terms of the preceding fill-in-the-blank exercise, we could write

economic performance causes presidential election outcomes,

or, more specifically, we could write

higher economic performance causes higher incumbent vote.

For now we'll refer to this theory, which has been widely advanced and tested by political scientists, as "the theory of economic voting."

To test the theory of economic voting in US presidential elections, we need to derive from it one or more testable hypotheses. Figure 1.2 provides a schematic diagram of the relationship between a theory and one of its hypotheses. At the top of this diagram are the components of the causal theory. As we move from the top part of this diagram (Causal theory) to the bottom part (Hypothesis), we are moving from a general statement about how we think the world works to a more specific statement about a relationship that we expect to find when we go out in the real world and measure (or **operationalize**) our variables.[5]

At the theory level at the top of Figure 1.2, our variables do not need to be explicitly defined. With the economic voting example, the independent variable, labeled "Economic Performance," can be thought of as a concept that ranges from values of very strong to very poor. The dependent variable, labeled "Incumbent Vote," can be thought of as a concept that ranges from values of very high to very low. Our causal theory is that a stronger economic performance causes the incumbent vote to be higher.

---

[5] Throughout this book we will use the terms "measure" and "operationalize" interchangeably. It is fairly common practice in the current political science literature to use the term "operationalize."

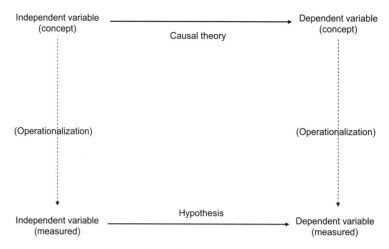

Figure 1.2 From theory to hypothesis

Because there are many ways in which we can measure each of our two variables, there are many different hypotheses that we can test to find out how well our theory holds up to real-world **data**. We can measure economic performance in a variety of ways. These measures include inflation, unemployment, real economic growth, and many others. "Incumbent Vote" may seem pretty straightforward to measure, but here there are also a number of choices that we need to make. For instance, what do we do in the cases in which the incumbent president is not running again? Or what about elections in which a third-party candidate runs? Measurement (or operationalization) of concepts is an important part of the scientific process. We will discuss this in greater detail in Chapters 5 and 6, which are devoted entirely to evaluating different variable measurements and variation in variables. For now, imagine that we are operationalizing economic performance with a variable that we will label "One-Year Real Economic Growth Per Capita." This measure, which is available from official US government sources, measures the one-year rate of inflation-adjusted (thus the term "real") economic growth per capita at the time of the election. The adjustments for inflation and population (per capita) reflect an important part of measurement – we want our measure of our variables to be comparable across cases. The values for this variable range from negative values for years in which the economy shrank to positive values for years in which the economy expanded. We operationalize our dependent variable with a variable that we label "Incumbent-Party Percentage of Major Party Vote." This variable takes on values based on the percentage of the popular vote, as reported in official election results, for the party that controlled the presidency at the time of the election, and thus has a possible range from 0 to 100.

Figure 1.3 Economic growth. What would you expect to see based on the theory of economic voting?

In order to make our measure of this dependent variable comparable across cases, votes for third-party candidates have been removed from this measure.[6]

Figure 1.3 shows the axes of the graph that we could produce if we collected the measures of these two variables. We could place each US presidential election on the graph in Figure 1.3 by identifying the point that corresponds to the value of both "One-Year Real Economic Growth" (the horizontal, or x, axis) and "Incumbent-Party Vote Percentage" (the vertical, or y, axis). For instance, if these values were (respectively) 0 and 50, the position for that election year would be exactly in the center of the graph. Based on our theory, what would you expect to see if we collected these measures for all elections? Remember that our theory is that a stronger *economic performance* causes the *incumbent vote* to be higher. And we can restate this theory in reverse such that a weaker *economic performance* causes the *incumbent vote* to be lower. So, what would this lead us to expect to see if we plotted real-world data onto Figure 1.3? To get this answer right, let's make sure that we know our way around this graph. If we move from left to right on the horizontal axis, which is labeled

---

[6] If you're questioning the wisdom of removing votes for third-party candidates, you are thinking in the right way – any time you read about a measurement you should think about different ways in which it might have been carried out. And, in particular, you should focus on the likely consequences of different measurement choices on the results of hypothesis tests. Evaluating measurement strategies is a major topic in Chapter 5.

"One-Year Real Economic Growth Per Capita," what is going on in real-world terms? We can see that, at the far left end of the horizontal axis, the value is –20. This would mean that the US economy had shrunk by 20 percent over the past year, which would represent a very poor performance (to say the least). As we move to the right on this axis, each point represents a better economic performance up to the point where we see a value of +20, indicating that the real economy has grown by 20 percent over the past year. The vertical axis depicts values of "Incumbent-Party Percentage of Major Party Vote." Moving upward on this axis represents an increasing share of the popular vote for the incumbent party, whereas moving downward represents a decreasing share of the popular vote.

Now think about these two axes together in terms of what we would expect to see based on the theory of economic voting. In thinking through these matters, we should always start with our independent variable. This is because our theory states that the value of the independent variable exerts a causal influence on the value of the dependent variable. So, if we start with a very low value of *economic performance* – let's say –15 on the horizontal axis – what does our theory lead us to expect in terms of values for the *incumbent vote*, the dependent variable? We would also expect the value of the dependent variable to be very low. This case would then be expected to be in the lower-left-hand corner of Figure 1.3. Now imagine a case in which economic performance was quite strong at +15. Under these circumstances, our theory would lead us to expect that the incumbent-vote percentage would also be quite high. Such a case would be in the upper-right-hand corner of our graph. Figure 1.4 shows two such hypothetical points plotted on the same graph as Figure 1.3. If we draw a line between these two points, this line would slope upward from the lower left to the upper right. We describe such a line as having a positive slope. We can therefore hypothesize that the relationship between the variable labeled "One-Year Real Economic Growth Per Capita" and the variable labeled "Incumbent-Party Percentage of Major Party Vote" will be a **positive relationship**. A positive relationship is one for which higher values of the independent variable tend to coincide with higher values of the dependent variable.

Let's consider a different operationalization of our independent variable. Instead of economic growth, let's use "Unemployment Percentage" as our operationalization of economic performance. We haven't changed our theory, but we need to rethink our hypothesis with this new measurement or operationalization. The best way to do so is to draw a picture like Figure 1.3 but with the changed independent variable on the horizontal axis. This is what we have in Figure 1.5. As we move from left to right on the horizontal axis in Figure 1.5, the percentage of the members of the

Figure 1.4 Economic growth. What would you expect to see based on the theory of economic voting? Two hypothetical cases

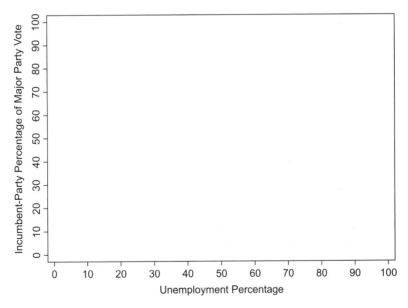

Figure 1.5 Unemployment. What would you expect to see based on the theory of economic voting?

workforce who are unemployed goes up. What does this mean in terms of economic performance? Rising unemployment is generally considered a poorer economic performance whereas decreasing unemployment is considered a better economic performance.

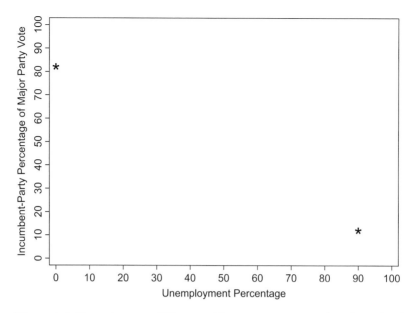

Figure 1.6 Unemployment. What would you expect to see based on the theory of economic voting? Two hypothetical cases

---

YOUR TURN: What would you expect?

Based on our theory, what should we expect to see in terms of incumbent vote percentage when unemployment is high? What about when unemployment is low?

Figure 1.6 shows two such hypothetical points plotted on our graph of unemployment and incumbent vote from Figure 1.5. The point in the upper-left-hand corner represents our expected vote percentage when unemployment equals zero. Under these circumstances, our theory of economic voting leads us to expect that the incumbent party will do very well. The point in the lower-right-hand corner represents our expected vote percentage when unemployment is very high. Under these circumstances, our theory of economic voting leads us to expect that the incumbent party will do very poorly. If we draw a line between these two points, this line would slope downward from the upper left to the lower right. We describe such a line as having a negative slope. We can therefore hypothesize that the relationship between the variable labeled "Unemployment Percentage" and the variable labeled "Incumbent-Party Percentage of Major Party Vote" will be a **negative relationship**. A negative relationship is one for which higher values of the independent variable tend to coincide with lower values of the dependent variable.

In this example we have seen that the same theory can lead to a hypothesis of a positive or a negative relationship. The theory to be tested, together with the operationalization of the independent and the dependent variables, determines the direction of the hypothesized relationship. The best way to translate our theories into hypotheses is to draw a picture like Figure 1.4 or 1.6. The first step is to label the horizontal axis with the variable label for the independent variable (as operationalized) and then label the left and right ends of the axis with appropriate value labels. The second step in this process is to label the vertical axis with the variable label for the dependent variable and then label the low and high ends of that axis with appropriate value labels. Once we have such a figure with the axes and minimum and maximum values for each properly labeled, we can determine what our expected value of our dependent variable should be if we observe both a low and a high value of the independent variable. And, once we have placed the two resulting points on our figure, we can tell whether our hypothesized relationship is positive or negative.

> **YOUR TURN: Developing another hypothesis to test the theory of economic voting**
>
> Think of a measure of the economy that is different from the two, economic growth and unemployment, that we have considered so far. Draw a picture like those in Figures 1.3 to 1.6 to decide whether you would expect a positive or negative relationship between this new independent variable and our dependent variable in this example.

Once we have figured out our hypothesized relationship, we can collect data from real-world cases and see how well these data reflect our expectations of a positive or negative relationship. This is a very important step that we can carry out fairly easily in the case of the theory of economic voting. Once we collect all of the data on economic performance and election outcomes, we will, however, still be a long way from confirming the theory that economic performance *causes* presidential election outcomes. Even if a graph like Figure 1.4 produces compelling visual evidence, we will need to see more rigorous evidence than that. Chapters 8–12 focus on the use of statistics to evaluate hypotheses. The basic logic of statistical hypothesis testing is that we assess the probability that the relationship we find could be due to random chance. The stronger the evidence that such a relationship *could not* be due to random chance, the more confident we would be in our hypothesis. The stronger the evidence that such a relationship *could* be due to random chance, the more confident we would be in the corresponding null hypothesis. This in turn reflects on our theory.

We also, at this point, need to be cautious about claiming that we have "confirmed" our theory, because social scientific phenomena (such as elections) are usually complex and cannot be explained completely with a single independent variable. Take a minute or two to think about what other variables, aside from economic performance, you believe might be causally related to US presidential election outcomes. If you can come up with at least one, you are on your way to thinking like a political scientist. Because there are usually other variables that matter, we can continue to think about our theories two variables at a time, but we need to qualify our expectations to account for other variables. We will spend Chapters 3 and 4 expanding on these important issues.

> **YOUR TURN: What other variables might matter?**
>
> What other variables, aside from economic performance, might be causally related to US presidential election outcomes?

1.4 MODELS OF POLITICS

When we think about the phenomena that we want to better understand as dependent variables and develop theories about the independent variables that causally influence them, we are constructing **theoretical models**. Political scientist James Rogers (2006) provides an excellent analogy between models and maps to explain how these abstractions from reality are useful to us as we try to understand the political world:

> The very unrealism of a model, if properly constructed, is what makes it useful. The models developed below are intended to serve much the same function as a street map of a city. If one compares a map of a city to the real topography of that city, it is certain that what is represented in the map is a highly unrealistic portrayal of what the city actually looks like. The map utterly distorts what is *really* there and leaves out numerous details about what a particular area looks like. But it is precisely *because* the map distorts reality – because it abstracts away from a host of details about what is really there – that it is a useful tool. A map that attempted to portray the full details of a particular area would be too cluttered to be useful in finding a particular location or would be too large to be conveniently stored. (Rogers, 2006, p. 276, emphasis in original)

The essential point is that models *are* simplifications. Whether or not they are useful to us depends on what we are trying to accomplish with the particular model. One of the remarkable aspects of models is that they are often more useful to us when they are inaccurate than when they are accurate. The process of thinking about the failure of a model to explain one or more cases can generate a new causal theory. Glaring inaccuracies often point us in the direction of fruitful theoretical progress.

1.5 RULES OF THE ROAD TO SCIENTIFIC KNOWLEDGE ABOUT POLITICS

In the chapters that follow, we will focus on particular tools of political science research. As we do this, try to keep in mind our larger purpose – trying to advance the state of scientific knowledge about politics. As scientists, we have a number of basic rules that should never be far from our thinking:

- Focus on causality.
- Don't let data alone drive your theories.
- Consider only empirical evidence.
- Avoid normative statements.
- Pursue both generality and parsimony.

1.5.1 Focus on Causality

All of Chapter 3 deals with the issue of causality and, specifically, how we identify causal relationships. When political scientists construct theories, it is critical that they always think in terms of the causal processes that drive the phenomena in which they are interested. For us to develop a better understanding of the political world, we need to think in terms of causes and not mere **covariation**. The term covariation is used to describe a situation in which two variables vary together (or **covary**). If we imagine two variables, A and B, then we would say that A and B covary if it is the case that, when we observe higher values of variable A, we generally also observe higher values of variable B. We would also say that A and B covary if it is the case that, when we observe higher values of variable A, we generally also observe lower values of variable B.[7] It is easy to assume that when we observe covariation we are also observing causality, but it is important not to fall into this trap. (More on this in Chapter 3.)

1.5.2 Don't Let Data Alone Drive Your Theories

This rule of the road is closely linked to the first. A longer way of stating it is "try to develop theories before examining the data on which you will perform your tests." The importance of this rule is best illustrated by a silly example. Suppose that we are looking at data on the murder rate (number

---

[7] A closely related term is **correlation**. For now we use these two terms interchangeably. In Chapter 8, you will see that there are precise statistical measures of covariance and correlation that are closely related to each other but produce different numbers for the same data.

of murders per 1000 people) in the city of Houston, Texas, by months of the year. This is our dependent variable, and we want to explain why it is higher in some months and lower in others. If we were to take as many different independent variables as possible and simply see whether they had a relationship with our dependent variable, one variable that we might find to strongly covary with the murder rate is the amount of money spent per capita on ice cream. If we perform some verbal gymnastics, we might develop a "theory" about how heightened blood sugar levels in people who eat too much ice cream lead to murderous patterns of behavior. Of course, if we think about it further, we might realize that both ice cream sales and the number of murders committed go up when temperatures rise. Do we have a plausible explanation for why temperatures and murder rates might be causally related? It is pretty well known that people's tempers tend to fray when the temperature is higher. People also spend a lot more time outside during hotter weather, and these two factors might combine to produce a causally plausible relationship between temperatures and murder rates.

What this rather silly example illustrates is that we don't want our theories to be crafted based entirely on observations from real-world data. We are likely to be somewhat familiar with empirical patterns relating to the dependent variables for which we are developing causal theories. This is normal; we wouldn't be able to develop theories about phenomena about which we know nothing. But we need to be careful about how much we let what we see guide our development of our theories. One of the best ways to do this is to think about the underlying causal process as we develop our theories and to let this have much more influence on our thinking than patterns that we might have observed. Chapter 2 is all about strategies for developing theories. One of these strategies is to identify interesting variation in our dependent variable. Although this strategy for theory development relies on data, it should not be done without thinking about the underlying causal processes.

1.5.3   Consider Only Empirical Evidence

As we previously outlined, we need to always remain open to the possibility that new evidence will come along that will decrease our confidence in even a well-established theory. A closely related rule of the road is that, as scientists, we want to base what we know on what we see from *empirical* evidence, which, as we have said, is simply "evidence based on observing the real world." Strong logical arguments are a good start in favor of a theory, but before we can be convinced, we need to see results from rigorous hypothesis tests.[8]

In science, empirical observation is the only admissible form of evidence in evaluating an argument. A logical extension of this is that your ideology or partisan identification or metaphysics cannot be a source of proof that something is or is not true. And closely related to this, as scientists, we should avoid **normative statements**. Normative statements are statements about how the world *ought* to be.

1.5.4 Check Your Ideology at the Door and Avoid Normative Statements

Whereas politicians make and break their political careers with normative statements, political scientists need to avoid them at all costs. Most political scientists care about political issues and have opinions about how the world ought to be. On its own, this is not a problem. But when normative preferences about how the world "should" be structured creep into their scientific work, the results can become highly problematic. The best way to avoid such problems is to conduct research and report your findings in such a fashion that it is impossible for the reader to tell what are your normative preferences about the world.

This does not mean that good political science research cannot be used to change the world. To the contrary, advances in our scientific knowledge about phenomena enable policy makers to bring about changes in an effective manner. For instance, if we want to rid the world of wars (normative), we need to understand the systematic dynamics of the international system that produce wars in the first place (empirical and causal). If we want to rid the United States of homelessness (normative), we need to understand the pathways into and out of being homeless (empirical and causal). If we want to help our favored candidate win elections (normative), we need to understand what characteristics make people vote the way they do (empirical and causal).

---

[8] It is worth noting that some political scientists use data drawn from experimental settings to test their hypotheses. There is some debate about whether such data are, strictly speaking, empirical or not. We discuss political science experiments and their limitations in Chapter 4. In recent years some political scientists have also made clever use of simulated data to gain leverage on their phenomena of interest, and the empirical nature of such data can certainly be debated. In the context of this textbook we are not interested in weighing in on these debates about exactly what is and is not empirical data. Instead, we suggest that one should always consider the overall quality of data on which hypothesis tests have been performed when evaluating causal claims.

1.5.5   Pursue Both Generality and Parsimony

Our final rule of the road is that we should always pursue generality and parsimony. These two goals can come into conflict. By "generality," we mean that we want our theories to be applied to as general a class of phenomena as possible. For instance, a theory that explains the causes of a phenomenon in only one country is less useful than a theory that explains the same phenomenon across multiple countries. Additionally, the more simple or **parsimonious** a theory is, the more appealing it becomes.[9] The term "parsimonious" is often used in a relative sense. So, if we are comparing two theories, the theory that is simpler would be the more parsimonious.

In the real world, however, we often face trade-offs between generality and parsimony. This is the case because, to make a theory apply more generally, we need to add caveats. The more caveats that we add to a theory, the less parsimonious it becomes.

1.6   A QUICK LOOK AHEAD

You now know the rules of the road. As we go through the next 11 chapters, you will acquire an increasingly complicated set of tools for developing and testing scientific theories about politics, so it is crucial that, at every step along the way, you keep these rules in the back of your mind. The rest of this book can be divided into three different sections. The first section, which includes this chapter through Chapter 4, is focused on the development of theories and research designs to study causal relationships about politics. In Chapter 2, "The Art of Theory Building," we discuss a range of strategies for developing theories about political phenomena. In Chapter 3, "Evaluating Causal Relationships," we provide a detailed explanation of the logic for evaluating causal claims about relationships between an independent variable, which we call "X," and a dependent variable, which we call "Y." In Chapter 4, "Research Design," we discuss the research strategies that political scientists use to investigate causal relationships.

In the second section of this book, we expand on the basic tools that political scientists need to test their theories. Chapter 5, "Measuring Concepts of Interest," is a detailed discussion of how we measure (or operationalize) our variables. Chapter 6, "Getting to Know Your Data," provides an introduction to a set of tools that can be used to summarize the characteristics of variables one at a time and thus get to know them.

---

[9] We use the words "parsimony" and "parsimonious" because they are widely used to describe theories.

Chapter 7, "Probability and Statistical Inference," introduces both the basics of probability theory as well as the logic of statistical hypothesis testing. In Chapter 8, "Bivariate Hypothesis Testing," we begin to apply the lessons from Chapter 7 to a series of empirical tests of the relationship between pairs of variables.

The third and final section of this book introduces the critical concepts of the regression model. Chapter 9, "Two-Variable Regression Models," introduces the two-variable regression model as an extension of the concepts from Chapter 8. In Chapter 10, "Multiple Regression: the Basics," we introduce the multiple regression model, with which researchers are able to look at the effects of independent variable X on dependent variable Y while controlling for the effects of other independent variables. Chapter 11, "Multiple Regression Model Specification," and Chapter 12, "Limited Dependent Variables and Time-Series Data," provide in-depth *discussions of* and *advice for* commonly encountered research scenarios involving multiple regression models.

CONCEPTS INTRODUCED IN THIS CHAPTER

- causal – implying causality; a central focus of this book is on theories about "causal" relationships
- correlation – a statistical measure of covariation which summarizes the direction (positive or negative) and strength of the linear relationship between two variables
- covary (or covariation) – when two variables vary together, they are said to "covary;" the term "covariation" is used to describe circumstances in which two variables covary
- data – a collection of variable values for at least two observations
- dependent variable – a variable for which at least some of the variation is theorized to be caused by one or more independent variables
- empirical – based on real-world observation
- hypothesis – a theory-based statement about what we would expect to observe if our theory is correct a hypothesis is a more explicit statement of a theory in terms of the expected relationship between a measure of the independent variable and a measure of the dependent variable
- hypothesis testing – the act of evaluating empirical evidence in order to determine the level of support for the hypothesis versus the null hypothesis
- independent variable – a variable that is theorized to cause variation in the dependent variable
- measure – a process by which abstract concepts are turned into real-world observations

- negative relationship – higher values of the independent variable tend to coincide with lower values of the dependent variable
- normal science – scientific research that is carried out under the shared set of assumptions and accepted theories of a paradigm
- normative statements – statements about how the world ought to be
- null hypothesis – a theory-based statement about what we would observe if there were no relationship between an independent variable and the dependent variable
- operationalize – another word for measurement; when a variable moves from the concept level in a theory to the real-world measure for a hypothesis test, it has been operationalized
- paradigm – a shared set of assumptions and accepted theories in a particular scientific field
- paradigm shift – when new findings challenge the conventional wisdom of a paradigm to the point where the set of shared assumptions and accepted theories in a scientific field is redefined
- parsimonious – synonym for simple or succinct
- positive relationship – higher values of the independent variable tend to coincide with higher values of the dependent variable
- theoretical model – the combination of independent variables, the dependent variable, and the causal relationships that are theorized to exist between them
- theory – a tentative conjecture about the causes of some phenomenon of interest
- variable – a definable quantity that can take on two or more values
- variable label – the label used to describe a particular variable
- variable values – the values that a particular variable can take on

EXERCISES

1. Pick another subject in which you have taken a course and heard mention of scientific theories. How is political science similar to and different from that subject?

2. Think about something in the political world that you would like to better understand. Try to think about this as a variable with high and low values. This is your dependent variable at the conceptual level. Now think about what might cause the values of your dependent variable to be higher or lower. Try to phrase this in terms of an independent variable, also at the conceptual level. Write a paragraph about these two variables and your theory about why they are causally related to each other.

3. Identify something in the world that you would like to see happen (normative). What scientific knowledge (empirical and causal) would help you to pursue this goal?

4. The 1992 US presidential election, in which challenger Bill Clinton defeated incumbent George H. W. Bush, has often been remembered as the "It's the economy, stupid," election. How can we restate the causal statement that embodies this conventional wisdom – "Clinton beat Bush because the economy had performed poorly" – into a more general theoretical statement?

For Exercises 5 and 6, consider the following statement about the world: "If you care about economic success in a country, you should also care about the peoples' political rights in that country. In a society in which people have more political rights, the victims of corrupt business practices will work through the system to get things corrected. As a result, countries in which people have more political rights will have less corruption. In countries in which there is less corruption, there will be more economic investment and more economic success."

5. Identify at least two causal claims that have been made in the preceding statement. For each causal claim, identify which variable is the independent variable and which variable is the dependent variable. These causal claims should be stated in terms of one of the following types of phrases in which the first blank should be filled by the independent variable and the second blank should be filled by the dependent variable:

_____ causes _____

higher _____ causes lower _____

higher _____ causes higher _____

6. Draw a graph like Figure 1.4 for each of the causal claims that you identified in Exercise 5. For each of your figures, do the following: Start on the left-hand side of the horizontal axis of the figure. This should represent a low value of the independent variable. What value of the dependent variable would you expect to find for such a case? Put a dot on your figure that represents this expected location. Now do the same for a case with a high value of the independent variable. Draw a line that connects these two points and write a couple of sentences that describe this picture.

7. Find an article in a political science journal that contains a model of politics. Provide the citation to the article, and answer the following questions:

(a) What is the dependent variable?

(b) What is one of the independent variables?

(c) What is the causal theory that connects the independent variable to the dependent variable?

(d) Does this seem reasonable?

8. For each of the following statements, identify which, if any, rule(s) of the road to scientific knowledge about politics has been violated:

(a) This study of the relationship between economic development and the level of autocracy is important because dictatorships are bad and we need to understand how to get rid of them.

(b) Did the European financial crisis of 2012 cause Nicolas Sarkozy to lose the subsequent French presidential election?

(c) It's just logical that poverty causes crime.

(d) This correlation supports the theory that bad weather drives down voter turnout.

2 The Art of Theory Building

OVERVIEW

In this chapter we discuss the art of theory building. Unfortunately there is no magical formula or cookbook for developing good theories about politics. But there are strategies that will help you to develop good theories. We discuss these strategies in this chapter.

Amat victoria curam. (Victory loves preparation.)
    —Latin proverb

If I have seen further, it is by standing on the shoulders of giants.
    —Isaac Newton

2.1 GOOD THEORIES COME FROM GOOD THEORY-BUILDING STRATEGIES

In Chapter 1 we discussed the role of theories in developing scientific knowledge. From that discussion, it is clear that a "good" theory is one that, after going through the rigors of the evaluation process, makes a contribution to scientific knowledge. In other words, a good theory is one that changes the way that we think about some aspect of the political world. We also know from our discussion of the rules of the road that we want our theories to be causal, not driven by data alone, empirical, non-normative, general, and parsimonious. This is a tall order, and a logical question to ask at this point is "How do I come up with such a theory?"

Unfortunately, there is neither an easy answer nor a single answer. Instead, what we can offer you is a set of strategies. "Strategies?" you may ask. Imagine that you were given the following assignment: "Go out and get struck by lightning."[1] There is no cut-and-dried formula that will show

---

[1] Our lawyers have asked us to make clear that this is an illustrative analogy and that we are in no way encouraging you to go out and try to get struck by lightning.

you how to get struck by lightning, but certainly there are actions that you can take that will make it more likely. The first step is to look at a weather map and find an area where there is thunderstorm activity; and if you were to go to such an area, you would increase your likelihood of getting struck. You would be even more likely to get struck by lightning if, once in the area of thunderstorms, you climbed to the top of a tall barren hill. But you would be still more likely to get struck if you carried with you a nine iron and, once on top of the barren hill, in the middle of a thunderstorm, you held that nine iron up to the sky. The point here is that, although there are no magical formulae that make the development of a good theory (or getting hit by lightning) a certain event, there are strategies that you can follow to increase the likelihood of it happening. That's what this chapter is about.

2.2   PROMISING THEORIES OFFER ANSWERS TO INTERESTING RESEARCH QUESTIONS

In the sections that follow, we discuss a series of strategies for developing theories. A reasonable question to ask before we depart on this tour of theory-building strategies is, "How will I know when I have a good theory?" Another way that we might think about this is to ask "What do good theories do?" We know from Chapter 1 that theories get turned into hypothesis tests, and then, if they are supported by empirical tests, they contribute to our scientific knowledge about what causes what. So a reasonable place to begin to answer the question of how one evaluates a new theory is to think about how that theory, if supported in empirical testing, would contribute to scientific knowledge. One of the main ways in which theories can be evaluated is in terms of the questions that they answer. If the question being answered by a theory is interesting and important, then that theory has potential.

Most of the influential research in any scientific field can be distilled into a soundbite-sized statement about the question to which it offers an answer, or the puzzle for which it offers a solution. Consider, for example, the ten most-cited articles published in the *American Political Science Review* between 1945 and 2005.[2] Table 2.1 lists these articles together with their research question. It is worth noting that, of these ten articles, all but one has as its main motivation the answer to a question or the solution

---

[2] This list comes from an article (Sigelman, 2006) published by the editor of the journal in which well-known researchers and some of the original authors reflected on the influence of the 20 most-cited articles published in the journal during that time period.

Table 2.1 Research questions of the ten most-cited papers in the *American Political Science Review*, 1945–2005	
Article	**Research question**
1) Bachrach and Baratz (1962)	How is political power created?
2) Hibbs (1977)	How do the interests of their core supporters effect governments' economic policies?
3) Walker (1969)	How do innovations in governance spread across US states?
4) Kramer (1971)	How do economic conditions impact US national elections?
5) Miller and Stokes (1963)	How do constituent attitudes influence the votes of US representatives?
6) March and Olsen (1984)	How do institutions shape politics?
7) Lipset (1959)	What are the necessary conditions for stable democratic politics?
8) Beck and Katz (1995)	What models should researchers use when they have pooled time-series data?
9) Cameron (1978)	Why has the government share of economic activity increased in some nations?
10) Deutsch (1961)	How does social mobilization shape politics in developing nations?

to a puzzle that is of interest to not just political science researchers.[3] This provides us with a valuable clue about what we should aim to do with our theories. It also provides a useful way of evaluating any theory that we are developing. If our theory doesn't propose an answer to an interesting question, it probably needs to be redeveloped. As we consider different strategies for developing theories, we will refer back to this basic idea of answering questions.

2.3 IDENTIFYING INTERESTING VARIATION

A useful first step in theory building is to think about phenomena that vary and to focus on general patterns. Because theories are designed to explain variation in the dependent variable, identifying some variation that is of interest to you is a good jumping-off point. In Chapter 4 we present a discussion of two of the most common research designs – cross-sectional and time-series observational studies – in some detail. For now, it is useful to give a brief description of each in terms of the types of variation in

---

[3] The Beck and Katz (1995) paper, which is one of the most influential technical papers in the history of political science, is the exception to this.

the dependent variable. These should help clarify the types of variation to consider as you begin to think about potential research ideas.

When we think about measuring our dependent variable, the first things that we need to identify are the time and spatial dimensions over which we would like to measure this variable. The **time dimension** identifies the point or points in time at which we would like to measure our variable. Depending on what we are measuring, typical time increments for political science data are annual, quarterly, monthly, or weekly measures. The **spatial dimension** identifies the physical units that we want to measure. There is a lot of variability in terms of the spatial units in political science data. If we are looking at survey data, the spatial unit will be the individual people who answered the survey (known as survey respondents). If we are looking at data on US state governments, the typical spatial unit will be the 50 US states. Data from international relations and comparative politics often take nations as their spatial units. Throughout this book, we think about measuring our dependent variable such that one of these two dimensions will be static (or constant). This means that our measures of our dependent variable will be of one of two types. The first is a **cross-sectional measure**, in which the time dimension is the same for all cases and the dependent variable is measured for multiple spatial units. The second is a **time-series measure**, in which the spatial dimension is the same for all cases and the dependent variable is measured at multiple points in time. Although it is possible for us to measure the same variable across both time and space, we strongly recommend thinking in terms of variation across only one of these two dimensions as you attempt to develop a theory about what causes this variation.[4] Let's consider an example of each type of dependent variable.

2.3.1   Cross-Sectional Example

In Figure 2.1 we see military spending as a percentage of gross domestic product (GDP) in 2005 for 22 randomly selected nations. We can tell that this variable is measured cross-sectionally, because it varies across spatial units (nations) but does not vary across time (it is measured for the year 2005 for each case). When we measure variables across spatial units like this, we have to be careful to choose appropriate measures that are comparable across spatial units. To better understand this, imagine that we had measured our dependent variable as the amount of money that each nation spent on its military. The problem would be that country

---

[4] As we mentioned in Chapter 1, we will eventually theorize about multiple independent variables simultaneously causing the same dependent variable to vary. Confining variation in the dependent variable to a single dimension helps to make such multivariate considerations tractable.

currencies – the Albanian Lek, the Bangladeshi Taka, and Chilean Peso – do not take on the same value. We would need to know the currency exchange rates in order to make these comparable across nations. Using currency exchange rates, we would be able to convert the absolute amounts of money that each nation had spent into a common measure. We could think of this particular measure as an operationalization of the concept of relative military "might." This would be a perfectly reasonable dependent variable for theories about what makes one nation more powerful than another. Why, you might ask, would we want to measure military spending as a percentage of GDP? The answer is that this comparison is our attempt to measure the percentage of the total budgetary effort available that a nation is putting into its armed forces. Some nations have larger economies than others, and this measure allows us to answer the question of how much of their total economic activity each nation is putting toward its military. With this variation in mind, we develop a theory to answer the question: "What *causes* a nation to put more or less of its available economic resources toward military spending?"

> **YOUR TURN: What causes military spending?**
>
> Thinking about data like those displayed in Figure 2.1, come up with some answers to the question: "What *causes* a nation to put more or less of its available economic resources toward military spending?"

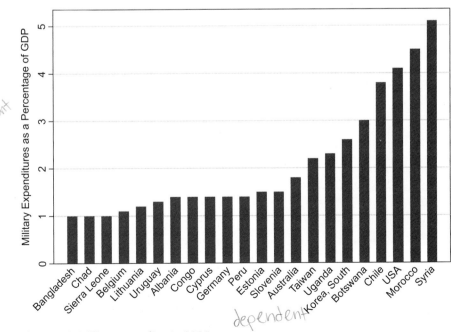

Figure 2.1 Military spending in 2005

If you just had a mental alarm bell go off telling you that we seemed to be violating one of our rules of the road from Chapter 1, then congratulations – you are doing a good job paying attention. Our second rule of the road is "don't let data alone drive your theories." Remember that we also can phrase this rule as "try to develop theories before examining the data on which you will perform your tests." Note, however, that in this example we are only examining variation in one of our variables, in this case the dependent variable. We would start to get into real problems if we plotted pairs of variables and then developed a theory only once we observed a pair of variables that varied together. If this still seems like we are getting too close to our data before developing our theory, we could develop a theory about military spending using Figure 2.1, but then test that theory with a different set of data that may or may not contain the data depicted in Figure 2.1.

2.3.2   Time-Series Example

In Figure 2.2 we see the monthly level of US presidential approval displayed from 1995 to 2005. We can tell that this variable is measured as a time series because the spatial unit is the same across all observations (the United States), but the variable has been measured at multiple points in time (each month). This measure is comparable across the cases; for each

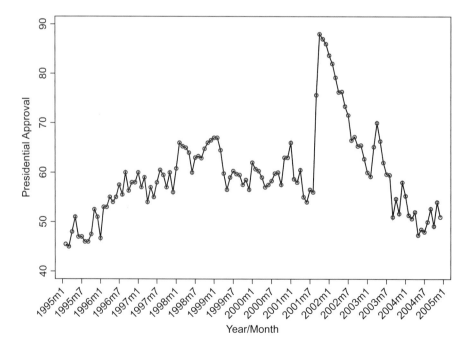

Figure 2.2 Presidential approval, 1995–2005

month we are looking at the percentage of people who reported that they approved of the job that the president was doing. Once we have a measure like this that is comparable across cases, we can start to think about what independent variable might *cause* the level of the dependent variable to be higher or lower. In other words, we are looking for answers to the research question: "What *causes* presidential approval to go up and down?"

> **YOUR TURN: What causes presidential approval?**
>
> Thinking about data like those displayed in Figure 2.2, come up with some answers to the question: "What *causes* presidential approval to go up and down?"

2.4 LEARNING TO USE YOUR KNOWLEDGE

One of the common problems that people have when trying to develop a theory about a phenomenon of interest is that they can't get past a particular political event in time or a particular place about which they know a lot. It is helpful to know some specifics about politics, but it is also important to be able to distance yourself from the specifics of one case and to think more broadly about the underlying causal process. To use an analogy, it's fine to know something about trees, but we want to theorize about the forest. Remember, one of our rules of the road is to try to make our theories general.

2.4.1 Moving from a Specific Event to More General Theories

For an example of this, return to Figure 2.2. What is the first thing that you think most people notice when they look at Figure 2.2? Once they have figured out what the dimensions are in this figure (US presidential approval over time), many people look at the fall of 2001 and notice the sharp increase in presidential approval that followed the terrorist attacks on the United States on September 11, 2001. This is a period of recent history about which many people have detailed memories. In particular, they might remember how the nation rallied around President Bush in the aftermath of these attacks. There are few people who would doubt that there was a causal linkage between these terrorist attacks and the subsequent spike in presidential approval.

At first glance, this particular incident might strike us as a unique event from which general theoretical insights cannot be drawn. After all, terrorist attacks on US soil are rare events, and attacks of this magnitude are even more rare. The challenge to the scientific mind when we have strong confidence about a causal relationship in one specific incident is to push the core concepts around in what we might call thought experiments: How might a less-effective terrorist attack affect public opinion? How might other types of international incidents shape public opinion? Do we think that terrorist attacks lead to similar reactions in public opinion toward leaders in other nations? Each of these questions is posed in general terms, taking the specific events of this one incident as a jumping-off point. The answers to these more general questions should lead us to general theories about the causal impact of international incidents on public opinion.

In the 1970s John Mueller moved from the specifics of particular international incidents and their influence on presidential approval toward a general theory of what causes rallies (or short-term increases) in presidential approval.[5] Mueller developed a theory that presidential approval would increase in the short term any time that there was international conflict. Mueller thought that this would occur because, in the face of international conflict, people would tend to put aside their partisan differences and other critiques that they may have of the president's handling of his job and support him as the commander in chief of the nation. In Mueller's statistical analysis of time-series data on presidential approval, he found that there was substantial support for his hypothesis that international conflicts would raise presidential approval rates, and this in turn gave him confidence in his theory of public opinion rallies.

2.4.2 Know Local, Think Global: Can You Drop the Proper Nouns?

Physicists don't have theories that apply only in France, and neither should we. Yet many political scientists write articles with one particular geographic context in mind. Among these, the articles that have the greatest impact are those that advance general theories from which the proper nouns have been removed.[6] An excellent example of this is Michael Lewis-Beck's (1997) "Who's the Chef?" Lewis-Beck, like many observers of French politics, had observed the particularly colorful period from 1986 to 1988 during which the president was a socialist named François Mitterand and the prime minister was Jacques Chirac, a right-wing politician from the Gaullist RPR party. The height of this political melodrama occurred when both leaders showed up to international summits of world leaders claiming to be the rightful representative of the French Republic. This led to a famous photo of the leaders of the G7 group of nations that contained eight people.[7]

---

[5] See Mueller (1973).

[6] By "proper nouns," we mean specific names of people or countries. But this logic can and should be pushed further to include specific dates, as we subsequently argue.

[7] The G7, now the G8 with the inclusion of Russia, is an annual summit meeting of the heads of government from the world's most powerful nations.

Although many people saw this as just another colorful anecdote about the ever-changing nature of the power relationship between presidents and prime ministers in Fifth Republic France, Lewis-Beck moved from the specifics of such events to develop and test a general theory about political control and public opinion. His theory was that changing the political control of the economy would cause public opinion to shift in terms of who was held accountable for the economy. In France, during times of unified political control of the top offices, the president is dominant, and thus according to Lewis-Beck's theory the president should be held accountable for economic outcomes. However, during periods of divided control, Lewis-Beck's theory leads to the expectation that the prime minister, because of his or her control of economic management during such periods, should be held accountable for economic outcomes. Through careful analysis of time-series data on political control and economic accountability, Lewis-Beck found that his theory was indeed supported.

Although the results of this study are important for advancing our understanding of French politics, the theoretical contribution made by Lewis-Beck was much greater because he couched it in general terms and without proper nouns. We also can use this logic to move from an understanding of a specific event to general theories that explain variation across multiple events. For example, although it might be tempting to think that every US presidential election is entirely unique – with different candidates (proper names) and different historical circumstances – the better scientific theory does *not* explain only the outcome of the 2016 US presidential election, but of US presidential elections in general. That is, instead of asking "Why did Trump beat Clinton in the 2016 election?" we should ask either "What causes the incumbent party to win or lose in US presidential elections?" or "What causes Republican candidates to fare better or worse than Democratic candidates in US presidential elections?"

2.5 THREE STRATEGIES TOWARD DEVELOPING AN ORIGINAL THEORY

One of the best ways to think about developing an original theory is to break the process down with a little mathematical notation. When we do this, we can see that most works in political science follow one of three strategies for developing a new theory. These strategies, to be sure, represent a simplification of the ways in which political scientists generate their own research programs. But sometimes simplifying things is helpful, especially when faced with a possibly daunting task.

Before we introduce these strategies, we will introduce some new notational conventions and a third variable type. Remember from Chapter 1 that we introduced the idea of thinking about the world in terms of variables. We also discussed theories as being about the causal relationship between an independent variable and a dependent variable. Moving forward in the book, we will find it useful to use notational shorthand in which we will represent independent variables as X or Z and dependent variables as Y. We can summarize a typical theory as "$X \rightarrow Y$," short for "X causes Y."

Using this notational shorthand, we can summarize the three strategies for developing a new theory as follows:

1. A new Y (and an existing X).
2. An existing Y and a new X.
3. A new Z which modifies an established $X \rightarrow Y$.

We take them in turn.

2.5.1   Theory Type 1: a New Y (and Some X)

The first type of theory involves the creation of, invention of, or discovery of some new type of dependent variable, and then theorizing about some independent variable that might cause the dependent variable to vary. What makes projects like this distinctive – and difficult! – is the word "new." A research project of this type is exceedingly creative, and also rather rare. Political scientists don't just arrive in their offices in the morning, take that first swig of coffee, and confront the day with the thought, "Okay, here we go. Today I'm going to create another new dependent variable to analyze." If only it were that simple!

The burden of creating a new concept to represent a brand-new dependent variable is considerable. Moreover, because research never occurs in a metaphorical vacuum, it has to be a concept that other scholars will find interesting. Otherwise, your work is unfortunately quite likely to be ignored.

If you can conceptualize something genuinely new, and then proceed to measure it, then the next (and critical) step is to theorize about some X that might cause this new Y to vary. Again, this is sometimes a formidable task, but, on the other hand, it's likely that, if you are able to imagine a new dependent variable, you might already have a clue about what force or forces might cause it to vary.

Projects of this type can break new paths toward scientific knowledge – paths that other scholars can follow, and that can lead to new theories and findings about how the world works. An example of a project like this is shown in Nelson Polsby's article "The Institutionalization of the U.S. House of Representatives," which appeared in the *American*

Political Science Review in 1968. Polsby developed a new variable, which he referred to as the "institutionalization" of an organization. As an organization becomes increasingly institutionalized, three things happen, he claimed. First, the organization becomes more clearly separated from the environment around it. Second, the organization becomes increasingly complex, with functions and roles that cannot simply be interchanged. Finally, the organization develops increasingly complex rules and procedures for handling its internal business. On all three levels, Polsby was able to show that, since the founding of the republic, the US Congress has become increasingly institutionalized. That is, his newly introduced concept became an interesting over-time variable that begged for scientific explanation – in other words: Why has the House become more institutionalized? In his article, Polsby offers some theoretical speculation about the causes of this phenomenon. The article exemplifies this type of project, since no previous scholars had thought of this as a possible dependent variable that needed explaining. And the article has been cited nearly one thousand times by subsequent scholars.

> **YOUR TURN: Thinking about the causes of institutionalization**
>
> Some states in the US have more institutionalized legislatures than do others. Can you think of any possible causes of this phenomenon?

So how do you find a new *Y*? First, you have to know that it is, indeed, *new*, by which we mean that no previous scholar has already conducted research on this particular dependent variable. This requires conducting a thorough research of the existing literature, likely using Google Scholar and some variations on keywords.[8] Beyond that, there is no magical formula, no recipe to follow that will lead to a new dependent variable that begs explanation. What we can say, to hark back to our analogy earlier in this chapter, is that the best way to get struck by metaphorical lightning is to read academic works. Read with a hunger that points toward questions like, "What *don't* we know yet?" This is a theme we'll return to later in this chapter.

2.5.2 Project Type 2: an Existing *Y* and a New *X*

Perhaps you will find that creating a new dependent variable from scratch is too challenging for now. If so, you're in very good company. Many researchers come to the conclusion that all of the good dependent variables

---

[8] Google Scholar is found at scholar.google.com, and is distinct from the main Google search engine, found at www.google.com. Be careful not to confuse the two. We discuss the use of Google Scholar to get a sense of the literature on a particular subject in Section 2.6.1.

are already taken. And if you find yourself in this position, perhaps it's time to consider our second type of new theory: taking an existing Y and theorizing how a new X might cause it.

You'll note that theories like these also have the word "new" in them – though this time, what's new isn't the dependent variable, but the independent variable. The burden of producing something new – by which we mean, a relationship between X and Y that some other scholar has not already examined in the same way that you're proposing – is still considerable. But in projects like this, the sense that a new scholar is "standing on the shoulders of giants" is far more evident. Previous scholars may have already examined a particular dependent variable, proposing several causes that might explain its variation. Those causes, to be sure, might be competing with one another, or they might complement one another. The heart of projects of this type is identifying some *other* possible cause of Y that has not been adequately examined.

The burden of novelty requires thorough canvassing of the existing literature on the particular phenomenon that interests you. For example, if you are interested in explaining cross-national variation in why citizens in some countries seem more trusting of government, whereas others seem less trusting of government, this means that you will have to consume that literature, systematically noting what independent variables – or categories of independent variables (like "the economy") – have already been examined by previous researchers.

2.5.3 A New Z which Modifies an Established $X \rightarrow Y$

A third path to an original theory is to start with an established $X \rightarrow Y$ relationship and think about how that relationship might vary across the values of a third variable Z. The first step is to figure out what the established $X \rightarrow Y$ relationship is and then to think about what factors might make that relationship different across cases. Those factors can then be thought of as your new variable, Z. So, if the established relationship is that X is positively related to Y, you might begin by thinking about circumstances in which it might be the case that that relationship is stronger or weaker. You might also imagine cases for which we wouldn't expect any relationship between X and Y or where the relationship between X and Y is negative. When you do so, whatever it is that you would use to describe what it is that causes the $X \rightarrow Y$ relationship to be different becomes your new variable Z. Again, notice the word "new" here; in order for your work to make an original contribution, something has to be new.

So, how do we come up with ideas about new modifying Z variables? One strategy is to think about a previously examined $X \rightarrow Y$ relationship in different contexts. Three ways to start your thinking along these lines would be to think about how $X \to Y$ might be different across different time periods, different types of individuals, or different geographic contexts. As you do so, it is important to ask yourself the question "What is it about these different times/individuals/geographic contexts that makes $X \to Y$ different?" Once you answer this question, you have your new variable Z, and once you have an explanation for *why* you think that Z modifies the $X \to Y$ connection, you have a new theory.

To take an example where the newness comes from a new time, consider that, at least since the work of Converse (1964), it has been noticed that among members of the American public there was not a particularly strong relationship between an individual's party identification (X) and their policy attitudes (Y). That is, researchers had found that Republicans express more conservative policy attitudes and Democrats express more liberal attitudes, but the established positive $X \to Y$ relationship was pretty weak. More recent research, though, particularly by Levendusky (2009), that investigates this same $X \to Y$ connection has shown that the relationship is quite a bit stronger in recent years. That is, in what Levendusky calls "the partisan sort," something has happened to make the relationship between an individual's partisanship and their policy preferences much more strong. This led Levendusky, of course, to ask what made this happen, and opened up considerable space for additional research in the study of American public opinion. Levendusky proposed that increasingly ideological behavior by elites in national politics, his Z, had provided partisan clarity and thus strengthened the established $X \to Y$ relationship between party identification and policy attitudes.

Other projects investigate an existing $X \to Y$ connection in different geographic contexts. Throughout this book we have used the example of the relationship between the US economy and incumbent-party electoral fortunes as one of our running examples. Indeed, much of the pioneering work on what is called economic voting took place in the US context. Those findings show that a strong economy clearly benefits the candidate of the incumbent party, and a weak economy hurts the incumbent party's electoral fortunes. Scholars naturally wondered if these patterns would also be found in other democracies. Fascinatingly, in some countries, an $X \to Y$ connection existed similar to that in the United States, but in others, no such connection could be found. Naturally, that led scholars to wonder why evidence of economic voting was strong in some countries, and absent in others. Powell and Whitten (1993) show that the strength of the economic vote is driven by a third variable, their Z, that they call the "clarity of responsibility" of the governing party's handling of the economy. In countries with coalition governments where multiple parties share power, for example, it's much less clear who deserves credit or blame for the health of the economy than it is in a country where control over the economic policy is concentrated in the hands of a single party.

YOUR TURN: Thinking about the impact of gender on the relationship between education and support for abortion rights

The literature on US public opinion toward abortion rights has established that there is a positive relationship between number of years of education and support for abortion rights. How do you think this established $X \rightarrow Y$ relationship might be different for men and women (i.e., treating gender as Z)?

2.6 USING THE LITERATURE WITHOUT GETTING BURIED IN IT

To assess the "newness" of a theory, you first have to be aware of what scholarly work has already been done in that area of inquiry. How do you go about doing that? This section is devoted to how to identify the giants whose shoulders you would like to stand upon.

2.6.1 Identifying the Important Work on a Subject – Using Citation Counts

One of the most daunting tasks faced by a researcher starting out is to identify what has been done before. Most keyword searches will yield a phone book-sized return of articles and other publications. Even the most avid reader will be overwhelmed. Thankfully, citations provide a powerful shortcut for sorting out which of the many published works on a topic are the most important.

By now you have probably had some experience with having to produce a written work with citations of sources. Citations are one of the most valued currencies in which scientific researchers conduct their business. To be cited is to be relevant; to be uncited is to be ignored. For this reason, citations have formed the basis for a wide range of indices by which individual scientists, scientific journals, academic departments, and even entire universities are ranked relative to each other. We can safely say that in academia today citations are very important.

As such, we recommend taking advantage of the fact that citations are a powerful tool for distinguishing among the many articles any time that you do a search using Google Scholar or similar tools. So, an obvious next question is: "How many citations does a publication need for it to be regarded as having a substantial impact?" As a rough rule of thumb, we suggest that you use 20 citations. Of course, as you might imagine, the number of citations that a publication has is, in part, a function of time.

Thus, an article that was published in 2015 that already has ten citations in 2017 is probably going to have a substantial influence.

2.6.2 Oh No! Someone Else Has Already Done What I Was Planning to Do. What Do I Do Now?

One of the most frustrating things that can happen during a search of the literature is that you find that someone else has already done what you had in mind and published an article or book testing your theory or something close to it. As frustrating as this may be at first, it is actually a good sign, because it means that what you had in mind was in fact a good idea. If this happens to you, you should read the work and think about how it can be improved upon. In Chapter 4, after we have introduced some critical concepts for doing so, we have an extensive section titled "Dissecting the Research by Other Scholars" (Section 4.4) which provides a roadmap for doing this.

2.6.3 Critically Examining Previous Research to Develop an Original Theory

Once you have identified an area in which you want to conduct research and dissected the influential works in that area, it is useful to ask a series of critical questions. As we discussed in Chapter 1, part of taking a scientific approach is to be skeptical of research findings, whether they are our own or those of other researchers. By taking a skeptical look at the research of others, we can develop new research ideas of our own and thus develop new theories.

We therefore suggest looking at research that seems interesting to you and, after you have done dissection of some of the most influential works along the lines described in Section 4.4, try to answer the following questions:

- What (if any) other causes of the dependent variable did the previous researchers miss?
- Can their theory be applied elsewhere?
- If we believe their findings, are there further implications?
- How might this theory work at different levels of aggregation (micro $\Longleftrightarrow$ macro)?

Let's elaborate on these.

What Did the Previous Researchers Miss?

Any time that we read the work of others, the first thing that we should do is break down their theory or theories in terms of the independent

(X and Z) and dependent variables (Y) that they claim are causally related to each other. We cannot overstate the importance of this endeavor. We understand that this can be a difficult task for a beginning student, but it gets easier with practice. A good way to start this process is to look at the figures or tables in an article and ask yourself, "What is the dependent variable here?" Once we have done this and also identified the key independent variable, we should think about whether the causal arguments that other researchers have advanced seem reasonable. (In Chapter 3 we present a detailed four-step process for doing this.) We should also be in the habit of coming up with other independent variables that we think might be causally related to the same dependent variable. Going through this type of mental exercise can lead to new theories that are worth pursuing.

Can Their Theory Be Applied Elsewhere?

When we read about the empirical research that others have conducted, we should be sure that we understand which specific cases they were studying when they tested their theory. We should then proceed with a mental exercise in which we think about what we might find if we tested the same theory on other cases. In doing so, we will probably identify some cases for which we expect to get the same results, as well as other cases for which we might have different expectations. Of course, we would have to carry out our own empirical research to know whether our speculation along these lines is correct, but replicating research can lead to interesting findings. The most useful theoretical development comes when we can identify systematic patterns in the types of cases that will fit and those that will not fit the established theory. As we discussed in Section 2.5, these systematic patterns can be the result of additional variables, Z, that shape how an established $X \rightarrow Y$ relationship works across an expanded set of cases.

If We Believe Their Findings, Are There Further Implications?

Beginning researchers often find themselves intimidated when they read convincing accounts of the research carried out by more established scholars. After all, how can we ever expect to produce such innovative theories and find such convincingly supportive results from extensive empirical tests? Instead of being intimidated by such works, we need to learn to view them as opportunities – opportunities to carry their logic further and think about what other implications might be out there. If, for example, another researcher has produced a convincing theory about how voters behave, we could ask "How might this new understanding alter the behavior of strategic politicians who understand that voters behave in this fashion?"

One of the best examples of this type of research extension in political science comes from our previous example of John Mueller's research on rallies in presidential popularity. Because Mueller (1973) had found such convincingly supportive evidence of this "rally round the flag effect" in his empirical testing, other researchers were able to think through the strategic consequences of this phenomenon. This led to a new body of research on a phenomenon called "diversionary use of force" (Richards et al., 1993). The idea of this new research is that, because strategic politicians will be aware that international conflicts temporarily increase presidential popularity, they will choose to generate international conflicts at times when they need such a boost.

How Might This Theory Work at Different Levels of Aggregation (Micro ⟺ Macro)?

As a final way to use the research of others to generate new theories, we suggest considering how a theory might work differently at varying levels of aggregation. In political science research, the lowest level of aggregation is usually at the level of individual people in studies of public opinion. As we saw in Section 2.6.3, when we find a trend in terms of individual-level behavior, we can develop new theoretical insights by thinking about how strategic politicians might take advantage of such trends. Sometimes it is possible to gain these insights by simply changing the level of aggregation. As we have seen, political scientists have often studied trends in public opinion by examining data measured at the national level over time. This type of study is referred to as the study of macro-politics. When we find trends in public opinion at higher (macro) levels of aggregation, it is always an interesting thought exercise to consider what types of patterns of individual-level or "micro-"level behavior are driving these aggregate-level findings.

As an example of this, return to the "rally round the flag" example and change the level of aggregation. We have evidence that, when there are international conflicts, public opinion toward the president becomes more positive. What types of individual-level forces might be driving this observed aggregate-level trend? It might be the case that there is a uniform shift across all types of individuals in their feelings about the president. It might also be the case that the shift is less uniform. Perhaps individuals who dislike the president's policy positions on domestic events are willing to put these differences aside in the face of international conflicts, whereas the opinions of the people who were already supporters of the president remain unchanged. Thinking about the individual-level dynamics that drive aggregate observations can be a fruitful source of new causal theories.

> **YOUR TURN: Thinking about time series ↔ cross-section**
>
> Think about what the data from Figure 2.1 would look like for a single country over multiple years. What do you think *causes* military spending to go up and down over time?
>
> Think about what the data from Figure 2.2 would look like for multiple countries in the same year. What do you think *causes* presidential approval to be higher or lower across countries?
>
> Notice how changing the type of data changes the research question?

2.7 THINK FORMALLY ABOUT THE CAUSES THAT LEAD TO VARIATION IN YOUR DEPENDENT VARIABLE

Thus far in this book we have discussed thinking about the political world in an organized, systematic fashion. By now, we hope that you are starting to think about politics in terms of independent variables and dependent variables and are developing theories about the causal relationships between them. The theories that we have considered thus far have come from thinking rigorously about the phenomena that we want to explain and deducing plausible causal explanations. One extension of this type of rigorous thinking is labeled "**formal theory**" or "**rational choice**."[9] Researchers have used this approach to develop answers to research questions about how people make strategic decisions. Put another way, if politics is a game, how do we explain the way that people play it?

To answer questions along these lines, the formal-theory approach to social science phenomena starts out with a fairly basic set of assumptions about human behavior and then uses game theory and other mathematical tools to build models of phenomena of interest. We can summarize these assumptions about human behavior by saying that formal theorists assume that all individuals are **rational utility maximizers** – that they attempt to maximize their self-interest. Individuals are faced with a variety of choices in political interactions, and those choices carry with them different consequences – some desirable, others undesirable. By thinking through the incentives faced by individuals, users of this approach begin with the strategic foundations of the decisions that individuals face. Formal theorists then deduce theoretical expectations of what individuals will do given their preferences and the strategic environment that they confront.

---

[9] The terms "formal theory" and "rational choice" have been used fairly interchangeably to describe the application of game theory and other formal mathematical tools to puzzles of human behavior. We have a slight preference for the term "formal theory" because it is a more overarching term describing the enterprise of using these tools, whereas "rational choice" describes the most critical assumption that this approach makes.

That sounds like a mouthful, we know. Let's begin with a simple example: If human beings are self-interested, then (by definition) members of a legislature are self-interested. This assumption suggests that members will place a high premium on reelection. Why is that? Because, first and foremost, a politician must be in office if she is going to achieve her political goals. And from this simple deduction flows a whole set of hypotheses about Congressional organization and behavior.[10]

This approach to studying politics is a mathematically rigorous attempt to think through what it would be like to be in the place of different actors involved in a situation in which they have to choose how to act. In essence, formal theory is a lot like the saying that we should not judge a person until we have walked a mile in his or her shoes. We use the tools of formal theory to try to put ourselves in the position of imagining that we are in someone else's shoes and thinking about the different choices that he or she has to make. In the following sections we introduce the basic tools for doing this by using an **expected utility** approach and then provide a famous example of how researchers used this framework to develop theories about why people vote.

2.7.1 Utility and Expected Utility

Think about the choice that you have made to read this chapter of this book. What are your expected benefits and what are the costs that you expect to incur? One benefit may be that you are genuinely curious about how we build theories of politics. Another expected benefit may be that your professor is likely to test you on this material, and you expect that you will perform better if you have read this chapter. There are, no doubt, also costs to reading this book. What else might you be doing with your time? This is the way that formal theorists approach the world.

Formal theorists think about the world in terms of the outcome of a collection of individual-level decisions about what to do. In thinking about an individual's choices of actions, formal theorists put everything in terms of **utility**. Utility is an intentionally vague quantity. The utility from a particular action is equal to the sum of all benefits minus the sum of all costs from that action. If we consider an action Y, we can summarize the utility from Y for individual i with the following formula:

$$U_i(Y) = \sum B_i(Y) - \sum C_i(Y),$$

where $U_i(Y)$ is the utility for individual i from action Y, $\sum B_i(Y)$ is the sum of the benefits B_i from action Y for individual i, and $\sum C_i(Y)$ is

---

[10] See Mayhew (1974) and Fiorina (1989).

the sum of the costs C_i from action Y for individual i. When choosing among a set of possible actions (including the decision not to act), a rational individual will choose that action that maximizes their utility. To put this formally,

$$\text{given a set of choices } Y = Y_1, Y_2, Y_3, \ldots, Y_n,$$
$$\text{individual } i \text{ will choose } Y_a \text{ such that } U_i(Y_a) > U_i(Y_b) \; \forall \; b \neq a,$$

which translates into, "given a set of choices of actions Y_1 through Y_n, individual i will choose that action (Y_a) such that the utility to individual i from that action is greater than the utility to individual i from any action (Y_b) for all ($\forall$) actions b not equal to a." In more straightforward terms, we could translate this into the individual choosing that action that he deems best for himself.

At this point, it is reasonable to look around the real world and think about exceptions. Is this really the way that the world works? What about altruism? During the summer of 2006, the world's second-richest man, Warren Buffett, agreed to donate more than 30 billion dollars to the Bill and Melinda Gates Foundation. Could this possibly have been rational utility-maximizing behavior? What about suicide bombers? The answers to these types of questions show both the flexibility and a potential problem of the concept of utility. Note that, in the preceding formulae, there is always a subscripted i under each of the referenced utility components, (U_i, B_i, C_i). This is because different individuals have *different* evaluations of the benefits (B_i) and costs (C_i) associated with a particular action. When the critic of this approach says, "How can this possibly be utility-maximizing behavior?", the formal theorist responds, "Because this is just an individual with an unusual utility structure."

Think of it another way. Criticizing formal theory because it takes preferences as "given" – that is, as predetermined, rather than the focus of inquiry – strikes us as beside the point. Other parts of political science can and should study preference formation; think about political psychology and the study of public opinion. What formal theory does, and does well, is to say, "Okay, once an individual has her preferences – regardless of where they came from – how do those preferences interact with strategic opportunities and incentives to produce political outcomes?" Because formal theory takes those preferences as given, it does not mean that the preference-formation process is unimportant. It merely means that formal theory is here to explain a different portion of social reality.

From a scientific perspective, this is fairly unsettling. As we discussed in Chapter 1, we want to build scientific knowledge based on real-world observation. How do we observe people's utilities? Although we can ask people questions about what they like and don't like, and even their perceptions of costs and benefits, we can never truly observe utilities. Instead, the assumption of utility maximization is just that – an assumption. This assumption is, however, a fairly robust assumption, and we can do a lot if we are willing to make it and move forward while keeping the potential problems in the back of our minds.

Another potentially troubling aspect of the rational-actor utility-maximizing assumption that you may have thought of is the assumption of **complete information**. In other words, what if we don't know exactly what the costs and benefits will be from a particular action? In the preceding formulae, we were operating under the assumption of complete information, for which we knew exactly what would be the costs, benefits, and thus the utility from each possible action. When we relax this assumption, we move our discussion from utility to expected utility. We represent this change in the assumptions about information by putting an "E" and square brackets around each term to which it applies. This type of transformation is known as "putting expectations" in front of all utilities. For example, the term $U_i(Y)$, which is read as "the utility for individual 'i' from action Y," becomes $E[U_i(Y)]$ under **incomplete information**, which is read as "the expected utility for individual 'i' from action Y." So, returning to our rational-actor assumption, under incomplete information, for an individual action Y,

$$E[U_i(Y)] = \sum E[B_i(Y)] - \sum E[C_i(Y)],$$

and a rational actor will maximize his expected utility thus:

given a set of choices $Y = Y_1, Y_2, Y_3, \ldots, Y_n,$
individual i will choose Y_a such that $E[U_i(Y_a)] > E[U_i(Y_b)] \; \forall \; b \neq a.$

2.7.2 The Puzzle of Turnout

One of the oldest and most enduring applications of formal theory to politics is known as the "paradox of voting." William Riker and Peter Ordeshook set out the core arguments surrounding this application in their influential 1968 article in the *American Political Science Review* titled "A Theory of the Calculus of Voting." Their paper was written to weigh in on a lively debate over the rationality of voting. In particular, Riker and Ordeshook presented a theory to answer the research question "Why do people vote?" In Riker and Ordeshook's notation (with subscripts added), the expected utility of voting was summarized as

$$R_i = (B_i P_i) - C_i,$$

where R_i is the reward that an individual receives from voting, B_i is the differential benefit that an individual voter receives "from the success of his more preferred candidate over his less preferred one" (Riker and Ordeshook, 1968, p. 25), P_i is the probability that that voter will cast the deciding vote that makes his preferred candidate the winner, and C_i is the sum of the costs that the voter incurs from voting.[11] If R_i is positive, the individual votes; otherwise, he abstains.[12]

We'll work our way through the right-hand side of this formula and think about the likely values of each term in this equation for an individual eligible voter in a US presidential election. The term B_i is likely to be greater than zero for most eligible voters in most US presidential elections. The reasons for this vary widely from policy preferences to gut feelings about the relative character traits of the different candidates. Note, however, that the B_i term is multiplied by the P_i term. What is the likely value of P_i? Most observers of elections would argue that P_i is extremely small and effectively equal to zero for every voter in most elections. In the case of a US presidential election, for one vote to be decisive, that voter must live in a state in which the popular vote total would be *exactly* tied if that individual did not vote, and this must be a presidential election for which that particular state would swing the outcome in the Electoral College to either candidate. Because P_i is effectively equal to zero, the entire term $(B_i P_i)$ is effectively equal to zero.

What about the costs of voting, C_i? Voting takes time for all voters. Even if a voter lives right next door to the polling place, he has to take some time to walk next door, perhaps stand in a line, and cast his ballot. The well-worn phrase "time is money" certainly applies here. Even if the voter in question is not working at the time that he votes, he could be doing something other than voting. Thus it is pretty clear that C_i is greater than zero. If C_i is greater than zero and $(B_i P_i)$ is effectively equal to zero, then R_i must be negative. How, then, do we explain the millions of people that vote in US presidential elections, or, indeed, elections around the world? Is this evidence that people are truly not rational? Or, perhaps, is it evidence that millions of people systematically overestimate P_i? Influential political economy scholars, including Anthony Downs and Gordon Tullock, posed these questions in the early years of formal theoretical analyses of politics.

Riker and Ordeshook's answer was that there must be some other benefit to voting that is not captured by the term $(B_i P_i)$. They proposed that the voting equation should be

[11] For simplicity in this example, consider an election in which there are only two candidates competing. Adding more candidates makes the calculation of B_i more complicated, but does not change the basic result of this model.

[12] For clarity, we follow Riker and Ordeshook's convention of using masculine pronouns.

$$R_i = (B_i P_i) - C_i + D_i,$$

where D_i is the satisfaction that individuals feel from participating in the democratic process, regardless of the impact of their participation on the final outcome of the election. Riker and Ordeshook argued that D_i could be made up of a variety of different efficacious feelings about the political system, ranging from fulfilling one's duties as a citizen to standing up and being counted.

Think of the contribution that Riker and Ordeshook made to political science, and that, more broadly, formal theory makes to political science, in the following way: Riker and Ordeshook's theory leads us to wonder why any individual will vote. And yet, empirically, we notice that close to half of the adult population votes in any given presidential election in recent history. What formal theory accomplishes for us is that it helps us to focus in on exactly *why* people do bother, rather than to assert, normatively, that people *should*.[13]

<table>
<tr><td>**2.8**</td><td>**THINK ABOUT THE INSTITUTIONS: THE RULES USUALLY MATTER**</td></tr>
</table>

In the previous section we thought about individuals and developing theoretical insights by thinking about their utility calculations. In this section we extend this line of thinking to develop theories about how people will interact with each other in political situations. One particularly rich source for theoretical insights along these lines comes from formal thinking about institutional arrangements and the influence that they have in shaping political behavior and outcomes. In other words, researchers have developed theories about politics by thinking about the rules under which the political game is played. To fully understand these rules and their impact, we need to think through some counterfactual scenarios in which we imagine how outcomes would be altered if there were different rules in place. This type of exercise can lead to some valuable theoretical insights. In the sections that follow, we consider two examples of thinking about the impact of institutions.

---

[13] Of course, Riker and Ordeshook did not have the final word in 1968. In fact, the debate over the rationality of turnout has been at the core of the debate over the usefulness of formal theory in general. In their 1994 book titled *Pathologies of Rational Choice Theory*, Donald Green and Ian Shapiro made it the first point of attack in their critique of the role that formal theory plays in political science. One of Green and Shapiro's major criticisms of this part of political science was that the linkages between formal theory and empirical hypothesis tests were too weak. In reaction to these and other critics, the National Science Foundation launched a new program titled "Empirical Implications of Theoretical Models" (EITM) that was designed to strengthen the linkage between formal theory and empirical hypothesis tests.

2.8.1 Legislative Rules

Considering the rules of the political game has yielded theoretical insights into the study of legislatures and other governmental decision-making bodies. This has typically involved thinking about the **preference orderings** of expected utility-maximizing actors. For example, let's imagine a legislature made up of three individual members, X, Y, and Z.[14] The task in front of X, Y, and Z is to choose between three alternatives A, B, and C. The preference orderings for these three rational individuals are as follows:

$$X : ABC,$$
$$Y : BCA,$$
$$Z : CAB.$$

An additional assumption that is made under these circumstances is that the preferences of rational individuals are **transitive**. This means that if individual X likes A better than B and B better than C, then, for X's preferences to be transitive, he or she must also like A better than C. Why is this an important assumption to make? Consider the alternative. What if X liked A better than B and B better than C, but liked C better than A? Under these circumstances, it would be impossible to discuss what X wants in a meaningful fashion because X's preferences would produce an infinite cycle. To put this another way, no matter which of the three choices X chose, there would always be some other choice that X prefers. Under these circumstances, X could not make a rational choice.

In this scenario, what would the group prefer? This is not an easy question to answer. If they each voted for their first choice, each alternative would receive one vote. If these three individuals vote between pairs of alternatives, and they vote according to their preferences, we would observe the following results:

$$A \text{ versus } B, X \text{ and } Z \text{ versus } Y, A \text{ wins;}$$
$$B \text{ versus } C, X \text{ and } Y \text{ versus } Z, B \text{ wins;}$$
$$C \text{ versus } A, Y \text{ and } Z \text{ versus } X, C \text{ wins.}$$

Which of these three alternatives does the group collectively prefer? This is an impossible question to answer because the group's preferences cycle across the three alternatives. Another way of describing this group's

---

[14] We know that, in practice, legislatures tend to have many more members. Starting with this type of miniature-scaled legislature makes formal considerations much easier to carry out. Once we have arrived at conclusions based on calculations made on such a small scale, it is important to consider whether the conclusions that we have drawn would apply to more realistically larger-scaled scenarios.

preferences is to say that they are **intransitive** (despite the fact that, as you can see, each individual's preferences are transitive).

This result should be fairly troubling to people who are concerned with the fairness of democratic elections. One of the often-stated goals of elections is to "let the people speak." Yet, as we have just seen, it is possible that, even when the people involved are all rational actors, their collective preferences may not be rational. Under such circumstances, a lot of the normative concepts concerning the role of elections simply break down. This finding is at the heart of Arrow's theorem, which was developed by Kenneth Arrow in his 1951 book titled *Social Choice and Individual Values* (second edition 1990). At the time of its publication, political scientists largely ignored this book. As formal theory became more popular in political science, Arrow's mathematical approach to these issues became increasingly recognized. In 1982 William Riker popularized Arrow's theorem in his book *Liberalism Against Populism*, in which he presented a more accessible version of Arrow's theorem and bolstered a number of Arrow's claims through mathematical expositions.

2.8.2 The Rules Matter!

Continuing to work with our example of three individuals, X, Y, and Z, with the previously described preferences, now imagine that the three individuals will choose among the alternatives in two different rounds of votes between pairs of choices. In the first round of voting, two of the alternatives will be pitted against each other. In the second round of voting, the alternative that won the first vote will be pitted against the alternative that was not among the choices in the first round. The winner of the second round of voting is the overall winning choice.

In our initial consideration of this scenario, we will assume that X, Y, and Z will vote according to their preferences. What if X got to decide on the order in which the alternatives got chosen? We know that X's preference ordering is ABC. Can X set things up so that A will win? What if X made the following rules:

1st round: *B* versus *C*;

2nd round: 1st round winner versus *A*.

What would happen under these rules? We know that both X and Y prefer B to C, so B would win the first round and then would be paired against A in the second round. We also know that X and Z prefer A to B, so alternative A would win and X would be happy with this outcome.

Does voting like this occur in the real world? Actually, the answer is "yes." This form of pairwise voting among alternatives is the way that legislatures typically conduct their voting. If we think of individuals X, Y, and Z as being members of a legislature, we can see that whoever controls the ordering of the voting (the rules) has substantial power. To explore these issues further, let's examine the situation of individual Y. Remember that Y's preference ordering is BCA. So Y would be particularly unhappy about the outcome of the voting according to X's rules, because it resulted in Y's least-favorite outcome. But remember that, for our initial consideration, we assumed that X, Y, and Z will vote according to their preferences. If we relax this assumption, what might Y do? In the first round of voting, Y could cast a **strategic vote** for C against B.[15] If both X and Z continued to vote (sincerely) according to their preferences, then C would win the first round. Because we know that both X and Z prefer C to A, C would win the second round and would be the chosen alternative. Under these circumstances, Y would be better off because Y prefers alternative C to A.

From the perspective of members of a legislature, it is clearly better to control the rules than to vote strategically to try to obtain a better outcome. When legislators face reelection, one of the common tactics of their opponents is to point to specific votes in which the incumbent appears to have voted contrary to the preferences of his constituents. It would seem reasonable to expect that legislator Y comes from a district with the same or similar preferences to those of Y. By casting a strategic vote for C over B, Y was able to obtain a better outcome but created an opportunity for an electoral challenger to tell voters that Y had voted against the preferences of his district.

In *Congressmen in Committees*, Richard Fenno's (1973) classic study of the US House of Representatives, one of the findings was that the Rules Committee – along with the Ways and Means and the Appropriations Committees – was one of the most requested committee assignments from the individual members of Congress. At first glance, the latter two committees make sense as prominent committees and, indeed, receive much attention in the popular media. By contrast, the Rules Committee very rarely gets any media attention. Members of Congress certainly understand and appreciate the fact that the rules matter, and formal theoretical thought exercises like the preceding one help us to see why this is the case.

---

[15] The concept of a "strategic" vote is often confusing. For our purposes, we define a strategic vote as a vote that is cast with the strategic context in mind. Note that for a particular individual in a particular circumstance, it might be the case that the best strategic decision for them is to vote according to their preferences. The casting of a strategic vote becomes particularly interesting, however, when the strategic context leads to the casting of a vote that is different from the individual's preferences.

2.8.3 Extensions

These examples represent just the beginning of the uses of formal theory in political science. We have not even introduced two of the more important aspects of formal theory – spatial models and game theory – that are beyond the scope of this discussion. In ways that mirror applications in microeconomics, political scientists have used spatial models to study phenomena such as the placement of political parties along the ideological spectrum, much as economists have used spatial models to study the location of firms in a market. Likewise, game theory utilizes a highly structured sequence of moves by different players to show how any particular actor's utility depends not only on her own choices, but also on the choices made by the other actors. It is easy to see hints about how game theory works in the preceding simple three-actor, two-stage voting examples: X's best vote in the first stage likely depends on which alternative Y and Z choose to support, and vice versa. Game theory, then, highlights how the strategic choices made in politics are interdependent.

2.9 CONCLUSION

We have presented a series of different strategies for developing theories of politics. Each of these strategies involves some type of thought exercise in which we arrange and rearrange our knowledge about the political world in hopes that doing so will lead to new causal theories. You have, we're certain, noticed that there is no simple formula for generating a new theory and hopefully, as a result, appreciate our description of theory building as an "art" in the chapter's title. Theoretical developments come from many places, and being critically immersed in the ongoing literature that studies your phenomenon of choice is a good place to start.

In Chapter 3, we develop tools that will help you critically evaluate the causal claims in the theories that you develop from going through the steps that we introduced in this chapter. Then, in Chapter 4, we provide an overview of the different research designs that can be employed to help you to test hypotheses that come from your refined theory.

CONCEPTS INTRODUCED IN THIS CHAPTER

- complete information – the situation in which each actor in a game knows the exact payoffs from each possible outcome
- cross-sectional measure – a measure for which the time dimension is the same for all cases and the cases represent multiple spatial units

- expected utility – a calculation equal to the sum of all expected benefits minus the sum of all expected costs from that action under this calculation, the exact benefits and costs are not known with certainty
- formal theory – the application of game theory and other formal mathematical tools to puzzles of human behavior (used interchangeably with "rational choice")
- incomplete information – the situation in which each actor in a game does not know the exact payoffs from each possible outcome
- intransitive – an illogical mathematical relationship such that, despite the fact that *A* is greater than *B* and *B* is greater than *C*, *C* is greater than *A*
- preference orderings – the ranking from greatest to least of an actor's preferred outcomes
- rational choice – the application of game theory and other formal mathematical tools to puzzles of human behavior (used interchangeably with "formal theory")
- rational utility maximizers – an assumption about human behavior that stipulates that individuals attempt to maximize their self-interest
- spatial dimension – the physical units on which a variable is measured
- strategic vote – a vote cast with a strategic context in mind
- time dimension – the point or points in time at which a variable is measured
- time-series measure – a measure for which the spatial dimension is the same for all cases and the cases represent multiple time units
- transitive – a mathematical relationship such that if *A* is greater than *B* and *B* is greater than *C*, then *A* must also be greater than *C*
- utility – a calculation equal to the sum of all benefits minus the sum of all costs from that action

EXERCISES

1. Table 2.2 contains the 11th through 20th most-cited papers from the *American Political Science Review*. Obtain a copy of one of these articles and figure out what is the research question.

2. Figure 2.3 shows gross US government debt as a percentage of GDP from 1960 to 2011. Can you think of a theory about what causes this variable to be higher or lower?

3. Figure 2.4 shows the percentage of a nation's members of parliament who were women for 20 randomly selected nations in 2004. Can you think of a theory about what causes this variable to be higher or lower?

4. Think about a political event with which you are familiar and follow these instructions:

(a) Write a short description of the event.

Table 2.2 The 11th through 20th most-cited papers in the *American Political Science Review*, 1945–2005

Article	Title
11) Riker and Ordeshook (1968)	"A Theory of the Calculus of Voting"
12) Shapley and Shubik (1954)	"A Method for Evaluating the Distribution of Power in a Committee System"
13) McClosky (1964)	"Consensus and Ideology in American Politics"
14) Miller (1974)	"Political Issues and Trust in Government: 1964–1970"
15) Axelrod (1986)	"An Evolutionary Approach to Norms"
16) Doyle (1986)	"Liberalism and World Politics"
17) Polsby (1968)	"The Institutionalization of the U.S. House of Representatives"
18) Inglehart (1971)	"The Silent Revolution in Europe: Intergenerational Change in Post-Industrial Societies"
19) Maoz and Russett (1993)	"Normative and Structural Causes of Democratic Peace, 1946–1986"
20) Tufte (1975)	"Determinants of the Outcomes of Midterm Congressional Elections"

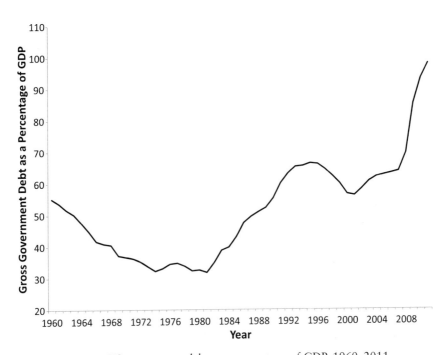

Figure 2.3 Gross US government debt as a percentage of GDP, 1960–2011

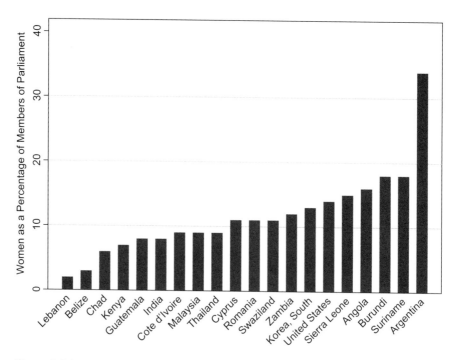

Figure 2.4 Women as a percentage of members of parliament, 2004

(b) What is your understanding of why this event happened the way that it happened?

(c) *Moving from local to global*: Reformulate your answer to part (b) into a general causal theory without proper nouns.

5. Find a political science journal article of interest to you, and of which your instructor approves, and answer the following items:

(a) What is the main dependent variable in the article?

(b) What is the main independent variable in the article?

(c) Briefly describe the causal theory that connects the independent and dependent variables.

(d) Can you think of another independent variable that is not mentioned in the article that might be causally related to the dependent variable? Briefly explain why that variable might be causally related to the dependent variable.

6. Imagine that the way in which the US House of Representatives is elected was changed from the current single-member district system to a system of national proportional representation in which any party that obtained at least 3 percent of the vote nationally would get a proportionate share of the seats in the House. How many and what types of parties would you expect to see represented in the House of Representatives under this different electoral system? What theories of politics can you come up with from thinking about this hypothetical scenario?

7. *Applying formal theory to something in which you are interested*. Think about something in the political world that you would like to better understand. Try to think about the individual-level decisions that play a role in deciding the outcome of this phenomenon. What are the expected benefits and costs that the individual who is making this decision must weigh?

For exercises 8 through 11, read Robert Putnam's (1995) article "Tuning In, Tuning Out: The Strange Disappearance of Social Capital in America."

8. What is the dependent variable in Putnam's study?

9. What other possible causes of the dependent variable can you think of?

10. Can Putnam's theory be applied in other countries? Why or why not?

11. If we believe Putnam's findings, are there further implications?

3 Evaluating Causal Relationships

OVERVIEW

Modern political science fundamentally revolves around establishing whether there are *causal relationships* between important concepts. This is rarely straightforward, and serves as the basis for almost all scientific controversies. How do we know, for example, if economic development causes democratization, or if democratization causes economic development, or both, or neither? To speak more generally, if we wish to evaluate whether or not some X causes some Y, we need to cross four causal hurdles: (1) Is there a credible causal mechanism that connects X to Y? (2) Can we eliminate the possibility that Y causes X? (3) Is there covariation between X and Y? (4) Have we controlled for all confounding variables Z that might make the association between X and Y spurious? Many people, especially those in the media, make the mistake that crossing just the third causal hurdle – observing that X and Y covary – is tantamount to crossing all four. In short, finding a relationship is not the same as finding a *causal* relationship, and causality is what we care about as political scientists.

I would rather discover one causal law than be King of Persia.
    —Democritus (quoted in Pearl, 2000)

3.1 CAUSALITY AND EVERYDAY LANGUAGE

Like that of most sciences, the discipline of political science fundamentally revolves around evaluating causal claims. Our theories – which may be right or may be wrong – typically specify that some independent variable causes some dependent variable. We then endeavor to find appropriate empirical evidence to evaluate the degree to which this theory is or is not supported. But how do we go about evaluating causal claims? In this chapter and the next, we discuss some principles for doing this. We focus on the logic of causality and on several criteria for establishing with some confidence the degree to which a causal connection exists between two variables. Then, in Chapter 4, we discuss various ways to design research that help us to investigate causal claims. As we pursue answers to questions about causal relationships, keep our "rules of the road" from Chapter 1 in your mind, in particular the admonition to consider only empirical evidence along the way.

It is important to recognize a distinction between the nature of most scientific theories and the way the world seems to be ordered. Most of our theories are limited to descriptions of relationships between a *single* cause (the independent variable) and a *single* effect (the dependent variable). Such theories, in this sense, are very simplistic representations of reality, and necessarily so. In fact, as we noted at the end of Chapter 1, theories of this sort are laudable in one respect: They are parsimonious, the equivalent of bite-sized, digestible pieces of information. We emphasize that the great majority of our theories about social and political phenomena are **bivariate** – that is, involving just two variables.

But social reality is *not* bivariate; it is **multivariate**, in the sense that any interesting dependent variable is caused by more than one factor. ("Multivariate" simply means "many variables," by which we mean involving more than two variables.) So although our theories describe the proposed relationship between some cause and some effect, we always have to keep in the forefront of our minds that the phenomenon we are trying to explain surely has many other possible causes. And when it comes time to design research to test our theoretical ideas – which is the topic of Chapter 4 – we have to try to account for, or "control for," those other causes. If we don't, then our causal inferences about whether our pet theory is right – whether X causes Y – may very well be wrong.[1] In this chapter we lay out some practical principles for evaluating whether or not, indeed, some X does cause Y. You also can apply these criteria when evaluating the causal claims made by others – be they a journalist, a candidate for office, a political scientist, a fellow classmate, a friend, or just about anyone else.

Nearly everyone, nearly every day, uses the language of causality – some of the time formally, but far more often in a very informal manner. Whenever we speak of how some event changes the course of subsequent events, we invoke causal reasoning. Even the word "because" implies that a

---

[1] Throughout this book, in the text as well as in the figures, we will use arrows as a shorthand for "causality." For example, the text "$X \rightarrow Y$" should be read as "X causes Y." Oftentimes, especially in figures, these arrows will have question marks over them, indicating that the existence of a causal connection between the concepts is uncertain.

causal process is in operation.[2] Yet, despite the ubiquitous use of the words "because," "affects," "impacts," "causes," and "causality," the meanings of these words are not exactly clear. Philosophers of science have long had vigorous debates over competing formulations of "causality."[3]

Although our goal here is not to wade too deeply into these debates, there is one feature of the discussions about causality that deserves brief mention. Most of the philosophy of science debates originate from the world of the physical sciences. The notions of causality that come to mind in these disciplines mostly involve **deterministic relationships** – that is, relationships such that if some cause occurs, then the effect will occur *with certainty*. In contrast, though, the world of human interactions consists of **probabilistic relationships** – such that increases in X are associated with increases (or decreases) in the probability of Y occurring, but those probabilities are not certainties. Whereas physical laws like Newton's laws of motion are deterministic – think of the law of gravity here – the social sciences (including political science) more closely resemble probabilistic causation like that in Darwin's theory of natural selection, in which random mutations make an organism more or less fit to survive and reproduce.[4]

What does it mean to say that, in political science, our conceptions of causality must be probabilistic in nature? When we theorize, for example, that an individual's level of wealth causes her opinions on optimal tax policy, we certainly do not mean that *every* wealthy person will want lower taxes, and *every* poor person will prefer higher taxes. Consider what would happen if we found a single rich person who favors high taxes or a single poor person who favors low taxes. (Perhaps you are, or know, such a person.) One case alone does not decrease our confidence in the theory, let alone disprove it entirely. In this sense, the relationship is probabilistic, not deterministic. Instead of saying deterministically that "wealthy people will prefer lower taxes, and poorer people will prefer higher taxes," we say, probabilistically, that "wealthy people are more likely to prefer lower taxes, whereas poorer individuals are more likely to prefer higher taxes."

---

[2] This use of terms was brought to our attention by Brady (2002).

[3] You can find an excellent account of the vigor of these debates in a 2003 book by David Edmonds and John Eidinow titled *Wittgenstein's Poker: The Story of a Ten-Minute Argument Between Two Great Philosophers.*

[4] Nevertheless, in reviewing three prominent attempts within the philosophy of science to elaborate on the probabilistic nature of causality, the philosopher Wesley Salmon (1993, p. 137) notes that "In the vast philosophical literature on causality [probabilistic notions of causality] are largely ignored." We borrow the helpful comparison of probabilistic social science to Darwinian natural selection from Brady (2004).

> **YOUR TURN: Deterministic or probabilistic?**
>
> Before the 2012 presidential election, many observers noted that no US president since World War II had been reelected with an unemployment rate above 8 percent.
>
> Identify the causal claim embedded in this statement. Is it deterministic or probabilistic? Is that a problem?

Take another example: Scholars of international conflict have noticed that there is a statistical relationship between the type of regime a country has and the likelihood of that country going to war. To be more precise, in a series of studies widely referred to as the "democratic peace" literature, many researchers have noticed that wars are much less likely to break out between two regimes that are democracies than between pairs of countries where at least one is a nondemocracy. To be perfectly clear, the literature does not suggest that democracies do not engage in warfare at all, but that democracies don't fight other democracies. A variety of mechanisms has been suggested to explain this correlation, but the point here is that, if two democracies start a war with one another next year, it would be a mistake to discard the theory. A deterministic theory would say that "democracies don't go to war with one another," but a more sensible probabilistic theory would say that "democracies are highly unlikely to go to war with one another."

In political science there will always be exceptions, because human beings are not deterministic robots whose behaviors always conform to lawlike statements. In other sciences in which the subjects of study do not have free will, it may make more sense to speak of laws that describe behavior. Consider the study of planetary orbits, in which scientists can precisely predict the movement of celestial bodies hundreds of years in advance. The political world, in contrast, is extremely difficult to predict. As a result, most of the time we are happy to be able to make statements about probabilistic causal relationships.

Indeed, approaches to studying causal relationships are still being refined today. For example, the statistician Donald Rubin (1974) has developed a rigorous framework for evaluating what are called "the effects of a cause." It is based on the understanding that a causal effect can be measured by examining the different potential outcomes for a case, depending on the assignment condition that a case receives. In an ideal setting, if we want to know if X causes Y, we would like to observe outcomes (Y) for the same cases with all values of the treatment (X).[5] The main problem with causal inference is that we cannot observe multiple

---

[5] Rubin would call the independent variable the "treatment."

outcomes for the same case. What must be done, then, is to formulate methods to facilitate comparisons between groups so that the assignment between groups does not affect our conclusions about the relationship between X and Y. More on this in Chapter 4.

What all of this boils down to is that the entire notion of what it means for something "to cause" something else is far from a settled matter. In the face of this, should social scientists abandon the search for causal connections? Not at all. What it means is that we should proceed cautiously and with an open mind, rather than in some exceedingly rigid fashion.

3.2 FOUR HURDLES ALONG THE ROUTE TO ESTABLISHING CAUSAL RELATIONSHIPS

If we wish to investigate whether some independent variable, which we will call X, "causes" some dependent variable, which we will call Y, what procedures must we follow before we can express our degree of confidence that a causal relationship does or does not exist? Finding some sort of covariation (or, equivalently, correlation) between X and Y is not sufficient for such a conclusion.

We encourage you to bear in mind that establishing causal relationships between variables is not at all akin to hunting for DNA evidence like some episode from a television crime drama. Social reality does not (often) lend itself to such simple, cut-and-dried answers. In light of the preceding discussion about the nature of causality itself, consider what follows to be guidelines as to what constitutes "best practice" in political science. With any theory about a causal relationship between X and Y, we should carefully consider the answers to the following four questions:

1. Is there a credible causal mechanism that connects X to Y?
2. Can we rule out the possibility that Y could cause X?
3. Is there covariation between X and Y?
4. Have we controlled for all **confounding variables** Z that might make the association between X and Y **spurious**?[6]

Let's discuss these in turn.

First, we must consider whether it is believable to claim that X *could* cause Y. In effect, this hurdle represents an effort to answer the "how" and "why" questions about causal relationships. To do this, we need to go through a thought exercise in which we evaluate the mechanics of how

---

[6] A "confounding variable" is simply a variable that is correlated with both the independent and dependent variables and that somehow alters the relationship between those two variables. "Spurious" means "not what it appears to be" or "false."

X would cause Y, or how varying the levels of X might cause the levels of Y to vary. What is the process or mechanism that, logically speaking, suggests that X might be a cause of Y? In other words, what is it specifically about having more (or less) of X that will in all probability lead to more (or less) of Y? The more outlandish these mechanics would have to be, the less confident we are that our theory has cleared this first hurdle. Failure to clear this first hurdle is a very serious matter; the result being that either our theory needs to be thrown out altogether, or we need to revise it after some careful rethinking of the underlying mechanisms through which it works.

What do we mean by a "credible causal mechanism"? Perhaps two examples will help shed some light on what is an admittedly cumbersome phrase. In our example from Chapter 1 on the theory of economic voting, which attempts to connect variations in economic performance (X) to an incumbent party's reelection vote percentage (Y), can we identify answers to this question? "How, specifically, might varying economic conditions cause an incumbent's vote shares to vary?" Yes, we can. If the population of a country values an economy that is performing well – with strong growth, low inflation, and low unemployment, for example – and if the voters hold the governing party, at least in part, responsible for the management of the economy, then voters might base their votes for or against the incumbent party on how well or how poorly the economy is doing. If the economy does well, more voters might reward the incumbent party for competent management of the economy with their votes; if the economy fares poorly, more voters might punish the incumbent party for inept management of the economy, and vote for the opposition. This series of statements would qualify as a "credible causal mechanism" in this case, and we would clear causal hurdle 1. However, just because something is "credible" – that is, believable – doesn't necessarily make it true, or show that the theory is right. It just means that we've identified a plausible, potentially true, mechanism of how X might cause Y.

To further illustrate the point, let's consider a different example. Ice cream consumption varies over the course of the year, as you might expect; most of us eat more ice cream in the hotter summer months, and less ice cream during the colder winter. Homicides, in many large cities, follow a similar pattern, with more murders in the summer months and fewer in the winter. What if we wanted to investigate the possibility that the monthly variation in ice cream consumption (X) *caused* the variation in homicides (Y)? As with any question about causality, our first step should be to ask if we can identify a credible causal mechanism that might connect changes in ice cream consumption with shifts in the murder rate. And that's really difficult, if not impossible, to do in this case. It's true, we acknowledge, that we could get a bit cheeky and say that, after all, when people eat more ice cream, they might get fueled rage from all of the high-fructose corn syrup, and therefore be more likely to commit murders. But even though that might make you chuckle, that's just not believable in any serious way. It's not something you can say with a straight face. So, in this case, our "theory" – note the scare quotes here, because we don't really have a proper theory – would not cross the first causal hurdle. We'd like to emphasize that it is only worth proceeding to the second question once we have a "yes" answer to this first question. That is, if you cannot specify a believable, potentially true process by which varying X might cause Y to vary, then stop now, and work on formulating a theoretical explanation about the relationship.

Second, and perhaps with greater difficulty, we must ask whether we can rule out the possibility that Y might cause X. As you will learn from the discussion of the various strategies for assessing causal connections in Chapter 4, this poses thorny problems for some forms of social science research, but is less problematic for others. Occasionally, this causal hurdle can be crossed logically. For example, when considering whether a person's gender (X) causes him or her to have particular attitudes about abortion policy (Y), it is a rock-solid certainty that the reverse-causal scenario can be dismissed: A person's attitudes about abortion does not "cause" them to be male or female. If our theory does not clear this particular hurdle, the race is not lost. Under these circumstances, we should proceed to the next question, while keeping in mind the possibility that our causal arrow might be reversed.

Throughout our consideration of the first two causal hurdles, we were concerned with only two variables, X and Y. The third causal hurdle can involve a third variable Z, and the fourth hurdle always does. Often it is the case that there are several Z variables.

For the third causal hurdle, we must consider whether X and Y covary (or, equivalently, whether they are correlated or associated). Generally speaking, for X to cause Y, there must be some form of measurable association between X and Y, such as "more of X is associated with more of Y," or "more of X is associated with less of Y." Demonstrating a simple bivariate connection between two variables is a relatively straightforward matter, and we will cover it in Chapters 8 and 9. Of course, you may be familiar with the dictum "Correlation does not prove causality," and we wholeheartedly agree. It is worth noting, though, that bivariate correlation is normally an essential component of a causal relationship.

But be careful. If you read the above paragraph carefully, you'll have noticed that we said that correlation is "normally" – not "universally" – a component of a causal relationship. It is possible for a causal relationship to exist between X and Y even if there is no bivariate association between

X and Y. Thus, even if we fail to clear this hurdle, we should not throw out our causal claim entirely. Instead, we should consider the possibility that there exists some confounding variable Z that we need to "control for" before we see a relationship between X and Y. Whether or not we find a bivariate relationship between X and Y, we should proceed to our fourth and final hurdle.

Fourth, in establishing causal connections between X and Y, we must face up to the reality that, as we noted at the outset of this chapter, we live in a world in which most of the interesting dependent variables are caused by more than one – often many more than one – independent variable. What problems does this pose for social science? It means that, when trying to establish whether a particular X causes a particular Y, we need to "control for" the effects of other causes of Y (and we call those other effects Z). If we fail to control for the effects of Z, we are quite likely to misunderstand the relationship between X and Y and make the wrong inference about whether X causes Y. This is the most serious mistake a social scientist can make. If we find that X and Y are correlated, but that, when we control for the effects of Z on both X and Y, the association between X and Y disappears, then the relationship between X and Y is said to be spurious. To return to our example about ice cream consumption (X) and homicide rates (Y), one obvious Z variable that might confound the relationship is "average monthly temperature." When it's warmer outside, people eat more ice cream. And when it's warmer outside, homicide rates rise. The association of both X and Y with Z can lead to the false appearance of a relationship between X and Y.

What does it mean to attempt to, as we have said, "control for" the effects of other variables? We'll eventually answer that question in two ways. Occasionally the control happens in the very design of the research plan; that possibility will be described in Chapter 4. More frequently, though, we will resort to statistical controls for these potentially confounding variables; that possibility, which happens far more frequently, will have to wait until Chapter 10.

3.2.1 Putting It All Together – Adding Up the Answers to Our Four Questions

As we have just seen, the process for evaluating a theoretical claim that X causes Y is complicated. Taken one at a time, each of the four questions in the introduction to this section can be difficult to answer decisively. But the challenge of evaluating a claim that X causes Y involves summing the answers to all four of these questions to determine our overall confidence about whether X causes Y. To understand this, think about the analogy that we have been using by calling these questions "hurdles." In track events that feature hurdles, runners must do their best to try to clear each hurdle as they make their way toward the finish line. Occasionally even the most experienced hurdler will knock over a hurdle. Although this slows them down and diminishes their chances of winning the race, all is not lost. If we think about putting a theory through the four hurdles posed by the preceding questions, there is no doubt our confidence will be greatest when we are able to answer all four questions the right way ("yes," "yes," "yes," "yes") and without reservation. As we described in the introduction to this section, failure to clear the first hurdle should give us pause. This is also the case if we find our relationship to be spurious. For the second and third hurdles, however, failure to clear them completely does not mean that we should discard the causal claim in question. Figure 3.1 provides a summary of this process. In the sections that follow, we will go through the process described in Figure 3.1 with a series of examples.

As we go through this process of answering the four questions, we will keep a **causal hurdles scorecard** as a shorthand for summarizing the answers to these four questions in square brackets. For now, we will limit our answers to "*y*" for "yes," "*n*" for "no," and "?" for "maybe." If a

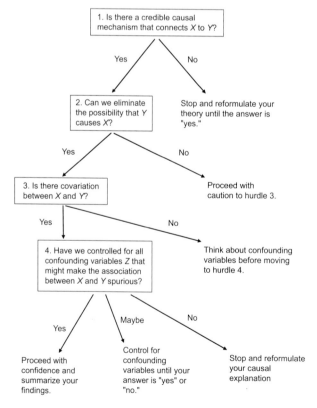

Figure 3.1 The path to evaluating a causal relationship

theory has cleared all four hurdles, the scorecard would read [y y y y] and the causal claim behind it would be strongly supported. As we described above, these hurdles are not all the same in terms of their impact on our assessments of causality. So, for instance, a causal claim for which the scorecard reads [n y y y] could be thrown out instantly. But, a claim for which it reads [y n y y] would have a reasonable level of evidence in its favor.

3.2.2 Identifying Causal Claims Is an Essential Thinking Skill

We want to emphasize that the logic just presented does not apply merely to political science research examples. Whenever you see a story in the news, or hear a speech by a candidate for public office, or, yes, read a research article in a political science class, it is almost always the case that some form of causal claim is embedded in the story, speech, or article. Sometimes those causal claims are explicit – indented and italicized so that you just can't miss them. Quite often, though, they are harder to spot, and most of the time not because the speaker or writer is trying to confuse you. What we want to emphasize is that spotting and identifying causal claims is a thinking skill. It does not come naturally to most people, but it can be practiced.

In our daily lives, we are often presented with causal claims by people trying to persuade us to adopt their point of view. Advocacy and attempts at persuasion, of course, are healthy features of a vibrant democracy. The health of public debate, though, will be further enhanced when citizens actively scrutinize the claims with which they are presented. Take, for example, debates in the media about the merits of private school choice programs, which have been implemented in several school districts. Among the arguments in favor of such programs is that the programs will improve student performance on standardized tests. Media reports about the successes and failures of programs like this are quite common. For example, an article by Jay Mathews in the *Washington Post* discusses a study that makes the argument that:

> African American students in the District [of Columbia] and two other cities have moved ahead of their public school classmates since they trans-ferred to private schools with the help of vouchers, according to a new study.... The study showed that those moving to private schools scored 6 percentile points higher than those who stayed in public schools in New York City, Dayton, Ohio, and the District. The effect was biggest in the District, where students with vouchers moved 9 percentile points ahead of public school peers.[7]

[7] Mathews, Jay. "Scores Improve for D.C. Pupils With Vouchers" *Washington Post*, August 28, (2000). A1.

Notice the causal claim here, which is: Participation (or not) in the school choice program (X) causes a child's test scores (Y) to vary. Often, the reader is presented with a bar chart of some sort in support of the argument. The reader is encouraged to think, sometimes subtly, that the differing heights of the bars, representing different average test scores for school choice children and public school children, means that the program *caused* the school choice children to earn higher scores. When we take such information in, we might take that nugget of evidence and be tempted to jump to the conclusion that a causal relationship exists. The key lesson here is that this is a premature conclusion.

Let's be clear: School choice programs may indeed cause students to do better on standardized tests. Our objective here is not to wade into that debate, but rather to sensitize you to the thinking skills required to evaluate the causal claim made in public by advocates such as those who support or oppose school choice programs. Evidence that students in school choice programs score higher on tests than do public school students is *one piece* of the causal puzzle – namely, it satisfies crossing hurdle 3 above, that there is covariation between X and Y. At this point in our evaluation, our scorecard reads [? ? y ?]. And thus, before we conclude that school choice does (or does not) cause student performance, we need to subject that claim to all four of the causal hurdles, not just the third one.

So let's apply all four causal hurdles to the question at hand. First, is there a mechanism that we can use to explain how and why attending a particular type of school – public or a voucher-sponsored private school – might affect a student's test scores? Certainly. Many private schools that participate in voucher programs have smaller class sizes (among other benefits), and smaller class sizes can translate to more learning and higher test scores. *The answer to the first question is "yes"* [y ? y ?].

Second, is it possible that the causal arrow might be reversed – that is, can we rule out the possibility that test scores cause a person to participate or not participate in a school choice program? Since the test scores occur months or even years after the person chooses a school to attend, this is not possible. *The answer to the second question is "yes"* [y y y ?].

Third, is there a correlation between participation in the program and test scores? The article quoted above just noted that, in the three cities considered, there is – voucher school students scored higher on standardized tests than their public school peers. *The answer to the third question is "yes"* [y y y ?].

Finally, have we controlled for all confounding variables that might make the association between participation in the program and test scores spurious? Remember, a potentially confounding variable is simply a variable that is related to the independent variable and is also a cause of the dependent variable. So, can we think of something that is both related to the type of school a child attends and is also a likely cause of that child's test scores? Sure. The variable "parental involvement" is a natural candidate to be a Z variable in this instance. Some children have highly involved parents – parents who read to their children, help them with homework, and take an active role in their education – while other children have parents who are much less involved. Highly involved parents are more likely than their uninvolved counterparts to learn about the existence of school choice programs in their cities, and are more likely to apply for such programs. (So Z is almost surely related to X.) And highly involved parents are more likely to create high expectations among their children, and to instill in their children a sense that achievement in school is important, all of which probably translate into having children who score better on standardized tests. (So Z is likely to be a cause of Y.) The key question then becomes: Did the study in question manage to *control for* those effects? We're a little ahead of the game here, because we haven't yet talked about the strategies that researchers employ to control for the effects of potentially confounding variables. (That task comes in Chapter 4.) But we hope you can see why controlling for the effects of parental involvement is so key in this particular situation (and in general): If our comparison of school choice children and public school children basically amounts to a comparison between the children of highly motivated parents and the children of poorly motivated parents, then it becomes very problematic to conclude that the difference between the groups' test scores was *caused by* the program. Without a control for parental involvement (Z), in other words, the relationship between school type (X) and test scores (Y) might be spurious. So, until we see evidence that this important Z has been controlled for, our scorecard for this causal claim is [y y y n] and we should be highly suspicious of the study's findings. More informally, without such a control, the comparison between those sets of test scores is an unfair one, because the groups would be so different in the first place. As it happens, the article from the *Washington Post* that we mentioned did include a control for parental involvement, because the students were chosen for the program by a random lottery. We'll wait until Chapter 4 to describe exactly why this makes such a big difference, but it does.

The same process can be applied to a wide variety of causal claims and questions that we encounter in our daily lives. Does drinking red wine cause a reduction in heart disease? Does psychotherapy help people with emotional and relational problems? Do increases in government spending spur or retard economic growth? In each of these and many other examples, we might be tempted to observe a correlation between two variables and conclude that the relationship is causal. It is important for us to resist that temptation, and subject each of these claims to the more rigorous criteria that we are suggesting here. If we think about such evidence on its own in terms of our causal hurdles scorecard, what we have is [? ? y ?]. This is a reasonable start to the evaluation of a causal claim, but a pretty poor place to stop and draw definitive conclusions. Thinking in terms of the hurdles depicted in the scorecard, whenever someone presents us with a causal claim but fails to address each of the hurdles, we will naturally ask further questions and, when we do that, we will be much smarter consumers of information in our everyday lives.

YOUR TURN: Does eating chocolate promote a healthy heart?

Go read the following article: http://www.nytimes.com/2009/09/15/health/15choc .html

　　Based solely on what appears in the article, complete a causal hurdles scorecard about the claim that eating chocolate (X) causes a person to have less heart disease (Y).

An important part of taking a scientific approach to the study of politics is that we turn the same skeptical logic loose on scholarly claims about causal relationships. Before we can evaluate a causal theory, we need to consider how well the available evidence answers each of the four questions about X, Y, and Z. Once we have answered each of these four questions, one at a time, we then think about the overall level of confidence that we have in the claim that X causes Y.

3.2.3   What Are the Consequences of Failing to Control for Other Possible Causes?

When it comes to any causal claim, as we have just noted, the fourth causal hurdle often trips us up, and not just for evaluating political rhetoric or stories in the news media. This is true for scrutinizing scientific research as well. In fact, a substantial portion of disagreements between scholars boils down to this fourth causal hurdle. When one scholar is evaluating another's work, perhaps the most frequent objection is that the researcher "failed to control for" some potentially important cause of the dependent variable.

　　What happens when we fail to control for some plausible other cause of our dependent variable of interest? Quite simply, it means that we have failed to cross our fourth causal hurdle. *So long as a reasonable case can be made that some uncontrolled-for Z might be related to both X and Y, we cannot conclude with full confidence that X indeed causes Y.* Because the main goal of science is to establish whether causal connections between variables exist, then failing to control for other causes of Y is a potentially serious problem.

One of the themes of this book is that statistical analysis should not be disconnected from issues of research design – such as controlling for as many causes of the dependent variable as possible. When we discuss multiple regression (in Chapters 10, 11, and 12), which is the most common statistical technique that political scientists use in their research, the entire point of those chapters is to learn how to control for other possible causes of the dependent variable. We will see that failures of research design, such as failing to control for all relevant causes of the dependent variable, have statistical implications, and the implications are always bad. Failures of research design produce problems for statistical analysis, but hold this thought. What is important to realize for now is that good research design will make statistical analysis more credible, whereas poor research design will make it harder for any statistical analysis to be conclusive about causal connections.

YOUR TURN: Exploring media reports of other social science studies

The media outlet NPR has a regular series in its broadcasts that they call "Hidden Brain" which explores some of the subconscious forces that shape human beliefs and behavior. They have an active Twitter feed (@*HiddenBrain*) and an extensive series of podcasts.

Go visit their web site: http://www.npr.org/podcasts/510308/hidden-brain

Pick a podcast on a topic that interests you, and listen to hear how the host describes whether or not the relationships uncovered are *causal* or *spurious*. It takes practice!

3.3 WHY IS STUDYING CAUSALITY SO IMPORTANT? THREE EXAMPLES FROM POLITICAL SCIENCE

Our emphasis on causal connections should be clear. We turn now to several active controversies within the discipline of political science, showing how debates about causality lie at the heart of precisely the kinds of controversies that got you (and most of us) interested in politics in the first place.

3.3.1 Life Satisfaction and Democratic Stability

One of the enduring controversies in political science is the relationship between *life satisfaction in the mass public* and *the stability of democratic institutions*. Life satisfaction, of course, can mean many different things, but for the current discussion let us consider it as varying along a continuum, from the public's being highly unsatisfied with day-to-day life to being highly satisfied. What, if anything, is the causal connection between the two concepts?

Political scientist Ronald Inglehart (1988) argues that life satisfaction (*X*) *causes* democratic system stability (*Y*). If we think through the first of the four questions for establishing causal relationships, we can see that there is a credible causal mechanism that connects *X* to *Y* – if people in a democratic nation are more satisfied with their lives, they will be less likely to want to overthrow their government. *The answer to our first question is "yes"* [y ? ? ?]. Moving on to our second question: Can we eliminate the possibility that democratic stability (*Y*) is what causes life satisfaction (*X*)? We cannot. It is very easy to conceive of a causal mechanism in which citizens living in stable democracies are likely to be more satisfied with their lives than citizens living in nations with a history of government instability and less-than-democratic governance. *The answer to our second question is "no"* [y n ? ?]. We now turn to the third question. Using an impressive amount of data from a wide variety of developed democracies, Inglehart and his colleagues have shown that there is, indeed, an association between average life satisfaction in the public and the length of uninterrupted democratic governance. That is, countries with higher average levels of life satisfaction have enjoyed longer uninterrupted periods of democratic stability. Conversely, countries with lower levels of life satisfaction have had shorter periods of democratic stability and more revolutionary upheaval. *The answer to our third question is "yes"* [y n y ?]. With respect to the fourth question, it is easy to imagine a myriad of other factors (*Z*) that lead to democratic stability, and whether Inglehart has done an adequate job of controlling for those other factors is the subject of considerable scholarly debate. *The answer to our fourth question is "maybe"* [y n y ?]. Inglehart's theory has satisfactorily answered questions 1 and 3, but it is the answers to questions 2 and 4 that have given skeptics substantial reasons to doubt his causal claim.

YOUR TURN: Other causes of democratic stability

Draw a diagram with the *X*, *Y*, and *Z* variables we identified in the Inglehart study on democratic stability.

Can you think of any other *Z* variables that are likely to be correlated with *X* (life satisfaction in a country) and are also likely to be a cause of *Y* (longevity of democracy)?

3.3.2   Race and Political Participation in the United States

Political participation – the extent to which individual citizens engage in voluntary political activity, such as voting, working for a campaign, or making a campaign contribution – represents one of the most frequently studied facets of mass political behavior, especially in the United States. And with good reason: Participation in democratic societies is viewed by some as one measure of the health of a democracy. After decades of studying the variation in Americans' rates of participation, several demographic characteristics consistently stood out as being correlated with participation, including an individual's racial classification. Anglos, surveys consistently showed, have participated in politics considerably more frequently than either Latinos or African Americans. A comprehensive survey, for example, shows that during a typical election cycle, Anglos engaged in 2.22 "participatory acts" – such as voting, working for a campaign, making a campaign contribution, attending a protest or demonstration, and similar such activities – whereas comparable rates for African Americans and Latino citizens were 1.90 and 1.41 activities (see Verba et al., 1993, figure 1).

Is the relationship between an individual's race (X) and the amount that the individual participates in politics (Y) a causal one? Before we accept the evidence above as conclusively demonstrating a *causal* relationship, we need to subject it to the four causal hurdles. Is there a reasonable mechanism that answers the "how" and "why" questions connecting race and political participation? There may be reason to think so. For long portions of US history, after all, some formal and many informal barriers existed prohibiting or discouraging the participation of non-Anglos. The notion that there might be residual effects of such barriers, even decades after they have been eradicated, is entirely reasonable. *The answer to our first question is "yes"* [y ? ? ?]. Can we eliminate the possibility that varying rates of participation cause an individual's racial classification? Obviously, yes. *The answer to our second question is "yes"* [y y ? ?]. Is there a correlation between an individual's race and their level of participation in the United States? The data above about the number of participatory acts among Anglos, African Americans, and Latinos clearly show that there is a relationship; Anglos participate the most. *The answer to our third question is "yes"* [y y y ?]. Finally, have we controlled for all possible confounding variables Z that are related to both race (X) and participation (Y) that might make the relationship spurious? Verba and his colleagues suggest that there might be just such a confounding variable: socio-economic status. Less so today than in the past, socio-economic status (Z) is nevertheless still correlated with race (X). And unsurprisingly, socio-economic status (Z) is also a cause of political participation (Y); wealthy people donate more, volunteer more, and the like, than their less wealthy counterparts. Once controlling for socio-economic status, the aforementioned relationship between race and political participation entirely vanishes (see Verba et al., 1993, table 8). In short, the correlation that we observe between race and political participation is spurious, or illusory; it is not a function of race, but instead a function of the disparities in wealth between Anglos and other races. Once we control for those socio-economic differences, the connection between race and participation goes away. *The answer to our fourth question is "no."* In this case, the effort to answer the fourth question actually changed our answer to the third question, moving our scorecard from [y y y ?] to [y y n n]. This is one of the important ways in which our conclusions about relationships can change when we move from a bivariate analysis in which we measure the relationship between one independent variable, X, and our dependent variable, Y, to a multiple variable analysis in which we measure the relationship between X and Y controlling for a second independent variable, Z. It is also possible for a lot of other things to happen when we move to controlling for Z. For instance, it is also possible for our scorecard to change from [y y n n] to [y y y y].

YOUR TURN: Other causes of participation

Draw a diagram with the X, Y, and Z variables we identified in the Verba et al. (1993) study on political participation.

Can you think of any other Z variables that are likely to be correlated with X (racial classification) and are also likely to be a cause of Y (political participation)?

3.3.3 Evaluating Whether "Head Start" Is Effective

In the 1960s, as part of the war on poverty, President Lyndon Johnson initiated the program "Head Start" to give economically underprivileged children a preschool experience that – the program hoped – would increase the chances that these poor children would succeed once they reached kindergarten and beyond. The program is clearly well intended, but, of course, that alone does not make it effective. Simply put: Does Head Start work? In this case, "work" would mean that Head Start could increase the chances that participants in the program would have better educational outcomes than nonparticipants.

It would be tempting, in this case, to simply compare some standardized test scores of the children who participated in Head Start with those who did not. If Head Start participants scored higher, then – voila! – case closed; the program works. If not, then not. But, as before, we need to stay focused on all four causal hurdles. First, is there some credible causal mechanism that would answer the "how" and "why" questions that connect Head Start participation (X) to educational outcomes (Y)? Yes. The theory behind the program is that exposure to a preschool environment that anticipates the actual school setting helps prepare children for what they will encounter in kindergarten and beyond. Head Start, in this sense, might help reduce discipline problems, and prepare students for reading and counting, among other skills. *The answer to our first question is "yes"* [y ? ? ?]. Is it possible, secondly, that the causal arrow might be reversed – in other words, can we rule out the possibility that educational outcomes (Y) could cause participation in Head Start (X)? Because testing would take place years after participation in the program, yes. *The answer to our second question is "yes"* [y y ? ?]. Is there an association between participation in the program and learning outcomes? Study after study has shown that Head Start participants fare better when tested, and have fewer instances of repeating a grade, than those who have no preschool experience. For example, a widely cited study shows that Head Start children do better on a vocabulary test suitable for young children than do students who have no preschool experience (Currie and Thomas, 1995). *The answer to our third question is "yes"* [y y y ?]. But, as was the case with the school-voucher example discussed previously, a potentially confounding variable – parental involvement (Z) – lurks nearby. Highly involved parents (Z) are more likely to seek out, be aware of, and enroll their children (X) in programs like Head Start that might benefit their children. Parents who are less involved in their children's lives are less likely to avail themselves of the potential opportunities that Head Start creates. And, as before, highly involved parents (Z) are likely to have positive effects on their children's educational outcomes. The key question, then, becomes: Do parental effects (Z) make the relationship between Head Start and later educational outcomes spurious? The aforementioned study by Currie and Thomas uses both statistical controls as well as controls in the design of their research to account for parental factors, and they find that Head Start has lasting educational effects only for Anglo children, but not for African American children (see their table 4). Again, that phrase "statistical controls" may not be quite as transparent as it will be later on in this book. For now, suffice it to say that these researchers used all of the techniques available to them to show that Head Start does, indeed, have positive effects for some, but not all, children. *The answer to our fourth question is a highly qualified "yes"* [y y y y].

3.4 WRAPPING UP

Learning the thinking skills required to evaluate causal claims as conclusively as possible requires practice. They are intellectual habits that, like a good knife, will sharpen with use.

Translating these thinking skills into actively designing new research that helps to address causal questions is the subject of Chapter 4. All of the "research designs" that you will learn in that chapter are strongly linked to issues of evaluating causal claims. Keeping the lessons of this chapter in mind as we move forward is essential to making you a better consumer of information, as well as edging you forward toward being a producer of research.

CONCEPTS INTRODUCED IN THIS CHAPTER

- bivariate – involving just two variables
- causal hurdles scorecard – a shorthand for summarizing evidence about whether an independent variable causes a dependent variable
- confounding variable – a variable that is correlated with both the independent and dependent variables and that somehow alters the relationship between those two variables
- deterministic relationship – if some cause occurs, then the effect will occur with certainty
- multivariate – involving more than two variables
- probabilistic relationship – increases in X are associated with increases (or decreases) in the probability of Y occurring, but those probabilities are not certainties
- spurious – not what it appears to be, or false

EXERCISES

1. Think back to a history class in which you learned about the "causes" of a particular historical event (for instance, the Great Depression, the French Revolution, or World War I). How well does each causal claim perform when you try to answer the four questions for establishing causal relationships?

2. Go to your local newspaper's web site (if it has one; if not, pick the web site of any media outlet you visit frequently). In the site's "Search" box, type the words "research cause" (without quotes). (*Hint*: You may need to limit the search time frame, depending on the site you visit.) From the search results, find two articles that make claims about causal relationships. Print them out, and include a brief synopsis of the causal claim embedded in the article.

3. For each of the following examples, imagine that some researcher has found the reported pattern of covariation between X and Y. Can you think of a variable Z that might make the relationship between X and Y spurious?

   (a) The more firefighters (X) that go to a house fire, the greater property damage that occurs (Y).
   (b) The more money spent by an incumbent member of Congress's campaign (X), the lower their percentage of vote (Y).

(c) Increased consumption of coffee (X) reduces the risk of depression among women (Y).

(d) The higher the salaries of Presbyterian ministers (X), the higher the price of rum in Havana, Cuba (Y).

4. For each of the following pairs of independent and dependent variables, write about both a probabilistic and a deterministic relationship to describe the likely relationship:

(a) A person's education (X) and voter turnout (Y).

(b) A nation's economic health (X) and political revolution (Y).

(c) Candidate height (X) and election outcome (Y).

5. Take a look at the codebook for the data set "BES 2005 Subset" (which is available on the textbook's web site at www.cambridge.org/fpsr) and write about your answers to the following items:

(a) Develop a causal theory about the relationship between an independent variable (X) and a dependent variable (Y) from this data set. Is it the credible causal mechanism that connects X to Y? Explain your answer.

(b) Could Y cause X? Explain your answer.

(c) What other variables (Z) would you like to control for in your tests of this theory?

6. Imagine causal claims for which the scorecards are listed below. Which of these three claims – (a), (b), or (c) – would you evaluate as most strongly supported? Explain your answer.

(a) [y n y y]

(b) [y y y n]

(c) [? y y y]

7. Researcher A and Researcher B are having a scientific debate. What are they arguing about if their argument is focused on each of the following?

(a) causal hurdle 1

(b) causal hurdle 2

(c) causal hurdle 3

(d) causal hurdle 4

8. Find a political science journal article of interest to you, and of which your instructor approves, and answer the following items (be sure to provide a full citation to the chosen article with your answers):

(a) Briefly describe the causal theory that connects the independent and dependent variables.

(b) Create a causal hurdles scorecard for this theory and write an explanation for each of your entries in the scorecard.

9. Consider the following possible causal relationships in political science. Following causal hurdle 4, come up with a list of some potentially confounding

variables (Z) that we would need to attempt to control for in order to successfully cross hurdle 4 and be confident in our conclusion about whether or not X causes Y:

(a) The relationship between the percentage of its budget that a country spends on social welfare programs (X) and economic inequality in that country (Y).

(b) The presence of a sanctions regime imposed by the international community on a rogue country (X) and the rogue country's compliance with the demands of the international community (Y).

4 Research Design

OVERVIEW

Given our focus on causality, what research strategies do political scientists use to investigate causal relationships? Generally speaking, the controlled experiment is the foundation for scientific research. And an increasing number of political scientists use experiments in their work. However, owing to the nature of our subject matter, most political scientists adopt one of two types of "observational" research designs that are intended to mimic experiments. The cross-sectional observational study focuses on variation across individual units (like people or countries). The time-series observational study focuses on variation in aggregate quantities (like presidential popularity) over time. What is an "experiment" and why is it so useful? How do observational studies try to mimic experimental designs? Most importantly, what are the strengths and weaknesses of each of these three research designs in establishing whether or not causal relationships exist between concepts? That is, how does each one help us to get across the four causal hurdles identified in Chapter 3? Relatedly, we introduce issues concerning the selection of samples of cases to study in which we are not able to study the entire population of cases to which our theory applies. This is a subject that will feature prominently in many of the subsequent chapters.

4.1 COMPARISON AS THE KEY TO ESTABLISHING CAUSAL RELATIONSHIPS

So far, you have learned that political scientists care about causal relationships. You have learned that most phenomena we are interested in explaining have multiple causes, but our theories typically deal with only one of them while ignoring the others. In some of the research examples in the previous chapters, we have noted that the multivariate nature of the world can make our first glances at evidence misleading. In the example dealing with race and political participation, at first it appeared that race might be causally related to participation rates, with Anglos participating more than those of other races. But, we argued, in this particular case, the first glance was potentially quite misleading.

Why? Because what appeared to be the straightforward comparisons between three groups – participation rates between Anglos, Latinos, and African Americans – ended up being far from simple. On some very important factors, our different groupings for our independent variable X were far from equal. That is, people of different racial groupings (X) had differing socio-economic statuses (Z), which are correlated with race (X) and also affected their levels of participation (Y). As convincing as those bivariate comparisons might have been, they would likely be misleading.

Comparisons are at the heart of science. If we are evaluating a theory about the relationship between some X and some Y, the scientist's job is to do everything possible to make sure that no other influences (Z) interfere with the comparisons that we will rely on to make our inferences about a possible causal relationship between X and Y.

The obstacles to causal inference that we described in Chapter 3 are substantial, but surmountable. We don't know whether, in reality, X causes Y. We may be armed with a theory that suggests that X does, indeed, cause Y, but theories can be (and often are) wrong or incomplete. So how do scientists generally, and political scientists in particular, go about testing whether X causes Y? There are several strategies, or **research designs**, that researchers can use toward that end. The goal of all types of research designs is to help us evaluate how well a theory fares as it makes its way over the four causal hurdles – that is, to answer as conclusively as is possible the question about whether X causes Y. In the next two sections we focus on the two strategies that political scientists use most commonly and effectively: **experiments** and **observational studies**.[1]

4.2   EXPERIMENTAL RESEARCH DESIGNS

Suppose that you were a candidate for political office locked in what seems to be a tight race. Your campaign budget has money for the end of the campaign, and you're deciding whether or not to make some television ad buys for a commercial that sharply contrasts your record with your opponent's – what some will surely call a negative, attack ad. The campaign manager has had a public relations firm craft the ad, and has shown it to

---

[1] Throughout this book, we will use the term "experiment" in the same way that researchers in medical science use the term "randomized control trial."

you in your strategy meetings. You like it, but you look to your staff and ask the bottom-line question: "Will the ad work with the voters?" In effect, you have two choices: run the attack ad, or do nothing.

We hope that you're becoming accustomed to spotting the causal questions embedded in this scenario: Exposure to a candidate's negative ad (X) may, or may not, affect a voter's likelihood of voting for that candidate (Y). And it is important to add here that the causal claim has a particular directional component to it; that is, exposure to the advertisement will *increase* the chances that a voter will choose that candidate.[2]

How might researchers in the social sciences evaluate such a causal claim? Those of you who are campaign junkies are probably thinking that your campaign would run a focus group to see how some real-life voters react to the ad. And that's not a bad idea. Let's informally define a focus group as a group of subjects selected to be exposed to some idea (like a new kitchen knife or a candidate's TV ad), and to try to gather the subjects' responses to the idea. There's a problem with the focus group, though, particularly in the case at hand of the candidate's TV ad: What would the subjects have said about the candidate had they *not* been exposed to the ad? There's nothing to use as a basis for comparison.

It is very important, and not at all surprising, to realize that voters may vote either for or against you for a variety of reasons (Z) that have nothing to do with exposure to the advertisements – varying socio-economic statuses, varying ideologies, and party identifications can all cause voters to favor one candidate over another. So how can we establish whether, among these other influences (Z), the advertisement (X) also causes voters to be more likely to vote for you (Y)?

Can we do better than the focus group? What would a more scientific approach look like? As the introduction to this chapter highlights, we will need a comparison of some kind, and we will want that comparison to isolate any potentially different effects that the ad has on a person's likelihood of voting for you.

The standard approach to a situation like this in the physical and medical sciences is that we would need to conduct an experiment. Because the word "experiment" has such common usage, its scientific meaning is frequently misunderstood. An experiment is *not* simply any kind of analysis that is quantitative in nature; neither is it exclusively the domain of laboratories and white-coated scientists with pocket protectors. We define

---

[2] There is a substantial literature in political science about the effects that negative advertisements have on both voter turnout and vote choice. For contrasting views on the effects of negative ads, see Ansolabehere and Iyengar (1997), Wattenberg and Brians (1999), and Geer (2006).

an experiment as follows: *An experiment is a research design in which the researcher both controls and randomly assigns values of the independent variable to the participants.*

Notice the twin components of the definition of the experiment: that the researcher both *controls* values of the independent variable – or *X*, as we have called it – as well as *randomly assigns* those values to the participants in the experiment. Together, these two features form a complete definition of an experiment, which means that there are no other essential features of an experiment beside these two.

What does it mean to say that a researcher "controls" the value of the independent variable that the participants receive? It means, most importantly, that the values of the independent variable that the participants receive are *not* determined either by the participants themselves or by nature. In our example of the campaign's TV ad, this requirement means that we cannot compare people who, by their own choice, already have chosen to expose themselves to the TV ad (perhaps because they're political junkies and watch a lot of cable news programs, where such ads are likely to air). It means that we, the researchers, have control over which of our experimental participants will see the ads and which ones will not.

But the definition of an experiment has one other essential component as well: We, the researchers, must not only control the values of the independent variable, but *we must also assign those values to participants randomly*. In the context of our campaign ad example, this means that we must toss coins, draw numbers out of a hat, use a random-number generator, or some other such mechanism to divide our participants into a **treatment group** (who will see the negative ad) and a **control group** (who will not see the ad, but will instead watch something innocuous, in a social science parallel to a **placebo**).

YOUR TURN: Start thinking experimentally

If we wanted to conduct an analysis that met the above definition of an experiment, what would a study look like that intended to examine whether a drug treatment program for people who are incarcerated (*X*) reduces subsequent recidivism (*Y*) once the prisoners are paroled?

What's the big deal here? Why is randomly assigning subjects to treatment groups important? What scientific benefits arise from the random assignment of people to treatment groups? To see why this is so crucial, recall that we have emphasized that all science is about comparisons, and also that just about every interesting phenomenon worth exploring – every interesting dependent variable – is caused by many factors, not just one. Random assignment to treatment groups ensures that the comparison we

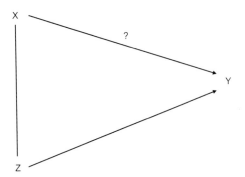

Figure 4.1 How does an experiment help cross the four causal hurdles?

make between the treatment group and the control group is as pure as possible, and that some other cause (Z) of the dependent variable will not pollute that comparison. By first taking a group of participants and then randomly splitting them into two groups on the basis of a coin flip, what we have ensured is that the two groups of participants will not be systematically different from one another. Indeed, provided that the participant pool is reasonably large, randomly assigning participants to treatment groups ensures that the groups, as a whole, are *identical*. If the two groups are identical, save for the coin flip, then we can be certain that any differences we observe between the groups must be because of the independent variable that we have assigned to them.

Put a different way, consider our simple diagram in Figure 4.1 of the relationship between our independent variable, X, our dependent variable, Y, and a potentially confounding variable, Z. Because, in an experiment, the researcher randomly assigns values of X, that means that two things happen. First, as a result of the fact that values of X are determined entirely randomly, then by definition that breaks the connection between Z and X in Figure 4.1. After all, if X is determined by pure randomness, then it should not be correlated with any variable, including Z. (That is the very definition of "randomness!") And if the connection between Z and X is broken, then Z cannot pollute the association between X and Y, which enables us to clear our fourth causal hurdle.[3]

Second, we can extend this logic to help us clear another of our four causal hurdles. If, in an experiment, values of X are caused only by pure randomness, then this means that, by definition, Y cannot be a cause of X.

---

[3] You will notice that this does not mean that the connection between Z and Y has been erased. Experiments do not remove the connection between other variables, Z, and our dependent variable, Y. They do, however, eliminate Z as a possible source of confounding between the X–Y relationship that makes the X–Y relationship spurious, which is what we care about in the first place.

In other words, the possible causal arrow between X and Y cannot be reversed, which means that we have also cleared our second causal hurdle.

Here is where experiments differ so drastically from any other kind of research design. What experimental research designs accomplish by way of random assignment to treatment groups, then, is to decontaminate the comparison between the treatment and control groups of all other influences. Before any stimulus (like a treatment or placebo) is administered, all of the participants are in the same pool. Researchers divide them by using some random factor like a coin flip, and that difference is the only difference between the two groups.

To see how this abstract discussion manifests itself in practical settings, let's return to our campaign advertising example. An experiment involving our new ad would involve finding a group of people – however obtained – and then randomly assigning them to view either our new ad or something that is not related to the campaign (like a cartoon or a public service announcement). We fully realize that there are other causes of people's voting behaviors, and that our experiment does not negate those factors. In fact, our experiment will have nothing whatsoever to say about those other causes. What it *will* do, and do well, is to determine whether our advertisement had a positive or negative effect, or none at all, on voter preferences. And that, you will recall, is precisely the question at hand.

Contrast the comparison that results from our hypothetical experiment with a comparison that arises from a non-experiment. (We'll discuss non-experimental designs in the next section.) Suppose that we don't do an experiment and just run the ad, and then spend the campaign money conducting a survey asking people if they've seen your ad, and for whom they plan to vote. Let's even assume that, in conducting the survey, we obtain a random sample of citizens in the district where the election will take place. If we analyze the results of the survey and discover that, as hoped, the people who say that they have seen the ad (X) are more likely to vote for you (Y) than are people who say they have not seen the ad, does that mean that the ad *caused* – see that word again? – people's opinions to shift in your favor? No, not necessarily. Why not? Because the people who saw your ad and the people who did not see your ad – that is, the varying values of our independent variable, X – might be *systematically different* from one another. What does that mean? It means that people who voluntarily watch a lot of politics on TV are (of course) more interested in politics than those who watch the rest of what appears on TV.

In this case, a person's level of interest in politics could be an important Z variable. Figure 4.2 shows this graphically. Interest in politics (Z) could very well be associated with a person's likelihood to vote for you (Y). What this means is that the simple comparison in a non-experiment between

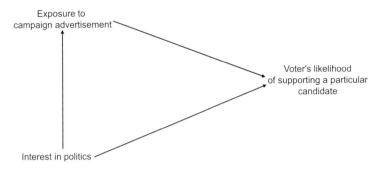

Figure 4.2 The possibly confounding effects of political interest in the advertisement viewing–vote intention relationship

those who do and those who do not see the ad is potentially misleading because it is confounded by other factors like interest in politics. So, is the higher support for you the result of the advertisement, or is it the result of the fact that people likely to see the ad in the first place are people with higher interest in politics? Because this particular non-experimental research design does not answer that question, it does not clear our fourth causal hurdle. It is impossible to know whether it was the ad that caused the voters to support you. In this non-experimental design just described, because there are other factors that influence support for a candidate – and, critically, because these factors are also related to whether or not people will see the advertisement – it is very difficult to say conclusively that the independent variable (ad exposure) causes the dependent variable (vote intention).[4]

Had we been able to conduct an experiment, we would have had considerably more confidence in our causal conclusion. Again, this is because the way that the confounding variables in Figure 4.2 are correlated with the independent variable is highly improbable in an experiment. Why? Because if exposure to the advertisement is determined by randomness, like a coin flip, then (by the very definition of randomness) it is exceedingly unlikely to be correlated with interest in politics (or any other possibly confounding variables Z). If we had been able to assign individuals to see or to not see the advertisement randomly, the comparison between the different groups will not be affected by the fact that other factors certainly do cause vote intentions, the dependent variable. In an experiment, then, because exposure to the ad would only be caused by randomness, it means that we can erase the connection between interest in politics (Z) and exposure to the ad (X) in Figure 4.2. And, recalling our definition of a confounding variable,

---

[4] We also note that such a design also fails to cross the second causal hurdle.

if interest in politics is not correlated with exposure to the ad, it cannot confound the relationship between the ad and vote intentions.

4.2.1 Experimental Designs and the Four Causal Hurdles

Recall our discussion from Chapter 3 about how researchers attempt to cross four hurdles in their efforts to establish whether some X causes Y. As we will see, experiments are not the only method that helps researchers cross the four causal hurdles, but they are uniquely capable in accomplishing important parts of that task. Consider each hurdle in turn. First, we should evaluate whether there is a credible causal mechanism before we decide to run the experiment. It is worth noting that the crossing of this causal hurdle is neither easier nor harder in experiments than in non-experiments. Coming up with a credible causal scenario that links X to Y heightens our dependence on theory, not on data or research design.

Second, in an experiment, it is impossible for Y to cause X – the second causal hurdle – for two reasons. First, assigning X occurs in time before Y is measured, which makes it impossible for Y to cause X. More importantly, though, as previously noted, if X is generated by randomness alone, then nothing (including Y) can cause it. So, in Figure 4.2, we could eliminate any possible reverse-causal arrow flowing from Y to X.

Establishing, third, whether X and Y are correlated is similarly easy regardless of chosen research design, experimental or non-experimental (as we will see in Chapter 8). What about our fourth causal hurdle? Have we controlled for all confounding variables Z that might make the association between X and Y spurious? Experiments are uniquely well equipped to help us answer this question definitively. An experiment does not, in any way, eliminate the possibility that a variety of other variables (that we call Z) might also affect Y (as well as X). What the experiment does, through the process of randomly assigning subjects to different values of X, is to equate the treatment and control groups on all possible factors. On every possible variable, whether or not it is related to X, or to Y, or to both, or to neither, the treatment and control groups should, in theory, be identical. That makes the comparison between the two values of X unpolluted by any possible Z variables because we expect the groups to be equivalent on all values of Z.

Remarkably, the experimental ability to control for the effects of outside variables (Z) applies to *all* possible confounding variables, regardless of whether we, the researchers, are aware of them. Let's make the example downright preposterous. Let's say that, 20 years from now, another team of scientists discovers that having attached (as opposed to detached) earlobes causes people to have different voting behaviors. Does that possibility threaten the inference that we draw from our experiment about our campaign ad? No, not at all. Why not? Because, whether or not we are aware of it, the random assignment of participants to treatment groups means that, whether we are paying attention to it or not, we would expect our treatment and control groups to have equal numbers of people with attached earlobes, and for both groups to have equal numbers of people with detached earlobes. The key element of an experimental research design – randomly assigning subjects to different values of X, the independent variable – controls for every Z in the universe, whether or not we are aware of that Z.

In summary, if we think back to the causal hurdles scorecard from the previous chapter, all properly set-up experiments start out with a scorecard reading [? y ? y]. The ability of experimental designs to cleanly and definitively answer "yes" to the fourth hurdle question – Have we controlled for all confounding variables Z that might make the association between X and Y spurious? – is a massive advantage.[5] All that remains for establishing a causal relationship is the answers to clear the first hurdle – Is there a credible causal mechanism that connects X to Y? – and hurdle three – Is there covariation between X and Y? The difficulty of clearing hurdle one is unchanged, but the third hurdle is much easier because we need only to make a statistical evaluation of the relationship between X and Y. As we will see in Chapter 8, such evaluations are pretty straightforward, especially when compared to statistical tests that involve controlling for other variables (Z).

Together, all of this means that experiments bring with them a particularly strong confidence in the causal inferences drawn from the analysis. In scientific parlance, this is called **internal validity**. If a research design produces high levels of confidence in the conclusions about causality among the cases that are specifically analyzed, it is said to have high internal validity. Conversely, research designs that do not allow for particularly definitive conclusions about whether X causes Y for those particular cases under consideration are said to have low degrees of internal validity.

4.2.2 "Random Assignment" versus "Random Sampling"

It is critical that you do not confuse *the experimental process of randomly assigning subjects to treatment groups*, on the one hand, with *the process of randomly sampling subjects for participation*, on the other hand. They

---

[5] After all, even the best designed and executed non-experimental designs must remain open to the possibility that, somewhere out there, there is a Z variable that has not yet been considered and controlled for.

are entirely different, and in fact have nothing more in common than that six-letter word "random." They are, however, quite often confused for one another. **Random assignment** to treatment and control groups occurs when the participants for an experiment are assigned randomly to one of several possible values of X, the independent variable. Importantly, this definition says nothing at all about how the subjects were selected for participation. But **random sampling** is, at its very heart, about how researchers select cases for inclusion in a study – they are selected at random, which means that every member of the underlying **population** has an equal probability of being selected. (This is common in survey research, for example.)

We emphasize that selecting participants for a study at random from the underlying population is never a bad idea. In fact, it helps researchers to generalize their findings from the sample that is under study to the general population. But, logically, it has nothing whatsoever to do with crossing any of the four causal hurdles.

Mixing up these two critical concepts will produce a good bit of confusion. In particular, confusing random sampling with random assignment to treatment groups will mean that the distinction between experiments and non-experiments has been lost, and this difference is among the more important ones in all of science. To understand how science works, keep these two very important concepts separate from one another.

4.2.3   Varieties of Experiments and Near-Experiments

Not all experiments take place in a laboratory with scientists wearing white lab coats. Some experiments in the social sciences are conducted by surveys that do use random samples (see above). Since 1990 or so, there has been a growing movement in the field of survey research – which has traditionally used random samples of the population – to use computers in the interviewing process, that includes experimental randomization of variations in survey questions, in a technique called a **survey experiment**. Such designs are intended to reap the benefits of both random assignment to treatment groups, and hence have high internal validity, as well as the benefits of a random sample, and hence have high **external validity**.[6] Survey experiments may be conducted over the phone or, increasingly, over the internet.

Another setting for an experiment is out in the natural world. A **field experiment** is one that occurs in the natural setting where the subjects normally lead their lives. Random assignment to treatment groups has

---

[6] See Piazza, Sniderman, and Tetlock (1990) and Sniderman and Piazza (1993).

enabled researchers in the social sciences to study subjects that seemed beyond the reach of experimentation. Economists have long sought conclusive evidence about the effectiveness (or the lack thereof) of economic development policies. For example, do government fertilizer subsidies (X) affect agricultural output (Y)? Duflo, Kremer, and Robinson (2011) report the results of an experiment in a region in western Kenya in which a subsidy of free delivery of fertilizer was offered only to randomly chosen farmers, but not to others.

YOUR TURN: Imagining a field experiment

Do the positions that elected officials espouse (X) shape their constituents' opinions (Y)? You can surely imagine why political scientists might be eager to answer such a question, as it touches on the ability (or inability) of politicians to shape public opinion.

Imagine, for a moment, what obstacles a field experiment that examines this question would have to overcome. Keep in mind the two-pronged definition of an experiment.

Now go see how it was done. Read Broockman and Butler (2017) here: http://rdcu.be/vXCV/

Field experiments can also take place in public policy settings, sometimes with understandable controversy. Does the police officer's decision whether or not to arrest the male at a domestic violence call (X) affect the incidence of repeat violence at the same address in the subsequent months (Y)? Sherman and Berk (1984) conducted a field experiment in Minneapolis, randomizing whether or not the male in the household would automatically (or not) be arrested when police arrived at the house.

On occasion, situations in nature that are not properly defined as experiments – because the values of X have not been controlled and assigned by the researcher – nevertheless resemble experiments in key ways. In a **natural experiment** – which, we emphasize, does not meet our definition of an experiment, hence the name is fairly misleading – values of the independent variable arise naturally in such a way as to make it seem as if true random assignment by a researcher has occurred. For example, does the size of an ethnic group within a population (X) affect inter-group conflict or cooperation (Y)? Posner (2004) investigates why the Chewa and Tumbuka peoples are allies in Zambia but are adversaries in Malawi. Because the sizes of the groups in the different countries seem to have arisen randomly, the comparison is treated *as if* the sizes of the respective populations were assigned randomly by the researcher, when (of course) they were not.

4.2.4   Are There Drawbacks to Experimental Research Designs?

Experiments, as we have seen, have a unique ability to get social scientists across our hurdles needed to establish whether X causes Y. But that does not mean they are without disadvantages. Many of these disadvantages are related to the differences between medical and physical sciences, on the one hand, and the social sciences, on the other. We now discuss four drawbacks to experimentation.

First, especially in the social sciences, not every independent variable (X) is controllable and subject to experimental manipulation. Suppose, for example, that we wish to study the effects of gender on political participation. Do men contribute more money, vote more, volunteer more in campaigns, than women? There are a variety of non-experimental ways to study this relationship, but it is impossible to experimentally manipulate a subject's gender. Recall that the definition of an experiment is that the researcher both controls and randomly assigns the values of the independent variable. In this case, the presumed cause (the independent variable) is a person's gender. Compared with drugs versus placebos, assigning a participant's gender is another matter entirely. It is, to put it mildly, impossible. People show up at an experiment with some gender identity, and it is not within the experimenter's power to "randomly assign" a gender to participants.

This is true in many, many political science examples. There are simply a myriad of substantive problems that are impossible to study in an experimental fashion. How does a person's partisanship (X) affect his issue opinions (Y)? How does a person's income level (X) affect her campaign contributions (Y)? How does a country's level of democratization (X) affect its openness to international trade (Y)? How does the level of military spending in India (X) affect the level of military spending in Pakistan (Y) – and, for that matter, vice versa? How does media coverage (X) in an election campaign influence voters' priorities (Y)? Does serving in the UK parliament (X) make members of parliament wealthy (Y)? In each of these examples that intrigue social scientists, the independent variable is simply not subject to experimental manipulation. Social scientists cannot, in any meaningful sense, "assign" people a party identification or an income, "assign" a country a level of democratization or level of military spending, "assign" a campaign-specific, long-term amount of media coverage, or "assign" different candidates to win seats in parliament. These variables simply exist in nature, and we cannot control exposure to them and randomly assign different values to different cases (that is, individual people or countries). And yet, social scientists feel compelled to study these phenomena, which means that, in those circumstances, we must turn to a non-experimental research design.

> **YOUR TURN: What would it take to investigate these research questions experimentally?**
>
> For each of the research questions in the previous paragraph, spell out what it would take in order to be able to investigate these questions using experimental methods. (Some of them will seem preposterous! Others less so, especially if you're clever.)

A second potential disadvantage of experimental research designs is that experiments often suffer from low degrees of external validity. We have noted that the key strength of experiments is that they typically have high levels of internal validity. That is, we can be quite confident that the conclusions about causality reached in the analysis are not confounded by other variables. External validity, in a sense, is the other side of the coin, as it represents the degree to which we can be confident that the results of our analysis apply not only to the participants in the study, but also to the population more broadly construed.

There are actually two types of concerns with respect to external validity. The first is the external validity of the sample itself. Recall that there is nothing whatsoever in our definition of an experiment that describes how researchers recruit or select people to participate in the experiment. To reiterate: *It is absolutely not the case that experiments require a random sample of the target population.* Indeed, it is extremely rare for experiments to draw a random sample from a population. In drug-trial experiments, for example, it is common to place advertisements in newspapers or on the radio to invite participation, usually involving some form of compensation to the participants. Clearly, people who see and respond to advertisements like this are not a random sample of the population of interest, which is typically thought of as all potential recipients of the drug. Similarly, when professors "recruit" people from their (or their colleagues') classes, the participants are not a random sample of *any* population.[7] The participant pool in this case represents what we would call a **sample of convenience**, which is to say, this is more or less the group of people we could beg, coerce, entice, or cajole to participate.

With a sample of convenience, it is simply unclear how, if at all, the results of the experiment generalize to a broader population. As we will learn in Chapter 7, this is a critical issue in the social sciences. Because most experiments make use of such samples of convenience, with any *single* experiment, it is difficult to know whether the results of that

---

[7] Think about that for a moment. Experiments in undergraduate psychology or political science classes are not a random sample of 18- to 22-year-olds, or even a random sample of undergraduate students, or even a random sample of students from your college or university. Your psychology class is populated with people more interested in the social sciences than in the physical sciences or engineering or the humanities.

analysis are in any way typical of what we would find in a different sample. With experimental designs, then, scientists learn about how their results apply to a broader population through the process of **replication**, in which researchers implement the same procedures repeatedly in identical form to see if the relationships hold in a consistent fashion. Over time, as scientists repeatedly use identical experimental procedures on different samples of participants, and those analyses produce the same pattern of results, we become increasingly convinced that the results generalize to a broader population.

There is a second external validity concern with experiments that is more subtle, but perhaps just as important. It concerns the external validity of the stimulus. To continue our example of whether the campaign ad affects voter intentions, if we were to run an experiment to address this question, what would we do? First, we would need to obtain a sample of volunteer subjects somehow. (Remember, they need not be a random sample.) Second, we would divide them, on a random basis, into experimental and control groups. We would then sit them in a lab in front of computers, and show the ad to the experimental group, and show something innocuous to the control group. Then we would ask the subjects from both groups their vote intentions, and make a comparison between our groups. Just as we might have concerns about how externally valid our sample is, because they may not be representative of the underlying population, we should also be concerned about how externally valid our stimulus is. What do we mean here? The stimulus is the X variable. In this case, it is the act of sitting the experimental and control subjects down and having them watch (different) video messages on the computer screens. How similar is that stimulus to one that a person experiences in his or her home – that is, in their more natural environment? In some critical respects it is quite different. In our hypothetical experiment, the individual does not choose what he or she sees. The exposure to the ad is forced (once the subject consents to participate in the experiment). At home? People who don't want to be exposed to political ads can avoid them rather easily if they so choose, simply by not watching particular channels or programs, or by not watching TV at all, or by flipping the channel when a political ad starts up. But the comparison in our hypothetical experiment is entirely insensitive to this key difference between the experimental environment and the subject's more natural environment. To the extent that an experiment creates an entirely artificial environment, we might be concerned that the results of that experiment will be found in a more real-world context.[8]

---

[8] For a discussion of the external validity of experiments embedded in national surveys, see Barabas and Jerit (2010). See also Morton and Williams (2010, p. 264), who refer to this problem as one of "ecological validity."

> **YOUR TURN: Thinking creatively to increase the external validity of the stimulus**
>
> In the example above about how lab experiments sometimes force exposure (of media content, for example) on to participants, can you think of any creative way that an experimenter might be able to circumvent this problem? Try to imagine how we could do the experiment differently.
>
> Now go see how it was done. Read Arceneaux, Johnson, and Murphy (2012) here: http://www.jstor.org/stable/10.1017/s002238161100123x
>
> What difference did it make on the results about media effects on public opinion?

Experimental research designs, at times, can be plagued with a third disadvantage, namely that they carry special ethical dilemmas for the researcher. Ethical issues about the treatment of human participants occur frequently with medical experiments, of course. If we wished to study experimentally the effects of different types of cancer treatments on survival rates, this would require obtaining a sample of patients with cancer and then randomly assigning the patients to differing treatment regimens. This is typically not considered acceptable medical practice. In such high-stakes medical situations, most individuals value making these decisions themselves, in consultation with their doctor, and would not relinquish the important decisions about their treatment to a random-number generator.

Ethical situations arise less frequently, and typically less dramatically, in social science experimentation, but they do arise on occasion. During the behavioral revolution in psychology in the 1960s, several famous experiments conducted at universities produced vigorous ethical debates. Psychologist Stanley Milgram (1974) conducted experiments on how easily he could make individuals obey an authority figure. In this case, the dependent variable was the willingness of the participant to administer what he or she believed to be a shock to another participant, who was in fact an employee of Milgram's. (The ruse was that Milgram told the participant that he was testing how negative reinforcement – electric shocks – affected the "learning" of the "student.") The independent variable was the degree to which Milgram conveyed his status as an authority figure. In other words, the X that Milgram manipulated was the degree to which he presented himself as an authority who must be obeyed. For some participants, Milgram wore a white lab coat and informed them that he was a professor at Yale University. For others, he dressed more casually and never mentioned his institutional affiliation. The dependent variable, then, was how strong the (fake) shocks would be before the subject simply refused to go on. At the highest extreme, the instrument that delivered the "shock" said "450 volts, XXX." The results of the experiment were fascinating because, to his surprise, Milgram found that the great majority of his participants were willing to administer even these extreme shocks to the "learners." But scientific review boards consider such experiments unethical today, because the experiment created a great degree of emotional distress among the true participants.

YOUR TURN: What do you think is ethical?

Though we are unaware of any experimental research situations in political science that approach the severity of the ethical problems of the Milgram experiment, consider the potential ethical risks of the following experimental situation:

If an experimenter wanted to investigate the potential influence of exposure to online political advertisements (X) on an individual's vote choice (Y), and in an effort to manipulate X experimentally, purchased advertising space on Facebook – randomly exposing some Facebook users to one type of advertisement, and randomly exposing others to a different type of advertisement – what would be the potential ethical considerations involved?

A fourth potential drawback of experimental research designs is that, when interpreting the results of an experiment, we sometimes make mistakes of emphasis. If an experiment produces a finding that some X does indeed cause Y, that does not mean that that particular X is the most prominent cause of Y. As we have emphasized repeatedly, a variety of independent variables are causally related to every interesting dependent variable in the social sciences. Experimental research designs often do not help to sort out which causes of the dependent variable have the largest effects and which ones have smaller effects.

4.3   OBSERVATIONAL STUDIES (IN TWO FLAVORS)

Taken together, the drawbacks of experiments mean that, for any given political science research situation, implementing an experiment often proves to be unworkable, and sometimes downright impossible. As a result, though its use is becoming more widespread, experimentation is not the most common research design used by political scientists. In some subfields, such as political psychology – which, as the name implies, studies the cognitive and emotional underpinnings of political decision making – experimentation is quite common. Experimentation is also becoming more common in the study of public opinion and electoral competition. And an increasing number of researchers are turning to experiments – either in laboratories or online – where participants engage in competitive or cooperative tasks in order to mimic the way nation states might interact in the international arena. But the experiment, for many researchers and for varying reasons, remains a tool that is not applicable to many of the phenomena that we seek to study.

Does this mean that researchers have to shrug their shoulders and abandon their search for causal connections before they even begin? Not at all. But what options do scholars have when they cannot control exposure to different values of the independent variables? In such cases, the only choice is to take the world as it already exists and make the comparison either between individual units – like people, political parties, or countries – or between an **aggregate** quantity that varies over time. These represent two variants of what is most commonly called an observational study. Observational studies are not experiments, but they seek to emulate them. They are known as observational studies because, unlike the controlled and somewhat artificial nature of most experiments, in these research designs, researchers simply take reality as it is and "observe" it, attempting to sort out causal connections without the benefit of randomly assigning participants to treatment groups. Instead, different values of the independent variable already exist in the world, and what scientists do is observe them and then evaluate their theoretical claims by putting them through the same four causal hurdles to discover whether X causes Y.

This leads to the definition of an observational study: An observational study is a research design in which the researcher does *not* have control over values of the independent variable, which occur naturally. However, it is necessary that there be some degree of variability in the independent variable across cases, as well as variation in the dependent variable.

Because there is no random assignment to treatment groups, as in experiments, some scholars claim that it is impossible to speak of causality in observational studies, and therefore sometimes refer to them as **correlational studies**. Along with most political scientists, we do not share this view. Certainly experiments produce higher degrees of confidence about causal matters than do observational studies. However, in observational studies, if sufficient attention is paid to accounting for all of the other possible causes of the dependent variable that are suggested by current understanding, then we can make informed evaluations of our confidence that the independent variable does cause the dependent variable.

Observational studies, as this discussion implies, face exactly the same four causal hurdles as do experiments. (Recall that those hurdles are present in any research design.) So how, in observational studies, do we cross these hurdles? The first causal hurdle – Is there a credible mechanism connecting X and Y? – is identical in experimental and observational studies.

In an observational study, however, crossing the second causal hurdle – Can we eliminate the possibility that Y causes X? – can sometimes be problematic. For example, do countries with higher levels of economic development (X) have, as a consequence, more stable democratic regimes (Y)? Crossing the second causal hurdle, in this case, is a rather dicey matter. It is clearly plausible that having a stable democratic government makes economic prosperity more likely, which is the reverse-causal scenario. After all, investors are probably more comfortable taking risks with their money in democratic regimes than in autocratic ones. Those risks, in turn, likely produce greater degrees of economic prosperity. It is possible, of course, that X and Y are mutually reinforcing – that is, X causes Y and Y causes X.

The third hurdle – Is there covariation between X and Y? – is, as we mentioned, no more difficult for an observational study than for an experiment. (The techniques for examining relationships between two variables are straightforward, and you will learn them in Chapters 8 and 9.) But, unlike in an experimental setting, if we fail to find covariation between X and Y in an observational setting, we should still proceed to the fourth hurdle because the possibility remains that we will find covariation between X and Y once we control for some variable Z.

The most pointed comparison between experiments and observational studies, though, occurs with respect to the fourth causal hurdle. The near-magic that happens in experiments because of random assignment to treatment groups – which enables researchers to know that no other factors interfere in the relationship between X and Y – is not present in an observational study. So, in an observational study, the comparison between groups with different values of the independent variable may very well be polluted by other factors, interfering with our ability to make conclusive statements about whether X causes Y.

Within observational studies, there are two pure types – **cross-sectional observational studies**, which focus on variation across **spatial units** at a single **time unit**, and **time-series observational studies**, which focus on variation within a single spatial unit over multiple time units. There are, in addition, hybrid designs, but for the sake of simplicity we will focus on the pure types.[9] Before we get into the two types of observational studies, we need to provide a brief introduction to observational data.

---

[9] The classic statements of observational studies appeared in 1963 in Donald Campbell and Julian Stanley's seminal work *Experimental and Quasi-Experimental Designs for Research*.

4.3.1 Datum, Data, Data Set

The word "data" is one of the most grammatically misused words in the English language. Why? Because most people use this word as though it were a singular word when it is, in fact, plural. Any time you read "the data is," you have found a grammatical error. Instead, when describing data, the phrasing should be "the data are." Get used to it: You are now one of the foot soldiers in the crusade to get people to use this word appropriately. It will be a long and uphill battle.

The singular form of the word data is "**datum.**" Together, a collection of datum produces data or a "**data set.**" We define observational data sets by the variables that they contain and the spatial and time units over which they are measured. Political scientists use data measured on a variety of different spatial units. For instance, in survey research, the spatial unit is the individual survey respondent. In comparative US state government studies, the spatial unit is the US state. In international relations, the spatial unit is often the nation. Commonly studied time units are months, quarters, and years. It is also common to refer to the spatial and time units that define data sets as the **data set dimensions.**

Two of the most common types of data sets correspond directly to the two types of observational studies that we just introduced. For instance, Table 4.1 presents a cross-sectional data set in which the time unit is the year 1972 and the spatial unit is nations. These data could be used to test the theory that unemployment percentage $(X) \rightarrow$ government debt as a percentage of gross national product (Y).

Time-series observational studies contain measures of X and Y across time for a single spatial unit. For instance, Table 4.2 displays a time-series data set in which the spatial unit is the United States and the time unit is months. We could use these data to test the theory that inflation $(X) \rightarrow$ presidential approval (Y). In a data set, researchers analyze only those data that contain measured values for both the independent variable (X) and the dependent variable (Y) to determine whether the third causal hurdle has been cleared.

4.3.2 Cross-Sectional Observational Studies

As the name implies, a cross-sectional observational study examines a cross-section of social reality, focusing on variation between *individual spatial units* – again, like citizens, elected officials, voting districts, or countries – and explaining the variation in the dependent variable across them.

For example, what, if anything, is the connection between the preferences of the voters from a district (X) and a representative's voting

Table 4.1 Example of cross-sectional data		
Nation	Government debt as a percentage of GNP	Unemployment rate
Finland	6.6	2.6
Denmark	5.7	1.6
United States	27.5	5.6
Spain	13.9	3.2
Sweden	15.9	2.7
Belgium	45.0	2.4
Japan	11.2	1.4
New Zealand	44.6	0.5
Ireland	63.8	5.9
Italy	42.5	4.7
Portugal	6.6	2.1
Norway	28.1	1.7
Netherlands	23.6	2.1
Germany	6.7	0.9
Canada	26.9	6.3
Greece	18.4	2.1
France	8.7	2.8
Switzerland	8.2	0.0
United Kingdom	53.6	3.1
Australia	23.8	2.6

Table 4.2 Example of time-series data		
Month	Presidential approval	Inflation
2002.01	83.7	1.14
2002.02	82.0	1.14
2002.03	79.8	1.48
2002.04	76.2	1.64
2002.05	76.3	1.18
2002.06	73.4	1.07
2002.07	71.6	1.46
2002.08	66.5	1.80
2002.09	67.2	1.51
2002.10	65.3	2.03
2002.11	65.5	2.20
2002.12	62.8	2.38

behavior (Y)? In a cross-sectional observational study, the strategy that a researcher would pursue in answering this question involves comparing the aggregated preferences of voters from a variety of districts (X) with the voting records of the representatives (Y). Such an analysis, of course, would have to be observational, instead of experimental, because this particular X is not subject to experimental manipulation. Such an analysis might take place within the confines of a single legislative session, for a variety of practical purposes (such as the absence of turnover in seats, which is an obviously complicating factor).

Bear in mind, of course, that observational studies have to cross the same four causal hurdles as do experiments. And we have noted that, unlike experiments, with their random assignment to treatment groups, observational studies will often get stuck on our fourth hurdle. That might indeed be the case here. Assuming the other three hurdles can be cleared, consider the possibility that there are confounding variables that cause Y and are also correlated with X, which make the X–Y connection spurious. How do cross-sectional observational studies deal with this critical issue? The answer is that, in most cases, this can be accomplished through a series of rather straightforward statistical controls. In particular, beginning in Chapter 10, you will learn the most common social science research tool for "controlling for" other possible causes of Y, namely the multiple regression model. What you will learn there is that multiple regression can allow researchers to see how, if at all, controlling for another variable (like Z) affects the relationship between X and Y.

YOUR TURN: Controlling for other variables in studying the opinion–policy connection

In the observational study of the connection between the policy preferences of voters from a district (X) and their representative's voting behavior (Y), can you think of any variables (Z) that we would need to control for in order to guard against the possibility that the observed relationship is spurious?

4.3.3 Time-Series Observational Studies

The other major variant of observational studies is the time-series observational study, which has, at its heart, a comparison over time within a single spatial unit. Unlike in the cross-sectional variety, which examines relationships between variables across individual units typically at a single time point, in the time-series observational study, political scientists typically examine the variation within one spatial unit over time.[10]

For example, how, if at all, do changes in media coverage about the economy (X) affect public concern about the economy (Y)?[11] To be a bit more specific, when the media spend more time talking about the potential problem of inflation, does the public show more concern about inflation,

---

[10] The spatial units analyzed in time-series observational studies are usually aggregated.
[11] See Iyengar and Kinder (2010).

and when the media spend less time on the subject of inflation, does public concern about inflation wane? We can measure these variables in aggregate terms that vary over time. For example, how many stories about inflation make it onto the nightly news in a given month? It is almost certain that that quantity will not be the same each and every month. And how much concern does the public show (through opinion polls, for example) about inflation in a given month? Again, the percentage of people who identify inflation as a pressing problem will almost certainly vary from month to month.

Of course, as with its cross-sectional cousin, the time-series observational study will require us to focus hard on that fourth causal hurdle. Have we controlled for all confounding variables (Z) that are related to the varying volume of news coverage about inflation (X) and public concern about inflation (Y)? If we can identify any other possible causes of why the public is sometimes more concerned about inflation, and why they are sometimes less concerned about it, then we will need to control for those factors in our analysis.

YOUR TURN: What do we need to control for?

Can you think of any relevant Z variables that we will need to control for, statistically, in such an analysis, to be confident that the relationship between X and Y is causal? That is, can you name a variable that might be a cause of Y and also correlated with X that might make the X–Y relationship spurious?

4.3.4   The Major Difficulty with Observational Studies

We noted that experimental research designs carry some drawbacks with them. So, too, do observational studies. Here, we focus only on one, but it is a big one. As the preceding examples demonstrate, when we need to control for the other possible causes of Y to cross the fourth causal hurdle, we need to control for *all of them*, not just one.[12] But how do we know whether we have controlled for all of the other possible causes of Y? In many cases, we don't know that for certain. We need to try, of course, to control statistically for all other possible causes that we can, which involves carefully considering the previous research on the subject and gathering as much data on those other causes as is possible. But in many cases, we will simply be unable to do this perfectly.

What all of this means, in our view, is that observational analysis must be a bit more tentative in its pronouncements about causality. Indeed, if

---

[12] As we will see in Chapter 10, technically we need to control only for the factors that might affect Y and are also related to X. In practice, though, that is a very difficult distinction to make.

we have done the very best we can to control for as many causes of Y, then the most sensible conclusion we can reach, in many cases, is that X causes Y. But in practice, our conclusions are rarely definitive, and subsequent research can modify them. That can be frustrating, we know, for students to come to grips with – and it can be frustrating for researchers, too. But the fact that conclusive answers are difficult to come by should only make us work harder to identify other causes of Y. An important part of being a scientist is that we very rarely can make definitive conclusions about causality; we must remain open to the possibility that some previously unconsidered (Z) variable will surface and render our previously found relationships to be spurious.

4.4 DISSECTING THE RESEARCH BY OTHER SCHOLARS

Once you have identified the influential work in your topic area, it is important to take each piece of research apart in order to be able to put it to work for your purposes. We recommend making notes on the answers to the following questions:

- What was the research question/puzzle?
- What was their theory?
- What was their research design?
- How did they do with the four hurdles?
- What did they conclude?

For example, consider a highly cited article about consumer confidence and presidential approval by MacKuen, Erikson, and Stimson (1992). A paragraph-long synopsis of that article might take the following form:

> In their article, MacKuen, Erikson, and Stimson (1992) address the question of how changes in the economy translate into shifts in presidential approval ratings. Whereas the conventional wisdom held that objective economic reality – usually in the form of inflation and unemployment – drives approval ratings, their theory argues that a more subjective measure, **consumer confidence**, is what causes approval to rise and fall over time. To test their theory, they conducted a time-series observational study over the period 1954–1988, controlling for a number of noneconomic factors that also shape approval. They found that, once controlling for consumer sentiment, inflation and unemployment no longer were statistically significant predictors of approval ratings, whereas consumer confidence was.

By systematically going through the important pieces of previous research, as we've done here, and summarizing each compactly, it becomes possible to see what the literature, as a collection, teaches us about what we do know, and what we don't know, about a particular phenomenon. Once you have done this, you are ready to critically evaluate previous research and ask questions that may lead you to a new theory.

YOUR TURN: Producing a summary of a published article

Using the itemized list above, produce a summary of an article published in a political science journal.

4.5 SUMMARY

For almost every phenomenon of interest to political scientists, there is more than one form of research design that they could implement to address questions of causal relationships. Before starting a project, researchers need to decide whether to use experimental or observational methods; and if they opt for the latter, as is common, they have to decide what type of observational study to use. And sometimes researchers choose more than one type of design.

Different research designs help shed light on different substantive questions. Focus, for the moment, on a simple matter like the public's preferences for a more liberal or conservative government policy. Cross-sectional and time-series approaches are both useful in this respect. They simply address distinct substantive questions. Cross-sectional approaches look to see why some individuals prefer more liberal government policies, and why some other individuals prefer more conservative government policies. That is a perfectly worthwhile undertaking for a political scientist: What causes some people to be liberals and others to be conservatives? But consider the time-series approach, which focuses on why the public as an aggregated whole prefers a more liberal or a more conservative government at a variety of points in time. That is simply a different question. Neither approach is inherently better or worse than the other – though scholars might have varying tastes about which is more interesting than the other – but they both shed light on different aspects of social reality. Which design researchers should choose depends on what type of question they intend to ask and answer.

CONCEPTS INTRODUCED IN THIS CHAPTER

- aggregate – a quantity that is created by combining the values of many individual cases

- consumer confidence – a subjective assessment by members of the mass public that registers the public's optimism or pessimism about the state of the economy
- control group – in an experiment, the subset of cases that is not exposed to the main causal stimulus under investigation
- correlational studies – synonymous with "observational studies"
- cross-sectional observational studies – a research design that focuses on variation across spatial units at a single time unit
- data set – a collection of variable values for at least two observations; synonym for "data"
- data set dimensions – the spatial and time units that define a data set
- datum – the singular form of the word "data"
- experiments – research designs in which the researcher both controls and randomly assigns values of the independent variable to the participants
- external validity – the degree to which we can be confident that the results of our analysis apply not only to the participants and circumstances in the study, but also to the population more broadly construed
- field experiment – an experimental study that occurs in the natural setting where the subjects normally lead their lives
- internal validity – the degree to which a study produces high levels of confidence about whether the independent variable causes the dependent variable
- natural experiment – situations in nature that are not properly defined as experiments but the values of the independent variable arise naturally in such a way as to make it seem as if true random assignment by a researcher has occurred
- observational studies – research designs in which the researcher does not have control over values of the independent variable, which occur naturally; it is necessary that there be some degree of variability in the independent variable across cases, as well as variation in the dependent variable
- placebo – in an experiment, an innocuous stimulus given to the control group
- population – the entire set of cases to which our theory applies
- random assignment – when the participants for an experiment are assigned randomly to one of several possible values of X, the independent variable
- random sampling – a method for selecting individual cases for a study in which every member of the underlying population has an equal probability of being selected

- replication – a scientific process in which researchers implement the same procedures repeatedly in identical form to see if the relationships hold in a consistent fashion
- research designs – the strategies that a researcher employs to make comparisons with the goal of evaluating causal claims
- sample of convenience – a sample of cases from the underlying population in which the mechanism for selecting cases is not random
- spatial unit – the physical unit that forms the basis for observation
- survey experiment – a survey research technique in which the interviewing process includes experimental randomization in the survey stimulus
- time-series observational studies – a research design that focuses on variation within a single spatial unit over multiple time units
- time unit – the time-based unit that forms the basis for observation
- treatment group – in an experiment, the subset of cases that is exposed to the main causal stimulus under investigation

EXERCISES

1. Consider the following proposed relationships between an independent and a dependent variable. In each case, would it be realistic for a researcher to perform an experiment to test the theory? If yes, briefly describe what would be randomly assigned in the experiment; if no, briefly explain why not.

   (a) An individual's level of religiosity (X) and his or her preferences for different political candidates (Y).
   (b) Exposure to negative political news (X) and political apathy (Y).
   (c) Military service (X) and attitudes toward foreign policy (Y).
   (d) A speaker's personal characteristics (X) and persuasiveness (Y).

2. Consider the relationship between education level (X) and voting turnout (Y). How would the design of a cross-sectional observational study differ from that of a time-series observational study?

3. In the previous chapter (specifically, Section 3.3 titled "Why Is Studying Causality So Important? Three Examples from Political Science"), we gave examples of research problems. For each of these examples, identify the spatial unit(s) and time unit(s). For each, say whether the study was an experiment, a cross-sectional observational study, or a time-series observational study.

4. Table 4.1 presents data for a test of a theory by use of a cross-sectional observational study. If this same theory were tested by use of a time-series observational study, what would the data table look like?

5. Compare the two designs for testing the preceding theory. Across the two forms of observational studies, what are the Z variables for which you want to control?

6. Table 4.2 presents data for a test of a theory by use of a time-series observational study. If this same theory were tested by use of a cross-sectional observational study, what would the data table look like?

7. Compare the two designs for testing the preceding theory. Across the two forms of observational studies, what are the Z variables for which you want to control?

8. Use your library's resources or Google Scholar (scholar.google.com) to look up the following articles and determine whether the research design used in each is an experiment, a cross-sectional observational study, or a time-series observational study. (*Note*: To access these articles, you might need to perform the search from a location based on your campus.)

(a) Clarke, Harold D., William Mishler, and Paul Whiteley. 1990. "Recapturing the Falklands: Models of Conservative Popularity, 1979–83." *British Journal of Political Science* 20(1):63–81.

(b) Gibson, James L., Gregory A. Caldeira, and Vanessa A. Baird. 1998. "On the Legitimacy of National High Courts." *American Political Science Review* 92(2):343–358.

(c) Druckman, James N. 2001. "The Implications of Framing Effects for Citizen Competence." *Political Behavior* 23(3):225–256.

5 Measuring Concepts of Interest

OVERVIEW

Although what political scientists care about is discovering whether causal relationships exist between concepts, what we *actually* examine is statistical associations between variables. Therefore, it is critical that we have a clear understanding of the concepts that we care about so we can measure them in a valid and reliable way. As we discuss the importance of measurement, we use several examples from the political science literature, such as the concept of political tolerance. We know that political tolerance (and intolerance) is a "real" thing – that it exists to varying degrees in the hearts and minds of people. But how do we go about measuring it? What are the implications of poor measurement?

I know it when I see it.
　　　　—Associate Justice of the United States Supreme Court Potter Stewart, in
　　　　　an attempt to define "obscenity" in a concurring opinion in *Jacobellis v.*
　　　　　Ohio (1964)

These go to eleven.
　　　　—Nigel Tufnel (played by Christopher Guest), describing the volume knob
　　　　　on his amplifier, in the movie *This Is Spinal Tap*

5.1　GETTING TO KNOW YOUR DATA

We have emphasized the role of theory in political science. That is, we care about causal relationships between concepts that interest us as political scientists. At this point, you are hopefully starting to develop theories of your own about politics. If these original theories are in line with the rules of the road that we laid out in Chapter 1, they will be causal, general, and parsimonious. They may even be elegant and clever.

But at this point, it is worth pausing and thinking about what a theory really *is* and *is not*. To help us in this process, take a look back at

Figure 1.2. A theory, as we have said, is merely a conjecture about the possible causal relationship between two or more concepts. As scientists, we must always resist the temptation to view our theories as somehow supported until we have evaluated evidence from the real world, and until we have done everything we can with empirical evidence to evaluate how well our theory clears the four causal hurdles we identified in Chapter 3. In other words, we cannot evaluate a theory until we have gone through the rest of the process depicted in Figure 1.2. The first part of this chapter deals with operationalization, or the movement of variables from the rather abstract conceptual level to the very real measured level. We can conduct hypothesis tests and make reasonable evaluations of our theories only after we have gone carefully through this important process with all of our variables.

If our theories are statements about relationships *between concepts*, when we look for evidence to test our theories, we are immediately confronted with the reality that we do not actually *observe* those concepts. Many of the concepts that we care about in political science, as we will see shortly, are inherently elusive and downright impossible to observe empirically in a direct way, and sometimes incredibly difficult to measure quantitatively. For this reason, we need to think very carefully about the data that we choose to evaluate our theories.

Until now, we have seen many examples of data, but we have not discussed the process of obtaining data and putting them to work. If we think back to Figure 1.2, we are now at the stage where we want to move from the theoretical–conceptual level to the empirical–measured level. For every theoretical concept, there are multiple operationalization or measurement strategies. As we discussed in the previous chapter, one of the first major decisions that one needs to make is whether to conduct an experiment or some form of observational study. In this chapter, we assume that you have a theory and that you are going to conduct an observational test of your theory.

A useful exercise, once you have developed an original theory, is to draw your version of Figure 1.2 and to think about what would be the ideal setup for testing your theory. What would be the best setup, a cross-sectional design or a time-series design? Once you have answered this question and have your ideal time and spatial dimensions in hand, what would be the ideal measure of your independent and dependent variables?

Having gone through the exercise of thinking about the ideal data, the first instinct of most students is to collect their own data, perhaps even to do so through a survey.[1] In our experience, beginning researchers almost

---

[1] A survey is a particularly cumbersome choice because, at least at most universities, you would need to have approval for conducting your survey from the Human Subjects Research Committee.

always underestimate the difficulties and the costs (in terms of both time and money) of collecting one's own data. We *strongly* recommend that you look to see what data are already available for you to use.

For a political science researcher, one of the great things about the era in which we live is that there is a nearly endless supply of data that are available from web sites and other easily accessible resources.[2] But a few words of caution: just because data are easily available on the web does not mean that these data will be perfectly suitable to the particular needs of your hypothesis test. What follows in the rest of this chapter is a set of considerations that you should have in mind to help you determine whether or not a particular set of data that you have found is appropriate for your purposes, and to help you to get to know your data once you have loaded them into a statistical program. We begin with the all-important topic of variable measurement. We describe the problems of measurement and the importance of measuring the concepts in which we are interested as precisely as possible. During this process, you will learn some thinking skills for evaluating the measurement strategies of scholarship that you read, as well as learn about evaluating the usefulness of measures that you are considering using to test your hypotheses.

We begin this chapter with a section on measurement in the social sciences generally. We focus on examples from economics and psychology, two social sciences that are at rather different levels of agreement about the measurement of their major variables. In political science, we have a complete range of variables in terms of the levels of agreement about how they should be measured. We discuss the core concepts of measurement and give some examples from political science research. Throughout our discussion of these core concepts, we focus on the measurements of variables that take on a numeric range of values we feel comfortable treating the way that we normally treat numeric values.

5.2   SOCIAL SCIENCE MEASUREMENT: THE VARYING CHALLENGES OF QUANTIFYING HUMAN BEHAVIOR

Measurement is a "problem" in all sciences – from the physical sciences of physics and chemistry to the social sciences of economics, political science, psychology, and the rest. But in the physical sciences, the problem of measurement is often reduced to a problem of instrumentation, in which scientists develop well-specified protocols for measuring, say, the

---

[2] One resource that is often overlooked is your school's library. While libraries may seem old-fashioned, your school's library may have purchased access to data sources, and librarians are often experts in the location of data from the web.

amount of gas released in a chemical reaction, or the amount of light given off by a star. The social sciences, by contrast, are younger sciences, and scientific consensus on how to measure our important concepts is rare. Perhaps more crucial, though, is the fact that the social sciences deal with an inherently difficult-to-predict subject matter: human beings.

The problem of measurement exists in all of the social sciences. It would be wrong, though, to say that it is equally problematic in all of the social science disciplines. Some disciplines pay comparatively little heed to issues of measurement, whereas others are mired nearly constantly in measurement controversies and difficulties.

Consider the subject matter in much research in economics: dollars (or euros, or yen, or what have you). If the concept of interest is "economic output" (or "Gross Domestic Product," GDP), which is commonly defined as the total sum of goods and services produced by labor and property in a given time period, then it is a relatively straightforward matter to obtain an empirical observation that is consistent with the concept of interest.[3] Such measures will not be controversial among the vast majority of scholars. To the contrary, once economists agree on a measure of economic output, they can move on to the next (and more interesting) step in the scientific process – to argue about what forces *cause* greater or less growth in economic output. (That's where the agreement among economists ends.)

Not every concept in economics is measured with such ease, however. Many economists are concerned with poverty: Why are some individuals poor whereas others are not? What forces cause poverty to rise or fall over time? Despite the fact that we all know that poverty is a very real thing, measuring who is poor and who is not poor turns out to be a bit tricky. The federal government defines the concept of poverty as "a set of income cutoffs adjusted for household size, the age of the head of the household, and the number of children under age 18."[4] The intent of the cutoffs is to describe "minimally decent levels of consumption."[5] There are difficulties in obtaining empirical observations of poverty, though. Among them, consider the reality that most Western democracies (including the United States) have welfare states that provide transfer payments – in the form of cash payments, food stamps, or services like subsidized health care – to their citizens below some income threshold. Such programs, of course,

---

[3] For details about how the federal government measures GDP, see http://www.bea.gov.

[4] See http://www.census.gov/hhes/www/poverty/poverty.html.

[5] Note a problem right off the bat: What is "minimally decent"? Do you suspect that what qualified as "minimally decent" in 1950 or 1985 would be considered "minimally decent" today? This immediately raises issues of how sensible it is to compare the poverty rates from the past with those of today. If the floor of what is considered minimally decent continues to rise, then the comparison is problematic at best, and meaningless at worst.

are designed to minimize or eliminate the problems that afflict the poor. When economists seek to measure a person's income level to determine whether or not he is poor, should they use a "pretransfer" definition of income – a person's or family's income level *before* receiving any transfer payments from the government – or a "posttransfer" definition? Either choice carries potentially negative consequences. Choosing a pretransfer definition of income gives a sense of how much the private sector of the economy is failing. On the other hand, a posttransfer definition gives a sense of how much welfare state programs are falling short and how people are actually living. As the Baby Boom generation in the United States continues to age, more and more people are retiring from work. Using a pretransfer measure of poverty means that researchers will not consider Social Security payments – the US's largest source of transfer payments by far – and therefore the (pretransfer) poverty rate should grow rather steadily over the next few decades, regardless of the health of the overall economy. This might not accurately represent what we mean by "poverty" (Danziger and Gottschalk, 1983).

YOUR TURN: Other sticky measurement issues in economics

While we contend that, generally, the discipline of economics does not often suffer from contentious measurement issues, we have offered at least one counterexample to this trend – measuring poverty. Can you think of other examples in economics where measurement of key concepts is not straightforward?

If, owing to their subject matter, economists rarely (but occasionally) have measurement obstacles, the opposite end of the spectrum would be the discipline of psychology. The subject matter of psychology – human behavior, cognition, and emotion – is rife with concepts that are extremely difficult to measure. Consider a few examples. We all know that the concept of "depression" is a real thing; some individuals are depressed, and others are not. Some individuals who are depressed today will not be depressed as time passes, and some who are not depressed today will become depressed. Yet how is it possible to assess scientifically whether a person is or is not depressed?[6] After all, it's not like there's some finger-prick blood test – at least not yet – that scientists can do to conclude whether or not a person is depressed. Why does it matter if we measure depression accurately? Recall the scientific stakes described at the

---

[6] Since 1952, the American Psychiatric Press, Inc., has published the *Diagnostic and Statistical Manual of Mental Disorders*, now in its fifth edition (published in 2013, and called DSM-5), which diagnoses depression by focusing on four sets of symptoms that indicate depression: mood, behavioral symptoms such as withdrawal, cognitive symptoms such as the inability to concentrate, and somatic symptoms such as insomnia.

beginning of this chapter: If we don't measure depression well, how can we know whether remedies like clinical therapy or chemical antidepressants are effective?[7] Psychology deals with a variety of other concepts that are notoriously slippery, such as the clinical focus on "anxiety," or the social-psychological focus on concepts such as "stereotyping" or "prejudice" (which are also of concern to political scientists).

Political science, in our view, lies somewhere between the extremes of economics and psychology in terms of how frequently we encounter serious measurement problems. Some subfields in political science operate relatively free of measurement problems. The study of political economy – which examines the relationship between the economy and political forces such as government policy, elections, and consumer confidence – has much the same feel as economics, for obvious reasons. Other subfields encounter measurement problems regularly. The subfield of political psychology – which studies the way that individual citizens interact with the political world – shares much of the same subject matter as social psychology, and hence, because of its focus on the attitudes and feelings of people, it shares much of social psychology's measurement troubles.

Consider the following list of critically important concepts in the discipline of political science that have sticky measurement issues:

- **Judicial activism:** In the United States, the role of the judiciary in the policy-making process has always been controversial. Some view the federal courts as the protectors of important civil liberties, whereas others view the courts as a threat to democracy, because judges are not elected. How is it possible to identify an "activist judge" or an "activist decision"? In this particular case, there could even be a disagreement over the conceptual definition of "activist." What a conservative and a liberal would consider to be "activist" might produce no agreement at all. And yet political scientists have worked on this important issue. In their 2009 book, Stefanie Lindquist and Frank Cross have conceived of three dimensions of activism: (1) the extent to which a decision of the Court defers to elected branches; (2) attempts by the Court to seek power for power's sake; and (3) the extent to which the Court embraces legal stability.[8]

---

[7] In fact, the effectiveness of clinical "talk" therapy is a matter of some contention among psychologists. See Susan Gilbert's article, "Married with Problems? Therapy May Not Help," *New York Times*, April 19, 2005.

[8] For a journalistic account of this issue, see Dahlia Lithwick's article, "Activist, Schmactivist," *New York Times*, August 15, 2004.

> **YOUR TURN: Expand your thinking on judicial activism**
>
> The above three-pronged definition of judicial activism by Lindquist and Cross (2009) represents a systematic effort to conceptualize and measure a slippery concept that scientists believe to be real. Can you – especially those of you who might be interested in careers in the law – think of any aspects of judicial activism that the above definition might have missed?

- **Congressional liberalism**: With each successive session of the US Congress, commentators often compare the level of liberalism and conservatism of the present Congress with that of its most recent predecessors. Using roll-call votes, is it possible to know if the Congress is becoming more or less liberal over time (Poole and Rosenthal, 1997)? Consider, in particular, the difficulty of knowing whether a single representative is becoming more or less liberal in successive years, or whether a Congress, collectively, is more or less liberal in successive years. After all, it's quite rare that votes happen on *identical* bills at multiple points in time.

> **YOUR TURN: Expand your thinking on Congressional liberalism**
>
> The famous Poole and Rosenthal scores in Congressional liberalism are based on an extensive analysis of roll-call votes. Can you think of a different way to measure how liberal or conservative a legislator is?
>
> Give it some thought, and then go see another ambitious effort to try to classify a legislator's liberalism or conservatism by Lauderdale and Herzog (2016) here: http://eprints.lse.ac.uk/66498/

- **Political legitimacy**: How can analysts distinguish between a "legitimate" and an "illegitimate" government? The key conceptual issue is more or less "how citizens evaluate governmental authority" (Weatherford, 1992). Some view it positively, others quite negatively. Is legitimacy something that can objectively be determined, or is it an inherently subjective property among citizens?
- **Political sophistication**: Some citizens know more about politics and are better able to process political information than other citizens who seem to know little and care less about political affairs. How do we distinguish politically sophisticated citizens from the politically unsophisticated ones? Moreover, how can we tell if a society's level of political sophistication is rising or falling over time (Luskin, 1987)?
- **Social capital**: Some societies are characterized by relatively high levels of interconnectedness, with dense networks of relationships that make the population cohesive. Other societies, in contrast, are characterized by high degrees of isolation and distrustfulness. How can we measure what

social scientists call *social capital* in a way that enables us to compare one society's level of connectedness with another's or one society's level of connectedness at varying points in time (Putnam, 2000)?

In Sections 5.4 and 5.5, we describe the measurement controversies surrounding two other concepts that are important to political science – democracy and political tolerance. But first, in the next section, we describe some key issues that political scientists need to grapple with when measuring their concepts of interest.

5.3 PROBLEMS IN MEASURING CONCEPTS OF INTEREST

We can summarize the problems of measuring concepts of interest in preparation for hypothesis testing as follows: First, you need to make sure that you have conceptual clarity. Next, settle on a reasonable level of measurement. Finally, ensure that your measure is both valid and reliable. After you repeat this process for each variable in your theory, you are ready to test your hypothesis.

Unfortunately, there is no clear map to follow as we go through these steps with our variables. Some variables are very easy to measure, whereas others, because of the nature of what we are trying to measure, will always be elusive. As we will see, debates over issues of measurement are at the core of many interesting fields of study in political science.

5.3.1 Conceptual Clarity

The first step in measuring any phenomenon of interest to political scientists is to have a clear sense of what the concept is that we are trying to measure. In some cases, like the ones we subsequently discuss, this is an exceedingly revealing and difficult task. It requires considerably disciplined thought to ferret out precisely what we mean by the concepts about which we are theorizing. But even in some seemingly easy examples, this is more difficult than might appear at first glance.

Consider a survey in which we needed to measure a person's *income*. That would seem easy enough. Once we draw our sample of adults, why not just ask each respondent, "What is your income?" and offer a range of values, perhaps in increments of $10,000 or so, on which respondents could place themselves. What could be the problem with such a measure? Imagine a 19-year-old college student whose parents are very wealthy, but who has never worked herself, answering such a question. How much income has that person earned in the last year? Zero. In such a circumstance, this is the true answer to such a question. But it is not a particularly valid measure of her income. We likely want a measure of income that reflects the fact that her parents earn a good deal of money, which affords her the luxury of not having to work her way through school as many other students do. That measure should place the daughter of wealthy parents ahead of a relatively poor student who carries a full load and works 40 hours a week just to pay her tuition. Therefore, we might reconsider our seemingly simple question and ask instead, "What is the total amount of income earned in the most recently completed tax year by you and any other adults in your household, including all sources of income?" This measure puts the nonworking child of wealthy parents ahead of the student from the less-well-off family. And, for most social science purposes, this is the measure of "income" that we would find most theoretically useful.[9]

At this point, it is worth highlighting that the _best_ measure of income – as well as that of most other concepts – depends on what our theoretical objectives are. The best measure of something as simple as a respondent's income depends on what we intend to relate that measure to in our hypothesis testing.

5.3.2 Reliability

An operational measure of a concept is said to be reliable to the extent that it is repeatable or consistent; that is, applying the same measurement rules to the same case or observation will produce identical results. An unreliable measure, by contrast, would produce inconsistent results for the same observation. For obvious reasons, all scientists want their measures to be reliable.

Perhaps the most simple example to help you understand this is your bathroom scale. Say you step up on the scale one morning and the scale tells you that you weigh 150 pounds. You step down off the scale and it returns to zero. But have you ever _not_ trusted that scale reading, and thought to yourself, "Maybe if I hop back up on the scale, I'll get a number I like better?" That is a **reliability** check. If you (immediately) step back on the scale, and it tells you that you now weigh 146 pounds, your scale is unreliable, because repeated measures of the same case – your body at that particular point in time – produced different results.

To take our bathroom scale example to the extreme, we should not confuse over-time variability with unreliability. If you wake up one week later and weigh 157 instead of 150 pounds, that does not necessarily mean that your scale is unreliable (though that might be true). Perhaps you

---

[9] The same issues would arise in assessing the income of retired people who no longer participate in the workforce.

substituted french fries for salads at dinner in the intervening week, and perhaps you exercised less vigorously or less often.

> **YOUR TURN: Reliability of income measures**
>
> Can you think of any reasons that our two survey questions to measure a respondent's income – "What is your income?" and "What is the total amount of income earned in the most recently completed tax year by you and any other adults in your household, including all sources of income?" – might (for different reasons) both be unreliable measures? *Hint*: Try answering the questions yourself.

Reliability is often an important issue when scholars need to code events or text for quantitative analysis. For example, if a researcher was trying to code the text of news coverage that was favorable or unfavorable toward a candidate for office, he would develop some specific coding rules to apply to the text – in effect, to count certain references as either "pro" or "con" with respect to the candidate. Suppose that, for the coding, the researcher employs a group of students to code the text – a practice that is common in political research. A *reliable* set of coding rules would imply that, when one student applies the rules to the text, the results would be the same as when another student takes the rules and applies them to the same text. An *unreliable* set of coding rules would imply the opposite, namely, that when two different coders try to apply the same rules to the same news articles, they reach different conclusions.[10] The same issues arise when one codes things such as events by using newspaper coverage.[11]

5.3.3 Measurement Bias and Reliability

One of the concerns that comes up with any measurement technique is **measurement bias**, which is the systematic over-reporting or under-reporting of values for a variable. Although measurement bias is a serious problem for anyone who wants to know the "true" values of variables for particular cases, it is less of a problem than you might think for theory-testing purposes. To better understand this, imagine that we have to choose between two different operationalizations of the same variable. Operationalization A is biased but reliable, and Operationalization B is unbiased but unreliable. For theory-testing purposes we would greatly prefer the biased but reliable Operationalization A!

---

[10] Of course, it is possible that the coding *scheme* is perfectly reliable, but the *coders themselves* are not.

[11] There is a variety of tools for assessing reliability, many of which are beyond the scope of this discussion.

You will be better able to see why this is the case once you have an understanding of statistical hypothesis testing from Chapter 8 and beyond. For now, though, keep in mind that as we test our theories we are looking for general patterns between two variables. For instance, with *higher* values of X do we tend to see *higher* values of Y, or with *higher* values of X do we tend to see *lower* values of Y? If the measurement of X was biased upward, the same general pattern of association with Y would be visible. But if the measurement of X was unreliable, it would obscure the underlying relationship between X and Y.

5.3.4   Validity

The most important feature of a measure is that it is valid. A valid measure accurately represents the concept that it is supposed to measure, whereas an invalid measure measures something other than what was originally intended. All of this might sound a bit circular, we realize.

Perhaps it is useful to think of some important concepts that represent thorny measurement examples in the social sciences. In both social psychology and political science, the study of the concept of *prejudice* has been particularly important. Among individuals, the level of prejudice can vary, from vanishingly small amounts to very high levels. Measuring prejudice can be important in social-psychological terms, so we can try to determine what factors cause some people to be prejudiced whereas others do not. In political science, in particular, we are often interested in the attitudinal and behavioral consequences of prejudice. Assuming that some form of truth serum is unavailable, how can we obtain a quantitative measure of prejudice that can tell us who harbors large amounts of prejudice, who harbors some, and who harbors none? It would be easy enough to ask respondents to a survey if they were prejudiced or not. For example, we could ask respondents: "With respect to people who have a different race or ethnicity than you, would you say that you are extremely prejudiced, somewhat prejudiced, mildly prejudiced, or not at all prejudiced toward them?" But we would have clear reasons to doubt the **validity** of their answers – whether their measured responses accurately reflected their true levels of prejudice.

There are a variety of ways to assess a measure's validity, though it is critical to note that all of them are theoretical and subject to large degrees of disagreement. There is no simple formula to check for a measure's validity on a scale of 0 to 100, unfortunately. Instead, we rely on several overlapping ways to determine a measure's validity. First, and most simply, we can examine a measure's **face validity**. When examining a measurement strategy, we can first ask whether or not, on its face, the measure appears to be measuring what it purports to be measuring. This is face validity. Second, and a bit more advanced, we can scrutinize a measure's **content validity**. What is the concept to be measured? What are all of the essential elements to that concept and the features that define it? And have you excluded all of the things that are not it? For example, the concept of democracy surely contains the element of "elections," but it also must incorporate more than mere elections, because elections are held in places like North Korea, which we know to be nondemocratic. What else must be in a valid measure of democracy? (More on this notion later on.) Basically, content validation is a rigorous process that forces the researcher to come up with a list of all of the critical elements that, as a group, define the concept we wish to measure. Finally, we can examine a measure's **construct validity**: the degree to which the measure is related to other measures that theory requires them to be related to. That is, if we have a theory that connects democratization and economic development, then a measure of democracy that is related to a measure of economic development (as our theory requires) serves simultaneously to confirm the theory and also to validate the measure of democracy. Of course, one difficulty with this approach is what happens when the expected association is not present. Is it because our measure of democracy is invalid or because the theory is misguided? There is no conclusive way to tell.

> **YOUR TURN: Measuring media exposure in a changing media environment**
>
> Some citizens consume a lot of news, and others consume very little. In the not-too-distant past, when scientists wanted to measure how much news a citizen took in, they would simply ask survey questions about how many days a week a person watched the news on TV, or read the newspaper. Obviously, things are very different today, with a wide variety of news apps on smartphones and news streaming through many users' social media feeds. This presents a measurement challenge that didn't really exist in the past. Can you propose a method that would be a reliable and valid way to measure how much news an individual citizen is exposed to in today's environment?

5.3.5   The Relationship between Validity and Reliability

What is the connection between validity and reliability? Is it possible to have a valid but unreliable measure? And is it possible to have a reliable but invalid measure? With respect to the second question, some scientific debate exists; there are some who believe that it is possible to have a reliable but invalid measure. In our view, that is possible in abstract terms. But because we are interested in measuring concepts in the interest of evaluating causal theories, we believe that, in all practical terms, any

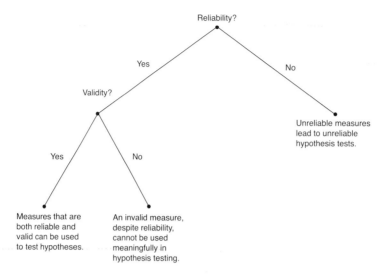

Figure 5.1   Reliability, validity, and hypothesis testing

conceivable measures that are reliable but invalid will not be useful in evaluating causal theories.

Similarly, it is theoretically possible to have valid but unreliable measures. But those measures also will be problematic for evaluating causal theories, because we will have no confidence in the hypothesis tests that we conduct. We present the relationship between reliability and validity in Figure 5.1, where we show that, if a measure is unreliable, there is little point in evaluating its validity. Once we have established that a measure is reliable, we can assess its validity; and only reliable and valid measures are useful for evaluating causal theories.

5.4   CONTROVERSY 1: MEASURING DEMOCRACY

Although we might be tempted to think of democracy as being similar to pregnancy – that is, a country either *is* or *is not* a democracy in much the same way that a woman either *is* or *is not* pregnant – on a bit of additional thought, we are probably better off thinking of democracy as a *continuum*.[12] That is, there can be varying degrees to which a government is democratic. Furthermore, within democracies, some countries are more democratic than others, and a country can become more or less democratic as time passes.

[12] This position, though, is controversial within political science. For an interesting discussion about whether researchers should measure democracy as a binary concept or a continuous one, see Elkins (2000).

But defining a continuum that ranges from democracy, on one end, to totalitarianism, on the other end, is not at all easy. We might be tempted to resort to the Potter Stewart "I know it when I see it" definition. As political scientists, of course, this is not an option. We have to begin by asking ourselves: What do we mean by democracy? What are the core elements that make a government more or less democratic? Political philosopher Robert Dahl (1971) persuasively argued that there are two core attributes to a democracy: "contestation" and "participation." That is, according to Dahl, democracies have competitive elections to choose leaders and broadly inclusive rules for and rates of participation.

Several groups of political scientists have attempted to measure democracy systematically in recent decades.[13] The best known – though by no means universally accepted – of these is the Polity IV measure.[14] The project measures democracy with annual scores ranging from -10 (strongly autocratic) to $+10$ (strongly democratic) for every country on Earth from 1800 to 2004.[15] In these researchers' operationalization, democracy has four components:

1. Regulation of executive recruitment
2. Competitiveness of executive recruitment
3. Openness of executive recruitment
4. Constraints on chief executive

For each of these dimensions, experts rate each country on a particular scale. For example, the first criterion, "Regulation of executive recruitment," allows for the following possible values:

- $+3$ = regular competition between recognized groups
- $+2$ = transitional competition
- $+1$ = factional or restricted patterns of competition
-   0 = no competition

Countries that have regular elections between groups that are more than ethnic rivals will have higher scores. By similar procedures, the scholars associated with the project score the other dimensions that comprise their democracy scale.

---

[13] For a useful review and comparison of these various measures, see Munck and Verkuilen (2002).

[14] The project's web site, which provides access to a vast array of country-specific over-time data, is http://www.systemicpeace.org/polityproject.html.

[15] They derive the scores on this scale from two separate ten-point scales, one for democracy and the other for autocracy. A country's Polity score for that year is its democracy score minus its autocracy score; thus, a country that received a 10 on the democracy scale and a 0 on the autocracy scale would have a net Polity score of 10 for that year.

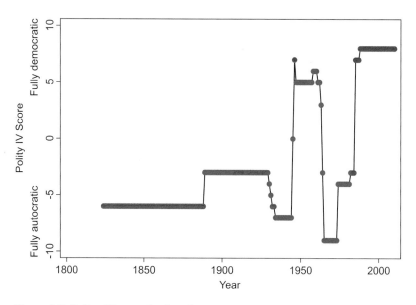

Figure 5.2 Polity IV score for Brazil

Figure 5.2 presents the Polity score for Brazil from 1824 through 2010.[16] Remember that higher scores represent points in time when Brazil was more democratic, and lower scores represent times when Brazil was more autocratic. There has been, as you can see, enormous variation in the democratic experience in Brazil since its declaration of independence from Portugal in 1822. If we make a rough comparison of these scores with the timeline of Brazil's political history, we can get an initial evaluation of the face validity of the Polity scores as a measure of democracy. After the declaration of independence from Portugal, Brazil was a constitutional monarchy headed by an emperor. After a coup in 1889, Brazil became a republic, but one in which politics was fairly strictly controlled by the elites from the two dominant states. We can see that this regime shift resulted in a move from a Polity score of −6 to a score of −3. Starting in 1930, Brazil went through a series of coups and counter-coups. Scholars writing about this period (e.g., Skidmore, 2009) generally agree that the nation's government became more and more autocratic during this era. The Polity scores certainly reflect this movement. In 1945, after another military coup, a relatively democratic government was put into place. This regime lasted until the mid-1960s, when another period of instability was ended by a military dictatorship. This period is widely recognized as the most politically repressive regime in Brazil's independent political history. It lasted until 1974 when the ruling military government began to allow limited

[16] Source: http://www.systemicpeace.org/inscr/p4v2016.xls.

political elections and other political activities. In 1985, Brazil elected a civilian president, a move widely seen as the start of the current democratic period. Each of these major moves in Brazil's political history is reflected in the Polity scores. So, from this rough evaluation, Polity scores have face validity.

The Polity measure is rich in historical detail, as is obvious from Figure 5.2. The coding rules are transparent and clear, and the amount of raw information that goes into a country's score for any given year is impressive. And yet it is fair to criticize the Polity measure for including only one part of Dahl's definition of democracy. The Polity measure contains rich information about what Dahl calls "contestation" – whether a country has broadly open contests to decide on its leadership. But the measure is much less rich when it comes to gauging a country's level of what Dahl calls "participation" – the degree to which citizens are engaged in political processes and activities. This may be understandable, in part, because of the impressive time scope of the study. After all, in 1800 (when the Polity time series begins), very few countries had broad electoral participation. Since the end of World War II, broadly democratic participation has spread rapidly across the globe. But if the world is becoming a more democratic place, owing to expansion of suffrage, our measures of democracy ought to incorporate that reality. Because the Polity measure includes one part ("contestation") of what it means, conceptually, to be democratic, but ignores the other part ("participation"), the measure can be said to lack content validity. The Polity IV measure, despite its considerable strengths, does not fully encompass what it means, conceptually, to be more or less democratic.

This problem is nicely illustrated by examining the Polity score for the United States presented in Figure 5.3, which shows its score for the time period 1800–2010. The consistent score of 10 for almost every year after the founding of the republic – the exception is during the Civil War, when President Lincoln suspended the writ of *habeas corpus* – belies the fact that the United States, in many important ways, has become a more democratic nation over its history, particularly on the participatory dimension not captured in the Polity measure. Even considering something as basic to democratic participation as the right to vote reveals this to be the case. Slavery prevented African Americans from many things, voting included, until after the Civil War, and Jim Crow laws in the South kept those prohibitions in place for nearly a century afterward. Women, too, were not allowed to vote until the 19th Amendment to the Constitution was ratified in 1920. It would be difficult to argue that these changes did not make the United States more democratic, but of course those changes are not reflected in Figure 5.3. This is not to say that the Polity measure is

Figure 5.3 Polity IV score for the United States

useless, but merely that it lacks content validity because one of the key components of democracy – participation – is nowhere to be found in the measure.

5.5   CONTROVERSY 2: MEASURING POLITICAL TOLERANCE

We know that some continuum exists in which, on the one end, some individuals are extremely "tolerant" and, on the other end, other individuals are extremely "intolerant." In other words, political tolerance and intolerance, at the conceptual level, are real things. Some individuals have more tolerance and others have less. It is easy to imagine why political scientists would be interested in political tolerance and intolerance. Are there systematic factors that cause some people to be tolerant and others to be intolerant?

Measuring political tolerance, on the other hand, is far from easy. Tolerance is not like cholesterol, for which a simple blood test can tell us how much of the good and how much of the bad we have inside of us. The naive approach to measuring political tolerance – conducting a survey and asking people directly "Are you tolerant or intolerant?" – seems silly right off the bat. Any such survey question would surely produce extremely high rates of "tolerance," because presumably very few people – even intolerant people – think of themselves as intolerant. Even those who are aware of their own intolerance are unlikely to admit that fact to a pollster. Given this situation, how have political scientists tackled this problem?

During the 1950s, when the spread of Soviet communism represented the biggest threat to America, Samuel Stouffer (1955) conducted a series of opinion surveys to measure how people reacted to the Red Scare. He asked national samples of Americans whether they would be willing to extend certain civil liberties – like being allowed to teach in a public school, to be free from having phones tapped, and the like – to certain unpopular groups like communists, socialists, and atheists. He found that a variety of people were, by these measures, intolerant; they were not willing to grant these civil liberties to members of those groups. The precise amount of intolerance varied, depending on the target group and the activity mentioned in the scenarios, but intolerance was substantial – at least 70 percent of respondents gave the intolerant response. Stouffer found that the best predictor of an individual's level of tolerance was how much formal education he or she had received; people with more education emerged as more tolerant, and people with less education were less tolerant. In the 1970s, when the Red Scare was subsiding somewhat, a new group of researchers asked the identical questions to a new sample of Americans. They found that the levels of intolerance had dropped considerably over the 20-odd years – in only one scenario did intolerance exceed 60 percent and in the majority of scenarios it was below 50 percent – leading some to speculate that political intolerance was waning.

However, also in the late 1970s, a different group of researchers led by political scientist John Sullivan questioned the *validity* of the Stouffer measures and hence questioned the conclusions that Stouffer reached. The concept of political tolerance, wrote Sullivan, Piereson, and Marcus (1979), "presupposes opposition." That is, unless a survey respondent actively opposed communists, socialists, and atheists, the issue of tolerance or intolerance simply does not arise. By way of example, consider asking such questions of an atheist. Is an atheist who agrees that atheists should be allowed to teach in public schools politically tolerant? Sullivan and his colleagues thought not.

The authors proposed a new set of survey-based questions that were, in their view, more consistent with a conceptual understanding of tolerance. If, as they defined it, tolerance presupposes opposition, then researchers need to *find out* who the survey respondent opposes; *assuming* that the respondent might oppose a particular group is not a good idea. They identified a variety of groups active in politics at the time – including racist groups, both pro- and anti-abortion groups, and even the Symbionese Liberation Army – and asked respondents which one they disliked the most. They followed this up with questions that looked very much like the Stouffer items, only directed at *the respondent's own* disliked groups instead of the ones Stouffer had picked out for them.

Among other findings, two stood out. First, the levels of intolerance were strikingly high. As many as 66 percent of Americans were willing to forbid members of their least-liked group from holding rallies, and fully 71 percent were willing to have the government ban the group altogether. Second, under this new conceptualization and measurement of tolerance, the authors found that an individual's perception of the threatening nature of the target group, and not their level of education, was the primary predictor of intolerance. In other words, individuals who found their target group to be particularly threatening were most likely to be intolerant, whereas those who found their most-disliked group to be less threatening were more tolerant. Education did not directly affect tolerance either way. In this sense, measuring an important concept differently produced rather different substantive findings about causes and effects.[17]

It is important that you see the connection to valid measurement here. Sullivan and his colleagues argued that Stouffer's survey questions were not valid measures of tolerance because the question wording did not accurately capture what it meant, in the abstract, to be intolerant (specifically, opposition). Creating measures of tolerance and intolerance that more truthfully mirrored the concept of interest produced significantly different findings about the persistence of intolerance, as well as about the factors that cause individuals to be tolerant or intolerant.

5.6   ARE THERE CONSEQUENCES TO POOR MEASUREMENT?

What happens when we fail to measure the key concepts in our theory in a way that is both valid and reliable? Refer back to Figure 1.2, which highlights the distinction between the abstract concepts of theoretical interest and the variables we observe in the real world. If the variables that we observe in the real world do not do a good job of mirroring the abstract concepts, then that affects our ability to evaluate conclusively a theory's empirical support. That is, how can we know if our theory is supported if we have done a poor job measuring the key concepts that we observe? If our empirical analysis is based on measures that do not capture the essence of the abstract concepts in our theory, then we are unlikely to have any confidence in the findings themselves.

5.7   CONCLUSIONS

How we measure the concepts that we care about matters. As we can see from the examples above, different measurement strategies can and

---

[17] But see Gibson (1992).

sometimes do produce different conclusions about causal relationships. And conclusions about causal relationships are what we care most about in science.

One of the take-home points of this chapter should be that measurement cannot take place in a theoretical vacuum. The *theoretical purpose* of the scholarly enterprise must inform the process of how we measure what we measure. For example, recall our discussion above about the various ways to measure poverty. How we want to measure this concept depends on what our objective is. In the process of measuring poverty, if our theoretical aim is to evaluate the effectiveness of different policies at combating poverty, we would have different measurement issues than would scholars whose theoretical aim is to study how being poor influences a person's political attitudes. In the former case, we would give strong consideration to pretransfer measures of poverty, whereas in the latter example, posttransfer measures would likely be more applicable.

CONCEPTS INTRODUCED IN THIS CHAPTER

- construct validity – the degree to which the measure is related to other measures that theory requires them to be related to
- content validity – the degree to which a measure contains all of the critical elements that, as a group, define the concept we wish to measure
- face validity – whether or not, on its face, the measure appears to be measuring what it purports to be measuring
- measurement bias – the systematic over-reporting or under-reporting of values for a variable
- reliability – the extent to which applying the same measurement rules to the same case or observation will produce identical results
- validity – the degree to which a measure accurately represents the concept that it is supposed to measure

EXERCISES

1. Suppose that a researcher wanted to measure the federal government's efforts to make the education of its citizens a priority. The researcher proposed to count the government's budget for education as a percentage of the total GDP and use that as the measure of the government's commitment to education. In terms of validity, what are the strengths and weaknesses of such a measure?

2. Suppose that a researcher wanted to create a measure of media coverage of a candidate for office, and therefore created a set of coding rules to code words in newspaper articles as either "pro" or "con" toward the candidate. Instead of hiring students to implement these rules, however, the researcher used a

computer to code the text, by counting the frequency with which certain words were mentioned in a series of articles. What would be the reliability of such a computer-driven measurement strategy, and why?

3. For each of the following concepts, identify whether there would, in measuring the concept, likely be a problem of measurement bias, invalidity, unreliability, or none of the above. Explain your answer.

(a) Measuring the concept of the public's approval of the president by using a series of survey results asking respondents whether they approve or disapprove of the president's job performance.

(b) Measuring the concept of political corruption as the percentage of politicians in a country in a year who are convicted of corrupt practices.

(c) Measuring the concept of democracy in each nation of the world by reading their constitution and seeing if it claims that the nation is "democratic."

4. Download a codebook for a political science data set in which you are interested.

(a) Describe the data set and the purpose for which it was assembled.

(b) What are the time and space dimensions of the data set?

Read the details of how one of the variables in which you are interested was coded. Write your answers to the following questions:

(c) Does this seem like a reliable method of operationalizing this variable? How might the reliability of this operationalization be improved?

(d) Assess the various elements of the validity for this variable operationalization. How might the validity of this operationalization be improved?

5. If you did not yet do Exercise 5 in Chapter 3, do so now. For the theory that you developed, evaluate the measurement of both the independent and dependent variables. Write about the reliability, and the various aspects of validity for each measure. Can you think of a better way to operationalize these variables to test your theory?

6 Getting to Know Your Data

OVERVIEW

Descriptive statistics and descriptive graphs are what they sound like – they are tools that describe variables. These tools are valuable because they can summarize a tremendous amount of information in a succinct fashion. In this chapter we discuss some of the most commonly used descriptive statistics and graphs, how we should interpret them, how we should use them, and their limitations.

6.1 GETTING TO KNOW YOUR DATA STATISTICALLY

Thus far we have discussed details of the measurement of variables. A lot of thought and effort goes into the measurement of individual variables. But once a researcher has collected data and become familiar and satisfied with how the variables were measured, it is important for them to get a good idea of the types of values that the individual variables take on before moving to testing for causal connections between two or more variables. For example, researchers might want to know, among other things: What do "typical" values for a variable look like? How tightly clustered (or widely dispersed) are these values?

Before proceeding to test for theorized relationships *between* two or more variables, it is essential to understand the properties and characteristics of each variable. To put it differently, we want to learn something about what the values of each variable "look like." How do we accomplish this? One possibility is to list all of the observed values of a measured variable. For example, the following are the percentages of popular votes for major party candidates that went to the candidate of the party of the sitting president during US presidential elections from 1876 to 2016:[1]

---

[1] This measure is constructed so that it is comparable across time. Although independent or third-party candidates have occasionally contested elections, we focus on only those votes

48.516, 50.220, 49.846, 50.414, 48.268, 47.760, 53.171, 60.006, 54.483, 54.708, 51.682, 36.148, 58.263, 58.756, 40.851, 62.226, 54.983, 53.778, 52.319, 44.710, 57.094, 49.913, 61.203, 49.425, 61.791, 48.951, 44.842, 59.123, 53.832, 46.379, 54.737, 50.262, 51.233, 46.311, 52.010, 51.111. We can see from this example that, once we get beyond a small number of observations, a listing of values becomes unwieldy. We will get lost in the trees and have no idea of the overall shape of the forest. For this reason, we turn to descriptive statistics and descriptive graphs, to take what would be a large amount of information and reduce it to bite-size chunks that summarize that information.

YOUR TURN: Identifying a typical value

Based on the listing of values for incumbent vote, what do you think is a typical value for this variable?

Descriptive statistics and graphs are useful tools for helping researchers to get to know their data before they move to testing causal hypotheses. They are also sometimes helpful when writing about one's research. You have to make the decision of whether or not to present descriptive statistics and/or graphs in the body of a paper on a case-by-case basis. It is scientifically important, however, that this information be made available to consumers of your research in some way.[2]

One major way to distinguish among variables is the **measurement metric**. A variable's measurement metric is the type of values that the variable takes on, and we discuss this in detail in the next section by describing three different variable types. We then explain that, despite the imperfect nature of the distinctions among these three variable types, we are forced to choose between two broad classifications of variables – categorical or continuous – when we describe them. The rest of this chapter discusses strategies for describing **categorical variables** and **continuous variables**.

6.2   WHAT IS THE VARIABLE'S MEASUREMENT METRIC?

There are no hard-and-fast rules for describing variables, but a major initial juncture that we encounter involves the metric in which we measure each

---

for the two major parties. Also, because we want to test the theory of economic voting, we need to have a measure of support for incumbents. In elections in which the sitting president is not running for reelection, there is still reason to expect that their party will be held accountable for economic performances.

[2] Many researchers will present this information in an appendix (often made available online) unless there is something particularly noteworthy about the characteristics of one or more of their variables.

variable. Remember from Chapter 1 that we can think of each variable in terms of its label and its values. The label is the description of the variable – such as "Gender of survey respondent" – and its values are the denominations in which the variable occurs – such as "Male" or "Female." For treatment in most statistical analyses, we are forced to divide our variables into two types according to the metric in which the values of the variable occur: categorical or continuous. In reality, variables come in at least three different metric types, and there are a lot of variables that do not neatly fit into just one of these classifications. To help you to better understand each of these variable types, we will go through each with an example. All of the examples that we are using in these initial descriptions come from survey research, but the same basic principles of measurement metric hold regardless of the type of data being analyzed.

6.2.1 Categorical Variables

Categorical variables are variables for which cases have values that are either different from or the same as the values for other cases, but about which we cannot make any universally holding ranking distinctions. If we consider a variable that we might label "Religious Identification," some values for this variable are "Catholic," "Muslim," "nonreligious," and so on. Although these values are clearly different from each other, we cannot make universally holding ranking distinctions across them. More casually, with categorical variables like this one, it is not possible to rank order the categories from least to greatest: The value "Muslim" is neither greater nor less than "nonreligious" (and so on), for example. Instead, we are left knowing that cases with the same value for this variable are the same, whereas those cases with different values are different. The term "categorical" expresses the essence of this variable type; we can put individual cases into categories based on their values, but we cannot go any further in terms of ranking or otherwise ordering these values.

6.2.2 Ordinal Variables

Like categorical variables, **ordinal variables** are also variables for which cases have values that are either different from or the same as the values for other cases. The distinction between ordinal and categorical variables is that we *can* make universally holding ranking distinctions across the variable values for ordinal variables. For instance, consider the variable labeled "Retrospective Family Financial Situation" that has commonly been used as an independent variable in individual-level economic voting studies. In the 2004 National Election Study (NES), researchers created this variable by first asking respondents to answer the following question: "We are interested in how people are getting along financially these days. Would you say that you (and your family living here) are better off or worse off than you were a year ago?" Researchers then asked respondents who answered "Better" or "Worse": "Much [better/worse] or somewhat [better/worse]?" The resulting variable was then coded as follows:

1. much better
2. somewhat better
3. same
4. somewhat worse
5. much worse

This variable is pretty clearly an ordinal variable because as we go from the top to the bottom of the list we are moving from better to worse evaluations of how individuals (and their families with whom they live) have been faring financially in the past year.

As another example, consider the variable labeled "Party Identification." In the 2004 NES researchers created this variable by using each respondent's answer to the question, "Generally speaking, do you usually think of yourself as a Republican, a Democrat, an Independent, or what?"[3] which we can code as taking on the following values:

1. Republican
2. Independent
3. Democrat

If all cases that take on the value "Independent" represent individuals whose views lie somewhere between "Republican" and "Democrat," we can call "Party Identification" an ordinal variable. If this is not the case, then this variable is a categorical variable.

> **YOUR TURN: Is that variable categorical or ordinal?**
>
> Choose a variable from the United States National Election Study 2016 post-election questionnaire (located at http://www.electionstudies.org/studypages/anes_timeseries_2016/anes_timeseries_2016_qnaire_post.pdf). Is that variable categorical or ordinal? Why?

---

[3] Almost all US respondents put themselves into one of the first three categories. For instance, in 2004, 1128 of the 1212 respondents (93.1 percent) to the post-election NES responded that they were a Republican, Democrat, or an Independent. For our purposes, we will ignore the "or what" cases. Note that researchers usually present partisan identification across seven values ranging from "Strong Republican" to "Strong Democrat" based on follow-up questions that ask respondents to further characterize their positions.

Continuous Variables

An important characteristic that ordinal variables *do not* have is **equal unit differences**. A variable has equal unit differences if a one-unit increase in the value of that variable *always* means the same thing. If we return to the examples from the previous section, we can rank order the five categories of "Retrospective Family Financial Situation" from 1 for the best situation to 5 for the worst situation. But we may not feel very confident working with these assigned values the way that we typically work with numbers. In other words, can we say that the difference between "somewhat worse" and "same" $(4 - 3)$ is the same as the difference between "much worse" and "somewhat worse" $(5 - 4)$? What about saying that the difference between "much worse" and "same" $(5 - 3)$ is twice the difference between "somewhat better" and "much better" $(2 - 1)$? If the answer to both questions is "yes," then "Retrospective Family Financial Situation" is a continuous variable.

If we ask the same questions about "Party Identification," we should be somewhat skeptical. We can rank order the three categories of "Party Identification," but we cannot with great confidence assign "Republican" a value of 1, "Independent" a value of 2, and "Democrat" a value of 3 and work with these values in the way that we typically work with numbers. We cannot say that the difference between an "Independent" and a "Republican" $(2 - 1)$ is the same as the difference between a "Democrat" and an "Independent" $(3 - 2)$ – despite the fact that both $3 - 2$ and $2 - 1 = 1$. Certainly, we cannot say that the difference between a "Democrat" and a "Republican" $(3 - 1)$ is twice the difference between an "Independent" and a "Republican" $(2 - 1)$ – despite the fact that 2 is twice as big as 1.

The metric in which we measure a variable has equal unit differences if a one-unit increase in the value of that variable indicates the same amount of change across *all values* of that variable. Continuous variables are variables that *do* have equal unit differences.[4] Imagine, for instance, a variable labeled "Age in Years." A one-unit increase in this variable *always* indicates an individual who is one year older; this is true when we are talking about a case with a value of 21 just as it is when we are talking about a case with a value of 55.

---

[4] We sometimes call these variables "interval variables." A further distinction you will encounter with continuous variables is whether they have a substantively meaningful zero point. We usually describe variables that have this characteristic as "ratio" variables.

> **YOUR TURN: Is the Polity IV measure of democracy continuous?**
>
> In the previous chapter, we discussed the way in which the Polity IV measure of democracy is constructed. Would you feel comfortable treating this measure as a continuous variable? Why or why not?

6.2.4   Variable Types and Statistical Analyses

As we saw in the preceding sections, variables do not always neatly fit into the three categories. When we move to the vast majority of statistical analyses, we must decide between treating each of our variables as though it is categorical or as though it is continuous. For some variables, this is a very straightforward choice. However, for others, this is a very difficult choice. If we treat an ordinal variable as though it is categorical, we are acting as though we know less about the values of this variable than we really know. On the other hand, treating an ordinal variable as though it is a continuous variable means that we are assuming that it has equal unit differences. Either way, it is critical that we be aware of our decisions. We can always repeat our analyses under a different assumption and see how robust our conclusions are to our choices.

With all of this in mind, we present separate discussions of the process of describing a variable's **variation** for categorical and continuous variables. A variable's variation is the distribution of values that it takes across the cases for which it is measured. It is important that we have a strong knowledge of the variation in each of our variables before we can translate our theory into hypotheses, assess whether there is covariation between two variables (causal hurdle 3 from Chapter 3), and think about whether or not there might exist a third variable that makes any observed covariation between our independent and dependent variables spurious (hurdle 4). As we just outlined, descriptive statistics and graphs are useful summaries of the variation for individual variables. Another way in which we describe distributions of variables is through measures of **central tendency**. Measures of central tendency tell us about typical values for a particular variable at the center of its distribution.

6.3   DESCRIBING CATEGORICAL VARIABLES

With categorical variables, we want to understand the frequency with which each value of the variable occurs in our data. The simplest way of seeing this is to produce a frequency table in which the values of the categorical variable are displayed down one column and the frequency with which it occurs (in absolute number of cases and/or in percentage terms) is displayed in (an)other column(s). Table 6.1 shows such a table for the variable "Religious Identification" from the NES survey measured during the 2004 national elections in the United States.

The only measure of central tendency that is appropriate for a categorical variable is the **mode**, which is defined as the most frequently occurring value. In Table 6.1, the mode of the distribution is "Protestant," because there are more Protestants than there are members of any other single category.

A typical way in which non-statisticians present frequency data is in a pie graph such as Figure 6.1. Pie graphs are one way for visualizing the percentage of cases that fall into particular categories. Many statisticians argue strongly against their use and, instead, advocate the use of bar graphs. Bar graphs, such as Figure 6.2, are another graphical way to illustrate frequencies of categorical variables. It is worth noting, however, that most of the

Table 6.1 "Religious Identification" from the NES survey measured during the 2004 national elections in the United States		
Category	**Number of cases**	**Percent**
Protestant	672	56.14
Catholic	292	24.39
Jewish	35	2.92
Other	17	1.42
None	181	15.12
Total	1197	99.99

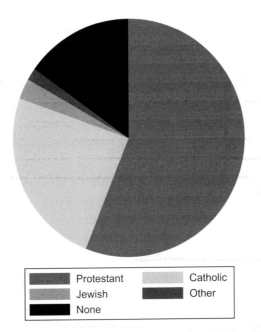

Figure 6.1 Pie graph of religious identification, NES 2004

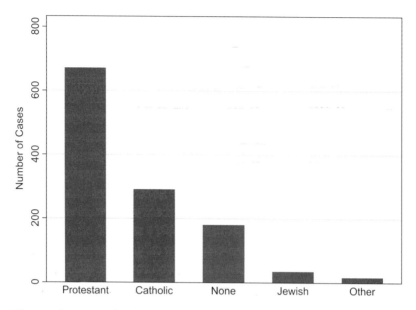

Figure 6.2 Bar graph of religious identification, NES 2004

information that we are able to gather from these two figures is very clearly and precisely presented in the columns of frequencies and percentages displayed in Table 6.1.

6.4 DESCRIBING CONTINUOUS VARIABLES

The statistics and graphs for describing continuous variables are considerably more complicated than those for categorical variables. This is because continuous variables are more mathematically complex than categorical variables. With continuous variables, we want to know about the central tendency and the spread or variation of the values around the central tendency. With continuous variables we also want to be on the lookout for outliers. Outliers are cases for which the value of the variable is extremely high or low relative to the rest of the values for that variable. When we encounter an outlier, we want to make sure that such a case is real and not created by some kind of error.

Most statistical software programs have a command for getting a battery of descriptive statistics on continuous variables. Figure 6.3 shows the output from Stata's "summarize" command with the "detail" option for the percentage of the major party vote won by the incumbent party in every US presidential election between 1876 and 2016.[5] The statistics

---

[5] These data come from a famous US forecasting model, developed by Ray Fair; see https://fairmodel.econ.yale.edu.

```
. summarize inc_vote, det

                                  inc_vote

        Percentiles      Smallest
 1%        36.148          36.148
 5%        40.851          40.851
10%        44.842          44.71       Obs                     36
25%        48.7335         44.842      Sum of Wgt.             36

50%        51.4575                     Mean              51.92569
                          Largest      Std. Dev.         5.785544
75%        54.86           60.006
90%        60.006          61.203      Variance          33.47252
95%        61.791          61.791      Skewness         -.3039279
99%        62.226          62.226      Kurtosis          3.274385
```

Figure 6.3 Example output from Stata's "summarize" command with "detail" option

on the left-hand side (the first three columns on the left) of the computer printout are what we call **rank statistics**, and the statistics on the right-hand side (the two columns on the right-hand side) are known as the **statistical moments**. Although both rank statistics and statistical moments are intended to describe the variation of continuous variables, they do so in slightly different ways and are thus quite useful together for getting a complete picture of the variation for a single variable.

6.4.1   Rank Statistics

The calculation of rank statistics begins with the ranking of the values of a continuous variable from smallest to largest, followed by the identification of crucial junctures along the way. Once we have our cases ranked, the midpoint as we count through our cases is known as the median case. Remember that earlier in the chapter we defined the variable in Figure 6.3 as the percentage of popular votes for major party candidates that went to the candidate from the party of the sitting president during US presidential elections from 1876 to 2016. We will call this variable "Incumbent Vote" for short. To calculate rank statistics for this variable, we need to first put the cases in order from the smallest to the largest observed value. This ordering is shown in Table 6.2. With rank statistics we measure the central tendency as the **median value** of the variable. The median value is the value of the case that sits at the exact center of our cases when we rank them from the smallest to the largest observed values. When we have an even number of cases, as we do in Table 6.2, we average the value of the two centermost ranked cases to obtain the median value (in our example we calculate the median as $\frac{1}{2}(51.233 + 51.682) = 51.4575$). This is also known as the value of the variable at the 50 percent rank. In a similar way, we can talk about the value of the variable at any other

Table 6.2 Values of "Incumbent Vote" ranked from smallest to largest		
Rank	**Year**	**Value**
1	1920	36.148
2	1932	40.851
3	1952	44.710
4	1980	44.842
5	2008	46.311
6	1992	46.379
7	1896	47.760
8	1892	48.268
9	1876	48.516
10	1976	48.951
11	1968	49.425
12	1884	49.846
13	1960	49.913
14	1880	50.220
15	2000	50.262
16	1888	50.414
17	2016	51.111
18	2004	51.233
19	1916	51.682
20	2012	52.010
21	1948	52.319
22	1900	53.171
23	1944	53.778
24	1988	53.832
25	1908	54.483
26	1912	54.708
27	1996	54.737
28	1940	54.983
29	1956	57.094
30	1924	58.263
31	1928	58.756
32	1984	59.123
33	1904	60.006
34	1964	61.203
35	1972	61.791
36	1936	62.226

percentage rank in which we have an interest. Other ranks that are often of interest are the 25 percent and 75 percent ranks, which are also known as the first and third "quartile ranks" for a distribution. The difference between the variable value at the 25 percent and the 75 percent ranks is known as the "interquartile range" or "IQR" of the variable. In our example variable, the 25 percent value is $\frac{1}{2}(48.516 + 48.951) = 48.7335$ and the 75 percent value is $\frac{1}{2}(54.737 + 54.983) = 54.8600$. This makes the IQR $= 54.8600 - 48.7335 = 6.1265$. In the language of rank statistics, the median value for a variable is a measure of its central tendency, whereas the IQR is a measure of the **dispersion**, or spread, of values.

With rank statistics, we also want to look at the smallest and largest values to identify outliers. Remember that we defined outliers at the beginning of this section as "cases for which the value of the variable is extremely high or low relative to the rest of the values for that variable." If we look at the highest values in Table 6.2, we can see that there aren't really any cases that fit this description. Although there are certainly some values that are a lot higher than the median value and the 75 percent value, they aren't "extremely" higher than the rest of the values. Instead, there seems to be a fairly even progression from the 75 percent value up to the highest value. The story at the lower end of the range of values in Table 6.2 is a little different. We can see that the two lowest values are pretty far from each other and from the rest of the low values. The value

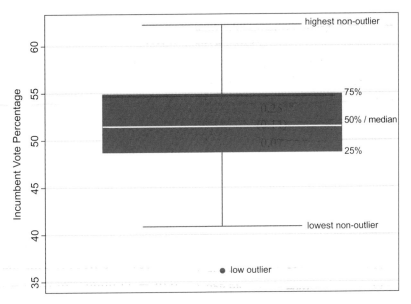

Figure 6.4 Box–whisker plot of incumbent-party presidential vote percentage, 1876–2016

of 36.148 in 1920 seems to meet our definition of an outlier. The value of 40.851 in 1932 is also a borderline case. Whenever we see outliers, we should begin by checking whether we have measured the values for these cases accurately. Sometimes we find that outliers are the result of errors when entering data. In this case, a check of our data set reveals that the outlier case occurred in 1920 when the incumbent-party candidate received only 36.148 percent of the votes cast for the two major parties. A further check of our data indicates that this was indeed a correct measure of this variable for 1920.[6]

Figure 6.4 presents a box–whisker plot of the rank statistics for our presidential vote variable. This plot displays the distribution of the variable along the vertical dimension. If we start at the center of the box in Figure 6.4, we see the median value (or 50 percent rank value) of our variable represented as the slight gap in the center of the box. The other two ends of the box show the values of the 25 percent rank and the 75 percent rank of our variable. The ends of the whiskers show the lowest and highest non-outlier values of our variable. Each statistical program has its own rules for dealing with outliers, so it is important to know whether

---

[6] An obvious question is "Why was 1920 such a low value?" This was the first presidential election in the aftermath of World War I, during a period when there was a lot of economic and political turmoil. The election in 1932 was at the very beginning of the large economic downturn known as "the Great Depression," so it makes sense that the party of the incumbent president would not have done very well during this election.

your box–whisker plot is or is not set up to display outliers. These settings are usually adjustable within the statistical program. The calculation of whether an individual case is or is not an outlier in this box–whisker plot is fairly standard. This calculation starts with the IQR for the variable. Any case is defined as an outlier if its value is either 1.5 times the IQR higher than the 75 percent value or if its value is 1.5 times the IQR lower than the 25 percent value. For Figure 6.4 we have set things up so that the plot displays the outliers, and we can see one such value at the bottom of our figure. As we already know from Table 6.2, this is the value of 36.148 from the 1920 election.

6.4.2 Moments

The statistical moments of a variable are a set of statistics that describe the central tendency for a single variable and the distribution of values around it. The most familiar of these statistics is known as the **mean value** or "average" value for the variable. For a variable Y, the mean value is calculated as

$$\bar{Y} = \frac{\sum_{i=1}^{n} Y_i}{n},$$

where $\bar{Y}$, read aloud as "Y-bar," indicates the mean of Y, which is equal to the sum of all values of Y across individual cases of Y, Y_i, divided by the total number of cases, n.[7] Although everyone is familiar with mean or average values, not everyone is familiar with the two characteristics of the mean value that make it particularly attractive to people who use statistics. The first is known as the **"zero-sum property"**:

$$\sum_{i=1}^{n} (Y_i - \bar{Y}) = 0,$$

which means the sum of the difference between each Y value, Y_i, and the mean value of Y, $\bar{Y}$, is equal to zero. The second desirable characteristic of the mean value is known as the **"least-squares property"**:

$$\sum_{i=1}^{n} (Y_i - \bar{Y})^2 < \sum_{i=1}^{n} (Y_i - c)^2 \quad \forall c \neq \bar{Y},$$

which means that the sum of the squared differences between each Y value, Y_i, and the mean value of Y, $\bar{Y}$, is less than the sum of the squared differences between each Y value, Y_i, and some value c, for all ($\forall$) c values not equal to ($\neq$) $\bar{Y}$. Because of these two properties, the mean value is

---

[7] To understand formulae like this, it is helpful to read through each of the pieces of the formula and translate them into words, as we have done here.

also referred to as the **expected value** of a variable. Think of it this way: If someone were to ask you to guess what the value for an individual case is without giving you any more information than the mean value, based on these two properties of the mean, the mean value would be the best guess.

The next statistical moment for a variable is the **variance** (var). We calculate the variance as follows:

$$\mathrm{var}(Y) = \mathrm{var}_Y = s_Y^2 = \frac{\sum_{i=1}^{n}(Y_i - \bar{Y})^2}{n-1},$$

which means that the variance of Y is equal to the sum of the squared differences between each Y value, Y_i, and its mean divided by the number of cases minus one.[8] If we look through this formula, what would happen if we had no variation on Y at all ($Y_i = \bar{Y} \ \forall \ i$)? In this case, variance would be equal to zero. But as individual cases are spread further and further from the mean, this calculation would increase. This is the logic of variance: It conveys the spread of the data around the mean. A more intuitive measure of variance is the **standard deviation** (sd):

$$\mathrm{sd}(Y) = \mathrm{sd}_Y = s_Y = \sqrt{\mathrm{var}(Y)} = \sqrt{\frac{\sum_{i=1}^{n}(Y_i - \bar{Y})^2}{n-1}}.$$

Roughly speaking, this is the average difference between values of Y (Y_i) and the mean of Y ($\bar{Y}$). At first glance, this may not be apparent. But the important thing to understand about this formula is that the purpose of squaring each difference from the mean and then taking the square root of the resulting sum of squared deviations is to keep the negative and positive deviations from canceling each other out.[9]

The variance and the standard deviation give us a numerical summary of the distribution of cases around the mean value for a variable.[10] We can also visually depict distributions. The idea of visually depicting distributions is to produce a two-dimensional figure in which the horizontal

[8] The "minus one" in this equation is an adjustment that is made to account for the number of "degrees of freedom" with which this calculation was made. We will discuss degrees of freedom in Chapter 8.

[9] An alternative method that would produce a very similar calculation would be to calculate the average value of the absolute value of each difference from the mean: $\left(\frac{\sum_{i=1}^{n}|Y_i - \bar{Y}|}{n}\right)$.

[10] The **skewness** and the **kurtosis** of a variable convey the further aspects of the distribution of a variable. The skewness calculation indicates the symmetry of the distribution around the mean. If the data are symmetrically distributed around the mean, then this statistic will equal zero. If skewness is negative, this indicates that there are more values below the mean than there are above; if skewness is positive, this indicates that there are more values above the mean than there are below. The kurtosis indicates the steepness of the statistical distribution. Positive kurtosis values indicate very steep distributions, or a concentration of values close to the mean value, whereas negative kurtosis values indicate a flatter distribution, or more cases further from the mean value. For the normal distribution, which we will discuss in Chapter 7, skewness = 0 and kurtosis = 3.

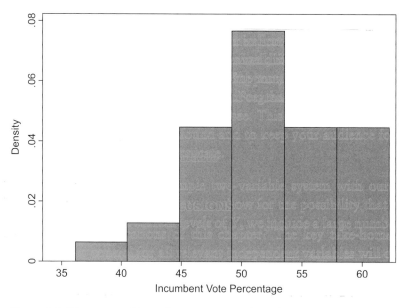

Figure 6.5 Histogram of incumbent-party presidential vote percentage, 1876–2016

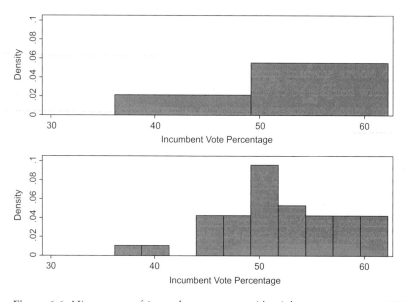

Figure 6.6 Histograms of incumbent-party presidential vote percentage, 1876–2016, depicted with two and then ten blocks

dimension (x axis) displays the values of the variable and the vertical dimension (y axis) displays the relative frequency of cases. One of the most popular visual depictions of a variable's distribution is the **histogram**, such as Figure 6.5. One problem with histograms is that we (or the computer program with which we are working) must choose how many rectangular blocks (called "bins") are depicted in our histogram. Changing the number of blocks in a histogram can change our impression of the distribution

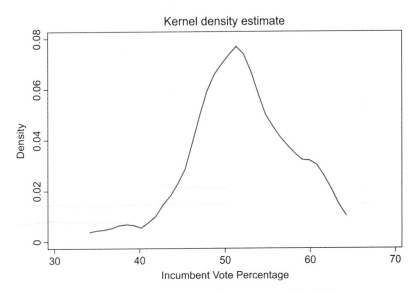

Figure 6.7 Kernel density plot of incumbent-party presidential vote percentage, 1876–2016

of the variable being depicted. Figure 6.6 shows the same variable as in Figure 6.5 with two and then ten blocks. Although we generate both of the graphs in Figure 6.6 from the same data, they are fairly different from each other.

Another option is the **kernel density plot**, as in Figure 6.7, which is based on a smoothed calculation of the density of cases across the range of values.

6.5 LIMITATIONS OF DESCRIPTIVE STATISTICS AND GRAPHS

The tools that we have presented in the last three sections of this chapter are helpful for providing a first look at data, one variable at a time. Taking a look at your data with these tools will help you to better know your data and make fewer mistakes in the long run. It is important, however, to note that we cannot test causal theories with a single variable. After all, as we have noted, a theory is a tentative statement about the possible causal relationship between two variables. Because we have discussed how to describe only a single variable, we have not yet begun to subject our causal theories to appropriate tests.

6.6 CONCLUSIONS

The tools that we have presented in this chapter are helpful for providing a first look at data, one variable at a time. Taking a look at your data with these tools will help you to better know your data and make less mistakes in the long run. It is important, however, to note that we cannot test causal theories with a single variable. After all, as we have noted, a theory is a tentative statement about the possible causal relationship between two variables. Since we have only discussed how to describe a single variable, we have not yet begun to subject our causal theories to appropriate tests.

CONCEPTS INTRODUCED IN THIS CHAPTER

- categorical variable – a variable for which cases have values that are either different from or the same as the values for other cases, but about which we cannot make any universally holding ranking distinctions
- central tendency – typical values for a particular variable at the center of its distribution
- continuous variable – a variable whose metric has equal unit differences such that a one-unit increase in the value of the variable indicates the same amount of change across all values of that variable
- dispersion – the spread or range of values of a variable
- equal unit differences – a variable has equal unit differences if a one-unit increase in the value of that variable always means the same thing
- expected value – a synonym for mean value
- histogram – a visual depiction of the distribution of a single variable that produces a two-dimensional figure in which the horizontal dimension (x axis) displays the values of the variable and the vertical dimension (y axis) displays the relative frequency of cases
- kernel density plot – a visual depiction of the distribution of a single variable based on a smoothed calculation of the density of cases across the range of values
- kurtosis – a statistical measure indicating the steepness of the statistical distribution of a single variable
- least-squares property – a property of the mean value for a single variable Y, which means that the sum of the squared differences between each Y value, Y_i, and the mean value of Y, $\bar{Y}$, is less than the sum of the squared differences between each Y value, Y_i, and some value c, for all ($\forall$) c values not equal to ($\neq$) $\bar{Y}$
- mean value – the arithmetical average of a variable equal to the sum of all values of Y across individual cases of Y, Y_i, divided by the total number of cases
- measurement metric – the type of values that the variable takes on
- median value – the value of the case that sits at the exact center of our cases when we rank the values of a single variable from the smallest to the largest observed values

- mode – the most frequently occurring value of a variable
- ordinal variable – a variable for which we can make universally holding ranking distinctions across the variable values, but whose metric does not have equal unit differences
- outlier – a case for which the value of the variable is extremely high or low relative to the rest of the values for that variable
- rank statistics – a class of statistics used to describe the variation of continuous variables based on their ranking from lowest to highest observed values
- skewness – a statistical measure indicating the symmetry of the distribution around the mean
- standard deviation – a statistical measure of the dispersion of a variable around its mean
- statistical moments – a class of statistics used to describe the variation of continuous variables based on numerical calculations
- variance – a statistical measure of the dispersion of a variable around its mean
- variation – the distribution of values that a variable takes across the cases for which it is measured
- zero-sum property – a property of the mean value for a single variable Y, which means that the sum of the difference between each Y value, Y_i, and the mean value of Y, $\bar{Y}$, is equal to zero

EXERCISES

1. *Collecting and describing a categorical variable.* Find data for a categorical variable in which you are interested. Get those data into a format that can be read by the statistical software that you are using. Produce a frequency table and describe what you see.

2. *Collecting and describing a continuous variable.* Find data for a continuous variable in which you are interested. Get those data into a format that can be read by the statistical software that you are using. Produce a table of descriptive statistics and either a histogram or a kernel density plot. Describe what you have found out from doing this.

3. In Table 6.1, why would it be problematic to calculate the mean value of the variable "Religious Identification"?

4. *Moving from mathematical formulae to textual statements.* Write a sentence that conveys what is going on in each of the following equations:

    (a) $Y = 3 \; \forall \; X_i = 2$.

    (b) $Y_{total} = \sum_{i=1}^{n} Y_i = n\bar{Y}$.

Table 6.3 Median incomes of the 50 states, 2004–2005

State	Income	State	Income
Alabama	37,502	Montana	36,202
Alaska	56,398	Nebraska	46,587
Arizona	45,279	Nevada	48,496
Arkansas	36,406	New Hampshire	57,850
California	51,312	New Jersey	60,246
Colorado	51,518	New Mexico	39,916
Connecticut	56,889	New York	46,659
Delaware	50,445	North Carolina	41,820
Florida	42,440	North Dakota	41,362
Georgia	44,140	Ohio	44,349
Hawaii	58,854	Oklahoma	39,292
Idaho	45,009	Oregon	43,262
Illinois	48,008	Pennsylvania	45,941
Indiana	43,091	Rhode Island	49,511
Iowa	45,671	South Carolina	40,107
Kansas	42,233	South Dakota	42,816
Kentucky	36,750	Tennessee	39,376
Louisiana	37,442	Texas	42,102
Maine	43,317	Utah	53,693
Maryland	59,762	Vermont	49,808
Massachusetts	54,888	Virginia	52,383
Michigan	44,801	Washington	51,119
Minnesota	56,098	West Virginia	35,467
Mississippi	34,396	Wisconsin	45,956
Missouri	43,266	Wyoming	45,817

5. *Computing means and standard deviations.* Table 6.3 contains the median income for each of the 50 US states for the years 2004–2005. What is the mean of this distribution, and what is its standard deviation? Show all of your work.

7 Probability and Statistical Inference

OVERVIEW

Researchers aspire to draw conclusions about the entire population of cases that are relevant to a particular research question. However, in almost all research situations, they must rely on data from only a sample of those cases to do so. In this chapter, we lay the foundation for how researchers make inferences about a population of cases while only observing a sample of data. This foundation rests on probability theory, which we introduce here with extensive examples. We conclude the chapter with an example familiar to political science students – namely, the "plus-or-minus" error figures in presidential approval polls, showing where such figures come from and how they illustrate the principles of building bridges from samples we know about with certainty to the underlying population of interest.

How dare we speak of the laws of chance? Is not chance the antithesis of all law?
   —Bertrand Russell

7.1 POPULATIONS AND SAMPLES

In Chapter 5, we learned how to measure our key concepts of interest, and in Chapter 6 how to use descriptive statistics to summarize large amounts of information about a single variable. In particular, you discovered how to characterize a distribution by computing measures of central tendency (like the mean or median) and measures of dispersion (like the standard deviation or IQR). For example, you can implement these formulae to characterize the distribution of income in the United States, or, for that matter, the scores of a midterm examination your professor may have just handed back.

But it is time to draw a critical distinction between two types of data sets that social scientists might use. The first type is data about the **population** – that is, data for every possible relevant case. In your experience, the example of population data that might come to mind first is that of the US Census, an attempt by the US government to gather some critical bits of data about the entire US population once every 10 years.[1] It is a relatively rare occurrence that social scientists will make use of data pertaining to the entire population. But we nevertheless aspire to make inferences about some population of interest, and it is up to the researcher to define explicitly what that population of interest is. Sometimes, as in the case of the US Census, the relevant population – all US residents – is easy to understand. Other times, it is a bit less obvious. Consider a pre-election survey, in which the researcher needs to decide whether the population of interest is all adult citizens, or likely voters, or something else.

The second type of data is drawn from a **sample** – a subset of cases that is drawn from an underlying population. Because of the proliferation of public opinion polls today, many of you might assume that the word "sample" implies a **random sample**.[2] It does not. Researchers *may* draw a sample of data on the basis of randomness – meaning that each member of the population has an equal probability of being selected in the sample. But samples may also be nonrandom, which we refer to as samples of convenience.

The vast majority of analyses undertaken by social scientists are done on sample data, not population data. Why make this distinction? Even though the overwhelming majority of social science data sets are comprised of a sample, not the population, it is critical to note that we are not interested in the properties of the sample *per se*; we are interested in the sample only insofar as it helps us to learn about the underlying population. In effect, we try to build a metaphorical bridge from what we know about the sample to what we believe, probabilistically, to be true about the broader population. That process is called **statistical inference**, because we use what we *know* to be true about one thing (the sample) to *infer* what is likely to be true about another thing (the population). That is what the word "inference" means: It means to draw an uncertain conclusion based on some limited information.

---

[1] The Bureau of the Census's web site is http://www.census.gov.

[2] When we discussed research design in Chapter 4, we distinguished between the experimental notion of random assignment to treatment groups, on the one hand, and random sampling, on the other. See Chapter 4 if you need a refresher on this difference.

> **YOUR TURN: Two sides of the same coin – "infer" and "imply"**
>
> If a friend of yours revealed *something* to you without saying their true feelings outright, we might say that he or she "implied" something to you. They revealed *some* information, but you had to fill in the gaps to draw the conclusion.
>
> So when your friend "implies" something, in order to fill in those gaps of understanding, you have to "infer" the rest.
>
> Think about how this applies to the concept that we've just defined above – "statistical inference."

There are implications for using sample data to learn about a population. First and foremost is that this process of statistical inference involves, by definition, some degree of uncertainty. That notion, we hope, is relatively straightforward: Any time that we wish to learn something general based on something specific, we are going to encounter some degree of uncertainty. For example, if we want to learn about an entire country's voting-age population, but we don't have the time or resources to interview every member of the voting-age population in that country, we can still learn something about what the population thinks *based upon the observations of a sample of that population*, provided that we know things about how that sample was selected, and provided that we recognize the uncertainty inherent in extrapolating what we know for sure about our sample to what is likely to be true about the population writ large.

In this chapter, we discuss this process of statistical inference, including the tools that social scientists use to learn about the population that they are interested in by using samples of data. Our first step in this process is to discuss the basics of probability theory, which, in turn, forms the basis for all of statistical inference.

7.2 SOME BASICS OF PROBABILITY THEORY

Let's start with an example.

Suppose that you take an empty pillowcase, and that, without anyone else looking, you meticulously count out 550 small blue beads, and 450 small red beads, and place all 1000 of them into the pillowcase. You twist the pillowcase opening a few times to close it up, and then give it a robust shake to mix up the beads. Next, you have a friend reach her hand into the pillowcase – no peeking! – and have her draw out 100 beads, and then count the number of red and blue beads.

Obviously, because she is observing the entire pillowcase and the process unfolding before her eyes, your friend knows that she is taking just a relatively small sample of beads from the population that is in the pillowcase. And because you shook that pillowcase vigorously, and forbade your friend from looking into the pillowcase while selecting the 100 beads, her selection of 100 (more or less) represents a random sample of that population. Importantly, your friend doesn't know, of course, how many red and blue beads are in the pillowcase. She only knows how many red and blue beads she observed in the sample that she plucked out of it.

Next, you ask her to count the number of red and blue beads. Let's imagine that she happened to draw 46 red beads and 54 blue ones. Once she does this, you then ask her the key question: Based on her count, what is her best guess about the *percentage* of red beads and blue beads in the entire pillowcase? The only way for your friend to know for sure how many red and blue beads are in the pillowcase, of course, is to dump out the entire pillowcase and count all 1000 beads. But, on the other hand, you're not exactly asking your friend to make some entirely random, wild guess. She has a decent amount of information, after all, and she can use that information to make a better guess than simply randomly picking a number between 0 and 100 percent.

Sensibly, given the results of her sample, she guesses that 46 percent of the beads in the entire pillowcase are red, and 54 percent are blue.

YOUR TURN: What would you guess in her situation?

Even though you know how many blue and red beads, overall, are in the pillowcase, and you know that your friend's guess based upon her sample is wrong, what should she have guessed, *given the information that she had at the time*?

Before telling her the true answer, you have her dump the 100 beads that she drew back into the pillowcase, re-mix the 1000 beads, and have her repeat the process from the get-go: reach into the pillowcase again, re-draw 100 beads, and count the number of reds and blues drawn again. This time, she draws 43 red beads and 57 blue ones.

You ask your friend if she'd like to revise her guess, and, based on some new information and some quick averaging on her part, she revises her guess to say that she thinks that 44.5 percent of the beads are red, and 55.5 percent of the beads are blue. (She does this by simply averaging the 46 percent of red beads from the first sample and 43 percent of red beads from the second sample.)

The laws of probability are useful in many ways – in calculating gambling odds, for example – but in the above example, they are useful for taking particular information about a characteristic of an observed sample of data and attempting to generalize that information to the underlying (and unobserved) population. The observed samples above, of course, are the two samples of 100 that your friend drew from the pillowcase. The underlying population is represented by the 1000 beads in the bag.

Of course, the example above has some limitations. In particular, in the example, you *knew, with certainty*, the actual population characteristic – there were 450 red and 550 blue beads. In social reality, there is no comparable knowledge of the value of the true characteristic of the underlying population. That's a pretty big difference between our contrived example and the reality that we experience daily.

Now, some definitions.

An **outcome** is the result of a random observation. Two or more outcomes can be said to be **independent outcomes** if the realization of one of the outcomes does not affect the realization of the other outcome. For example, the roll of two dice represents independent outcomes, because the outcome of the first die – did you roll a 1, 2, 3, 4, 5, or 6 – does not affect the outcome of the second die. Rolling a 3 on the first die has no bearing on the outcome of the second die. Hence the outcomes are, by definition, independent, in the sense that one does not depend on the other.

Probability has several key properties. First, all outcomes have some probability ranging from 0 to 1. A probability value of 0 for an outcome means that the outcome is impossible, and a probability value of 1 for an outcome means that the outcome is absolutely certain to happen. As an example of an outcome that cannot possibly happen, consider taking two fair dice, rolling them, and adding up the sides facing up. The probability that the sum will equal 13 is 0, since the highest possible outcome is 12.

Second, the sum of all possible outcomes must be exactly 1. A different way of putting this is that, once you undertake a random observation, you must observe something. If you flip a fair coin, the probability of it landing heads is $1/2$, and the probability of it landing tails is $1/2$, and the probability of landing either a head or a tail is 1, because $1/2 + 1/2 = 1$.

Third, if (but only if!) two outcomes are independent, then the probability of those events both occurring is equal to the product of them individually. So, if we have our fair coin, and toss it three times, the probability of tossing three tails is $1/2 \times 1/2 \times 1/2 = 1/8$. (Be mindful that each toss is an independent outcome, because seeing a tail on one toss has no bearing on whether the next toss will be a head or a tail.)

Of course, many of the outcomes in which we are interested are not independent. And in these circumstances, more complex rules of probability are required that are beyond the scope of this discussion.

Why is probability relevant for scientific investigations, and in particular, for political science? For several reasons. First, because political scientists typically work with samples (not populations) of data, the rules of probability tell us how we can generalize from what we know with certainty about our sample to what is likely to be true about the broader population. Second, and relatedly, the rules of probability are the key to identifying which relationships are "statistically significant" (a concept that we define in the next chapter). Put differently, we use probability theory to decide whether the patterns of relationships we observe in a sample could have occurred simply by chance.

LEARNING ABOUT THE POPULATION FROM A SAMPLE: THE CENTRAL LIMIT THEOREM

The reasons that social scientists rely on sample data instead of on population data – in spite of the fact that we care about the results in the population instead of in the sample – are easy to understand. Consider an election campaign, in which the media, the public, and the politicians involved all want a sense of which candidates the public favors and by how much. Is it practicable to take a census in such circumstances? Of course not. The adult population in the United States is well over 200 million people, and it is an understatement to say that we can't interview each and every one of these individuals. We simply don't have the time or the money to do that; and even if we tried, opinion might shift over the time period it would take making the attempt. There is a reason why the US government conducts a **census** only once every ten years.[3]

Of course, anyone familiar with the ubiquitous public opinion polls knows that scholars and news organizations conduct surveys on a sample of Americans routinely and use the results of these surveys to generalize about the people as a whole. When you think about it, it seems a little audacious to think that you can interview perhaps as few as 800 or 1000 people and then use the results of those interviews to generalize to the beliefs and opinions of the entire 200 million. How is that possible?

The answer lies in a fundamental result from statistics called the **central limit theorem**, which Dutch statistician Henk Tijms (2004) calls "the unofficial sovereign of probability theory." Before diving into what the theorem demonstrates, and how it applies to social science research, we need to explore one of the most useful probability distributions in statistics, the **normal distribution**.

7.3.1 The Normal Distribution

To say that a particular distribution is "normal" is *not* to say that it is "typical" or "desirable" or "good." A distribution that is not "normal"

---

[3] You might not be aware that, even though the federal government conducts only one census per ten years, it conducts sample surveys with great frequency in an attempt to measure population characteristics such as economic activity.

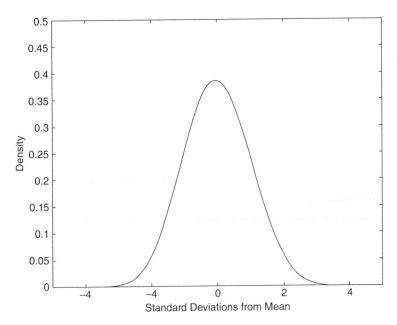

Figure 7.1 The normal probability distribution

is not something odd like the "deviant" or "abnormal" distribution. It is worth emphasizing, as well, that normal distributions are not necessarily common in the real world. Yet, as we will see, they are incredibly useful in the world of statistics.

The normal distribution is often called a "bell curve" in common language. It is shown in Figure 7.1 and has several special properties. First, it is symmetrical about its mean,[4] such that the mode, median, and mean are the same. Second, the normal distribution has a predictable area under the curve within specified distances of the mean. Starting from the mean and going one standard deviation in each direction above and below the mean will capture 68 percent of the area under the curve. Going one additional standard deviation in each direction will capture a shade over 95 percent of the total area under the curve.[5] And going a third standard deviation in each direction will capture more than 99 percent of the total area under the curve. This is commonly referred to as the **68–95–99 rule** and is illustrated in Figure 7.2. You should bear in mind that this is a special feature of the normal distribution and *does not apply to any other-shaped*

---

[4] Equivalently, but a bit more formally, we can characterize the distribution by its mean and variance (or standard deviation) – which implies that its skewness and excess kurtosis are both equal to zero.

[5] To get exactly 95 percent of the area under the curve, we would actually go 1.96, not 2, standard deviations in each direction from the mean. Nevertheless, the rule of two is a handy rule of thumb for many statistical calculations.

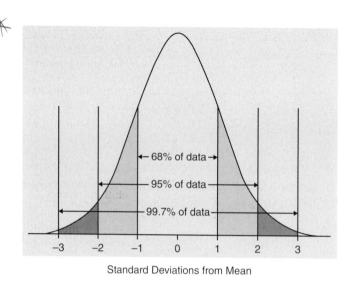

Standard Deviations from Mean

Figure 7.2 The 68–95–99 rule

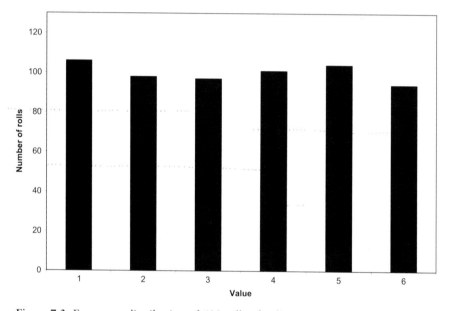

Figure 7.3 Frequency distribution of 600 rolls of a die

distributions. What do the normal distribution and the 68–95–99 rule have to do with the process of learning about population characteristics based on a sample?

A distribution of actual scores in a sample – called a **frequency distribution**, to represent the frequency of each value of a particular variable – on any variable might be shaped normally, or it might not be. Consider the frequency distribution of 600 rolls of a six-sided (and unbiased) die, presented in Figure 7.3. Note something about Figure 7.3

right off the bat: that frequency distribution does not even remotely resemble a normal distribution.[6] If we roll a fair six-sided die 600 times, how many 1s, 2s, etc., should we see? On average, 100 of each, right? That's *pretty close* to what we see in the figure, but only pretty close. Purely because of chance, we rolled a couple too many 1s, for example, and a couple too few 6s.

What can we say about this sample of 600 rolls of the die? And, more to the point, from these 600 rolls of the die, what can we say about the underlying population of all rolls of a fair six-sided die? Before we answer the second question, which will require some inference, let's answer the first, which we can answer with certainty. We can calculate the mean of these rolls of dice in the straightforward way that we learned in Chapter 6: Add up all of the "scores" – that is, the 1s, 2s, and so on – and divide by the total number of rolls, which in this case is 600. That will lead to the following calculation:

$$\bar{Y} = \frac{\sum_{i=1}^{n} Y_i}{n}$$

$$= \frac{\sum(1 \times 106) + (2 \times 98) + (3 \times 97) + (4 \times 101) + (5 \times 104) + (6 \times 94)}{600}$$

$$= 3.47.$$

Following the formula for the mean, for our 600 rolls of the die, in the numerator we must add up all of the 1s (106 of them), all of the 2s (98 of them), and so on, and then divide by 600 to produce our result of 3.47.

We can also calculate the standard deviation of this distribution:

$$s_Y = \sqrt{\frac{\sum_{i=1}^{n}(Y_i - \bar{Y})^2}{n-1}} = \sqrt{\frac{1753.40}{599}} = 1.71.$$

Looking at the numerator for the formula for the standard deviation that we learned in Chapter 6, we see that $\sum(Y_i - \bar{Y})^2$ indicates that, for each observation (a 1, 2, 3, 4, 5, or 6) we subtract its value from the mean (3.47), then square that difference, then add up all 600 squared deviations from the mean, which produces a numerator of 1753.40 beneath the square-root sign. Dividing that amount by 599 (that is, $n-1$), then taking the square root, produces a standard deviation of 1.71.

As we noted, the sample mean is 3.47, but what should we have *expected* the mean to be? If we had exactly 100 rolls of each side of the die, the mean would have been 3.50, so our sample mean is a bit lower than we would have expected. But then again, we can see that we rolled a few "too many" 1s and a few "too few" 6s, so the fact that our mean is a bit below 3.50 makes sense.

---

[6] In fact, the distribution in the figure very closely resembles a uniform (or flat) distribution.

What would happen, though, if we rolled that same die another 600 times? What would the mean value of those rolls be? We can't say for certain, of course. Perhaps we would come up with another sample mean of 3.47, or perhaps it would be a bit above 3.50, or perhaps the mean would hit 3.50 on the nose. Suppose that we rolled the die 600 times like this not once, and not twice, but an infinite number of times. Let's be clear: We do not mean *an infinite number of rolls*, but instead we mean *rolling the die 600 times for an infinite number of times.* That distinction is critical. We are imagining that we are taking a sample of 600, not once, but an infinite number of times. We can refer to a hypothetical distribution of sample means, such as this, as a **sampling distribution**. It is hypothetical because scientists almost never actually draw more than one sample from an underlying population at one given point in time.

If we followed this hypothetical procedure, we could take those sample means and plot them. Some would be above 3.50, some below, and a few right on it. Here is the key outcome, though: The sampling distribution would be normally shaped, even though the underlying frequency distribution is clearly not normally shaped.

> **YOUR TURN: High and low scores in frequency versus sampling distributions**
>
> With a frequency distribution of 600 rolls of a die that is distributed uniformly, it's not unusual to get extremely high or extremely low rolls of 6 or 1, is it? But if we took the mean of a sample of 600 rolls, what would have to happen in order to get a *sample mean* of 6 or 1?

That is the insight of the central limit theorem. If we can envision an infinite number of random samples and plot our sample means for each of these random samples, those sample means would be distributed normally. Furthermore, the mean of the sampling distribution would be equal to the true population mean. Last, the central limit theorem shows that the standard deviation of the sampling distribution is:

$$\sigma_{\bar{Y}} = \frac{s_Y}{\sqrt{n}},$$

where n is the sample size. The standard deviation of the sampling distribution of sample means, which is known as the **standard error of the mean** (or simply "standard error"), is simply equal to the sample standard deviation of the observed sample divided by the square root of the sample size. In the preceding die-rolling example, the standard error of the mean is

$$\sigma_{\bar{Y}} = \frac{1.71}{\sqrt{600}} = 0.07.$$

Recall that our goal here is to learn what we can about the underlying population based on what we know with certainty about our sample. We know that the mean of our sample of 600 rolls of the die is 3.47, and its standard deviation is 1.71. From those characteristics, we can imagine that, if we rolled that die 600 times an infinite number of times, the resulting sampling distribution would have a standard deviation of 0.07. Our best approximation of the population mean is 3.47, because that is the result that our sample generated.[7] But we realize that our sample of 600 might be different from the true population mean by a little bit, either too high or too low, for no reason other than randomness. What we can do, then, is use our knowledge that the sampling distribution is shaped normally and invoke the 68–95–99 rule to create a **confidence interval** about the likely location of the population mean.

How do we do that? First, we choose a degree of confidence that we want to have in our estimate. Although we can choose any confidence range up from just above 0 to just below 100, social scientists traditionally rely on the 95 percent confidence level. If we follow this tradition – and, critically, because our sampling distribution is normally shaped – we would merely start at our mean (3.47) and move *two* standard errors of the mean in each direction to produce the interval that we are approximately 95 percent confident that the population mean lies within. Why *two* standard errors? Because just over 95 percent of the area under a normal curve lies within two standard errors of the mean. Again, to be precisely 95 percent confident, we would move 1.96, not 2, standard errors in each direction. But the rule of thumb of two is commonly used in practice. In other words,

$$\bar{Y} \pm (2 \times \sigma_{\bar{Y}}) = 3.47 \pm (2 \times 0.07) = 3.47 \pm 0.14.$$

That means, from our sample, we are 95 percent confident that the population mean for our rolls of the die lies somewhere on the interval between 3.33 and 3.61.

YOUR TURN: From 95 to 99 percent confidence intervals

For a variety of reasons, we might like to have more confidence that our estimate lies on a particular interval. Say that, instead of being 95 percent confident, we would be more comfortable with a 99 percent level of confidence. Using what you know about normal distributions, and the procedure we just practiced, can you construct the 99 percent confidence interval?

Is it possible that we're wrong and that the true population mean lies outside that interval? Absolutely. Moreover, we know exactly *how* likely.

---

[7] One might imagine that our best guess should be 3.50 because, in theory, a fair die ought to produce such a result.

There is a 2.5 percent chance that the population mean is less than 3.33, and a 2.5 percent chance that the population mean is greater than 3.61, for a total of a 5 percent chance that the population mean is not in the interval from 3.33 to 3.61.

Throughout this example we have been helped along by the fact that we knew the underlying characteristics of the data-generating process (a fair die). In the real world, social scientists almost never have this advantage. In the next section we consider such a case.

7.4   EXAMPLE: PRESIDENTIAL APPROVAL RATINGS

Between September 14 and 18, 2017, NBC News and the *Wall Street Journal* sponsored a survey in which 900 randomly selected adult US citizens were interviewed about their political beliefs. Among the questions they were asked was the following item intended to tap into a respondent's evaluation of the president's job performance:

> In general, do you approve or disapprove of the job Donald Trump is doing as president?

This question wording is the industry standard, used for over a half-century by almost all polling organizations.[8] In September of 2017, 43 percent of the sample approved of Trump's job performance, 52 percent disapproved, and 5 percent were unsure.[9]

These news organizations, of course, are not inherently interested in the opinions of those 900 Americans who happened to be in the sample, except insofar as they tell us something about the adult population as a whole. But we can use these 900 responses to do precisely that, using the logic of the central limit theorem and the tools previously described.

To reiterate, we know the properties of our randomly drawn sample of 900 people with absolute certainty. If we consider the 387 approving responses to be 1s and the remaining 513 responses to be 0s, then we calculate our sample mean, $\bar{Y}$, as follows:[10]

$$\bar{Y} = \frac{\sum_{i=1}^{n} Y_i}{n} = \frac{\sum(387 \times 1) + (513 \times 0)}{900} = 0.43.$$

---

[8] The only changes, of course, are for the name of the current president.

[9] The source for the survey was http://www.pollingreport.com/djt_job.htm, accessed October 15, 2017.

[10] There are a variety of different ways in which to handle mathematically the 5 percent of "uncertain" responses. In this case, because we are interested in calculating the "approval" rating for this example, it is reasonable to lump the disapproving and unsure answers together. When we make decisions like this in our statistical work, it is very important to communicate exactly what we have done so that the scientific audience can make a reasoned evaluation of our work.

We calculate the sample standard deviation, s_Y, in the following way:

$$s_Y = \sqrt{\frac{\sum_{i=1}^{n}(Y_i - \bar{Y})^2}{n-1}} = \sqrt{\frac{387(1-0.43)^2 + 513(0-0.43)^2}{900-1}}$$

$$= \sqrt{\frac{212.27}{899}} = 0.49.$$

But what can we say about the population as a whole? Obviously, unlike the sample mean, the population mean cannot be known with certainty. But if we imagine that, instead of one sample of 900 respondents, we had an infinite number of samples of 900, then the central limit theorem tells us that those sample means would be distributed normally. Our best guess of the population mean, of course, is 0.43, because it is our sample mean. The standard error of the mean is

$$\sigma_{\bar{Y}} = \frac{0.49}{\sqrt{900}} = 0.016,$$

which is our measure of uncertainty about the population mean. If we use the rule of thumb and calculate the 95 percent confidence interval by using two standard errors in either direction from the sample mean, we are left with the following interval:

$$\bar{Y} \pm (2 \times \sigma_{\bar{Y}}) = 0.43 \pm (2 \times 0.016) = 0.43 \pm 0.032,$$

or between 0.398 and 0.462, which translates into being 95 percent confident that the population value of Trump approval during September 14–18, 2017 was between 39.8 and 46.2 percent.

And this is where the "plus-or-minus" figures that we always see in public opinion polls come from.[11] The best guess for the population mean value is the sample mean value, plus or minus two standard errors. So the plus-or-minus figures we are accustomed to seeing are built, typically, on the 95 percent interval.

7.4.1   What Kind of Sample Was That?

If you read the preceding example carefully, you will have noted that the NBC–*Wall Street Journal* poll we described used a *random* sample of 900 individuals. That means that they used some mechanism (like random-digit telephone dialing) to ensure that all members of the population had an equal probability of being selected for the survey. We want to reiterate the importance of using random samples. The central limit theorem applies

---

[11] In practice, most polling firms have their own additional adjustments that they make to these calculations, but they start with this basic logic.

only to samples that are selected randomly. With a sample of convenience, by contrast, we cannot invoke the central limit theorem to construct a sampling distribution and create a confidence interval.

This lesson is critical: A nonrandomly selected sample of convenience does very little to help us build bridges between the sample and the population about which we want to learn. This has all sorts of implications about "polls" that news organizations conduct on their web sites. Only certain types of people – high in political interest, with a particular ideological bent – look at these web sites and click on those surveys. As a result, what do such "surveys" say about the population as a whole? Because their samples are clearly not random samples of the underlying population, the answer is "nothing."

There is a related lesson involved here. The preceding example represents an entirely straightforward connection between a sample (the 900 people in the survey) and the population (all adults in the United States). Often the link between the sample and the population is less straightforward. Consider, for example, an examination of votes in a country's legislature during a given year. Assuming that it's easy enough to get all of the roll-call voting information for each member of the legislature (which is our sample), we are left with a slightly perplexing question: What is the population of interest? The answer is not obvious, and not all social scientists would agree on the answer. Some might claim that these data don't represent a sample, but a population, because the data set contains the votes of every member of the legislature. Others might claim that the sample is a sample of one year's worth of the legislature since its inception. Others still might say that the sample is one realization of the infinite number of legislatures that could have happened in that particular year. Suffice it to say that there is no clear scientific consensus, in this example, of what would constitute the "sample" and what would constitute the "population." Still, treating these data as a sample represents the more cautious approach, and hence one we recommend.

7.4.2   Obtaining a Random Sample in the Cellphone Era

In today's era of constant technological advances, you might think that drawing a random sample of adult Americans would be easier than ever. Actually, it's getting harder, and here's why. Let's pretend for the moment that the year is 1988. If a survey-research company wanted to call 900 random US households to conduct a survey, they would use random-digit telephone dialing in a simple way. The phone company (there was only one) told the survey-research company how many numbers were in each three-digit area code. (Some, like (212) for New York City, had more than others, like (402) for the entire state of Nebraska.) Then the phone company would tell you which three-digit prefixes were for households (instead of businesses). And then, armed with those figures, you would call the last four digits randomly. It was not particularly complicated to identify a household. And at the time, over 99 percent of US households had landlines, so very few people would be missed by such a procedure. Lastly, in 1988, the now ubiquitous technology of caller-ID had not yet been made available to households. So a pollster would call a home number, and if someone was home, they picked up, because they didn't know who was calling. In short, random-digit dialing and a little cooperation from the phone company made it easy to get a random sample of the public.

How times have changed! While it is legal for polling companies to call cellphones for survey purposes, it is against US law for those numbers to be auto-dialed by a computer. So the numbers have to be dialed by hand, which takes more time, and costs survey companies more money. Fewer and fewer households – especially younger households, and non-white households – have landlines any more. And caller-ID is everywhere, which means that when you see a number from a polling organization – or simply any number not in your "contacts" list on your cellphone – you might think, "uh, no, I'm not picking up." Or maybe your reaction is the opposite – "Cool, a polling firm! Have I got an opinion for you!" Hopefully you see that even this last point makes pollsters wonder just how "representative" of the population as a whole, or the population of likely voters, their sample of people who answer the phone and agree to be interviewed happens to be.

> **YOUR TURN: Obtaining a random sample in the 2016 election season**
>
> News media organizations have a reputational interest in getting an accurate read of public opinion. And some even try to explain to their audience the process of how they try to guarantee that their samples are indeed representative.
>
> First, go watch the following video from Fox News, and note that the date of the segment is November 30, 2015 – before a single vote was cast during the 2016 primaries or general election: http://video.foxnews.com/v/4638558543001/?#sp=show-clips
>
> Now go watch a video segment from the day after the 2016 general election for an analysis of their polls in the aftermath of the election: http://video.foxnews.com/v/5203990293001/?playlist_id=2127351621001#sp=show-clips

7.4.3 A Note on the Effects of Sample Size

As the formula for the confidence interval indicates, the smaller the standard errors, the "tighter" our resulting confidence intervals will be; larger standard errors will produce "wider" confidence intervals. If we are interested in estimating population values, based on our samples, with as much precision as possible, then it is desirable to have tighter instead of wider confidence intervals.

How can we achieve this? From the formula for the standard error of the mean, it is clear through simple algebra that we can get a smaller quotient by having either a smaller numerator or a larger denominator. Because obtaining a smaller numerator – the sample standard deviation – is not something we can do in practice, we can consider whether it is possible to have a larger denominator – a larger sample size.

Larger sample sizes will reduce the size of the standard errors, and smaller sample sizes will increase the size of the standard errors. This, we hope, makes intuitive sense. If we have a large sample, then it should be easier to make inferences about the population of interest; smaller samples should produce less confidence about the population estimate.

In the preceding example, if instead of having our sample of 900, we had a much larger sample – say, 2500 – our standard errors would have been

$$\sigma_{\bar{Y}} = \frac{0.49}{\sqrt{2500}} = 0.010,$$

which is less than two-thirds the size of our actual standard errors of 0.016. You can do the math to see that going two standard errors of 0.010 in either direction produces a narrower interval than going two standard errors of 0.016. But note that the cost of reducing our error by about 1.2 percent in either direction is the addition of another 1600 respondents, and in many cases that reduction in error will not be worth the financial and time costs involved in obtaining all of those extra interviews.

Consider the opposite case. If, instead of interviewing 900 individuals, we interviewed only 400, then our standard errors would have been

$$\sigma_{\bar{Y}} = \frac{0.49}{\sqrt{400}} = 0.024,$$

which, when doubled to get our 95 percent confidence interval, would leave a plus-or-minus 0.048 (or 4.8 percent) in each direction.

We could be downright silly and obtain a random sample of only 64 people if we liked. That would generate some rather wide confidence intervals. The standard error would be

$$\sigma_{\bar{Y}} = \frac{0.49}{\sqrt{64}} = 0.061,$$

which, when doubled to get the 95 percent confidence interval, would leave a rather hefty plus-or-minus 0.122 (or 12.2 percent) in each direction. In this circumstance, we would guess that Trump's approval in the population was 43 percent, but we would be 95 percent confident that it was between 30.8 and 55.2 percent – and that alarmingly wide interval would be just too wide to be particularly informative.

In short, the answer to the question, "How big does my sample need to be?" is another question: "How tight do you want your confidence intervals to be?"

YOUR TURN: A margin of error of plus-or-minus 1 percent

If the pollsters in the above example for President Trump's approval ratings were willing to tolerate only a margin of error of plus-or-minus 1 percent (for a 95 percent confidence interval), how large would their sample size need to be? Assume, for the moment, that the sample standard deviation remains unchanged at $\sigma_{\bar{Y}} = 0.49$.

7.5 A LOOK AHEAD: EXAMINING RELATIONSHIPS BETWEEN VARIABLES

Let's take stock for a moment. In this book, we have emphasized that political science research involves evaluating causal explanations, which entails examining the relationships between two or more variables. Yet, in this chapter, all we have done is talk about the process of statistical inference with a *single* variable. This was a necessary tangent, because we had to teach you the logic of statistical inference – that is, how we use samples to learn something about an underlying population.

In Chapter 8, you will learn three different ways to move into the world of bivariate hypothesis testing. We will examine relationships between two variables, typically in a sample, and then make probabilistic assessments of the likelihood that those relationships exist in the population. The logic is identical to what you have just learned; we merely extend it to cover relationships between two variables. After that, in Chapter 9, you will learn one other way to conduct hypothesis tests involving two variables – the bivariate regression model.

CONCEPTS INTRODUCED IN THIS CHAPTER

- 68–95–99 rule – a useful characteristic of the normal distribution which states that moving ± 1, ± 2, and ± 3 standard deviations from the mean will leave 68, 95, and 99 percent of the distribution's area under the curve
- census – an accounting of a population
- central limit theorem – a fundamental result from statistics indicating that if one were to collect an infinite number of random samples and plot the resulting sample means, those sample means would be distributed normally around the true population mean

- confidence interval – a probabilistic statement about the likely value of a population characteristic based on the observations in a sample
- frequency distribution – a distribution of actual scores in a sample
- independent outcomes – two or more outcomes such that the realization of one of the outcomes does not affect the realization of the other outcomes
- normal distribution – a bell-shaped statistical distribution that can be entirely characterized by its mean and standard deviation
- outcome – the result of a random observation
- population – data for every possible relevant case
- random sample – a sample such that each member of the underlying population has an equal probability of being selected
- sample – a subset of cases that is drawn from an underlying population
- sampling distribution – a hypothetical distribution of sample means
- standard error of the mean – the standard deviation of the sampling distribution of sample means
- statistical inference – the process of using what we know about a sample to make probabilistic statements about the broader population

EXERCISES

1. Go to http://www.pollingreport.com and find a polling statistic that interests you most. Be sure to click on the "full details" option, where available, to get the sample size for the survey item. Then calculate the 95 percent and 99 percent confidence intervals for the population value of the statistic you have in mind, showing all of your work. Print the page from the web site and turn it in with your homework.

2. For the same survey item, what would happen to the confidence interval if the sample size were cut in half? What would happen instead if it were doubled? Assume that the sample standard deviation does not change and show your work.

3. Are larger sample sizes always better than smaller sample sizes? Explain your answer.

4. Refer back to Table 6.2, which shows the incumbent vote percentage in US presidential elections. Calculate the standard error of the mean for that distribution, and then construct the 95 percent confidence interval for the population mean. Show your work. What does the 95 percent confidence interval tell us in this particular case?

5. If we take a representative draw of 1000 respondents from the population of the United States for a particular survey question and obtain a 95 percent confidence margin, how many respondents would you need to draw from the population of Maine to obtain the same interval, assuming that the distribution of responses is the same for both populations?

8 Bivariate Hypothesis Testing

OVERVIEW

Once we have set up a hypothesis test and collected data, how do we evaluate what we have found? In this chapter we provide hands-on discussions of the basic building blocks used to make statistical inferences about the relationship between two variables. We deal with the often-misunderstood topic of "statistical significance" – focusing both on what it is and what it is not – as well as the nature of statistical uncertainty. We introduce three ways to examine relationships between two variables: tabular analysis, difference of means tests, and correlation coefficients. (We will introduce a fourth technique, two-variable regression analysis, in Chapter 9.)

8.1 BIVARIATE HYPOTHESIS TESTS AND ESTABLISHING CAUSAL RELATIONSHIPS

In the preceding chapters we introduced the core concepts of hypothesis testing. In this chapter we discuss the basic mechanics of hypothesis testing with three different examples of bivariate hypothesis testing. It is worth noting that, although this type of analysis was the main form of hypothesis testing in the professional journals up through the 1970s, it is seldom used as the *primary* means of hypothesis testing in the professional journals today.[1] This is the case because these techniques are good at helping us with clearing only the first of the four hurdles for establishing

---

[1] By definition, researchers conducting bivariate hypothesis tests are making one of two assumptions about the state of the world. They are assuming either that there are no other variables that are causally related to the dependent variable in question, or that, if there are such omitted variables, they are unrelated to the independent variable in the model. We will have much more to say about omitting independent variables from causal models in Chapter 10. For now, bear in mind that, as we have discussed in previous chapters, these assumptions rarely hold when we are describing the political world.

causal relationships. Namely, bivariate hypothesis tests help us to answer the question, "Are X and Y related?" By definition – "bivariate" means "two variables" – these tests cannot help us with the important question, "Have we controlled for all confounding variables Z that might make the observed association between X and Y spurious?"

Despite their limitations, the techniques covered in this chapter are important starting points for understanding the underlying logic of statistical hypothesis testing. In the sections that follow we discuss how one chooses which bivariate test to conduct and then provide detailed discussions of three such tests. Throughout this chapter, try to keep in mind the main purpose of this exercise: We are attempting to apply the lessons of the previous chapters to real-world data. We will eventually do this with more appropriate and more sophisticated tools, but the lessons that we learn in this chapter will be crucial to our understanding of these more advanced methods. Put simply, we are trying to get up and walk in the complicated world of hypothesis testing with real-world data. Once we have mastered walking, we will then begin to work on running with more advanced techniques.

8.2   CHOOSING THE RIGHT BIVARIATE HYPOTHESIS TEST

As we discussed in previous chapters, and especially in Chapters 5, 6, and 7, researchers make a number of critical decisions before they test their hypotheses. Once they have collected their data and want to conduct a bivariate hypothesis test, they need to consider the nature of their dependent and independent variables. As we discussed in Chapter 6, we can classify variables in terms of the types of values that cases take on. Table 8.1 shows four different scenarios for testing a bivariate hypothesis; which one is most appropriate depends on the variable type of the independent variable and the dependent variable. For each case, we have listed one or more appropriate type of bivariate hypothesis tests. In cases in which we can

Table 8.1 Variable types and appropriate bivariate hypothesis tests			
		Independent variable type	
		Categorical	Continuous
Dependent variable type	Categorical	*tabular analysis*	probit/logit (Ch. 12)
	Continuous	*difference of means; regression extensions* (Ch. 11)	*correlation coefficient; two-variable regression model* (Ch. 9)

Note: Tests in italics are discussed in this chapter.

describe both the independent and dependent variables as categorical, we use a form of analysis referred to as **tabular analysis** to test our hypothesis. When the dependent variable is continuous and the independent variable is categorical, we use either a **difference of means test** or a regression model (we show some examples of regression models with a continuous dependent variable and categorical independent variables in Chapter 11). When the independent variable is continuous and the dependent variable is categorical, analysts typically use either a probit or logit model. (These types of statistical models are discussed in Chapter 12.) Finally, when both the dependent and independent variables are continuous, we use a **correlation coefficient** in this chapter, and, in Chapter 9, we will discuss the bivariate regression model.

8.3   ALL ROADS LEAD TO p

One common element across a wide range of statistical hypothesis tests is the p-value (the p stands for "probability"). This value, ranging between 0 and 1, is the closest thing that we have to a bottom line in statistics. But it is often misunderstood and misused. In this section we discuss the basic logic of the p-value and relate it back to our discussion in Chapter 7 of using sample data to make inferences about an underlying population.

8.3.1   The Logic of p-Values

If we think back to the four principles for establishing causal relationships that were discussed in Chapter 3, the third hurdle is the question "Is there covariation between X and Y?" To answer this question, we need to apply standards to real-world data for determining whether there appears to be a relationship between our two variables, the independent variable X and the dependent variable Y. The tests listed in the cells in Table 8.1 are commonly accepted tests for each possible combination of variable type. In each of these tests, we follow a common logic: We compare the actual relationship between X and Y in sample data with what we would expect to find if X and Y *were not* related in the underlying population. The *more different* the empirically observed relationship is from what we would expect to find if there were *not* a relationship, the more confidence we have that X and Y are related in the population. The logic of this inference from sample to population is the same as what we used in Chapter 7 to make inferences about the population mean from sample data.

The statistic that is most commonly associated with this type of logical exercise is the *p*-value. The p-value, which ranges between 0 and 1, is the probability that we would see the relationship that we are finding because of random chance. Put another way, the p-value tells us the probability that we would see the observed relationship between the two variables in our sample data if there were truly no relationship between them in the unobserved population. Thus, the lower the p-value, the greater confidence we have that there *is* a systematic relationship between the two variables for which we estimated the particular p-value.

One common characteristic across most statistical techniques is that, for a particular measured relationship, the more data on which the measurement is based, the lower our p-value will be. This is consistent with one of the lessons of Chapter 7 about sample size: The larger the sample size, the more confident we can be that our sample will more accurately represent the population.[2] (See Section 7.4.2 for a reminder.)

8.3.2 The Limitations of p-Values

Although p-values are powerful indicators of whether or not two variables are related, they are limited. In this section we review those limitations. It is important that we also understand what a p-value is not: The logic of a p-value is not reversible. In other words, $p = 0.001$ does not mean that there is a 0.999 chance that something systematic is going on. Also, it is important to realize that, although a p-value tells us something about our confidence that there is a relationship between two variables, it does not tell us whether that relationship is causal.

In addition, it might be tempting to assume that, when a p-value is very close to zero, this indicates that the relationship between X and Y is very *strong*. This is not necessarily true (though it might be true). As we previously noted, p-values represent our degree of confidence that there is a relationship in the underlying population. So we should naturally expect smaller p-values as our sample sizes increase. But a larger sample size does not magically make a relationship stronger; it *does* increase our confidence that the observed relationship in our sample accurately represents the underlying population. We saw a similar type of relationship in Chapter 7 when we calculated standard errors. Because the number of cases is in the denominator of the standard error formula, an increased number of cases leads to a smaller standard error and a more narrow confidence interval for our inferences about the population.

Another limitation of p-values is that they do not directly reflect the quality of the measurement procedure for our variables. Thus, if we are

---

[2] Also, the smaller the sample size, the more likely it is that we will get a result that is not very representative of the population.

more confident in our measurement, we should be more confident in a particular p-value. The flip side of this is that, if we are not very confident in our measurement of one or both of our variables, we should be less confident in a particular p-value.

Finally, we should keep in mind that p-values are always based on the assumption that you are drawing a random sample from the underlying population. Mathematically, this is expressed as

$$p_i = P \quad \forall \, i.$$

This translates into "the probability of an individual case from our population ending up in our sample, p_i, is assumed to equal the same value, P, for all of the individual cases i." If this assumption were valid, we would have a truly random sample. Because this is a standard that is almost never met, we should use this in our assessment of a particular p-value. The further we are from a truly random sample, the less confidence we should have in our p-value.

8.3.3 From p-Values to Statistical Significance

As we outlined in the preceding section, lower p-values increase our confidence that there is indeed a relationship between the two variables in question. A common way of referring to such a situation is to state that the relationship between the two variables is **statistically significant**. Although this type of statement has a ring of authoritative finality, it is always a qualified statement. In other words, an assertion of statistical significance depends on a number of other factors. One of these factors is the set of assumptions from the previous section. "Statistical significance" is achieved only to the extent that the assumptions underlying the calculation of the p-value hold. In addition, there are a variety of different standards for what is a statistically significant p-value. Most social scientists use the standard of a p-value of 0.05. If p is less than 0.05, they consider a relationship to be statistically significant. Others use a more stringent standard of 0.01, or a more loose standard of 0.1.[3]

We cannot emphasize strongly enough that finding that X and Y have a statistically significant relationship does *not* necessarily mean that the relationship between X and Y is strong or, especially, that the relationship is causal. To evaluate whether or not a relationship is strong, we need to use our substantive knowledge about what it means for the value of Y to change by a particular amount. We will discuss assessments of the strength

---

[3] More recently, there has been a trend toward reporting the estimated p-value and letting readers make their own assessments of statistical significance.

of relationships in greater detail in Chapter 10. To evaluate the case for a causal relationship, we need to evaluate how well our theory has performed in terms of all four of the causal hurdles from Chapter 3.

8.3.4   The Null Hypothesis and p-Values

In Chapter 1 we introduced the concept of the null hypothesis: A null hypothesis is a theory-based statement about what we would expect to observe if our theory were incorrect. Thus, following the logic that we previously outlined, if our theory-driven hypothesis is that there is covariation between X and Y, then the corresponding null hypothesis is that there is no covariation between X and Y. In this context, another interpretation of the p-value is that it conveys the level of confidence with which we can reject the null hypothesis.

8.4   THREE BIVARIATE HYPOTHESIS TESTS

We now turn to three specific bivariate hypothesis tests. In each case, we are testing for whether there is a relationship between X and Y. We are doing this with sample data, and then, based on what we find, making inferences about what is likely to be true in the underlying population.

8.4.1   Example 1: Tabular Analysis

Tabular presentations of data on two variables are still used quite widely. In the more recent political science literature, scholars use them as stepping stones on the way to multivariate analyses. It is worth noting at this point in the process that, in tables, it is customary for the dependent variable to be displayed in the rows, and the independent variable to be displayed in the columns. Any time that you see a table, it is very important to take some time to make sure that you understand what information is being conveyed. We can break this into the following three-step process:

1. Figure out what the variables are that define the rows and columns of the table.
2. Figure out what the individual cell values represent. Sometimes they will be the number of cases that take on the particular row and column values; other times the cell values will be proportions (ranging from 0 to 1.0) or percentages (ranging from 0 to 100). Less commonly, cell values can also represent the proportion or percentage of cases in the whole table. If this is the case, it is critical that you figure out whether the

	Table 8.2 Union households and vote in the 2016 US presidential election		
Candidate	Not from a union household	From a union household	Row total
Clinton	51.2	58.1	52.2
Trump	48.8	41.9	47.8
Column total	100.0	100.0	100.0

Note: Cell entries are column percentages.

researcher calculated the percentages or proportions for the entire table or for each column or row.

3. Figure out what, if any, general patterns you see in the table.

Let's go through these steps with Table 8.2. In this table we are testing the theory that affiliation with trade unions makes people more likely to support left-leaning candidates. We can tell from the title and the column and row headings that this table is comparing the votes of people from union households with those not from union households in the 2016 US presidential election. We can use the information in this table to test the hypothesis that voters from union households were more likely to support Democratic Party presidential candidate Hillary Clinton.[4] As the first step in reading this table, we determine that the columns indicate values for the independent variable (whether or not the individual was from a union household) and that the rows indicate values for the dependent variable (presidential vote). The second step is fairly straightforward; the table contains a footnote that tells us that the "cell entries are column percentages." This is the easiest format for pursuing step 3, because the column percentages correspond to the comparison that we want to make. We want to compare the presidential votes of people from union households with the presidential votes of people not from union households. The pattern is fairly clear: People from the union households overwhelmingly supported Clinton (58.1 percent for Clinton and 41.9 percent for Trump), whereas people from the nonunion households only marginally favored Clinton (51.2 percent for Clinton and 48.8 percent for Trump). If we think in terms of independent (X) and dependent (Y) variables, the comparison that we have made is between the distribution of the dependent variable ($Y =$ Presidential Vote) across values of the independent variable ($X =$ Type of Household).

---

[4] What do you think about the operationalization of these two variables? How well does it stand up to what we discussed in Chapter 5?

> **YOUR TURN: Assessing the theory behind Table 8.2**
>
> Take a moment to assess this theory behind Table 8.2 in terms of the first two of the four hurdles that we discussed in Chapter 3. The theory is that affiliation with trade unions makes people more likely to support left-leaning candidates. The causal mechanism is that left-leaning candidates tend to support policies favored by trade unions, and therefore voters from union households will favor these left-leaning candidates. Is this credible? What about hurdle 2? Can we rule out the possibility that support for left-leaning candidates makes one more likely to be affiliated with a trade union?

In Table 8.2, we follow the simple convention of placing the values of the independent variable in the columns and the values of the dependent variable in the rows. Then, by calculating column percentages for the cell values, this makes comparing across the columns straightforward. It is wise to adhere to these norms, because it is the easiest way to make the comparison that we want, and because it is the way many readers will expect to see the information.

In our next example we are going to go step-by-step through a bivariate test of the hypothesis that gender (X) is related to vote (Y) in US presidential elections. To test this hypothesis about gender and presidential vote, we are going to use data from the 2016 American National Election Study (ANES from here on). This is an appropriate set of data for testing this hypothesis because these data are from a randomly selected sample of cases from the underlying population of interest (US adults). In Table 8.3, we see the results of interest for this hypothesis test. A quick glance at the column percentages in this table seems to confirm our expectations – male respondents did indeed vote for Trump more than Clinton while female respondents voted more for Clinton than for Trump.

Let's back up a step here. Think briefly about the measurement of the variables of interest and what we would expect to find if there were no relationship between the two variables. Table 8.4 shows partial information from a hypothetical example in which we know that 48.0 percent of our sample respondents report having voted for Donald Trump, and 52.0

Table 8.3 Gender and vote in the 2016 US presidential election

Candidate	Male	Female	Row total
Clinton	47.2	56.2	52.0
Trump	58.8	43.8	48.0
Column total	100.0	100.0	100.0

Note: Cell entries are column percentages.

Table 8.4 Gender and vote in the 2016 US presidential election: hypothetical scenario

Candidate	Male	Female	Row total
Clinton	?	?	52.0
Trump	?	?	48.0
Column total	100.0	100.0	100.0

Note: Cell entries are column percentages.

Table 8.5 Gender and vote in the 2016 US presidential election: expectations for hypothetical scenario if there were no relationship

Candidate	Male	Female	Row total
Clinton	52.0	52.0	52.0
Trump	48.0	48.0	48.0
Column total	100.0	100.0	100.0

Note: Cell entries are column percentages.

percent of our sample respondents report having voted for Hillary Clinton. If there were no relationship between gender and presidential voting in 2016, consider what we would expect to see given what we know from Table 8.4. In other words, what values should replace the question marks in Table 8.4 if there were no relationship between our independent variable (X) and dependent variable (Y)?

If there were not a relationship between gender and presidential vote, then we should expect to see no major differences between males and females in terms of how they voted for Donald Trump and Hillary Clinton. Because we know from Table 8.3 that 48.0 percent of our cases voted for Trump and 52.0 percent for Clinton, what should we expect to see for males and for females? We should expect to see the same proportions of males and females voting for each candidate. In other words, we should expect to see the question marks replaced with the values in Table 8.5. This table displays the expected cell values for the null hypothesis that there is no relationship between gender and presidential vote. Think through this a minute. Were you tempted to say that the "?" marks in Table 8.4 should all be replaced by "50.0"? That would be wrong. Why? Because we know from Table 8.3 that 52.0 percent of all individuals reported voting for Clinton. So, if there is no relationship between gender and vote, we should expect 52.0 for both men and women.

Table 8.6 shows the total number of respondents who fit into each column and row from the 2016 ANES. If we do the calculations, we can

Table 8.6 Gender and vote in the 2016 US presidential election

Candidate	Male	Female	Row total
Clinton	?	?	1269
Trump	?	?	1171
Total	1128	1312	2440

Note: Cell entries are number of respondents.

Table 8.7 Gender and vote in the 2016 US presidential election: calculating the expected cell values if gender and presidential vote were unrelated

Candidate	Male	Female
Clinton	(52% of 1128) $= 0.52 \times 1128 = 586.56$	(52% of 1312) $= 0.52 \times 1312 = 682.24$
Trump	(48% of 1128) $= 0.48 \times 1128 = 541.44$	(48% of 1312) $= 0.48 \times 1312 = 629.76$

Note: Cell entries are expectation calculations if these two variables were unrelated.

Table 8.8 Gender and vote in the 2016 US presidential election

Candidate	Male	Female	Row total
Clinton	532	737	1269
Trump	596	575	1171
Column total	1128	1312	2440

Note: Cell entries are number of respondents.

see that the numbers in the rightmost column of Table 8.6 correspond with the percentages from Table 8.4. We can now combine the information from Table 8.6 with our expectations from Table 8.5 to calculate the number of respondents that we would expect to see in each cell if gender and presidential vote were unrelated. We display these calculations in Table 8.7. In Table 8.8, we see the actual number of respondents from the survey that fell into each of the four cells.

Finally, in Table 8.9, we compare the observed number of cases in each cell (O) with the number of cases that we would expect to see if there were no relationship between our independent and dependent variables (E).

We can see a pattern. Among males, the proportion observed voting for Clinton is lower than what we would expect if there were no relationship between the two variables. Also, among men, the proportion

Table 8.9 Gender and vote in the 2016 US presidential election		
Candidate	Male	Female
Clinton	$O = 532; E = 586.56$	$O = 737; E = 682.24$
Trump	$O = 596; E = 541.44$	$O = 575; E = 629.76$

Note: Cell entries are the number observed (O); and the number expected if there were no relationship (E).

voting for Trump is higher than what we would expect if there were no relationship. For females this pattern is reversed – the proportion voting for Clinton (Trump) is higher (lower) than we would expect if there were no relationship between gender and vote for US president. The pattern of these differences is in line with the theory that women support Democratic Party candidates more than men do. Although these differences are present, we have not yet determined that they are of such a magnitude that we should now have increased confidence in our theory. In other words, we want to know whether or not these differences are statistically significant.

To answer this question, we turn to the **chi-squared (χ^2) test for tabular association**. Karl Pearson originally developed this test when he was testing theories about the influence of nature versus nurture at the beginning of the twentieth century. His formula for the χ^2 statistic is

$$\chi^2 = \sum \frac{(O - E)^2}{E},$$

where O is the observed number of cases in each cell, E is the expected number in each cell if there were no relationship, and hence $(O - E)^2$ are the numbers in the cells in Table 8.9.

The summation sign in this formula signifies that we sum over each cell in the table; so a 2×2 table would have four cells to add up. If we think about an individual cell's contribution to this formula, we can see the underlying logic of the χ^2 test. If the value observed, O, is exactly equal to the expected value if there were no relationship between the two variables, E, then we would get a contribution of zero from that cell to the overall formula (because $O - E$ would be zero). Thus, if all observed values were exactly equal to the values that we expect if there were no relationship between the two variables, then $\chi^2 = 0$. The more the O values differ from the E values, the greater the value will be for χ^2. Because the numerator on the right-hand side of the χ^2 formula $(O - E)$ is squared, any difference between O and E will contribute positively to the overall χ^2 value.

Here are the calculations for χ^2 made with the values in Table 8.9:

$$\chi^2 = \sum \frac{(O - E)^2}{E}$$

$$= \frac{(532 - 586.56)^2}{586.56} + \frac{(737 - 682.24)^2}{682.24} + \frac{(596 - 541.44)^2}{541.44} + \frac{(575 - 629.76)^2}{629.76}$$

$$= \frac{2976.8}{586.56} + \frac{2998.7}{682.24} + \frac{2976.8}{541.44} + \frac{2998.7}{629.76}$$

$$= 5.075 + 5.498 + 4.395 + 4.762 = 19.73.$$

So our calculated value of χ^2 is 19.73 based on the observed data. What do we do with this? We need to compare that 19.73 with some predetermined standard, called a **critical value**, of χ^2. If our calculated value is greater than the critical value, then we conclude that there is a relationship between the two variables; and if the calculated value is less than the critical value, we cannot make such a conclusion.

How do we obtain this critical value? First, we need a piece of information known as the **degrees of freedom** (df) for our test.[5] In this case, the df calculation is very simple: df $= (r - 1)(c - 1)$, where r is the number of rows in the table, and c is the number of columns in the table. In the example in Table 8.9, there are two rows and two columns, so df $= (2 - 1)(2 - 1) = 1$.

You can find a table with critical values of χ^2 in Appendix A. If we adopt the standard p-value of 0.05, we see that the critical value of χ^2 for df $= 1$ is 3.841. Therefore a calculated χ^2 value of 19.73 is well over the minimum value needed to achieve a p-value of 0.05. In fact, continuing out in this table, we can see that we have exceeded the critical value needed to achieve a p-value of 0.001.

At this point, we have established that the relationship between our two variables meets a conventionally accepted standard of statistical significance (i.e., $p < 0.05$). Although this result is supportive of our hypothesis, we have not yet established a causal relationship between gender and presidential voting. To see this, think back to the four hurdles along the route to establishing causal relationships that we discussed in Chapter 3. Thus far, we have cleared the third hurdle, by demonstrating that X (gender) and Y (vote) covary. From what we know about politics, we can easily cross hurdle 1, "Is there a credible causal mechanism that links X to Y?" Women might be more likely to vote for candidates like Clinton because, among other things, women depend on the social safety net of the welfare state more than men do. If we turn to hurdle 2, "Can we rule out the possibility that Y could cause X?," we can pretty easily see that we

---

[5] We define degrees of freedom in the next section.

Table 8.10 Union households and vote in the 2016 US presidential election			
Candidate	Not from a union household	From a union household	Row total
Clinton	1068	218	1286
Trump	1019	157	1176
Column total	2087	375	2462

Note: Cell entries are number of respondents.

have met this standard through basic logic. We know with confidence that changing one's vote does not lead to a change in one's gender. We hit the most serious bump in the road to establishing causality for this relationship when we encounter hurdle 4, "Have we controlled for all confounding variables Z that might make the association between X and Y spurious?" Unfortunately, our answer here is "no." In fact, with a bivariate analysis, we cannot know whether some other variable Z is relevant because, by definition, there are only two variables in such an analysis. So, until we see evidence that Z variables have been controlled for, our scorecard for this causal claim is [y y y n].

> **YOUR TURN: Is the relationship between union household affiliation and vote significant?**
>
> In Table 8.10 we present the raw numbers that generated Table 8.2. Is this relationship statistically significant?

8.4.2 Example 2: Difference of Means

In our second example, we examine a situation in which we have a continuous dependent variable and a categorical independent variable. In this type of bivariate hypothesis test, we are looking to see if the means are different across the values of the independent variable. We follow the basic logic of hypothesis testing: comparing our real-world data from our sample with what we would expect to find if there were no relationship between our independent and dependent variables in the population. We use the sample means and standard deviations to make inferences about the unobserved population.

Our theory in this section will come from the study of parliamentary governments. When political scientists study phenomena across different forms of government, one of the fundamental distinctions that they draw between different types of democracies is whether the regime is parliamentary or not. A democratic regime is labeled "parliamentary" when the lower house of the legislature is the most powerful branch of government and directly selects the head of the government.[6] One of the interesting features of most parliamentary regimes is that a vote in the lower house of the legislature can remove the government from power. As a result, political scientists have been very interested in the determinants of how long parliamentary governments last when the possibility of such a vote exists.

One factor that is an important difference across parliamentary democracies is whether the party or parties that are in government occupy a majority of the seats in the legislature.[7] By definition, the opposition can vote out of office a minority government, because a minority government does not control a majority of the seats in the legislature. Thus a pretty reasonable theory about government duration is that majority governments will last longer than minority governments.

We can move from this theory to a hypothesis test by using a data set produced by Michael D. McDonald and Silvia M. Mendes titled "Governments, 1950–1995." Their data set covers governments from 21 Western countries. For the sake of comparability, we will limit our sample to those governments that were formed after an election.[8] Our independent variable, "Government Type," takes on one of two values: "majority government" or "minority government." Our dependent variable, "Government Duration," is a continuous variable measuring the number of days that each government lasted in office. Although this variable has a hypothetical

---

[6] An important part of research design is determining which cases are and are not covered by our theory. In this case, our theory, which we will introduce shortly, is going to apply to only parliamentary democracies. As an example, consider whether or not the United States and the United Kingdom fit this description at the beginning of 2007. In the United States in 2007, the head of government was President George W. Bush. Because Bush was selected by a presidential election and not by the lower branch of government, we can already see that the United States at the beginning of 2007 is not covered by our theory. In the United Kingdom, we might be tempted at first to say that the head of government at the beginning of 2007 was Queen Elizabeth II. But, if we consider that British queens and kings have been mostly ceremonial in UK politics for some time now, we then realize that the head of government was the prime minister, Tony Blair, who was selected from the lower house of the legislature, the House of Commons. If we further consider the relative power of the House of Commons compared with the other branches of government at the beginning of 2007, we can see that the United Kingdom met our criteria for being classified as parliamentary.

[7] Researchers usually define a party as being in government if its members occupy one or more cabinet posts, whereas parties not in government are in opposition.

[8] We have also limited the analyses to cases in which the governments had a legal maximum of four years before they must call for new elections. These limitations mean that, strictly speaking, we are only able to make inferences about the population of cases that also fit these criteria.

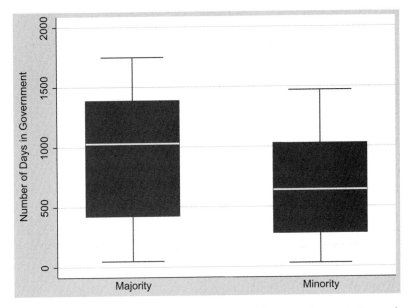

Figure 8.1 Box–whisker plot of government duration for majority and minority governments

range from 1 day to 1461 days, the actual data vary from an Italian government that lasted for 31 days in 1953 to a Dutch government that lasted for 1749 days in the late 1980s and early 1990s.

To get a better idea of the data that we are comparing, we can turn to two graphs that we introduced in Chapter 6 for viewing the distribution of continuous variables. Figure 8.1 presents a box–whisker plot of government duration for minority and majority governments, and Figure 8.2 presents a kernel density plot of government duration for minority and majority governments. From both of these plots, it appears that majority governments last longer than minority governments.

To determine whether the differences from these figures are statistically significant, we turn to a difference of means test. In this test we compare what we have seen in the two figures with what we would expect if there were no relationship between government type and government duration. If there were no relationship between these two variables, then the world would be such that the duration of governments of both types were drawn from the same underlying distribution. If this were the case, the mean or average value of government duration would be the same for minority and majority governments.

To test the hypothesis that these means are drawn from the same underlying distribution, we use another test developed by Karl Pearson

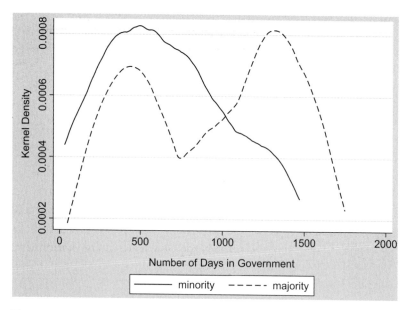

Figure 8.2 Kernel density plot of government duration for majority and minority governments

for these purposes. The test statistic for this is known as a *t*-test because it follows the *t*-distribution. The formula for this particular *t*-test is

$$t = \frac{\bar{Y}_1 - \bar{Y}_2}{\text{se}(\bar{Y}_1 - \bar{Y}_2)},$$

where $\bar{Y}_1$ is the mean of the dependent variable for the first value of the independent variable, $\bar{Y}_2$ is the mean of the dependent variable for the second value of the independent variable, and se(...) is the standard error of the difference between the two means (see below). We can see from this formula that the greater the difference between the mean value of the dependent variable across the two values of the independent variable, the further the value of *t* will be from zero.

In Chapter 7 we introduced the notion of a standard error, which is a measure of uncertainty about a statistical estimate. The basic logic of a standard error is that the larger it is, the more uncertainty (or less confidence) we have in our ability to make precise statements. Similarly, the smaller the standard error, the greater our confidence about our ability to make precise statements about the population.

To better understand the contribution of the top and bottom parts of the *t*-calculation for a difference of means, look again at Figures 8.1 and 8.2. The further apart the two means are and the less dispersed the

Table 8.11 Government type and government duration			
Government type	Number of observations	Mean duration	Standard deviation
Majority	124	930.5	466.1
Minority	53	674.4	421.4
Combined	177	853.8	467.1

distributions (as measured by the standard deviations s_1 and s_2), the greater confidence we have that $\bar{Y}_1$ and $\bar{Y}_2$ are different from each other.

Table 8.11 presents the descriptive statistics for government duration by government type. From the values displayed in this table we can calculate the t-test statistic for our hypothesis test. The standard error of the difference between two means ($\bar{Y}_1$ and $\bar{Y}_2$), se($\bar{Y}_1 - \bar{Y}_2$), is calculated from the following formula:

$$se(\bar{Y}_1 - \bar{Y}_2) = \sqrt{\left(\frac{(n_1 - 1)s_1^2 + (n_2 - 1)s_2^2}{n_1 + n_2 - 2}\right) \times \sqrt{\left(\frac{1}{n_1} + \frac{1}{n_2}\right)}},$$

where n_1 and n_2 are the sample sizes, and s_1^2 and s_2^2 are the sample variances. If we label the number of days in government for majority governments Y_1 and the number of days in government for minority governments Y_2, then we can calculate the standard error as

$$se(\bar{Y}_1 - \bar{Y}_2) = \sqrt{\left(\frac{(124 - 1)(466.1)^2 + (53 - 1)(421.4)^2}{124 + 53 - 2}\right) \times \sqrt{\left(\frac{1}{124} + \frac{1}{53}\right)}}$$
$$= 74.39.$$

Now that we have the standard error, we can calculate the t-statistic:

$$t = \frac{\bar{Y}_1 - \bar{Y}_2}{se(\bar{Y}_1 - \bar{Y}_2)} = \frac{930.5 - 674.4}{74.39} = \frac{256.1}{74.39} = 3.44.$$

Now that we have calculated this t-statistic, we need one more piece of information before we can get to our p-value. This is called the degrees of freedom (df). Degrees of freedom reflect the basic idea that we will gain confidence in an observed pattern as the amount of data on which that pattern is based increases. In other words, as our sample size increases, we become more confident about our ability to say things about the underlying population. If we turn to Appendix B, which is a table of critical values for t, we can see that it reflects this logic. This table also follows the same basic logic as the χ^2 table. The way to read such a table is that the columns are defined by targeted p-values, and, to achieve a particular target p-value, you need to obtain a particular value of t. The rows in the t-table indicate the number of degrees of freedom. As the number of degrees of freedom goes up, the t-statistic we need to obtain a particular p-value goes down. We calculate the degrees of freedom for a difference of means t-statistic based on the sum of total sample size minus two. Thus our degrees of freedom is

$$n_1 + n_2 - 2 = 124 + 53 - 2 = 175.$$

From the p-value, we can look across the row for which df $= 100$ and see the minimum t-value needed to achieve each targeted value of p.[9] In the second column of the t-table, we can see that, to have a p-value of 0.10 (meaning that there is a 10 percent, or 1 in 10, chance that we would see this relationship randomly in our sample if there were no relationship between X and Y in the underlying population), we must have a t-statistic greater than or equal to 1.29. Because $3.44 > 1.29$, we can proceed to the next column for $p = 0.05$ and see that 3.44 is also greater than 1.66. In fact, if we go all the way to the end of the row for df $= 100$, we can see that our t-statistic is greater than 3.174, which is the t-value needed to achieve $p = 0.001$ (meaning that there is a 0.1 percent, or 1 in 1000, chance that we would see this relationship randomly in our sample if there were no relationship between X and Y in the underlying population). This indicates that we have very confidently cleared the third hurdle in our assessment of whether or not there is a causal relationship between majority status and government duration.

8.4.3 Example 3: Correlation Coefficient

In our final example of bivariate hypothesis testing we look at a situation in which both the independent variable and the dependent variable are continuous. We test the hypothesis that there is a positive relationship between economic growth and incumbent-party fortunes in US presidential elections.

In Chapter 6 we discussed the variation (or variance) of a single variable, and in Chapter 1 we introduced the concept of covariation. In the three examples that we have looked at so far, we have found there to be covariation between being from a union household and presidential vote, between gender and presidential vote, and between government type and government duration. All of these examples used at least one categorical variable. By contrast, when we have an independent variable and a dependent variable that are both continuous, we can visually detect covariation

---

[9] Although our degrees of freedom equal 175, we are using the row for df $= 100$ to get a rough idea of the p-value. With a computer program, we can calculate an exact p-value.

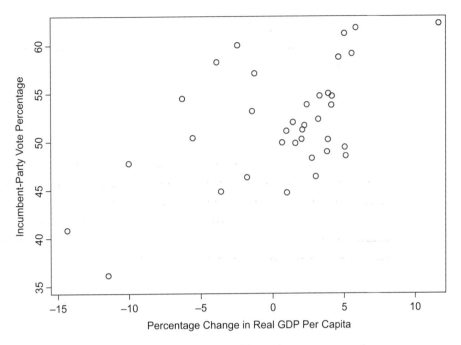

Figure 8.3 Scatter plot of change in GDP and incumbent-party vote share

pretty easily in graphs. Consider the graph in Figure 8.3, which shows a scatter plot of incumbent vote and economic growth. Scatter plots are useful for getting an initial look at the relationship between two continuous variables. Any time that you examine a scatter plot, you should determine what the axes are and then what each point in the scatter plot represents. In these plots, the dependent variable (in this case, incumbent vote) should be displayed on the vertical axis while the independent variable (in this case, economic growth) should be displayed on the horizontal axis. Each point in the scatter plot should represent the values of the two variables for an individual case. So, in Figure 8.3, we are looking at the values of incumbent vote and economic growth for each US presidential election year on which we have data for both variables.

When we look at this graph, we want to assess whether or not we see a pattern. Since our theory implies that the independent variable causes the dependent variable, we should move from left to right on the horizontal axis (representing increasing values of the independent variable) and see whether there is a corresponding increase or decrease in the values of the dependent variable. In the case of Figure 8.3, as we move from left to right, we generally see a pattern of increasing values on the vertical axis. This indicates that, as expected by our theory, when the economy is doing better (more rightward values on the horizontal axis), we also tend to see higher vote percentages for the incumbent party in US presidential elections (higher values on the vertical axis).

Covariance is a statistical way of summarizing the general pattern of association (or the lack thereof) between two continuous variables. The formula for covariance between two variables X and Y is

$$\text{cov}_{XY} = \frac{\sum_{i=1}^{n}(X_i - \bar{X})(Y_i - \bar{Y})}{n - 1}.$$

To better understand the intuition behind the covariance formula, it is helpful to think of individual cases in terms of their values relative to the mean of X ($\bar{X}$) and the mean of Y ($\bar{Y}$). If an individual case has a value for the independent variable that is greater than the mean of X (such that $X_i - \bar{X} > 0$) and its value for the dependent variable is greater than the mean of Y (such that $Y_i - \bar{Y} > 0$), that case's contribution to the numerator in the covariance equation will be positive. If an individual case has a value for the independent variable that is less than the mean of X (such that $X_i - \bar{X} < 0$) and a value of the dependent variable that is less than the mean of Y (such that $Y_i - \bar{Y} < 0$), that case's contribution to the numerator in the covariance equation will also be positive, because multiplying two negative numbers yields a positive product. If a case has a combination of one value greater than the mean and one value less than the mean, its contribution to the numerator in the covariance equation will be negative because multiplying a positive number by a negative number yields a negative product. Figure 8.4 illustrates this; we see the same plot of

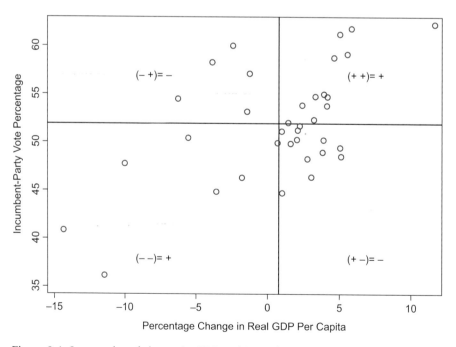

Figure 8.4 Scatter plot of change in GDP and incumbent-party vote share with mean-delimited quadrants

growth versus incumbent vote, but with the addition of lines showing the mean value of each variable. In each of these mean-delimited quadrants we can see the contribution of the cases to the numerator. If a plot contains cases in mostly the upper-right and lower-left quadrants, the covariance will tend to be positive. On the other hand, if a plot contains cases in mostly the lower-right and upper-left quadrants, the covariance will tend to be negative. If a plot contains a nearly equal balance of cases in all four quadrants, the covariance calculation will be close to zero because the positive and negative values will cancel each other out. When the covariance between two variables is positive, we describe this situation as a positive relationship between the variables, and when the covariation between two variables is negative, we describe this situation as a negative relationship.

Table 8.12 presents the calculations for each year in the covariance formula for the data that we presented in Figure 8.4. For each year, we have started out by calculating the difference between each X and $\bar{X}$ and the difference between each Y and $\bar{Y}$. If we begin with the year 1876, we can see that the value for growth (X_{1876}) was 5.11 and the value for vote (Y_{1876}) was 48.516. The value for growth is greater than the mean and the value for vote is less than the mean, $X_{1876} - \bar{X} = 5.11 - 0.7635 = 4.3465$ and $Y_{1876} - \bar{Y} = 48.516 - 51.92569 = -3.409691$. In Figure 8.4, the point for 1876 is in the lower-right quadrant. When we multiply these two mean deviations together, we get $(X_{1876} - \bar{X})(Y_{1876} - \bar{Y}) = -14.82022$.

We repeat this same calculation for every case (presidential election year). Each negative calculation like this contributes evidence that the overall relationship between X and Y is negative, whereas each positive calculation contributes evidence that the overall relationship between X and Y is positive. The sum across all 36 election years in Table 8.12 is 606.51276, indicating that the positive values have outweighed the negative values. When we divide this by 35, $(n - 1)$, we have the sample covariance, which equals 17.3289. This tells us that we have a positive relationship (because $17.3289 > 0$), but it does not tell us how confident we can be that this relationship is different from what we would see if our independent and dependent variables were not related in our underlying population of interest. To see this, we turn to a third test developed by Karl Pearson, Pearson's correlation coefficient. This is also known as **Pearson's r**, the formula for which is

$$r = \frac{\text{cov}_{XY}}{\sqrt{\text{var}_X \text{var}_Y}}.$$

Table 8.13 is a covariance table. In a covariance table, the cells across the main diagonal (from upper-left to lower-right) are cells for which the column and the row reference the same variable. In this case the cell entry

Table 8.12 Contributions of individual election years to the covariance calculation					
Year	Growth (X_i)	Vote (Y_i)	$X_i - \bar{X}$	$Y_i - \bar{Y}$	$(X_i - \bar{X})(Y_i - \bar{Y})$
1876	5.11	48.516	4.3465	−3.409691	−14.82022
1880	3.879	50.220	3.1155	−1.705689	−5.314074
1884	1.589	49.846	0.8255	−2.079689	−1.716784
1888	−5.553	50.414	−6.3165	−1.511689	9.548581
1892	2.763	48.268	1.9995	−3.657688	−7.313548
1896	−10.024	47.760	−10.7875	−4.165692	44.9374
1900	−1.425	53.171	−2.1885	1.245311	−2.725364
1904	−2.421	60.006	−3.1845	8.080311	−25.73175
1908	−6.281	54.483	−7.0445	2.557312	−18.01498
1912	4.164	54.708	3.4005	2.78231	9.461246
1916	2.229	51.682	1.4655	−0.2436908	−0.3571289
1920	−11.463	36.148	−12.2265	−15.77769	192.9059
1924	−3.872	58.263	−4.6355	6.33731	−29.3766
1928	4.623	58.756	3.8595	6.83031	26.36158
1932	−14.35	40.851	−15.1135	−11.07469	167.3773
1936	11.682	62.226	10.9185	10.30031	112.464
1940	3.913	54.983	3.1495	3.057312	9.629004
1944	4.122	53.778	3.3585	1.85231	6.220983
1948	3.214	52.319	2.4505	0.3933102	0.9638067
1952	0.997	44.710	0.2335	−7.215691	−1.684864
1956	−1.252	57.094	−2.0155	5.168312	−10.41673
1960	0.674	49.913	−0.0895	−2.012692	0.1801359
1964	5.03	61.203	4.2665	9.277309	39.58164
1968	5.045	49.425	4.2815	−2.500691	−10.70671
1972	5.834	61.791	5.0705	9.865311	50.02206
1976	3.817	48.951	3.0535	−2.97469	−9.083215
1980	−3.583	44.842	−4.3465	−7.083691	30.78926
1984	5.55	59.123	4.7865	7.197311	34.44993
1988	2.403	53.832	1.6395	1.906311	3.125397
1992	3.035	46.379	2.2715	−5.546689	−12.5993
1996	3.315	54.737	2.5515	2.81131	7.173057
2000	2.031	50.262	1.2675	−1.663689	−2.108726
2004	2.086	51.233	1.3225	−0.6926883	−0.9160802
2008	−1.787	46.311	−2.5505	−5.614689	14.32026
2012	1.422	52.010	0.6585001	0.0843083	0.055517
2016	0.97	51.111	0.2065	−0.8146899	−0.1682335
	$\bar{X} = 0.7635$	$\bar{Y} = 51.92569$			$\sum (X_i - \bar{X})(Y_i - \bar{Y})$ $= 606.51276$

is the variance for the referenced variable. Each of the cells off of the main diagonal displays the covariance for a pair of variables. In covariance tables, the cells above the main diagonal are often left blank, because the values in these cells are a mirror image of the values in the corresponding

Table 8.13 Covariance table for economic growth and incumbent-party presidential vote, 1880–2016

	Vote	Growth
Vote	33.4725	
Growth	17.3289	27.7346

cells below the main diagonal. For instance, in Table 8.13 the covariance between growth and vote is the same as the covariance between vote and growth, so the upper-right cell in this table is left blank.

Using the entries in Table 8.13, we can calculate the correlation coefficient:

$$r = \frac{\text{cov}_{XY}}{\sqrt{\text{var}_X \, \text{var}_Y}}$$
$$= \frac{17.3289}{\sqrt{33.4725 \times 27.7346}}$$
$$= \frac{17.3289}{\sqrt{928.3463985}}$$
$$= \frac{17.3289}{30.468777}$$
$$= 0.56874288.$$

There are a couple of points worth noting about the correlation coefficient. If all of the points in the plot line up perfectly on a straight, positively sloping line, the correlation coefficient will equal $+1$. If all of the points in the plot line up perfectly on a straight, negatively sloping line, the correlation coefficient will equal -1. Otherwise, the values will lie between $+1$ and -1. This standardization of correlation coefficient values is a particularly useful improvement over the covariance calculation. Additionally, we can calculate a t-statistic for a correlation coefficient as

$$t_r = \frac{r\sqrt{n-2}}{\sqrt{1-r^2}},$$

with $n-2$ degrees of freedom, where n is the number of cases. In this case, our degrees of freedom equal $36 - 2 = 34$.

For the current example,

$$t_r = \frac{r\sqrt{n-2}}{\sqrt{1-r^2}}$$
$$= \frac{0.56874288\sqrt{36-2}}{\sqrt{1-(0.56874288)^2}}$$
$$= \frac{0.56874288 \times 5.830951}{\sqrt{1-(0.3234684)}}$$
$$= \frac{3.31631}{\sqrt{0.67653153}}$$

$$= \frac{3.31631}{0.82251536}$$
$$= 4.03191.$$

With the degrees of freedom equal to 36 ($n = 36$) minus two, or 34, we can now turn to the t-table in Appendix B. Looking across the row for df = 30, we can see that our calculated t of 4.03 is greater even than the critical t at the p-value of 0.001 (which is 3.385). This tells us that the probability of seeing this relationship due to random chance is less than 0.001, or 1 in 1000. When we estimate our correlation coefficient with a computer program, we get a more precise p-value of 0.0003. Thus we can be quite confident that there is covariation between economic growth and incumbent-party vote share and that our theory has successfully cleared our third causal hurdle.[10]

8.5   WRAPPING UP

We have introduced three methods to conduct bivariate hypothesis tests – tabular analysis, difference of means tests, and correlation coefficients. Which test is most appropriate in any given situation depends on the measurement metric of your independent and dependent variables. Table 8.1 should serve as a helpful reference for you on this front.

We have yet to introduce the final method for conducting bivariate hypothesis tests covered in this book, namely bivariate regression analysis. That is the topic of our next chapter, and it serves as the initial building block for multiple regression (which we will cover in Chapter 10).

CONCEPTS INTRODUCED IN THIS CHAPTER

- chi-squared (χ^2) test for tabular association – a statistical test for a relationship between two categorical variables
- correlation coefficient – a measure of linear association between two continuous variables
- covariance – an unstandardized statistical measure summarizing the general pattern of association (or the lack thereof) between two continuous variables

---

[10] The first causal hurdle is pretty well cleared if we refer back to the discussion of the theory of economic voting in earlier chapters. The second causal hurdle also can be pretty well cleared logically by the timing of the measurement of each variable. Because economic growth is measured prior to incumbent vote, it is difficult to imagine that Y caused X.

- critical value – a predetermined standard for a statistical test such that, if the calculated value is greater than the critical value, then we conclude that there is a relationship between the two variables; and if the calculated value is less than the critical value, we cannot make such a conclusion
- degrees of freedom – the number of pieces of information we have beyond the minimum that we would need to make a particular inference
- difference of means test – a method of bivariate hypothesis testing that is appropriate for a categorical independent variable and a continuous dependent variable
- Pearson's r – the most commonly employed correlation coefficient
- p-value – the probability that we would see the relationship that we are finding because of random chance
- statistically significant relationship – a conclusion, based on the observed data, that the relationship between two variables is not due to random chance, and therefore exists in the broader population
- tabular analysis – a type of bivariate analysis that is appropriate for two categorical variables

EXERCISES

1. What form of bivariate hypothesis test would be appropriate for the following research questions:

   (a) You want to test the theory that being female causes lower salaries.

   (b) You want to test the theory that a state's percentage of college graduates is positively related to its turnout percentage.

   (c) You want to test the theory that individuals with higher incomes are more likely to vote.

2. Explain why each of the following statements is either true or false:

   (a) The computer program gave me a p-value of 0.000, so I know that my theory has been verified.

   (b) The computer program gave me a p-value of 0.02, so I know that I have found a very strong relationship.

   (c) The computer program gave me a p-value of 0.07, so I know that this relationship is due to random chance.

   (d) The computer program gave me a p-value of 0.50, so I know that there is only a 50 percent chance of this relationship being systematic.

3. Take a look at Figure 8.5. What is the dependent variable? What are the independent variables? What does this table tell us about politics?

4. What makes the table in Figure 8.5 so confusing?

MORAL VALUES – THE TRANSATLANTIC GULF

Q How often do you go to church?	BRITAIN				US	
	All Voters	Labour voters	Tory voters	Lib Dem voters	Bush voters	Kerry voters
More than weekly	2%	2%	3%	1%	63%	35%
Weekly	10%	10%	13%	7%	58%	41%
Monthly	5%	6%	4%	6%	50%	50%
A few times a year	36%	36%	38%	40%	44%	55%
Never	47%	46%	43%	44%	34%	64%

Q Which of the following is closest to your view of what the law should say about abortion?						
Always legal: absolute right to choose	38%	45%	34%	46%	24%	74%
Mostly legal: some restrictions	36%	35%	40%	32%	37%	62%
Mostly illegal: only in exceptional circumstances	19%	14%	18%	17%	72%	27%
Always illegal	4%	4%	3%	3%	77%	22%

Q Which of the following is closest to your view of what the law should be towards same-sex couples?						
Legal right to marry	28%	33%	18%	31%	22%	77%
Legally civil union but not marriage	37%	37%	39%	47%	51%	48%
No legal recognition of same sex couples	29%	23%	39%	20%	69%	30%

Sources: for British figures, Populus poll for The Times (Nov 5–7); for American figures, exit polls conducted by National Election Poll (Nov 2)

Figure 8.5 What is wrong with this table?

5. Conduct a tabular analysis from the information presented in the following hypothetical discussion of polling results: "We did a survey of 800 respondents who were likely Democratic primary voters in the state. Among these respondents, 45 percent favored Obama whereas 55 percent favored Clinton. When we split the respondents in half at the median age of 40, we found some stark differences: Among the younger half of the sample respondents, we found that 72.2 percent favored Obama to be the nominee and among the older sample respondents, we found that 68.2 percent favored Clinton."

6. For the example in Exercise 5, test the theory that age is related to preference for a Democratic nominee.

7. A lot of people in the United States think that the Watergate scandal in 1972 caused a sea change in terms of US citizens' views toward incumbent politicians. Use the data in Table 8.14 to produce a difference of means test of the null hypothesis that average reelection rates were the same before and after the Watergate scandal. Because of the timing of the elections and the scandal, 1972 should be coded as a pre-scandal case. Do this test once for the House and once for the Senate. Show all of your work.

8. Using the data set "BES2005 Subset" (which is available on the textbook's web site at www.cambridge.org/fpsr), produce a table that shows the combination values for the variables "LabourVote" (Y) and "IraqWarApprovalDich" (X). Read the descriptions of these two variables and write about what this table tells you about politics in the United Kingdom in 2005. Compute a χ^2 hypothesis test for these two variables. Write about what this tells you about politics in the United Kingdom in 2005.

Table 8.14 Incumbent reelection rates in US congressional elections, 1964–2006		
Year	House	Senate
1964	87	85
1966	88	88
1968	97	71
1970	85	77
1972	94	74
1974	88	85
1976	96	64
1978	94	60
1980	91	55
1982	90	93
1984	95	90
1986	98	75
1988	98	85
1990	96	96
1992	88	83
1994	90	92
1996	94	91
1998	98	90
2000	98	79
2002	96	86
2004	98	96
2006	94	79

9. Using the data set "BES2005 Subset," test the hypothesis that values for "Blair-Feelings" (Y) are different across different values of "IraqWarApprovalDich" (X). Read the descriptions of these two variables and write about what this table tells you about politics in the United Kingdom in 2005.

10. Using the data set "BES2005 Subset," produce a scatter plot of the values for "BlairFeelings" (Y) and "SelfLR" (X). Calculate a correlation coefficient and p-value for the hypothesis that these two variables are related to each other. Read the descriptions of these two variables and write about what this table tells you about politics in the United Kingdom in 2005.

9 Two-Variable Regression Models

OVERVIEW

Regression models are the workhorses of data analysts in a wide range of fields in the social sciences. We begin this chapter with a discussion of fitting a line to a scatter plot of data, and then we discuss the additional inferences that can be made when we move from a correlation coefficient to a two-variable regression model. We include discussions of measures of goodness-of-fit and on the nature of hypothesis testing and statistical significance in regression models. Throughout this chapter, we present important concepts in text, mathematical formulae, and graphical illustrations. This chapter concludes with a discussion of the assumptions of the regression model and minimal mathematical requirements for estimation.

9.1 TWO-VARIABLE REGRESSION

In Chapter 8 we introduced three different bivariate hypothesis tests. In this chapter we add a fourth, two-variable regression. This is an important first step toward the multiple regression model – which is the topic of Chapter 10 – in which we are able to "control for" another variable (Z) as we measure the relationship between our independent variable of interest (X) and our dependent variable (Y). It is crucial to develop an in-depth understanding of two-variable regression before moving to multiple regression. In the sections that follow, we begin with an overview of the two-variable regression model, in which a line is fit to a scatter plot of data. We then discuss the uncertainty associated with the line and how we use various measures of this uncertainty to make inferences about the underlying population. This chapter concludes with a discussion of the assumptions of the regression model and the minimal mathematical requirements for model estimation.

9.2 FITTING A LINE: POPULATION ⇔ SAMPLE

The basic idea of two-variable regression is that we are fitting the "best" line through a scatter plot of data. This line, which is defined by its slope and y-intercept, serves as a **statistical model** of reality. In this sense, two-variable regression is very different from the three hypothesis-testing techniques that we introduced in Chapter 8; although those techniques allow hypothesis testing, they do not produce a statistical model. You may remember from a math course the formula for a line expressed as

$$Y = mX + b,$$

where b is the y-intercept and m is the slope – often explained as the "rise-over-run" component of the line formula. For a one-unit increase (run) in X, m is the corresponding amount of rise in Y (or fall in Y, if m is negative). Together these two elements (m and b) are described as the line's **parameters**.[1] You may remember exercises from junior high or high school math classes in which you were given the values of m and b and then asked to draw the resulting line on graph paper. Once we know these two parameters for a line, we can draw that line across any range of X values.[2]

In a two-variable regression model, we represent the y-intercept parameter by the Greek letter alpha (α) and the slope parameter by the Greek letter beta (β).[3] As foreshadowed by all of our other discussions of variables, Y is the dependent variable and X is the independent variable. Our theory about the underlying population in which we are interested is expressed in the **population regression model**:

$$Y_i = \alpha + \beta X_i + u_i.$$

Note that in this model there is one additional component, u_i, which does not correspond with what we are used to seeing in line formulae from math classes. This term is the **stochastic** or "random" component of our dependent variable. We have this term because we do not expect all of our data points to line up perfectly on a straight line. This corresponds directly with our discussion in earlier chapters about the probabilistic (as opposed to deterministic) nature of causal theories about political phenomena. We are, after all, trying to explain processes that involve human behavior. Because human beings are complex, there is bound to be a fair amount

---

[1] The term "parameter" is a synonym for "boundary" with a more mathematical connotation. In the description of a line, the parameters (m and b in this case) are fixed whereas the variables (X and Y in this case) vary.

[2] If this is not familiar to you, or if you merely want to refresh your memory, you may want to complete Exercise 1 at the end of this chapter before you continue reading.

[3] Different textbooks on regression use slightly different notation for these parameters, so it is important not to assume that all textbooks use the same notation when comparing across them.

of random noise in our measures of their behavior. Thus we think about the values of our dependent variable Y_i as having a systematic component, $\alpha + \beta X_i$, and a stochastic component, u_i.

As we have discussed, we rarely work with population data. Instead, we use sample data to make inferences about the underlying population of interest. In two-variable regression, we use information from the **sample regression model** to make inferences about the unseen population regression model. To distinguish between these two, we place hats (^) over terms in the sample regression model that are estimates of terms from the unseen population regression model. Because they have hats, we can describe $\hat{\alpha}$ and $\hat{\beta}$ as being **parameter estimates**. These terms are our best guesses of the unseen population parameters α and β. Thus the sample regression model is written as

$$Y_i = \hat{\alpha} + \hat{\beta} X_i + \hat{u}_i.$$

Note that, in the sample regression model, α, β, and u_i get hats, but Y_i and X_i do not. This is because Y_i and X_i are values for cases in the population that ended up in the sample. As such, Y_i and X_i are values that are *measured* rather than *estimated*. We use them to estimate α, β, and the u_i values. The values that define the line are the estimated systematic components of Y. For each X_i value, we use $\hat{\alpha}$ and $\hat{\beta}$ to calculate the predicted value of Y_i, which we call $\hat{Y}_i$, where

$$\hat{Y}_i = \hat{\alpha} + \hat{\beta} X_i.$$

This can also be written in terms of expectations,

$$E(Y|X_i) = \hat{Y}_i = \hat{\alpha} + \hat{\beta} X_i,$$

which means that the expected value of Y given X_i (or $\hat{Y}_i$) is equal to our formula for the two-variable regression line. So we can now talk about each Y_i as having an estimated systematic component, $\hat{Y}_i$, and an estimated stochastic component, $\hat{u}_i$. We can thus write our model as

$$Y_i = \hat{Y}_i + \hat{u}_i,$$

and we can rewrite this in terms of $\hat{u}_i$ to get a better understanding of the estimated stochastic component:

$$\hat{u}_i = Y_i - \hat{Y}_i.$$

From this formula, we can see that the estimated stochastic component ($\hat{u}_i$) is equal to the difference between the actual value of the dependent variable (Y_i) and the predicted value of the dependent variable from our two-variable regression model. Another name for the estimated stochastic component is the **residual**. "Residual" is another word for "leftover," and this is appropriate, because $\hat{u}_i$ is the leftover part of Y_i after we have drawn the line defined by $\hat{Y}_i = \hat{\alpha} + \hat{\beta} X_i$. Another way to refer to $\hat{u}_i$, which follows from the formula $\hat{u}_i = Y_i - \hat{Y}_i$, is to call it the **sample error term**. Because $\hat{u}_i$ is an estimate of u_i, a corresponding way of referring to u_i is to call it the **population error term**.

9.3 WHICH LINE FITS BEST? ESTIMATING THE REGRESSION LINE

Consider the scatter plot of data in Figure 9.1. Our task is to draw a straight line that describes the relationship between our independent variable X and our dependent variable Y. By "straight line," we mean a line with a single slope that does not change as we move from left to right in our figure. So, for instance, consider the line that we've drawn through this plot of data in Figure 9.2. It certainly meets the criteria of having a single slope that doesn't change. In fact, we can see from the figure that the formula for this line is $Y_i = 51 - 0.6 X_i$. But, if we look around Figure 9.2, we can see that there are a lot of points that this line misses by a long distance. In fact, we can see a pattern: the points that are furthest from the line in Figure 9.2 are all in the lower-left and upper-right quadrants. This is because, as we know from our work with these same data in Chapter 8, the relationship between growth and presidential vote is positive.

So, how do we draw a better line? We clearly want to draw a line that comes as close as possible to the cases in our scatter plot of data. And because the data have a general pattern from lower-left to upper-right, we

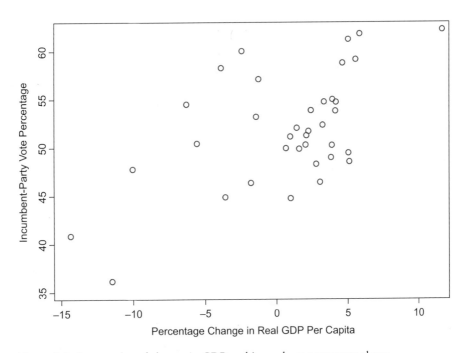

Figure 9.1 Scatter plot of change in GDP and incumbent-party vote share

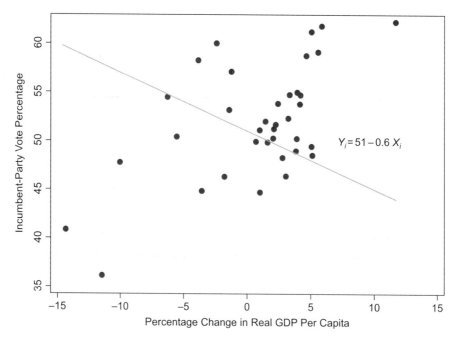

Figure 9.2 Scatter plot of change in GDP and incumbent-party vote share with a negatively sloped line

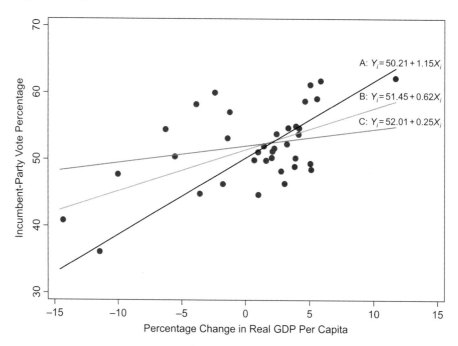

Figure 9.3 Three possible regression lines

know that our slope will be positive. In Figure 9.3, we have drawn three lines with positive slopes – labeled A, B, and C – through the scatter plot of growth and vote and written the corresponding parametric formula above each line on the right-hand side of the figure. So, how do we decide which

Line	Parametric formula	$\sum_{i=1}^{n} |\hat{u}_i|$	$\sum_{i=1}^{n} \hat{u}_i^2$
A	$Y_i = 50.21 + 1.15X_i$	150.18	1085.58
B	$Y_i = 51.45 + 0.62X_i$	139.17	792.60
C	$Y_i = 52.01 + 0.25X_i$	148.22	931.68

Table 9.1 Measures of total residuals for three different lines

line "best" fits the data that we see in our scatter plot of X_i and Y_i values? Because we are interested in explaining our dependent variable, we want our residual values, $\hat{u}_i$, which are vertical distances between each Y_i and the corresponding $\hat{Y}_i$, to be as small as possible. But, because these vertical distances come in both positive and negative values, we cannot just add them up for each line and have a good summary of the "fit" between each line and our data.[4]

So we need a method of assessing the fit of each line in which the positive and negative residuals do not cancel each other out. One possibility is to add together the absolute value of the residuals for each line:

$$\sum_{i=1}^{n} |\hat{u}_i|.$$

Another possibility is to add together the squared value of each of the residuals for each line:

$$\sum_{i=1}^{n} \hat{u}_i^2.$$

With either choice, we want to choose the line that has the smallest total value. Table 9.1 presents these calculations for the three lines in Figure 9.3.

From both calculations, we can see that line B does a better job of fitting the data than lines A and C. Although the absolute-value calculation is just as valid as the squared residual calculation, statisticians have tended to prefer the latter (both methods identify the same line as being "best"). Thus we draw a line that minimizes the sum of the *squared* residuals $\sum_{i=1}^{n} \hat{u}_i^2$. This technique for estimating the parameters of a regression model is known as **ordinary least-squares (OLS) regression**. For a two-variable OLS regression, the formulae for the parameter estimates of the line that meet this criterion are[5]

---

[4] Initially, we might think that we would want to minimize the sum of our residuals. But the line that minimizes the sum of the residuals is actually a flat line parallel to the x-axis. Such a line does not help us to explain the relationship between X and Y.

[5] The formulae for OLS parameter estimates come from setting the sum of squared residuals equal to zero and using differential calculus to solve for the values of $\hat{\beta}$ and $\hat{\alpha}$.

$$\hat{\beta} = \frac{\sum_{i=1}^{n}(X_i - \bar{X})(Y_i - \bar{Y})}{\sum_{i=1}^{n}(X_i - \bar{X})^2},$$

$$\hat{\alpha} = \bar{Y} - \hat{\beta}\bar{X}.$$

If we examine the formula for $\hat{\beta}$, we can see that the numerator is the same as the numerator for calculating the covariance between X and Y. Thus the logic of how each case contributes to this formula, as displayed in Figure 9.3, is the same. The denominator in the formula for $\hat{\beta}$ is the sum of squared deviations of the X_i values from the mean value of X ($\bar{X}$). Thus, for a given covariance between X and Y, the more (less) spread out X is, the less (more) steep the estimated slope of the regression line.

One of the mathematical properties of OLS regression is that the line produced by the parameter estimates goes through the sample mean values of X and Y. This makes the estimation of $\hat{\alpha}$ fairly simple. If we start out at the point defined by the mean value of X and the mean value of Y and then use the estimated slope ($\hat{\beta}$) to draw a line, the value of X where Y equals zero is $\hat{\alpha}$. Figure 9.4 shows the OLS regression line through the scatter plot of data. We can see from this figure that the OLS regression line passes through the point where the line depicting the mean value of X meets the line depicting the mean value of Y.

Using the data presented in Table 8.12 in the preceding formulae, we have calculated $\hat{\alpha} = 51.45$ and $\hat{\beta} = 0.62$, making our sample regression

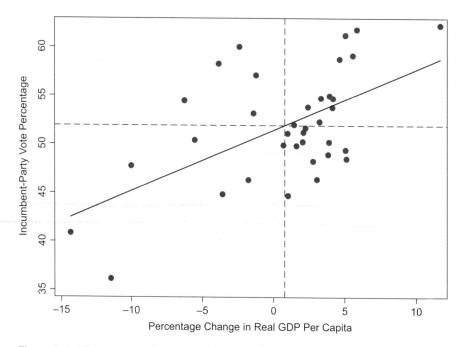

Figure 9.4 OLS regression line through scatter plot with mean-delimited quadrants

line formula $Y = 51.45 + 0.62X$. If we think about what this tells us about politics, we first need to remember that Y is the incumbent party's share of the major party vote, and X is the real per capita growth in GDP. So, if our measure of growth equals zero, we would expect the incumbent party to obtain 51.45 percent of the vote. If growth is not equal to zero, we multiply the value of growth by 0.62 and add (or subtract, if growth is negative) the result to 51.45 to obtain our best guess of the value of the vote. Moving to the right or the left along our sample regression line in Figure 9.4 means that we are increasing or decreasing the value of growth. For each right–left movement, we see a corresponding rise or decline in the value of the expected level of incumbent vote. If we go back to the logic of rise-over-run, our estimated slope parameter answers the question of how much change in Y we expect to see from a one-unit increase in X. In other words, a one-unit increase in our independent variable, growth, is expected to lead to a 0.62 increase in our dependent variable, incumbent vote.[6]

We can tell from Figure 9.4 that there are points that lie above and below our regression line. We therefore know that our model does not perfectly fit the real world. In the next section we discuss a series of inferences that we can make about the uncertainty associated with our sample regression model.

9.4 MEASURING OUR UNCERTAINTY ABOUT THE OLS REGRESSION LINE

As we have seen in Chapters 7 and 8, inferences about the underlying population of interest from sample data are made with varying degrees of uncertainty. In Chapter 8 we discussed the role of p-values in expressing this uncertainty. With an OLS regression model, we have several different ways in which to quantify our uncertainty. We discuss these measures in terms of the overall fit between X and Y first and then discuss the uncertainty about individual parameters. Our uncertainty about individual parameters is used in the testing of our hypotheses. Throughout this discussion, we refer to our example of fitting a regression line to our data on US presidential elections in order to test the theory of economic voting. Numerical results from Stata for this model are displayed in Figure 9.5. These numerical results can be partitioned into three separate areas. The

---

[6] Be sure not to invert the independent and dependent variables in describing results. It is *not* correct to interpret these results to say "for every 0.62-point change in growth rate in the US economy, we should expect to see, on average, an extra 1 percent in vote percentage for the incumbent party in presidential elections." Be sure that you can see the difference between those descriptions.

```
. reg inc_vote g
```

Source	SS	df	MS		Number of obs	=	36
					F(1, 34)	=	16.26
Model	378.957648	1	378.957648		Prob > F	=	0.0003
Residual	792.580681	34	23.3111965		R-squared	=	0.3235
					Adj R-squared	=	0.3036
Total	1171.53833	35	33.4725237		Root MSE	=	4.8282

inc_vote	Coef.	Std. Err.	t	P>|t|	[95% Conf.	Interval]
g	.624814	.1549664	4.03	0.000	.3098843	.9397437
_cons	51.44865	.8133462	63.26	0.000	49.79573	53.10157

Figure 9.5 Stata results for two-variable regression model between "vote" (inc_vote) and "growth" (g): $inc\_vote = \alpha + \beta \times g$

table in the upper-left corner of Figure 9.5 gives us measures of the variation in our model. The set of statistics listed in the upper-right corner of Figure 9.5 gives us a set of summary statistics about the entire model. Across the bottom of Figure 9.5 we get a table of statistics on the model's parameter estimates. The name of the dependent variable, "inc_vote," is displayed at the top of this table. Underneath we see the name of our independent variable, "g," which is short for "growth," and "_cons," which is short for "constant" (another name for the y-intercept term), which we also know as $\hat{\alpha}$. Moving to the right in the table at the bottom of Figure 9.5, we see that the next column heading here is "Coef.," which is short for "coefficient," which is another name for parameter estimate. In this column we see the values of $\hat{\beta}$ and $\hat{\alpha}$, which are 0.62 and 51.45 when we round these results to the second decimal place.[7]

9.4.1   Goodness-of-Fit: Root Mean-Squared Error

Measures of the overall fit between a regression model and the dependent variable are called goodness-of-fit measures. One of the most intuitive of these measures (despite its name) is **root mean-squared error** (root MSE). This statistic is sometimes referred to as the standard error of the regression model. It provides a measure of the average accuracy of the model in the metric of the dependent variable. This statistic ("Root MSE" in Figure 9.5) is calculated as

$$\text{root MSE} = \sqrt{\frac{\sum_{i=1}^{n} \hat{u}_i^2}{n}}.$$

[7] The choice of how many decimal places to report should be decided based on the value of the dependent variable. In this case, because our dependent variable is a vote percentage, we have chosen the second decimal place. Political scientists usually do not report election results beyond the first two decimal places.

The squaring and then taking the square root of the quantities in this formula are done to adjust for the fact that some of our residuals will be positive (points for which Y_i is above the regression line) and some will be negative (points for which Y_i is below the regression line). Once we realize this, we can see that this statistic is basically the average distance between the data points and the regression line.

From the numeric results depicted in Figure 9.5, we can see that the root MSE for our two-variable model of incumbent-party vote is 4.83. This value is found on the sixth line of the column of results on the right-hand side of Figure 9.5. It indicates that, on average, our model is off by 4.83 points in predicting the percentage of the incumbent party's share of the major party vote. It is worth emphasizing that the root MSE is always expressed in terms of the metric in which the dependent variable is measured. The only reason why this particular value corresponds to a percentage is because the metric of the dependent variable is vote percentage.

> **YOUR TURN: Evaluating a root MSE**
>
> In your opinion, is that root MSE "good"? Why or why not?

9.4.2 Goodness-of-Fit: *R*-Squared Statistic

Another commonly used indicator of the model's goodness-of-fit is the **R-squared statistic** (typically written as R^2). The R^2 statistic ranges between zero and one, indicating the proportion of the variation in the dependent variable that is accounted for by the model. The basic idea of the R^2 statistic is shown in Figure 9.6, which is a Venn diagram depiction

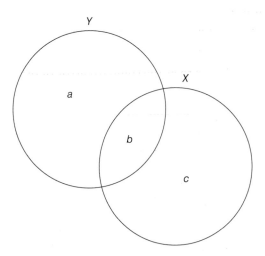

Figure 9.6 Venn diagram of variance and covariance for X and Y

of variation in X and Y as well as covariation between X and Y. The idea behind this diagram is that we are depicting variation in each variable with a circle. The larger the circle for a particular variable, the larger the variation for that variable. In this figure, the variation in Y consists of two areas, a and b, and variation in X consists of areas b and c. Area a represents variation in Y that is not related to variation in X, and area b represents covariation between X and Y. In a two-variable regression model, area a is the residual or stochastic variation in Y. The R^2 statistic is equal to area b over the total variation in Y, which is equal to the sum of areas a and b. Thus smaller values of area a and larger values of area b lead to a larger R^2 statistic. The formula for total variation in Y (areas a and b in Figure 9.6), also known as the total sum of squares (TSS), is

$$\text{TSS} = \sum_{i=1}^{n}(Y_i - \bar{Y})^2.$$

The formula for the residual variation in Y, area a that is not accounted for by X, called the residual sum of squares (RSS), is

$$\text{RSS} = \sum_{i=1}^{n}\hat{u}_i^2.$$

Once we have these two quantities, we can calculate the R^2 statistic as

$$R^2 = 1 - \frac{\text{RSS}}{\text{TSS}}.$$

The formula for the other part of TSS that is not the RSS, called the model sum of squares (MSS), is

$$\text{MSS} = \sum_{i=1}^{n}(\hat{Y}_i - \bar{Y})^2.$$

This can also be used to calculate R^2 as

$$R^2 = \frac{\text{MSS}}{\text{TSS}}.$$

From the numeric results depicted in Figure 9.5, we can see that the R^2 statistic for our two-variable model of incumbent-party vote is 0.324. This number appears on the fourth line of the column of results on the right-hand side of Figure 9.5. It indicates that our model accounts for about 32 percent of the variation in the dependent variable. We can also see in Figure 9.5 the values for the MSS, RSS, and TSS under the column labeled "SS" in the table in the upper-left-hand corner.

> **YOUR TURN: Evaluating an R-squared statistic**
>
> In your opinion, is that R-squared "good"? Why or why not?

9.4.3 Is That a "Good" Goodness-of-Fit?

A logical question to ask when we see a measure of a model's goodness-of-fit is "What is a good or bad value for the root MSE and/or R^2?" This is not an easy question to answer. In part, the answer depends on what you are trying to do with the model. If you are trying to predict election outcomes, saying that you can predict the outcome with a typical error of 4.83 may not seem very good. After all, most presidential elections are fairly close and, in the scheme of things, 4.83 percent is a lot of votes. In fact, we can see that in 21 of the 36 elections that we are looking at, the winning margin was less than 4.83 percent, making over one-half of our sample of elections too close to call with this model. On the other hand, looking at this another way, we can say that we are able to come this close and, in terms of R^2, explain just over 32 percent of the variation in incumbent vote from 1876 to 2016 with just one measure of the economy. When we start to think of all of the different campaign strategies, personalities, scandals, wars, and everything else that is not in this simple model, this level of accuracy is rather impressive. In fact, we would suggest that this tells us something pretty remarkable about politics in the United States – the economy is massively important.

9.4.4 Uncertainty about Individual Components of the Sample Regression Model

Before we go through this section, we want to warn you that there are a lot of formulae in it. To use a familiar metaphor, as you go through the formulae in this section it is important to focus on the contours of the forest and not to get caught up in the details of the many trees that we will see along the way. Instead of memorizing each formula, concentrate on what makes the overall values generated by these equations larger or smaller.

A crucial part of the uncertainty in OLS regression models is the degree of uncertainty about individual estimates of population parameter values from the sample regression model. We can use the same logic that we discussed in Chapter 7 for making inferences from sample values about population values for each of the individual parameters in a sample regression model.

One estimate that factors into the calculations of our uncertainty about each of the population parameters is the estimated variance of the population stochastic component, u_i. This unseen variance, σ^2, is estimated from the residuals $(\hat{u}_i)$ after the parameters for the sample regression model have been estimated by the following formula:

$$\hat{\sigma}^2 = \frac{\sum_{i=1}^{n} \hat{u}_i^2}{n-2}.$$

Looking at this formula, we can see two components that play a role in determining the magnitude of this estimate. The first component comes from the individual residual values $(\hat{u}_i)$. Remember that these values (calculated as $\hat{u}_i = Y_i - \hat{Y}_i$) are the vertical distance between each observed Y_i value and the regression line. The larger these values are, the further the individual cases are from the regression line. The second component of this formula comes from n, the sample size. By now, you should be familiar with the idea that the larger the sample size, the smaller the variance of the estimate. This is the case with our formula for $\hat{\sigma}^2$.

Once we have estimated $\hat{\sigma}^2$, the variance and standard errors for the slope parameter estimate $(\hat{\beta})$ are then estimated from the following formulae:

$$\text{var}(\hat{\beta}) = \frac{\hat{\sigma}^2}{\sum_{i=1}^{n}(X_i - \bar{X})^2},$$

$$\text{se}(\hat{\beta}) = \sqrt{\text{var}(\hat{\beta})} = \frac{\hat{\sigma}}{\sqrt{\sum_{i=1}^{n}(X_i - \bar{X})^2}}.$$

Both of these formulae can be broken into two components that determine their magnitude. In the numerator, we find $\hat{\sigma}$ values. So the larger these values are, the larger will be the variance and standard error of the slope parameter estimate. This makes sense, because the farther the points representing our data are from the regression line, the less confidence we will have in the value of the slope. If we look at the denominator in this equation, we see the term $\sum_{i=1}^{n}(X_i - \bar{X})^2$, which is a measure of the variation of the X_i values around their mean $(\bar{X})$. The greater this variation, the smaller will be the variance and standard error of the slope parameter estimate. This is an important property; in real-world terms it means that the more variation we have in X, the more precisely we will be able to estimate the relationship between X and Y.

The variance and standard errors for the intercept parameter estimate $(\hat{\alpha})$ are then estimated from the following formulae:

$$\text{var}(\hat{\alpha}) = \frac{\hat{\sigma}^2 \sum_{i=1}^{n} X_i^2}{n \sum_{i=1}^{n}(X_i - \bar{X})^2},$$

$$\text{se}(\hat{\alpha}) = \sqrt{\text{var}(\hat{\alpha})} = \sqrt{\frac{\hat{\sigma}^2 \sum_{i=1}^{n} X_i^2}{n \sum_{i=1}^{n}(X_i - \bar{X})^2}}.$$

The logic for taking apart the components of these formulae is slightly more complicated because we can see that the sum of the squared X_i values appears in the numerator. We can see, however, that the denominator contains the measure of the variation of the X_i values around their mean ($\bar{X}$) multiplied by n, the number of cases. Thus the same basic logic holds for these terms: The larger the $\hat{u}_i$ values are, the larger will be the variance and standard error of the intercept parameter estimate; and the larger the variation of the X_i values around their mean, the smaller will be the variance and standard error of the intercept parameter estimate.

Less obvious – but nevertheless true – from the preceding formulae is the fact that larger sample sizes will also produce smaller standard errors.[8] So, just as we learned about the effects of sample size when calculating the standard error of the mean in Chapter 7, there is an identical effect here. Larger sample sizes will, other things being equal, produce smaller standard errors of our estimated regression coefficients.

9.4.5 Confidence Intervals about Parameter Estimates

In Chapter 7 we discussed how we use the normal distribution (supported by the central limit theorem) to estimate confidence intervals for the unseen population mean from sample data. We go through the same logical steps to estimate confidence intervals for the unseen parameters from the population regression model by using the results from the sample regression model. The formulae for estimating confidence intervals are

$$\hat{\beta} \pm [t \times \text{se}(\hat{\beta})],$$
$$\hat{\alpha} \pm [t \times \text{se}(\hat{\alpha})],$$

where the value for t is determined from the t-table in Appendix B. So, for instance, if we want to calculate a 95 percent confidence interval, this means that we are looking down the column for 0.025.[9] Once we have determined the appropriate column, we select our row based on the number of degrees of freedom. The number of degrees of freedom for this t-test is equal to the number of observations (n) minus the number of parameters estimated (k). In the case of the regression model presented in Figure 9.5, $n = 36$ and $k = 2$, so our degrees of freedom equal 34. Looking down the column for 0.025 and across the row for 30 in the t-table, we can see that $t = 2.042$. However, because we have 34 degrees

---

[8] It is true because the numerator of the expression contains $\hat{\sigma}$, which, as seen previously, has the sample size n in its denominator.

[9] To understand this, think back to Chapter 7, where we introduced confidence intervals. A 95 percent confidence interval would mean that would leave a total of 5 percent in the tails. Because there are two tails, we are going to use the 0.025 column.

of freedom, the t-values that leave 0.025 in each tail is 2.032.[10] Thus our 95 percent confidence intervals are

$$\hat{\beta} \pm [t \times se(\hat{\beta})] = 0.624814 \pm (2.032 \times 0.1549664) = 0.31 \text{ to } 0.94,$$
$$\hat{\alpha} \pm [t \times se(\hat{\alpha})] = 51.44865 \pm (2.032 \times 0.8133462) = 49.80 \text{ to } 53.10.$$

These values are displayed in the lower right-hand corner of the table at the bottom of Figure 9.5.

The traditional approach to hypothesis testing with OLS regression is that we specify a null hypothesis and an **alternative hypothesis** and then compare the two. Although we can test hypotheses about either the slope or the intercept parameter, we are usually more concerned with tests about the slope parameter. In particular, we are usually concerned with testing the hypothesis that the population slope parameter is equal to zero. The logic of this hypothesis test corresponds closely with the logic of the bivariate hypothesis tests introduced in Chapter 8. We observe a sample slope parameter, which is an estimate of the population slope. Then, from the value of this parameter estimate, the confidence interval around it, and the size of our sample, we evaluate how likely it is that we observe this sample slope if the true but unobserved population slope is equal to zero. If the answer is "very likely," then we conclude that the population slope is equal to zero.

To understand why we so often focus on a slope value of zero, think about what this corresponds to in the formula for a line. Remember that the slope is the change in Y from a one-unit increase in X. If that change is equal to zero, resulting in a flat line, then there is no covariation between X and Y, and we have failed to clear our third causal hurdle.

These types of tests are either one- or two-tailed. Most statistical computer programs report the results from two-tailed hypothesis tests that the parameter in question is not equal to zero. Despite this, many political science theories are more appropriately translated into one-tailed hypothesis tests, which are sometimes referred to as "directional" hypothesis tests. We review both types of hypothesis tests with the example regression from Figure 9.5.

9.4.6   Two-Tailed Hypothesis Tests

The most common form of statistical hypothesis tests about the parameters from an OLS regression model is a two-tailed hypothesis test that the slope parameter is equal to zero. It is expressed as

[10] The exact value of t is calculated automatically by statistical packages. For an online tool that gives exact values of t, go to https://www.danielsoper.com/statcalc/calculator.aspx?id=10.

$$H_0: \quad \beta = 0,$$
$$H_1: \quad \beta \neq 0,$$

where H_0 is the null hypothesis and H_1 is the alternative hypothesis. Note that these two rival hypotheses are expressed in terms of the slope parameter from the population regression model. To test which of these two hypotheses is supported, we calculate a *t*-ratio in which β is set equal to the value specified in the null hypothesis (in this case zero because $H_0: \beta = 0$), which we represent as β^*:

$$t_{n-k} = \frac{\hat{\beta} - \beta^*}{\text{se}(\hat{\beta})}.$$

For the slope parameter in the two-variable regression model presented in Figure 9.5, we can calculate this as

$$t_{34} = \frac{\hat{\beta} - \beta^*}{\text{se}(\hat{\beta})} = \frac{0.624814 - 0}{0.1549664} = 4.03.$$

From what we have seen in previous chapters, we can tell that this *t*-ratio is quite large. Remember that a typical standard for statistical significance in the social sciences is when the *p*-value is less than 0.05. If we look across the row for degrees of freedom equal to 30 in Appendix B, we can see that, to have a *p*-value of less than 0.05, we would need a *t*-ratio of 2.042 or larger (2.032 if we use the exact degrees of freedom). We clearly have exceeded this standard.[11] In fact, if we look at the far-right-hand column in Appendix B for 30 degrees of freedom, we can see that this *t*-ratio exceeds the value for *t* needed for *p* to be less than 0.002 (we get this by looking down the column labeled "0.001" and seeing a required *t*-value of at least 3.385 for 30 degrees of freedom). This means that it is extremely unlikely that H_0 is the case, which in turn greatly increases our confidence in H_1. If we look at the table at the bottom of Figure 9.5, we can see that the *t*-ratio and resulting *p*-value for this hypothesis test are presented in the fourth and fifth columns of the growth g row. It is worth noting that, although the reported *p*-value is 0.000, this does not mean that the probability of the null hypothesis being the case is actually equal to zero. Instead, this means that it is a very small number that gets rounded to zero when we report it to three decimal places.

The exact same logic is used to test hypotheses about the *y*-intercept parameter. The formula for this *t*-ratio is

---

[11] Because this is a two-tailed hypothesis test, for the standard of $p < 0.05$ we need to look down the column labeled "0.025." This is the case because we are going to leave 0.025 in each tail.

$$t_{n-k} = \frac{\hat{\alpha} - \alpha^*}{se(\hat{\alpha})}.$$

In Figure 9.5 we see the calculation for the following null hypothesis and alternative:

$$H_0: \quad \alpha = 0,$$
$$H_1: \quad \alpha \neq 0.$$

The resulting t-ratio is a whopping 63.26! This makes sense when we think about this quantity in real-world terms. Remember that the y-intercept is the expected value of the dependent variable Y when the independent variable X is equal to zero. In our model, this means we want to know the expected value of incumbent-party vote when growth equals zero. Even when the economy is shrinking, there are always going to be some diehard partisans who will vote for the incumbent party. Thus it makes sense that the null hypothesis $H_0: \alpha = 0$ would be pretty easy to reject.

Perhaps a more interesting null hypothesis is that the incumbents would still obtain 50 percent of the vote if growth were equal to zero. In this case,

$$H_0: \quad \alpha = 50,$$
$$H_1: \quad \alpha \neq 50.$$

The corresponding t-ratio is calculated as

$$t_{34} = \frac{\hat{\alpha} - \alpha^*}{se(\hat{\alpha})} = \frac{51.44865 - 50}{0.8133462} = 1.78.$$

Looking at the row for degrees of freedom equal to 30 in the t-table, we can see that this t-ratio is smaller than 2.042, which is the value for $p < 0.05$ (from the column labeled "0.025") but is larger than the 1.697 value for $p < 0.10$ (from the column labeled "0.05"). With a more detailed t-table or a computer, we could calculate the exact p-value for this hypothesis test, which is 0.08. Thus from these results, we are in a bit of a gray area. We can be pretty confident that the intercept is not equal to 50, but we can only reject the null hypothesis ($H_0: \alpha = 50$) at the 0.10 level instead of the widely accepted standard for statistical significance of 0.05. Let's think for a second, however, about our interest in the value of 50 for the intercept. While the hypothesis test for the alternative hypothesis that we just tested ($H_1: \alpha \neq 50$) is of interest to us, might we be more interested in whether or not incumbents would "win" the popular vote if the growth equaled zero? Before we approach this question, we will explain the relationship between confidence intervals and two-tailed hypothesis tests.

9.4.7 The Relationship between Confidence Intervals and Two-Tailed Hypothesis Tests

In the previous three sections, we introduced confidence intervals and hypothesis tests as two of the ways for making inferences about the parameters of the population regression model from our sample regression model. These two methods for making inferences are mathematically related to each other. We can tell this because they each rely on the t-table. The relationship between the two is such that, if the 95 percent confidence interval does not include a particular value, then the null hypothesis that the population parameter equals that value (a two-tailed hypothesis test) will have a p-value smaller than 0.05. We can see this for each of the three hypothesis tests that we discussed in the section on two-tailed hypothesis tests:

- Because the 95 percent confidence interval for our slope parameter does not include 0, the p-value for the hypothesis test that $\beta = 0$ is less than 0.05.
- Because the 95 percent confidence interval for our intercept parameter does not include 0, the p-value for the hypothesis test that $\alpha = 0$ is less than 0.05.
- Because the 95 percent confidence interval for our intercept parameter does include 50, the p-value for the hypothesis test that $\alpha = 50$ is greater than 0.05.

9.4.8 One-Tailed Hypothesis Tests

As we pointed out in previous sections, the most common form of statistical hypothesis tests about the parameters from an OLS regression model is a two-tailed hypothesis test that the slope parameter is equal to zero. That this is the most common test is something of a fluke. By default, most statistical computer programs report the results of this hypothesis test. In reality, though, *most political science hypotheses are that a parameter is either positive or negative and not just that the parameter is different from zero.* This is what we call a **directional hypothesis.** Consider, for instance, the theory of economic voting and how we would translate it into a hypothesis about the slope parameter in our current example. Our theory is that the *better* the economy is performing, the *higher* will be the vote percentage for the incumbent-party candidate. In other words, we expect to see a positive relationship between economic growth and the incumbent-party vote percentage, meaning that we expect β to be greater than zero.

When our theory leads to such a directional hypothesis, it is expressed as

$$H_0: \quad \beta \leq 0,$$
$$H_1: \quad \beta > 0,$$

where H_0 is the null hypothesis and H_1 is the alternative hypothesis. As was the case with the two-tailed test, these two rival hypotheses are expressed in terms of the slope parameter from the population regression model. To test which of these two hypotheses is supported, we calculate a t-ratio where β is set equal to the value specified in the null hypothesis[12] (in this case zero because $H_0: \beta \leq 0$), which we represent as β^*:

$$t_{n-k} = \frac{\hat{\beta} - \beta^*}{se(\hat{\beta})}.$$

For the slope parameter in the two-variable regression model presented in Figure 9.5, we can calculate this as

$$t_{34} = \frac{\hat{\beta} - \beta^*}{se(\hat{\beta})} = \frac{0.624814 - 0}{0.1549664} = 4.03.$$

Do these calculations look familiar to you? They should, because this t-ratio is calculated exactly the same way that the t-ratio for the two-sided hypothesis about this parameter was calculated. The difference comes in how we use the t-table in Appendix B to arrive at the appropriate p-value for this hypothesis test. Because this is a one-tailed hypothesis test, we use the column labeled "0.05" instead of the column labeled "0.025" to assess whether we have achieved a t-ratio such that $p < 0.05$. In other words, we would need a t-ratio of only 1.697 for 30 degrees of freedom (1.691 for 34 degrees of freedom) to achieve this level of significance for a one-tailed hypothesis test. For a two-tailed hypothesis test, we needed a t-ratio of 2.047 (2.032).

Now, returning to our hypothesis test about the intercept and the value of 50, if we change from a two-tailed to a one-tailed hypothesis test,

$$H_0: \quad \alpha \leq 50,$$
$$H_1: \quad \alpha > 50,$$

we still get

$$t_{34} = \frac{\hat{\alpha} - \alpha^*}{se(\hat{\alpha})} = \frac{51.44865 - 50}{0.8133462} = 1.78.$$

---

[12] We choose 0 when the null hypothesis is $H_0: \beta \leq 0$ because this is the critical value for the null hypothesis. Under this null hypothesis, zero is the threshold, and evidence that β is equal to any value less than or equal to zero is supportive of this null hypothesis.

But, with 34 degrees of freedom, this one-tailed hypothesis test yields a *p*-value of 0.04. In other words, this is a case where the formulation of our hypothesis test as one-tailed versus two-tailed makes a pretty major difference, especially since many scholars judge 0.05 to be the standard for statistical significance.

We can see from these examples and from the *t*-table that, when we have a directional hypothesis, we can more easily reject a null hypothesis. One of the quirks of political science research is that, even when they have directional hypotheses, researchers often report the results of two-tailed hypothesis tests. We'll discuss the issue of how to present regression results in greater detail in Chapter 10.

9.5 ASSUMPTIONS, MORE ASSUMPTIONS, AND MINIMAL MATHEMATICAL REQUIREMENTS

If assumptions were water, you'd need an umbrella right now. Any time that you estimate a regression model, you are implicitly making a large set of assumptions about the unseen population model. In this section, we break these assumptions into assumptions about the population stochastic component and assumptions about our model specification. In addition, there are some minimal mathematical requirements that must be met before a regression model can be estimated. In this final section we list these assumptions and requirements and briefly discuss them as they apply to our working example of a two-variable regression model of the impact of economic growth on incumbent-party vote.

9.5.1 Assumptions about the Population Stochastic Component

The most important assumptions about the population stochastic component u_i are about its distribution. These can be summarized as

$$u_i \sim N(0, \sigma^2),$$

which means that we assume that u_i is distributed normally ($\sim N$) with the mean equal to zero and the variance equal to σ^2.[13] This compact mathematical statement contains three of the five assumptions that we make about the population stochastic component any time we estimate a regression model. We now go over each one separately.

---

[13] Strictly speaking we do not need to make all of these assumptions to estimate the parameters of an OLS model. But we do need to make all of these assumptions to interpret the results from an OLS model in the standard fashion.

u_i Is Normally Distributed

The assumption that u_i is normally distributed allows us to use the t-table to make probabilistic inferences about the population regression model from the sample regression model. The main justification for this assumption is the central limit theorem that we discussed in Chapter 7.

$E(u_i) = 0$: No Bias

The assumption that u_i has a mean or expected value equal to zero is also known as the assumption of zero bias. Consider what it would mean if there was a case for which $E(u_i) \neq 0$. In other words, this would be a case for which we would *expect* our regression model to be off. If we have cases like this, we would essentially be ignoring some theoretical insight that we have about the underlying causes of Y. Remember, this term is supposed to be random. If $E(u_i) \neq 0$, then there must be some nonrandom component to this term. It is important to note here that we do not expect *all* of our u_i values to equal zero because we know that some of our cases will fall above and below the regression line. But this assumption means that our best guess or expected value for each individual u_i value is zero.

If we think about the example in this chapter, this assumption means that we do not have any particular cases for which we expect our model, with economic growth as the independent variable, to overpredict or underpredict the value of the incumbent-party vote percentage. If, on the other hand, we had some expectation along these lines, we would not be able to make this assumption. Say, for instance, that we expected that during times of war the incumbent party would fare better than we would expect them to fare based on the economy. Under these circumstances, we would not be able to make this assumption. The solution to this problem would be to include another independent variable in our model that measured whether or not the nation was at war at the time of each election. Once we control for all such potential sources of bias, we can feel comfortable making this assumption. The inclusion of additional independent variables is the main subject covered in Chapter 10.

u_i Has Variance σ^2: Homoscedasticity

The assumption that u_i has variance equal to σ^2 seems pretty straightforward. But, because this notation for variance does not contain an i subscript, it means that the variance for every case in the underlying population is assumed to be the same. The word for describing this situation is "homoscedasticity," which means "uniform error variance." If this assumption does not hold, we have a situation in which the variance of u_i is σ_i^2, known as "heteroscedasticity," which means "unequal error variance." When we have heteroscedasticity, our regression model fits some of the cases in the population better than others. This can potentially cause us problems when we are estimating confidence intervals and testing hypotheses.

In our example for this chapter, this assumption would be violated if, for some reason, some elections were harder than others for our model to predict. In this case, our model would be heteroscedastic. It could, for instance, be the case that elections that were held after political debates became televised are harder to predict with our model in which the only independent variable is economic performance. Under these circumstances, the assumption of homoscedasticity would not be reasonable.

No Autocorrelation

We also assume that there is no autocorrelation. Autocorrelation occurs when the stochastic terms for any two or more cases are systematically related to each other. This clearly cuts against the grain of the idea that these terms are stochastic or random. Formally, we express this assumption as

$$\text{cov}_{u_i, u_j} = 0 \quad \forall\ i \neq j;$$

in words, this means that the covariance between the population error terms u_i and u_j is equal to zero for all i not equal to j (for any two unique cases).

The most common form of autocorrelation occurs in regression models of time-series data. As we discussed in Chapter 4, time-series data involve measurement of the relevant variables across time for a single spatial unit. In our example for this chapter, we are using measures of economic growth and incumbent-party vote percentage measured every four years for the United States. If, for some reason, the error terms for adjacent pairs of elections were correlated, we would have autocorrelation.

X Values Are Measured without Error

At first, the assumption that X values are measured without error may seem to be out of place in a listing of assumptions about the population stochastic component. But this assumption is made to greatly simplify inferences that we make about our population regression model from our sample regression model. By assuming that X is measured without error, we are assuming that any variability from our regression line is due to the stochastic component u_i and not to measurement problems in X. To put it another way, if X also had a stochastic component, we would need to model X before we could model Y, and that would substantially complicate matters.

With just about any regression model that we estimate with real-world data, we will likely be pretty uncomfortable with this assumption. In the example for this chapter, we are assuming that we have exactly correct measures of the percentage change in real GDP per capita from 1876 to 2016. If we think a little more about this measure, we can think of all kinds of potential errors in measurement. What about illegal economic activities that are hard for the government to measure? Because this is per capita, how confident are we that the denominator in this calculation, population, is measured exactly correctly?

Despite the obvious problems with this assumption, we make it every time that we estimate an OLS model. Unless we move to considerably more complicated statistical techniques, this is an assumption that we have to live with and keep in the back of our minds as we evaluate our overall confidence in what our models tell us.

Recall from Chapter 5, when we discussed measuring our concepts of interest, that we argued that measurement is important because if we mismeasure our variables we may make incorrect causal inferences about the real world. This assumption should make the important lessons of that chapter crystal clear.

9.5.2   Assumptions about Our Model Specification

The assumptions about our model specification can be summarized as a single assumption that we have *the* correct model specification. We break this into two separate assumptions to highlight the range of ways in which this assumption might be violated.

No Causal Variables Left Out; No Noncausal Variables Included

This assumption means that if we specify our two-variable regression model of the relationship between X and Y there cannot be some other variable Z that also causes Y.[14] It also means that X must cause Y. In other words, this is just another way of saying that the sample regression model that we have specified *is* the true underlying population regression model.

As we have gone through the example in this chapter, we have already begun to come up with additional variables that we theorize to be causally related to our dependent variable. To comfortably make this assumption,

---

[14] One exception to this is the very special case in which there is a Z variable that is causally related to Y but Z is uncorrelated with X and u_i. In this case, we would still be able to get a reasonable estimate of the relationship between X and Y despite leaving Z out of our model. More on this in Chapter 10.

we will need to include all such variables in our model. Adding additional independent variables to our model is the subject of Chapter 10.

Parametric Linearity

The assumption of parametric linearity is a fancy way of saying that our population parameter β for the relationship between X and Y does not vary. In other words, the relationship between X and Y is the same across all values of X.

In the context of our current example, this means that we are assuming that the impact of a one-unit increase in change in real GDP per capita is always the same. So moving from a value of -10 to -9 has the same effect as moving from a value of 1 to 2. In Chapter 11 we discuss some techniques for relaxing this assumption.

9.5.3 Minimal Mathematical Requirements

For a two-variable regression model, we have two minimal requirements that must be met by our sample data before we can estimate our parameters. We will add to these requirements when we expand to multiple regression models.

X Must Vary

Think about what the scatter plot of our sample data would look like if X did not vary. Basically, we would have a stack of Y values at the same point on the x-axis. The only reasonable line that we could draw through this set of points would be a straight line parallel to the y-axis. Remember that our goal is to explain our dependent variable Y. Under these circumstances we would have failed miserably because any Y value would be just as good as any other given our single value of X. Thus we need some variation in X in order to estimate an OLS regression model.

$n > k$

To estimate a regression model, the number of cases (n) must exceed the number of parameters to be estimated (k). Thus, as a minimum, when we estimate a two-variable regression model with two parameters (α and β) we must have *at least* three cases.

9.5.4 How Can We Make All of These Assumptions?

The mathematical requirements to estimate a regression model aren't too severe, but a sensible question to ask at this point is, "How can we reasonably make all of the assumptions just listed every time that we run a regression model?" To answer this question, we refer back to the discussion in Chapter 1 of the analogy between models and maps. We *know* that all of our assumptions cannot possibly be met. We also know that we are trying to simplify complex realities. The only way that we can do this is to make a large set of unrealistic assumptions about the world. It is crucial, though, that we never lose sight of the fact that we are making these assumptions. In the next chapter we relax one of these most unrealistic assumptions made in the two-variable regression model by controlling for a second variable, Z.

CONCEPTS INTRODUCED IN THIS CHAPTER

- alternative hypothesis – the theory-based expectation that is the opposite of the null hypothesis
- directional hypothesis – an alternative hypothesis in which the expected relationship is either positive or negative
- ordinary least-squares – often abbreviated to "OLS," the most popular method for computing sample regression models
- parameter – a synonym for "boundary" with a more mathematical connotation; in the context of statistics, the value of an unknown population characteristic
- parameter estimate – a sample-based calculation of a population characteristic
- population error term – in the population regression model, the difference between the model-based predicted value of the dependent variable and the true value of the dependent variable
- population regression model – a theoretical formulation of the proposed linear relationship between at least one independent variable and a dependent variable
- residual – same as population error term
- root mean-squared error – sometimes shortened to "root MSE," a calculation of goodness-of-fit made by squaring each sample error term, summing them up, dividing by the number of cases, and then taking the square root; also known as the "model standard error"
- *R*-squared statistic – a goodness-of-fit measure that varies between 0 and 1 representing the proportion of variation in the dependent variable that is accounted for by the model
- sample error term – in the sample regression model, the sample-based estimate of the residual
- sample regression model – a sample-based estimate of the population regression model

- statistical model – a numerical representation of a relationship between at least one independent variable and a dependent variable
- stochastic – random
- *t*-ratio – the ratio of an estimated parameter to its estimated standard error

EXERCISES

1. Draw an X–Y axis through the middle of a 10 × 10 grid. The point where the X and Y lines intersect is known as the "origin" and is defined as the point at which both X and Y are equal to zero. Draw each of the following lines across the values of X from −5 to 5 and write the corresponding regression equation:

   (a) *y*-intercept = 2, slope = 2;
   (b) *y*-intercept = −2, slope = 2;
   (c) *y*-intercept = 0, slope = −1;
   (d) *y*-intercept = 2, slope = −2.

2. Solve each of the following mathematical expressions to yield a single component of the two-variable sample regression model:

   (a) $\hat{\alpha} + \hat{\beta} X_i + \hat{u}_i$
   (b) $Y_i - E(Y|X_i)$
   (c) $\hat{\beta} X_i + \hat{u}_i - Y_i$

3. Using the data set "state_data.dta" (which is available on the textbook's web site at www.cambridge.org/fpsr), we estimated a two-variable regression model using data from each US state and the District of Columbia with per capita income ("*pcinc*" in our data set) as our dependent variable and the percentage of state residents with a college degree ("*pctba*" in our data set) as the independent variable. The estimated equation was:

$$pcinc_i = 11519.78 + 1028.96pctba_i.$$

   Interpret the parameter estimate for the effect of a state's level of education on average income levels.

4. In the data set described in Exercise 3, the value of *pctba* for Illinois equals 29.9. What is the model's predicted per capita income for Illinois?

5. The estimated standard error for the slope parameter in the model described in Exercise 3 was 95.7. Construct a 95 percent confidence interval for this parameter estimate. Show your work. What does this tell you about the estimated relationship?

6. Test the hypothesis that the parameter for *pctba* is not equal to zero. Show your work. What does this tell you about the estimated relationship?

7. Test the hypothesis that the parameter for *pctba* is greater than zero. Show your work. What does this tell you about the estimated relationship?

8. The *R*-squared statistic for the model described in Exercise 3 is 0.70 and the root MSE = 3773.8. What do these numbers tell us about our model?

9. Estimate and interpret the results from a two-variable regression model different from the model in Exercise 3 using the data set "state_data.dta."

10. Think through the assumptions that you made when you carried out Exercise 9. Which do you feel least and most comfortable making? Explain your answers.

11. In Exercise 10 for Chapter 8, you calculated a correlation coefficient for the relationship between two continuous variables. Now, estimate a two-variable regression model for these same two variables. Produce a table of the results and write about what this table tells you about politics in the United Kingdom in 2005.

10 Multiple Regression: the Basics

Despite what we have learned in the preceding chapters on hypothesis testing and statistical significance, we have not yet crossed all four of our hurdles for establishing causal relationships. Recall that all of the techniques we have learned in Chapters 8 and 9 are simply bivariate, X- and Y-type analyses. But, to fully assess whether X causes Y, we need to control for other possible causes of Y, which we have not yet done. In this chapter, we show how multiple regression – which is an extension of the two-variable model we covered in Chapter 9 – does exactly that. We explicitly connect the formulae that we include to the key issues of research design that tie the entire book together. We also discuss some of the problems in multiple regression models when key causes of the dependent variable are omitted, which ties this chapter to the fundamental principles presented in Chapters 3 and 4. Lastly, we will incorporate an example from the political science literature that uses multiple regression to evaluate causal relationships.

10.1 MODELING MULTIVARIATE REALITY

From the very outset of this book, we have emphasized that almost all interesting phenomena in social reality have more than one cause. And yet most of our theories are simply bivariate in nature.

We have shown you (in Chapter 4) that there are distinct methods for dealing with the nature of reality in our designs for social research. If we are fortunate enough to be able to conduct an experiment, then the process of randomly assigning our participants to treatment groups will automatically "control for" those other possible causes that are not a part of our theory.

But in observational research – which represents the vast majority of political science research – there is no automatic control for the other possible causes of our dependent variable; we have to control for them statistically. The main way that social scientists accomplish this is through multiple regression. The math in this model is an extension of the math involved in the two-variable regression model you just learned in Chapter 9.

In this book, we have made quite a big deal out of the need to "control for" alternative explanations. And before we introduce the idea of *statistical* control for Z – which we'll do starting in the next section – we want to distinguish between the *statistical control* that you're about to learn about and the *experimental control* that arises from controlling and randomly assigning values of X in an experiment.[1] Both terms, of course, feature the word "control," and therefore you might be tempted to equate "statistical control" with "experimental control." Experimental control is the far stronger version of control; in fact, as we have emphasized, it is the gold standard for scientific investigations of causality. Statistical control is an imperfect kind of control, and considerably less strong than its experimental counterpart. We'll draw your attention to this again below where it is appropriate, but we want to be sure you're on the lookout for those signs.

10.2   THE POPULATION REGRESSION FUNCTION

We can generalize the population regression model that we learned in Chapter 9,

$$\text{bivariate population regression model:} \quad Y_i = \alpha + \beta X_i + u_i,$$

to include more than one systematic cause of Y, which we have been calling Z throughout this book:

$$\text{multiple population regression model:} \quad Y_i = \alpha + \beta_1 X_i + \beta_2 Z_i + u_i.$$

The interpretation of the slope coefficients in the three-variable model is similar to interpreting bivariate coefficients, with one very important difference. In both, the coefficient in front of the variable X (β in the two-variable model, β_1 in the multiple regression model) represents the "rise-over-run" effect of X on Y. In the multiple regression case, though, β_1 actually represents the effect of X on Y *while holding constant the effects of Z*. If this distinction sounds important, it is. We show how these differences arise in the next section.

---

[1] You will recall, from Chapter 4, that the two components of the definition of an experiment are that the researcher be in control of the values of X that the participants are exposed to, and that those values are assigned to the participants randomly.

10.3 FROM TWO-VARIABLE TO MULTIPLE REGRESSION

Recall from Chapter 9 that the formula for a two-variable regression line (in a sample) is

$$Y_i = \hat{\alpha} + \hat{\beta}X_i + \hat{u}_i.$$

And recall that, to understand the nature of the effect that X has on Y, the estimated coefficient $\hat{\beta}$ tells us, on average, how many units of change in Y we should expect given a one-unit increase in X. The formula for $\hat{\beta}$ in the two-variable model, as we learned in Chapter 9, is

$$\hat{\beta} = \frac{\sum_{i=1}^{n}(X_i - \bar{X})(Y_i - \bar{Y})}{\sum_{i=1}^{n}(X_i - \bar{X})^2}.$$

Given that our goal is to control for the effects of some third variable, Z, how exactly is that accomplished in regression equations? If a scatter plot in two dimensions (X and Y) suggests the formula for a *line*, then adding a third dimension suggests the formula for a *plane*. And the formula for that plane is

$$Y_i = \alpha + \beta_1 X_i + \beta_2 Z_i.$$

That might seem deceptively simple. A formula representing a plane simply adds the additional $\beta_2 Z_i$ term to the formula for a line.[2]

Pay attention to how the notation has changed. In the two-variable formula for a line, there were no numeric subscripts for the β coefficient – because, well, there was only one of them. But now we have two independent variables, X and Z, that help to explain the variation in Y, and therefore we have two different β coefficients, and so we subscript them β_1 and β_2 to be clear that the values of these two effects are different from one another.[3]

The key message from this chapter is that, in the preceding formula, the coefficient β_1 represents more than the effect of X on Y; in the multiple regression formula, it represents *the effect of X on Y while controlling for the effect of Z*. Simultaneously, the coefficient β_2 represents *the effect of Z on Y while controlling for the effect of X*. And in observational research,

---

[2] All of the subsequent math about adding one more independent variable, Z, generalizes quite easily to adding still more independent variables. We use the two-independent-variable case for ease of illustration.

[3] In many other textbooks on regression analysis, just as we distinguish between β_1 and β_2, the authors choose to label their independent variables X_1, X_2, and so forth. We have consistently used the notation of X, Y, and Z to emphasize the concept of controlling for other variables while examining the relationship between an independent and a dependent variable of theoretical interest. Therefore we will stick with this notation throughout this chapter.

this is the key to crossing our fourth causal hurdle that we introduced all the way back in Chapter 3.

How is it the case that the coefficient for β_1 actually controls for Z? After all, β_1 is not connected to Z in the formula; it is, quite obviously, connected to X. The first thing to realize here is that the preceding multiple regression formula for β_1 is different from the two-variable formula for β from Chapter 9. (We'll get to the formula shortly.) The key consequence of this is that the value of β derived from the two-variable formula, representing the effect of X on Y, will almost always be different – perhaps only trivially different, or perhaps wildly different – from the value of β_1 derived from the multiple regression formula, representing the effect of X on Y while controlling for the effects of Z.

But how does β_1 control for the effects of Z? Let's assume that X and Z are correlated. They need not be related in a *causal* sense, and they need not be related *strongly*. They simply have to be correlated with one another – that is, for this example, their covariance is not exactly equal to zero. Now, assuming that they are related somehow, we can write their relationship just like that of a two-variable regression model:

$$X_i = \hat{\alpha}' + \hat{\beta}'Z_i + \hat{e}_i.$$

Note some notational differences here. Instead of the parameters $\hat{\alpha}$ and $\hat{\beta}$, we are calling the estimated parameters $\hat{\alpha}'$ and $\hat{\beta}'$ just so you are aware that their values will be different from the $\hat{\alpha}$ and $\hat{\beta}$ estimates in previous equations. And note also that the residuals, which we labeled $\hat{u}_i$ in previous equations, are now labeled $\hat{e}_i$ here.

If we use Z to predict X, then the predicted value of X (or $\hat{X}$) based on Z is simply

$$\hat{X}_i = \hat{\alpha}' + \hat{\beta}'Z_i,$$

which is just the preceding equation, but without the error term, because it is expected (on average) to be zero. Now, we can just substitute the left-hand side of the preceding equation into the previous equation, and get

$$X_i = \hat{X}_i + \hat{e}_i$$

or, equivalently,

$$\hat{e}_i = X_i - \hat{X}_i.$$

These $\hat{e}_i$, then, are the exact equivalents of the residuals from the two-variable regression of Y on X that you learned from Chapter 9. So their interpretation is identical, too. That being the case, the $\hat{e}_i$ are the portion of the variation in X that Z cannot explain. (The portion of X that Z *can* explain is the predicted portion – the $\hat{X}_i$.)

So what have we done here? We have just documented the relationship between Z and X and partitioned the variation in X into two parts – the portion that Z *can* explain (the $\hat{X}_i$) and the portion that Z *cannot* explain (the $\hat{e}_i$). Hold this thought.

We can do the exact same thing for the relationship between Z and Y that we just did for the relationship between Z and X. The process will look quite similar, with a bit of different notation to distinguish the processes. So we can model Y as a function of Z in the following way:

$$Y_i = \hat{\alpha}^* + \hat{\beta}^* Z_i + \hat{v}_i.$$

Here, the estimated slope is $\hat{\beta}^*$ and the error term is represented by $\hat{v}_i$.

Just as we did with Z and X, if we use Z to predict Y, then the predicted value of Y (or $\hat{Y}$) (which we will label $\hat{Y}^*$) based on Z is simply

$$\hat{Y}_i^* = \hat{\alpha}^* + \hat{\beta}^* Z_i,$$

which, as before, is identical to the preceding equation, but without the error term, because the residuals are expected (on average) to be zero. And again, as before, we can substitute the left-hand side of the preceding equation into the previous equation, and get

$$Y_i = \hat{Y}_i^* + \hat{v}_i$$

or, equivalently,

$$\hat{v}_i = Y_i - \hat{Y}_i^*.$$

These $\hat{v}_i$, then, are interpreted in an identical way to that of the preceding $\hat{e}_i$. They represent the portion of the variation in Y that Z cannot explain. (The portion of Y that Z *can* explain is the predicted portion – the $\hat{Y}_i^*$.)

Now what has this accomplished? We have just documented the relationship between Z and Y and partitioned the variation in Y into two parts – the portion that Z *can* explain and the portion that Z *cannot* explain.

So we have now let Z try to explain X and found the residuals (the $\hat{e}_i$ values); similarly, we have also now let Z try to explain Y, and found those residuals as well (the $\hat{v}_i$ values). Now back to our three-variable regression model that we have seen before, with Y as the dependent variable, and X and Z as the independent variables:

$$Y_i = \hat{\alpha} + \hat{\beta}_1 X_i + \hat{\beta}_2 Z_i + \hat{u}_i.$$

The formula for $\hat{\beta}_1$, representing the effect of X on Y while controlling for Z, is

$$\hat{\beta}_1 = \frac{\sum_{i=1}^n \hat{e}_i \hat{v}_i}{\sum_{i=1}^n \hat{e}_i^2}.$$

Now, we know what $\hat{e}_i$ and $\hat{v}_i$ are from the previous equations. So, substituting, we get

$$\hat{\beta}_1 = \frac{\sum_{i=1}^{n}(X_i - \hat{X}_i)(Y_i - \hat{Y}_i^*)}{\sum_{i=1}^{n}(X_i - \hat{X}_i)^2}.$$

Pay careful attention to this formula. The "hatted" components in these expressions are from the two-variable regressions involving Z that we previously learned about. The key components of the formula for the effect of X on Y, while controlling for Z, are the $\hat{e}_i$ and $\hat{v}_i$, which, as we just learned, are the portions of X and Y (respectively) that Z cannot account for. And that is how, in the multiple regression model, the parameter β_1, which represents the effects of X on Y, *controls for* the effects of Z. How? Because the only components of X and Y that it uses are components that Z cannot account for – that is, the $\hat{e}_i$ and $\hat{v}_i$.

Comparing this formula for estimating β_1 with the two-variable formula for estimating β is very revealing. Instead of using the factors $(X_i - \bar{X})$ and $(Y_i - \bar{Y})$ in the numerator, which were the components of the *two-variable* regression of Y on X from Chapter 9, in the multiple regression formula that controls for Z, the factors in the numerator are $(X_i - \hat{X}_i)$ and $(Y_i - \hat{Y}_i^*)$, where, again, the hatted portions represent X as predicted by Z and Y as predicted by Z.

Note something else in the comparison of the two-variable formula for estimating β and the multiple regression formula for estimating β_1. The result of $\hat{\beta}$ in the two-variable regression of Y and X and $\hat{\beta}_1$ in the three-variable regression of Y on X while controlling for Z will be different almost all the time. In fact, it is quite rare – though mathematically possible in theory – that those two values will be identical.[4]

And the formula for estimating β_2, likewise, represents the effects of Z on Y while controlling for the effects of X. These processes, in fact, happen simultaneously.

It's been a good number of chapters – six of them, to be precise – between the first moment when we discussed the importance of controlling for Z and the point, just above, when we showed you precisely how to do it. The fourth causal hurdle has never been too far from front-and-center since Chapter 3, and now you know the process of crossing it for observational data.

Don't get too optimistic too quickly, though. First, as we noted, the three-variable setup we just mentioned can easily be generalized to more than three variables. But the formula for estimating β_1 controls only for

---

[4] Later in this chapter, you will see that there are two situations in which the two-variable and multiple regression parameter estimates of β will be the same.

the effects of the Z variable that are included in the regression equation. It does not control for other variables that are not measured and not included in the model. And what happens when we fail to include a relevant cause of Y in our regression model? Bad things. (Those bad things will come into focus a bit later in this chapter.)

Second, as we foreshadowed at the beginning of this chapter, the type of control that we have just introduced for observational studies, what we call "statistical control," is not as strong as the experimental control that we described in Chapter 4. We hope that you can see that the type of control that is present in multiple regression is more akin to an accounting device based on the amounts of shared variance between X, Y, and Z. "Controlling for" Z in the regression sense involves identifying the variation that is shared between Z and the other two variables, and discounting it, and then looking at the relationship that remains between X and Y after the shared variation with Z is removed. This does represent a type of control, to be sure, but it is not as powerful as randomly assigning values of X to participants in an experiment. As we described back in Chapter 4, the reason that experimental control is so powerful is that we know exactly the process that generates values of X. (That process is simple randomness, and nothing more.) With statistical control in observational studies, by contrast, we do not know anything specific about the data-generating process of X. In such studies without experimental control, participants might choose or somehow acquire their own values of X, or there might be a complex causal process that sorts cases into different values of X. And it is possible that that very causal process is somehow polluted by some Z that we have failed to control for, or by Y (and, if this is true, it has even more severely negative consequences). All of this, though, is a normal part of the scientific process. It is always possible that there is another, uncontrolled-for Z out there. But, as a part of this process, it is best to put the results out in the open and see how well they stand the test of time.

10.4 INTERPRETING MULTIPLE REGRESSION

For an illustration of how to interpret multiple regression coefficients, let's return to our example from Chapter 9, in which we showed you the results of a regression of US presidential election results on the previous year's growth rate in the US economy (see Figure 9.5). The model we estimated, you will recall, was inc_vote $= \alpha + \beta \times$ g, where inc_vote is "vote" and g is "growth," and the estimated coefficients there were $\hat{\alpha} = 51.45$ and $\hat{\beta} = 0.62$. For the purposes of this example, we need to drop the observation from the presidential election of 1876. Doing this

Table 10.1 Three regression models of US presidential elections

	A	B	C
Growth	0.65*	—	0.58*
	(0.15)	—	(0.15)
Good News	—	0.87*	0.63*
	—	(0.32)	(0.28)
Intercept	51.61*	47.63*	48.47*
	(0.81)	(1.87)	(1.58)
R-squared	0.35	0.18	0.44
Number of cases	35	35	35

Notes: The dependent variable is the percentage of the two major parties' vote for the incumbent party's candidate.
Standard errors are in parentheses.
*$p < 0.05$, two-tailed t-test.

changes our estimates slightly so that $\hat{\alpha} = 51.61$ and $\hat{\beta} = 0.65$.[5] Those results are in column A of Table 10.1.

In column A, you see the parameter estimate (0.65) for the annual growth rate in the US economy (in the row labeled "Growth"), and the standard error of that estimated slope, 0.15. In the row labeled "Intercept," you see the estimated y-intercept for that regression, 51.61, and its associated standard error, 0.81. Both parameter estimates are statistically significant, as indicated by the asterisk and the note at the bottom of the table.

Recall that the interpretation of the slope coefficient in a two-variable regression indicates that, for every one-unit increase in the independent variable, we expect to see β units of change in the dependent variable. In the current context, $\hat{\beta} = 0.65$ means that, for every extra one percentage point in growth rate in the US economy, we expect to see, on average, an extra 0.65 percent in the vote percentage for the incumbent party in presidential elections.

But recall our admonition, throughout this book, about being too quick to interpret any bivariate analysis as evidence of a causal relationship. We have not shown, in column A of Table 10.1, that higher growth rates in the economy *cause* incumbent-party vote totals to be higher. To be sure, the evidence in column A is consistent with a causal connection,

---

[5] We had to drop 1876 because Fair's data do not include a measure for the new variable that we are adding in this example, "Good News," for that year. When making comparisons across different models of the same data, it is extremely important to have exactly the same cases.

but it does not *prove* it. Why not? Because we have not controlled for other possible causes of election outcomes. Surely there are other causes, in addition to how the economy has (or has not) grown in the last year, of how well the incumbent party will fare in a presidential election. Indeed, we can even imagine other *economic* causes that might bolster our statistical explanation of presidential elections.[6]

Consider the fact that the growth variable accounts for economic growth over the past year. But perhaps the public rewards or punishes the incumbent party for *sustained* economic growth over the long run. In particular, it does not necessarily make sense for the public to reelect a party that has presided over three years of subpar growth in the economy but a fourth year with solid growth. And yet, with our single measure of growth, we are assuming – rather unrealistically – that the public would pay attention to the growth rate only in the past year. Surely the public does pay attention to recent growth, but the public might also pay heed to growth over the long run.

In column B of Table 10.1, we estimate another two-variable regression model, this time using the number of consecutive quarters of strong economic growth leading up to the presidential election – the variable is labeled "Good News" – as our independent variable.[7] (Incumbent-party vote share remains our dependent variable.) In the row labeled "Good News," we see that the parameter estimate is 0.87, which means that, on average, for every additional consecutive quarter of good economic news, we expect to see a 0.87 percent increase in incumbent-party vote share. The coefficient is statistically significant at the usual standard of 0.05.

Our separate two-variable regressions each show a relationship between the independent variable in the particular model and incumbent-party vote shares. But none of the parameter estimates in columns A or B was estimated while controlling for the other independent variable. We rectify that situation in column C, in which we estimate the effects of both the "Growth" and "Good News" variables on vote shares simultaneously.

Compare column C with columns A and B. In the row labeled "Good News," we see that the estimated parameter of $\hat{\beta} = 0.63$ indicates that, for every extra quarter of a year with strong growth rates, the incumbent party should expect to see an additional 0.63 percent of the national vote share, *while controlling for the effects of Growth*. Note the additional clause in the interpretation as well as the emphasis that we place on it. Multiple

---

[6] And, of course, we can imagine variables relating to success or failure in foreign policy, for example, as other, noneconomic causes of election outcomes.

[7] Fair's operationalization of this variable is "the number of quarters in the first 15 quarters of the administration in which the growth rate of real per capita GDP is greater than 3.2 percent."

regression coefficients always represent the effects of a one-point increase in that particular independent variable on the dependent variable, *while controlling for the effects of all other independent variables in the model.* The higher the number of quarters of continuous strong growth in the economy, the higher the incumbent-party vote share should be in the next election, controlling for the previous year's growth rate.

But, critical to this chapter's focus on multiple regression, notice in column C how including the "Good News" variable changes the estimated effect of the "Growth" variable from an estimated 0.65 in column A to 0.58 in column C. The effect in column C is different because it *controls for the effects of Good News.* That is, when the effects of long-running economic expansions are controlled for, the effects of short-term growth falls a bit. The effect is still quite strong and is still statistically significant, but it is more modest once the effects of long-term growth are taken into account.[8] Note also that the R^2 statistic rises from 0.35 in column A to 0.44 in column C, which means that adding the "Good News" variable increased the proportion of the variance of our dependent variable that we have explained by 9 percent.[9]

In this particular example, the whole emphasis on controlling for other causes might seem like much ado about nothing. After all, comparing the three columns in Table 10.1 did not change our interpretation of whether short-term growth rates affect incumbent-party fortunes at the polls. But we didn't know this until we tested for the effects of long-term growth. And later in this chapter, we will see an example in which controlling for new causes of the dependent variable substantially changes our interpretations about causal relationships. We should be clear about one other

---

[8] And we can likewise compare the bivariate effect of Good News on vote shares in column B with the multivariate results in column C, noting that the effect of Good News, in the multivariate context, appears to have fallen by approximately one-fourth.

[9] It is important to be cautious when reporting contributions to R^2 statistics by individual independent variables, and this table provides a good example of why this is the case. If we were to estimate Model A first and C second, we might be tempted to conclude that Growth explains 35 percent of Vote and Good News explains 9 percent. But if we estimated Model B first and then C, we might be tempted to conclude that Growth explains 26 percent of Vote and Good News explains 18 percent. Actually, both of these sets of conclusions are faulty. The R^2 is always a measure of the overall fit of the model to the dependent variable. So, all that we can say about the R^2 for Model C is that Growth, Good News, and the intercept term together explain 44 percent of the variation in Vote. So, although we can talk about how the addition or subtraction of a particular variable to a model increases or decreases the model's R^2, we should not be tempted to attribute particular values of R^2 to specific independent variables. If we examine Figure 10.1 (in Section 10.7), we can get some intuition on why this is the case. The R^2 statistic for the model represented in this figure is $(f + d + b)/(a + f + d + b)$. It is the presence of area d that confounds our ability to make definitive statements about the contribution of individual variables to R^2.

thing regarding Table 10.1: Despite controlling for another variable, we still have a long way to go before we can say that we've controlled for all other possible causes of the dependent variable. As a result, we should be cautious about interpreting those results as proof of causality. However, as we continue to add possibly confounding independent variables to our regression model, we inch closer and closer to saying that we've controlled for every other possible cause that comes to mind. Recall that, all the way back in Chapter 1, we noted that one of the "rules of the road" of the scientific enterprise is to always be willing to consider new evidence. New evidence – in the form of controlling for other independent variables – can change our inferences about whether any particular independent variable is causally related to the dependent variable.

10.5 WHICH EFFECT IS "BIGGEST"?

In the preceding analysis, we might be tempted to look at the coefficients in column C of Table 10.1 for Growth (0.58) and for Good News (0.63) and conclude that the effect for Good News is larger than the effect for Growth. As tempting as such a conclusion might be, it must be avoided, for one critical reason: The two independent variables are measured in different metrics, which makes that comparison misleading. Short-run growth rates are measured in a different metric – ranging from negative numbers for times during which the economy shrunk, all the way through stronger periods during which growth exceeded 5 percent per year – than are the number of quarters of consecutive strong growth – which ranges from 0 in the data set through 10. That makes comparing the coefficients misleading.

Because the coefficients in Table 10.1 each exist in the native metric of each variable, they are referred to as **unstandardized coefficients**. Although they are normally not easy to compare to one another, there is a rather simple method to remove the metric of each variable to make them comparable with one another. As you might imagine, such coefficients, because they are on a standardized metric, are referred to as **standardized coefficients**. We compute them, quite simply, by taking the unstandardized coefficients and taking out the metrics – in the forms of the standard deviations – of both the independent and dependent variables:

$$\hat{\beta}_{\text{Std}} = \hat{\beta}\frac{s_X}{s_Y},$$

where $\hat{\beta}_{\text{Std}}$ is the standardized regression coefficient, $\hat{\beta}$ is the unstandardized coefficient (as in Table 10.1), and s_X and s_Y are the standard deviations of X and Y, respectively. The interpretation of the standardized coefficients changes, not surprisingly. Whereas the unstandardized coefficients represent the expected change in Y given a one-unit increase in X, the standardized coefficients represent the expected *standard deviation* change in Y given a *one-standard-deviation* increase in X. Now, because all parameter estimates are in the same units – that is, in expected standard deviation changes of the dependent variable – they become more readily comparable.

Implementing this formula for the unstandardized coefficients in column C of Table 10.1 produces the following results. First, for Growth, where standard deviations are calculated using the last equation in Subsection 6.4.2, we have

$$\hat{\beta}_{\text{Std}} = 0.58 \left(\frac{5.50}{6.02} \right) = 0.53.$$

Next, for Good News,

$$\hat{\beta}_{\text{Std}} = 0.63 \left(\frac{2.95}{6.02} \right) = 0.31.$$

These coefficients would be interpreted as follows: For a one-standard-deviation increase in Growth, on average, we expect a 0.53-standard-deviation increase in the incumbent-party vote share, controlling for the effect of Good News. And for a one-standard-deviation increase in Good News, we expect to see, on average, a 0.31-standard-deviation increase in the incumbent-party vote shares, controlling for the effect of Growth. Note how, when looking at the unstandardized coefficients, we might have mistakenly thought that the effect of Good News was larger than the effect of Growth. But the standardized coefficients (correctly) tell the opposite story: The estimated effect of Growth is 170 percent of the size of the effect of Good News.[10]

YOUR TURN: Interpreting standardized coefficients

What would be the substantive interpretation for the effect of Good News if $\hat{\beta}_{\text{Std}} = -0.31$?

---

[10] Some objections have been raised about the use of standardized coefficients (King, 1986). From a technical perspective, because standard deviations can differ across samples, this makes the results of standardized coefficients particularly sample specific. Additionally, and from a broader perspective, one-unit or one-standard-deviation shifts in different independent variables have different substantive meanings regardless of the metrics in which the variables are measured. We might therefore logically conclude that there isn't much use in trying to figure out which effect is biggest.

10.6 STATISTICAL AND SUBSTANTIVE SIGNIFICANCE

Related to the admonition about which effect is "biggest," consider the following, seemingly simpler, question: Are the effects found in column C of Table 10.1 "big"? A tempting answer to that question is "Well of course they're big. Both coefficients are statistically significant. Therefore, they're big."

That logic, although perhaps appealing, is faulty. Recall the discussion from Chapter 7 on the effects of sample size on the magnitude of the standard error of the mean. And we noted in Chapter 9 that the same effects of sample size are present on the magnitude of the standard error of our regression coefficients. What this means is that, even if the strength of the relationship (as measured by our coefficient estimates) remains constant, by merely increasing our sample size we can affect the statistical significance of those coefficients. Why? Because statistical significance is determined by a t-test in which the standard error is in the denominator of that quotient. What you can remember is that larger sample sizes will shrink standard errors and therefore make finding statistically significant relationships more likely.[11] It is also apparent from Appendix B that, when the number of degrees of freedom is greater, it is easier to achieve statistical significance.

We hope that you can see that arbitrarily increasing the size of a sample, and therefore finding statistically significant relationships, does not in any way make an effect "bigger" or even "big." Recall, such changes to the standard errors have no bearing on the rise-over-run nature of the slope coefficients themselves.

How, then, should you judge whether an effect of one variable on another is "big?" One way is to use the method just described – using standardized coefficients. By placing the variances of X and Y on the same metric, it is possible to come to a judgment about how big an effect is. This is particularly helpful when the independent variables X and Z, or the dependent variable Y, or both, are measured in metrics that are unfamiliar or artificial.

When the metrics of the variables in a regression analysis are intuitive and well known, however, rendering a judgment about whether an effect is large or small becomes something of a matter of interpretation. For example, in Chapter 11, we will see an example relating the effects of changes in the unemployment rate (X) on a president's approval rating (Y). It is very simple to interpret that a slope coefficient of, say, -1.51, means

---

[11] To be certain, it's not always possible to increase sample sizes, and, even when possible, it is nearly always costly to do so. The research situations in which increasing sample size is most likely, albeit still expensive, is in mass-based survey research.

that, for every additional point of unemployment, we expect approval to go down by 1.51 points, controlling for other factors in the model. Is that effect large, small, or moderate? There is something of a judgment call to be made here, but at least, in this case, the metrics of both X and Y are quite familiar; most people with even an elementary familiarity with politics will need no explanation as to what unemployment rates mean or what approval polls mean. Independent of the statistical significance of that estimate – which, you should note, we have not mentioned here – discussions of this sort represent attempts to judge the **substantive significance** of a coefficient estimate. Substantive significance is more difficult to judge than statistical significance because there are no numeric formulae for making such judgments. Instead, substantive significance is a judgment call about whether or not statistically significant relationships are "large" or "small" in terms of their real-world impact.

From time to time we will see a "large" parameter estimate that is not statistically significant. Although it is tempting to describe such a result as substantively significant, it is not. We can understand this by thinking about what it means for a particular result to be statistically significant. As we discussed in Chapter 9, in most cases we are testing the null hypothesis that the population parameter is equal to zero. In such cases, even when we have a large parameter estimate, if it is statistically insignificant this means that it is not statistically distinguishable from zero. Therefore a parameter estimate can be substantively significant only when it is also statistically significant.

10.7   WHAT HAPPENS WHEN WE FAIL TO CONTROL FOR Z?

Controlling for the effects of other possible causes of our dependent variable Y, we have maintained, is critical to making the correct causal inferences. Some of you might be wondering something like the following: "How does omitting Z from a regression model affect my inference of whether X causes Y? Z isn't X, and Z isn't Y, so why should omitting Z matter?"

Consider the following three-variable regression model involving our now-familiar trio of X, Y, and Z:

$$Y_i = \alpha + \beta_1 X_i + \beta_2 Z_i + u_i.$$

And assume, for the moment, that this is the *correct* model of reality. That is, the only systematic causes of Y are X and Z; and, to some degree, Y is also influenced by some random error component, u.

Now let's assume that, instead of estimating this correct model, we fail to estimate the effects of Z. That is, we estimate

$$Y_i = \alpha + \beta_1^* X_i + u_i^*.$$

As we previously hinted, the value of β_1 in the correct, three-variable equation and the value of β_1^* will not be identical under most circumstances. (We'll see the exceptions in a moment.) And that, right there, should be enough to raise red flags. For, if we know that the three-variable model is the *correct* model – and what that means, of course, is that the estimated value of β_1 that we obtain from the data will be equal to the true population value – and if we know that β_1 will not be equal to β_1^*, then there is a problem with the estimated value of β_1^*. That problem is a statistical problem called **bias**, which means that the expected value of the parameter estimate that we obtain from a sample will not be equal to the true population parameter. The specific type of bias that results from the failure to include a variable that belongs in our regression model is called **omitted-variables bias**.

Let's get specific about the nature of omitted-variables bias. If, instead of estimating the true three-variable model, we estimate the incorrect two-variable model, the formula for the slope β_1^* will be

$$\hat{\beta}_1^* = \frac{\sum_{i=1}^{n}(X_i - \bar{X})(Y_i - \bar{Y})}{\sum_{i=1}^{n}(X_i - \bar{X})^2}.$$

Notice that this is simply the two-variable formula for the effect of X on Y. (Of course, the model we just estimated is a two-variable model, in spite of the fact that we know that Z, as well as X, affects Y.) But because we know that Z *should* be in the model, and we know from Chapter 9 that regression lines travel through the mean values of each variable, we can figure out that the following is true:

$$(Y_i - \bar{Y}) = \beta_1(X_i - \bar{X}) + \beta_2(Z_i - \bar{Z}) + (u_i - \bar{u}).$$

We can do this because we know that the plane will travel through each variable's mean.

Now notice that the left-hand side of the preceding equation, the $(Y_i - \bar{Y})$, is identical to one portion of the numerator of the slope for $\hat{\beta}_1^*$. Therefore we can substitute the right-hand side of the preceding equation – yes, that entire mess – into the numerator of the formula for $\hat{\beta}_1^*$.

The resulting math isn't anything that is beyond your skills in algebra, but it is cumbersome, so we won't derive it here. After a few lines of multiplying and reducing, though, the formula for $\hat{\beta}_1^*$ will reduce to

$$E(\hat{\beta}_1^*) = \beta_1 + \beta_2 \frac{\sum_{i=1}^{n}(X_i - \bar{X})(Z_i - \bar{Z})}{\sum_{i=1}^{n}(X_i - \bar{X})^2}.$$

This might seem like a mouthful – a fact that's rather hard to deny – but there is a very important message in it. What the equation says is that the estimated effect of X on Y, $\hat{\beta}_1^*$, in which we do not include the effects of Z on Y (but should have), will be equal to the true β_1 – that is, the effect with Z taken into account – plus a bundle of other stuff. That other stuff, strictly speaking, is bias. And because this bias came about as a result of omitting a variable (Z) that should have been in the model, this type of bias is known as omitted-variables bias.

Obviously, we'd like the expected value of our $\hat{\beta}_1^*$ (estimated without Z) to equal the true β_1 (as if we had estimated the equation with Z). And if the product on the right-hand side of the "+" sign in the preceding equation equals zero, it will. When will that happen?[12] In two circumstances, neither of which is particularly likely. First, $\hat{\beta}_1^* = \beta_1$ if $\beta_2 = 0$. Second, $\hat{\beta}_1^* = \beta_1$ if the large quotient at the end of the equation, the

$$\frac{\sum_{i=1}^{n}(X_i - \bar{X})(Z_i - \bar{Z})}{\sum_{i=1}^{n}(X_i - \bar{X})^2},$$

is equal to zero. What is that quotient? It should look familiar; in fact, it is the bivariate slope parameter of a regression of Z on X.

In the first of these two special circumstances, the bias term will equal zero if and only if the effect of Z on Y – that is, the parameter β_2 – is zero. Okay, so it's safe to omit an independent variable from a regression equation if it has no effect on the dependent variable. (If that seems obvious to you, good.) The second circumstance is a bit more interesting: It's safe to omit an independent variable Z from an equation if it is entirely unrelated to the other independent variable X. Of course, if we omit Z in such circumstances, we'll still be deprived of understanding how Z affects Y; but at least, so long as Z and X are absolutely unrelated, omitting Z will not adversely affect our estimate of the effect of X on Y.[13]

We emphasize that this second condition is unlikely to occur in practice. Therefore, if Z affects Y, and Z and X are related, then if we omit Z from our model, our bias term will not equal zero. In the end, omitting Z will cause us to misestimate the effect of X on Y.

This result has many practical implications. Foremost among them is the fact that, even if you aren't interested theoretically in the connection between Z and Y, you need to control for it, statistically, in order to get an unbiased estimate of the impact of X, which is the focus of the theoretical investigation.

---

[12] To be very clear, for a mathematical product to equal zero, either one or both of the components must be zero.

[13] Omitting Z from our regression model also drives down the R^2 statistic.

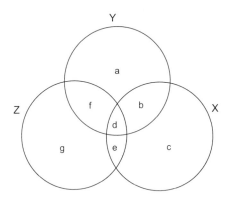

Figure 10.1 Venn diagram in which X, Y, and Z are correlated

That might seem unfair, but it's true. If we estimate a regression model that omits an independent variable (Z) that belongs in the model, then the effects of that Z will somehow work their way into the parameter estimates for the independent variable that we do estimate (X) and pollute our estimate of the effect of X on Y.

The preceding equation also suggests when the magnitude of the bias is likely to be large and when it is likely to be small. If either or both of the components of the bias term

$$\beta_2 \quad \text{and} \quad \frac{\sum_{i=1}^{n}(X_i - \bar{X})(Z_i - \bar{Z})}{\sum_{i=1}^{n}(X_i - \bar{X})^2}$$

are *close to* zero, then the bias is likely to be small (because the bias term is the product of both components); but if both are likely to be large, then the bias is likely to be quite large.

Moreover, the equation also suggests the likely *direction* of the bias. All we have said thus far is that the coefficient $\hat{\beta}_1^*$ will be biased – that is, it will not equal its true value. But will it be too large or too small? If we have good guesses about the values of β_2 and the correlation between X and Z – that is, whether or not they are positive or negative – then we can suspect the direction of the bias. For example, suppose that β_1, β_2, and the correlation between X and Z are all positive. That means that our estimated coefficient $\hat{\beta}_1^*$ will be larger than it is supposed to be, because a positive number plus the product of two positive numbers will be a still-larger positive number. And so on.[14]

To better understand the importance of controlling for other possible causes of the dependent variable and the importance of the relationship (or the lack of one) between X and Z, consider the following graphical illustrations. In Figure 10.1, we represent the total variation of Y, X, and Z each with a circle.[15] The covariation between any of these two variables – or among all three – is represented by the places where the circles overlap.

---

[14] With more than two independent variables, it becomes more complex to figure out the direction of the bias.

[15] Recall from Chapter 9 how we introduced Venn diagrams to represent variation (the circles) and covariation (the overlapping portion of the circles).

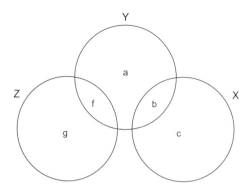

Figure 10.2 Venn diagram in which X and Z are correlated with Y, but not with each other

Thus, in the figure, the total variation in Y is represented as the sum of the area $a + b + d + f$. The covariation between Y and X is represented by the area $b + d$.

Note in Figure 10.1, though, that the variable Z is related to both Y and X (because the circle for Z overlaps with both Y and X). In particular, the relationship between Y and Z is accounted for by the area $f + d$, and the relationship between Z and X is accounted for by the area $d + e$. As we have already seen, d is also a portion of the relationship between Y and X. If, hypothetically, we erased the circle for Z from the figure, we would (incorrectly) attribute all of the area $b + d$ to X, when in fact the d portion of the variation in Y is shared by *both* X and Z. This is why, when Z is related to both X and Y, if we fail to control for Z, we will end up with a biased estimate of X's effect on Y.

Consider the alternative scenario, in which both X and Z affect Y, but X and Z are completely unrelated to one another. That scenario is portrayed graphically in Figure 10.2. There, the circles for both X and Z overlap with the circle for Y, but they do not overlap at all with one another. In that case – which, we have noted, is unlikely in applied research – we can safely omit consideration of Z when considering the effects of X on Y. In that figure, the relationship between X and Y, the area b, is unaffected by the presence (or absence) of Z in the model.[16]

10.7.1   An Additional Minimal Mathematical Requirement in Multiple Regression

We outlined a set of assumptions and minimal mathematical requirements for the two-variable regression model in Chapter 9. In multiple regression, all of these assumptions are made and all of the same minimal mathematical requirements remain in place. In addition to those, however, we need to add one more minimal mathematical requirement to be able to estimate our multiple regression models: It must be the case that *there is no exact linear relationship* between any two or more of our independent variables (which we have called X and Z). This is also called the assumption of

---

[16] For identical reasons, we could safely estimate the effect of Z on Y, the area f, without considering the effect of X.

no **perfect multicollinearity** (by which we mean that X and Z cannot be *perfectly* collinear, with a correlation coefficient of $r = 1.0$).

What does it mean to say that X and Z cannot exist in an exact linear relationship? Refer back to Figure 10.1. If X and Z had an *exact* linear relationship, instead of having some degree of overlap – that is, some imperfect degree of correlation – the circles would be exactly on top of one another. In such cases, it is literally impossible to estimate the regression model, as separating out the effects of X on Y from the effects of Z on Y is impossible.

This is not to say that we must assume that X and Z are entirely uncorrelated with one another (as in Figure 10.2). In fact, in almost all applications, X and Z will have some degree of correlation between them. Things become complicated only as that correlation approaches 1.0; and when it hits 1.0, the regression model will fail to be estimable with both X and Z as independent variables. In Chapter 11 we will discuss these issues further.

10.8 AN EXAMPLE FROM THE LITERATURE: COMPETING THEORIES OF HOW POLITICS AFFECTS INTERNATIONAL TRADE

What are the forces that affect international trade? Economists have long noted that there are economic forces that shape the extent to which two nations trade with one another.[17] The size of each nation's economy, the physical distance between them, and the overall level of development have all been investigated as economic causes of trade.[18] But in addition to economic forces, does politics help to shape international trade?

Morrow, Siverson, and Tabares (1998) investigate three competing (and perhaps complementary) political explanations for the extent to which two nations engage in international trade. The first theory is that states with friendly relations are more likely to trade with one another than are states engaged in conflict. Conflict, in this sense, need not be militarized disputes (though it may be).[19] Conflict, they argue, can dampen trade in several ways. First, interstate conflict can sometimes produce embargoes

---

[17] Theories of trade and, indeed, many theories about other aspects of international trade are usually developed with pairs of nations in mind. Thus all of the relevant variables, like trade, are measured in terms of pairs of nations, which are often referred to as "dyads" by international relations scholars. The resulting **dyadic data** sets are often quite large because they encompass each relevant pair of nations.

[18] Such models are charmingly referred to as "gravity models," because, according to these theories, the forces driving trade resemble the forces that determine gravitational attraction between two physical objects.

[19] See Pollins (1989) for an extended discussion of this theory.

(or prohibitions on trade). Second, conflict can reduce trade by raising the risks for firms that wish to engage in cross-border trading.

The second theory is that trade will be higher when both nations are democracies and lower when one (or both) is an autocracy.[20] Because democracies have more open political and judicial systems, trade should be higher between democracies because firms in one country will have greater assurance that any trade disputes will be resolved openly and fairly in courts to which they have access. In contrast, firms in a democratic state may be more reluctant to trade with nondemocratic countries, because it is less certain how any disagreements will be resolved. In addition, firms may be wary of trading with nondemocracies for fear of having their assets seized by the foreign government. In short, trading with an autocratic government should raise the perceived risks of international trade.

The third theory is that states that are in an alliance with one another are more likely to trade with one another than are states that are not in such an alliance.[21] For states that are not in an alliance, one nation may be reluctant to trade with another nation if the first thinks that the gains from trade may be used to arm itself for future conflict. In contrast, states in an alliance stand to gain from each other's increased wealth as a result of trade.

To test these theories, Morrow, Siverson, and Tabares (1998) look at trade among all of the major powers in the international system – the United States, Britain, France, Germany, Russia, and Italy – during most of the twentieth century. They consider each pair of states – called *dyads* – separately and examine exports to each country on an annual basis.[22] Their dependent variable is the amount of exports in every dyadic relationship in each year.

Table 10.2 shows excerpts from the analysis of Morrow, Siverson, and Tabares.[23] In column A, they show that, as the first theory predicts, increases in interstate peace are associated with higher amounts of trade between countries, controlling for economic factors. In addition, the larger the economy in general, the more trade there is. (This finding is consistent across all estimation equations.) The results in column B indicate that pairs of democracies trade at higher rates than do pairs involving at least one nondemocracy. Finally, the results in column C show that trade is higher

---

[20] See Dixon and Moon (1993) for an elaboration of this theory.

[21] See Gowa (1989) and Gowa and Mansfield (1993) for an extended discussion, including distinctions between bipolar and multipolar organizations of the international system.

[22] This research design is often referred to as a time-series cross-section design, because it contains both variation between units and variation across time. In this sense, it is a hybrid of the two types of quasi-experiments discussed in Chapter 3.

[23] Interpreting the precise magnitudes of the parameter estimates is a bit tricky in this case, because the independent variables were all transformed by use of natural logarithms.

Table 10.2 Excerpts from Morrow, Siverson, and Tabares's table on the political causes of international trade

	A	B	C	D
Peaceful relations	1.12*	—	—	1.45*
	(0.22)	—	—	(0.37)
Democratic partners	—	1.18*	—	1.22*
	—	(0.12)	—	(0.13)
Alliance partners	—	—	0.29*	−0.50*
	—	—	(0.03)	(0.16)
GNP of exporter	0.67*	0.57*	0.68*	0.56*
	(0.07)	(0.07)	(0.07)	(0.08)
R^2	0.77	0.78	0.77	0.78
N	2631	2631	2631	2631

Notes: Other variables were estimated as a part of the regression model but were excluded from this table for ease of presentation.
Standard errors are in parentheses.
*$p < 0.05$.

between alliance partners than between states that are not in an alliance with one another. All of these effects are statistically significant.

So far, each of the theories received at least some support. But, as you can tell from looking at the table, the results in columns A through C do not control for the other explanations. That is, we have yet to see results of a full multiple regression model, in which the theories can compete for explanatory power. That situation is rectified in column D, in which all three political variables are entered in the same regression model. There, we see that the effects of reduced hostility between states is actually enhanced in the multiple regression context – compare the coefficient of 1.12 with the multiple regression 1.45. Similarly, the effects of democratic trading partners remains almost unchanged in the fully multivariate framework. However, the effect of alliances changes. Before controlling for conflict and democracy, the effect of alliances was (as expected) positive and statistically significant. However, in column D, in which we control for conflict and democracy, the effect flips signs and is now *negative* (and statistically significant), which means that, when we control for these factors, states in an alliance are less (not more) likely to trade with one another.

The article by Morrow, Siverson, and Tabares (1998) represents a case in which synthesizing several competing explanations for the same phenomenon – international trade – produces surprising findings. By using a data set that allowed them to test all three theories simultaneously,

Morrow, Siverson, and Tabares were able to sort out which theories received support and which did not.

10.9   MAKING EFFECTIVE USE OF TABLES AND FIGURES

At this point in your class, it's likely that you've spent time in a computer lab learning how to conduct your own analyses. We understand – because we experienced it ourselves when we were your age – that it can feel like a pretty big leap to go from understanding how a statistical formula works algebraically from a book or a class presentation, to understanding how to critique how these methods are applied in work like that by Morrow, Siverson, and Tabares (1998) that we just described in the previous section, to understanding how things work when you're looking at statistical software output on your own computer.

We realize, too, that many of you have interests in conducting your own analyses to investigate problems that you find to be interesting. Good! Perhaps you have an independent study or an honors thesis to work on, or some other project that you want to include as a writing sample for applications to graduate school. And you want to learn to communicate your ideas and findings clearly for your intended audience. That's what this section is about.

We strongly recommend that you spend a lot of time constructing the tables and figures that you include in your projects. When readers first encounter your written work, many of them will take a quick look at the title and introduction and then go directly to your tables and figures. This is certainly a reasonable thing to do when someone is trying to evaluate whether or not they should invest further time reviewing your work. Thus, although they may appear at the back of your project, tables and figures often determine the first impression that potential readers have of your project. As such, we recommend that you construct your tables and figures so they stand on their own and draw readers in. With these two considerations in mind, we have a set of recommendations for what you should and should not do as you put your tables and figures together. We also recommend that you tell readers in the text of your project what they should see in your tables and figures. Some of this can be learned by reading other scholars' work on similar subjects: Take time, when you read, to think about what works and what doesn't work in terms of other scholars' use of tables and figures.

10.9.1   Constructing Regression Tables

As we have made clear, multiple regression analyses are the main tool that researchers in political science use to test their causal claims in observational research. Consumers of political science research are well-trained to read regression tables and make assessments based on what they see in them. In addition to making assessments about the specific results presented in a table, readers will also use what they see – and don't see – in regression tables to make assessments about the technical competence of the person who has constructed the table. Since this will have a major impact on the overall assessment of your project, you will want to be careful and thorough in your construction of regression tables.

The construction of regression tables involves moving back and forth between results in a statistics program and the table-making facilities in whatever word-processing program you are using. The easiest and *worst* way to do this is to simply copy and paste your statistical output into your word-processing program. This is a bad way to proceed for at least six reasons. First of all, it just doesn't look good, and (if you do this) makes you look transparently lazy. Second, statistical programs tend to give you an overabundance of information when you estimate a regression model. This information is often way more than what you will need to report in your regression table. Third, the default reporting of results that the statistical program reports may be different from what is appropriate for your purposes. For instance, as we discussed in Chapter 9, almost all statistical programs report the results from two-tailed hypothesis tests when most of our hypotheses in political science are directional (and thus should be assessed with one-tailed tests). Fourth, statistical programs report the names of your variables as they appear in your data sets. While the abbreviations that you have chosen for your variables probably make sense to you, they will almost surely be confusing to your readers. Fifth, computer programs usually report statistics with a number of digits past the decimal point that go way beyond what you need to report. We recommend rounding to two decimal places. And sixth, computer programs report model results with variables in a particular order, but that order may not be the best for emphasizing the important aspects of your results.

Having established what you *should not* do in constructing your tables, let's now talk about what you *should* do. Remember that your goals are to make your table of results stand on its own and draw potential readers in. As such, you want your tables to transmit to other researchers what you have done. Your regression table should include:

- a title that communicates the purpose of the model and/or the most important implications,
- names for the independent variables that are as clear as possible,
- a listing of your independent variables in an order that suits your purposes (usually with your main theoretical variable(s) at the top and control variables listed below),

- the estimated effect of each independent variable (usually the estimated parameter),
- some indication of the uncertainty/statistical significance of each estimated effect (standard errors or t-statistics in parentheses underneath a parameter estimate),
- some indication of which results have been found to be statistically significant according to a particular standard (e.g., putting stars next to results for which $p < 0.05$),
- some indication of what is the dependent variable,
- some overall diagnostics to communicate the model's fit and the number of cases on which the model was estimated,
- a set of notes to help readers decode anything they need to decode (e.g., that "**" means "$p < 0.01$)," and
- any other information that needs to be communicated in order to convey the importance of the findings.

As an example of a table of regression results, consider Table 10.3.[24] If we go through the list of what a table should contain, we can evaluate how well this table does with each item. The title is fairly informative about what is going on in the model depicted in the table, but certainly conveys the most important implications. The names of the independent variables could certainly be more clear. For instance, we don't know exactly what "Growth" or "Unemployment" represent, though we could probably make a good guess. We also don't know from the table alone what "Government Change" is, and it would be hard to make a good guess. The table clearly contains parameter estimates and an indication (in the form of standard errors) of the uncertainty about them. In addition, we can tell from the note beneath the table that the stars in the table convey different levels of statistical significance. The notes beneath the table also make it fairly clear what the dependent variable is, though we would have to figure out on our own that these data are from monthly surveys. So, overall, while this table is fairly clear, it could certainly be improved upon.

As we have seen in this chapter, it is often the case that we will want to report the results from several regression models in the same table. When we do this, it is important to make sure that we are setting up our comparisons across models in a fashion that conveys exactly what we want. There are two types of comparisons that we typically make when we are presenting multiple regression models in the same table: comparisons of different model specifications with the same sample of data or comparisons of the same model specification across different samples of data. In tables

---

[24] Tables 10.3 and 10.5 are based on tables contained in Palmer, Whitten, and Williams (2013).

Table 10.3 Economic models of monthly UK government support, 2004–2011 objective economic measures only	
Independent variable	Parameter estimate (standard error)
Growth	0.25**
	(0.11)
Unemployment	0.07
	(0.20)
Δ Inflation	-2.72***
	(0.75)
Government Change	12.46***
	(2.27)
Support_{t-1}	0.78***
	(0.06)
Constant	6.37***
	(2.13)
R^2	0.81
N	89

Notes: The dependent variable is the percentage of each sample that reported that they would vote for the government if an election was held at the time of the survey.
***$p < 0.01$, **$p < 0.05$, *$p < 0.1$ (two-tailed tests, despite directional hypotheses).

that show the results from multiple models, it is important to only make one of these two types of changes at a time.

Consider, for instance, Tables 10.1 and 10.2. In these tables we presented *different* model specifications across the *same* sample. What we can see very well as we move across the columns in these tables is the changes in the estimated effects of our variables as we change our model. But, it is important to note that, if the sample in Table 10.1 or 10.2 was not *exactly* the same across the columns, we would not know why the estimated effects were changing. In such a case, changes could be due to a change in the sample or a change in the model.

As an example of the second type of comparison, where we look at the same model specification but across different samples, consider Tables 10.4 and 10.5. Both of these tables are examples of the type of research strategy discussed in Chapter 2 where we are interested in differences across subpopulations of cases in terms of the relationship between X and Y. The key variable of interest in the first table is how coolly or warmly (on a 0-to-100 scale) survey respondents report feeling about a particular

Table 10.4 Alternative presentation of the effects of gender and feelings toward the women's movement on Hillary Clinton Thermometer scores

Independent variable	Sample		
	All	**Male**	**Female**
Women's Movement Thermometer	0.70***	0.75***	0.62***
	(0.03)	(0.05)	(0.04)
Intercept	8.52	1.56	16.77***
	(2.10)	(3.03)	(2.89)
n	1466	656	810
R^2	0.25	0.27	0.21

Notes: The dependent variable in both models is the respondent's thermometer score for Hillary Clinton.
Standard errors in parentheses.
Two-sided t-tests: $***p < 0.01$, $**p < 0.05$, $*p < 0.10$.

person or group – in this case feelings about Hillary Clinton. Table 10.4 shows such a comparison looking at the relationship between Women's Movement Thermometer scores across men and women.[25] We can see from this table that, although the sample changes across the columns, the model specification is the same. And we can tell from this comparison that there are differences across the columns in terms of the estimated relationships. The key variable in Table 10.5 is the percentage of a sample in the UK that reported that, were an election held that day, they would vote for the party that currently controls the government. The table shows that when we estimate the model for three different subpopulations defined by their income levels, we also see substantial differences in the ways in which the economic variables, the main Xs in this model, impact support for the government.

10.9.2 Writing about Regression Tables

Although our goal in constructing tables is to make them stand well on their own, when writing about regression tables, it is important to do

---

[25] As we will show in Chapter 11, we can also get leverage on this type of difference in the relationship between X and Y across subpopulations through the use of an interactive model specification. But here we show this difference in the relationship between X and Y by presenting the bivariate regression model with thermometer scores for Hillary Clinton as the dependent variable and Women's Movement Thermometer scores as the independent variable on the entire sample, and then subsamples of cases defined by the gender of the respondent.

Table 10.5 Economic models of monthly UK government support across groups of voters, 2004–2011 objective economic measures only

Independent variable	All	Upper income	Middle income	Low income
Growth	0.25**	0.61***	0.35**	0.33*
	(0.11)	(0.21)	(0.15)	(0.20)
Unemployment	0.07	1.18**	−0.24	−1.76***
	(0.20)	(0.47)	(0.31)	(0.51)
Δ Inflation	−2.72***	−3.40**	−4.21***	−3.38**
	(0.75)	(1.46)	(1.12)	(1.59)
Government Change	12.46***	19.60***	6.28*	−5.11
	(2.27)	(4.56)	(3.42)	(4.84)
Support_{t-1}	0.78***	0.58***	0.56***	0.28***
	(0.06)	(0.09)	(0.08)	(0.10)
Constant	6.37***	5.30**	15.95***	34.61***
	(2.13)	(2.65)	(3.66)	(5.74)
R^2	0.81	0.66	0.58	0.48
N	89	89	89	89

Notes: The dependent variable is the percentage of each sample that reported that they would vote for the government if an election was held at the time of the survey.
***$p < 0.01$, **$p < 0.05$, *$p < 0.1$ (two-tailed tests, despite directional hypotheses).

a little bit of handholding. In other words, *tell* your readers what they should take away from each table. Consider the way in which we just ended the above section. Although this table is competently constructed, we don't know for sure which parts of the table are going to catch the eye of our readers. All that we have told readers is that there are substantial differences across groups. Instead of leaving this up to chance, we should tell them what they should see from this table – for instance, that the largest effect of growth appears to happen among the high income group. We should also point out that the effect of unemployment is in the opposite direction of our theoretical expectations for the highest income group, statistically insignificant for the middle income group, and statistically significant in the expected direction for the lowest income group. We should point out that the effects of inflation are roughly the same across the three groups, all statistically significant in the expected (negative) direction, while for only the high income group is there a statistically significant and positive effect for the switch in government from the Labour Party to the Conservative/Liberal Democratic coalition represented by the variable named "Government Change." Finally, we should point out that these effects that we just discussed are only the short-term effects and that all of these variables have long-term effects as well, because these models include a lagged dependent variable, labeled "Support$_{t-1}$," in the table.[26]

The bottom line with writing about regression tables is that you want to tell your readers what they should see. This will help you to maximize the impact of what you have found and to keep your audience focused on what you are trying to communicate.

10.10 IMPLICATIONS AND CONCLUSIONS

What are the implications of this chapter? The key take-home point – that failing to control for all relevant independent variables will often lead to mistaken causal inferences for the variables that do make it into our models – applies in several contexts. If you are reading a research article in one of your other classes, and it shows a regression analysis between two variables, but fails to control for the effects of some other possible cause of the dependent variable, then you have some reason to be skeptical about the reported findings. In particular, if you can think of another independent variable that is likely to be related to *both* the independent variable and the dependent variable, then the relationship that the article does show that fails to control for that variable is likely to be plagued with bias. And if that's the case, then there is substantial reason to doubt the findings. The findings *might* be right, but you can't know that from the evidence presented in the article; in particular, you'd need to control for the omitted variable to know for sure.

But this critical issue isn't just encountered in research articles. When you read a news article from your favorite media web site that reports a relationship between some presumed cause and some presumed effect – news articles don't usually talk about "independent variables" or "dependent variables" – but fails to account for some other cause that you can imagine might be related to both the independent and dependent variables, then you have reason to doubt the conclusions.

It might be tempting to react to omitted-variables bias by saying, "Omitted-variables bias is such a potentially serious problem that I don't want to use regression analysis." That would be a mistake. In fact, the logic of omitted-variables bias applies to any type of research, no matter what type of statistical technique is used – in fact, no matter whether the research is qualitative or quantitative.

---

[26] We will learn more about the way to discuss time-series models in Chapter 12.

Sometimes, as we have seen, controlling for other causes of the dependent variable changes the discovered effects only at the margins. That happens on occasion in applied research. At other times, however, failure to control for a relevant cause of the dependent variable can have serious consequences for our causal inferences about the real world.

In Chapters 11 and 12, we present you with some crucial extensions of the multiple regression model that you are likely to encounter when consuming or conducting research.

CONCEPTS INTRODUCED IN THIS CHAPTER

- bias – a statistical problem that occurs when the expected value of the parameter estimate that we obtain from a sample will not be equal to the true population parameter
- dyadic data – data that reflect the characteristics of pairs of spatial units and/or the relationships between them
- omitted-variables bias – the specific type of bias that results from the failure to include a variable that belongs in our regression model
- perfect multicollinearity – when there is an exact linear relationship between any two or more of a regression model's independent variables
- standardized coefficients – regression coefficients such that the rise-over-run interpretation is expressed in standard-deviation units of each variable
- substantive significance – a judgment call about whether or not statistically significant relationships are "large" or "small" in terms of their real-world impact
- unstandardized coefficients – regression coefficients such that the rise-over-run interpretation is expressed in the original metric of each variable

EXERCISES

1. Identify an article from a prominent web site that reports a causal relationship between two variables. Can you think of another variable that is related to both the independent variable and the dependent variable? Print and turn in a copy of the article with your answers.

2. In Exercise 1, estimate the direction of the bias resulting from omitting the third variable.

3. Fill in the values in the third column of Table 10.6.

4. In your own research you have found evidence from a bivariate regression model that supports your theory that your independent variable X_i is positively related to your dependent variable Y_i (the slope parameter for X_i was statistically significant and positive when you estimated a bivariate regression

Table 10.6 Bias in $\hat{\beta}_1$ when the true population model is $Y_i = \alpha + \beta_1 X_i + \beta_2 Z_i + u_i$ but we leave out Z

β_2	$\dfrac{\sum_{i=1}^{n}(X_i - \bar{X})(Z_i - \bar{Z})}{\sum_{i=1}^{n}(X_i - \bar{X})^2}$	Resulting bias in $\hat{\beta}_1$
0	+	?
0	−	?
+	0	?
−	0	?
+	+	?
−	−	?
+	−	?
−	+	?

Table 10.7 Three regression models of teacher salaries in the US states and the District of Columbia

	A	B	C
Percentage of state residents with a college degree	704.02* (140.22)	— —	24.56 (231.72)
Per capita income	— —	0.68* (0.11)	0.66* (0.19)
Intercept	28768.01* (3913.27)	21168.11* (4102.40)	21161.07* (4144.96)
R^2	0.34	0.47	0.47
N	51	51	51

Notes: The dependent variable is the average salary of public elementary and secondary school teachers.

Standard errors are in parentheses.

*$p < 0.05$ (two-tailed t-test).

model). You go to a research presentation in which other researchers present a theory that their independent variable Z_i is negatively related to their dependent variable Y_i. They report the results from a bivariate regression model in which the slope parameter for Z_i was statistically significant and negative. Your Y_i and their Y_i are the same variable. What would be your reaction to these findings under each of the following circumstances?

(a) You are confident that the correlation between Z_i and X_i is equal to zero.

(b) You think that the correlation between Z_i and X_i is positive.

(c) You think that the correlation between Z_i and X_i is negative.

5. Using the results depicted in Table 10.7, interpret the results of the bivariate models displayed in columns A and B.

6. Using the results depicted in Table 10.7, interpret the results of the multiple regression model displayed in column C. Compare the results in column C with those in both columns A and B.

7. Draw a Venn diagram that depicts what is going on between the three variables based on the results in Table 10.7.

11 Multiple Regression Model Specification

OVERVIEW

In this chapter we provide introductory *discussions of* and *advice for* commonly encountered research scenarios involving multiple regression models. Issues covered include dummy independent variables, interactive specifications, influential cases, and multicollinearity.

All models are wrong, but some are useful.
    —George E.P. Box

11.1 EXTENSIONS OF ORDINARY LEAST-SQUARES

In the previous two chapters we discussed in detail various aspects of the estimation, interpretation, and presentation of OLS regression models. In this chapter we go through a series of research scenarios commonly encountered by political science researchers as they attempt to test their hypotheses within the OLS framework. The purpose of this chapter is twofold – first, to help you to identify when you encounter these issues and, second, to help you to figure out what to do to continue on your way.

We begin with a discussion of "dummy" independent variables and how to properly use them to make inferences. We then discuss how to test interactive hypotheses with dummy variables. We next turn our attention to two frequently encountered problems in OLS – outliers and multicollinearity. With both of these topics, at least half of the battle is identifying that you have the problem.

11.2 BEING SMART WITH DUMMY INDEPENDENT VARIABLES IN OLS

In Chapter 5 we discussed how an important part of knowing your data involves knowing the metric in which each of your variables is measured.

Throughout the examples that we have examined thus far, almost all of the variables, both the independent and dependent variables, have been continuous. This is not by accident. We chose examples with continuous variables because they are, in many cases, easier to interpret than models in which the variables are noncontinuous. In this section, though, we consider a series of scenarios involving independent variables that are *not* continuous. We begin with a relatively simple case in which we have a categorical independent variable that takes on one of two possible values for all cases. Categorical variables like this are commonly referred to as **dummy variables**. Although any two values will do, the most common form of dummy variable is one that takes on values of one or zero. These variables are also sometimes referred to as "indicator variables" when a value of one indicates the presence of a particular characteristic and a value of zero indicates the absence of that characteristic. After considering dummy variables that reflect two possible values, we then consider more complicated examples in which we have an independent variable that is categorical with more than two values. We conclude this section with an examination of how to handle models in which we have multiple dummy variables representing multiple and overlapping classifications of cases.

11.2.1 Using Dummy Variables to Test Hypotheses about a Categorical Independent Variable with Only Two Values

During the 1996 US presidential election between incumbent Democrat Bill Clinton and Republican challenger Robert Dole, Clinton's wife Hillary was a prominent and polarizing figure. Throughout the next couple of examples, we will use her "thermometer ratings" by individual respondents to the National Election Study (NES) survey as our dependent variable. As we discussed briefly in Chapter 10, a thermometer rating is a survey respondent's answer to a question about how they *feel* (as opposed to how they *think*) toward particular individuals or groups on a scale that typically runs from 0 to 100. Scores of 50 indicate that the individual feels neither warm nor cold about the individual or group in question. Scores from 50 to 100 represent increasingly warm (or favorable) feelings, and scores from 50 to 0 represent increasingly cold (or unfavorable) feelings.

During the 1996 campaign, Ms. Clinton was identified as being a left-wing feminist. Given this, we theorize that there may have been a causal relationship between a respondent's family income and their thermometer rating of Ms. Clinton – with wealthier individuals, holding all else constant, liking her less – as well as a relationship between a respondent's gender and their thermometer rating of Ms. Clinton – with women, holding

```
. reg hillary_thermo income male female
note: female omitted because of collinearity
```

Source	SS	df	MS			
Model	80916.663	2	40458.3315	Number of obs	=	1,542
Residual	1266234.71	1,539	822.764595	F(2, 1539)	=	49.17
				Prob > F	=	0.0000
				R-squared	=	0.0601
Total	1347151.37	1,541	874.205954	Adj R-squared	=	0.0588
				Root MSE	=	28.684

hillary_th~o	coef.	Std. Err.	t	P>|t|	[95% Conf. Interval]	
income	-.8407732	.117856	-7.13	0.000	-1.071949	-.6095978
male	-8.081448	1.495216	-5.40	0.000	-11.01432	-5.148572
female	0	(omitted)				
_cons	69.26185	1.92343	36.01	0.000	0.65.48903	73.03467

Figure 11.1 Stata output when we include both gender dummy variables in our model

all else constant, liking her more. For the sake of this example, we are going to assume that both our dependent variable and our income independent variable are continuous.[1] Each respondent's gender was coded as equaling either 1 for "male" or 2 for "female." Although we could leave this gender variable as it is and run our analyses, we chose to use this variable to create two new dummy variables, "male" equaling 1 for "yes" and 0 for "no," and "female" equaling 1 for "yes" and 0 for "no."

Our first inclination is to estimate an OLS model in which the specification is the following:

$$\text{Hillary Thermometer}_i = \alpha + \beta_1 \text{Income}_i + \beta_2 \text{Male}_i + \beta_3 \text{Female}_i + u_i.$$

But if we try to estimate this model, our statistical computer program will revolt and give us an error message.[2] Figure 11.1 shows a screen shot of what this output looks like in Stata. We can see that Stata has reported the results from the following model instead of what we asked for:

$$\text{Hillary Thermometer}_i = \alpha + \beta_1 \text{Income}_i + \beta_3 \text{Female}_i + u_i.$$

Instead of the estimates for β_2 on the second row of parameter estimates, we get a note that this variable was "dropped." This is the case because we have failed to meet the additional minimal mathematical criteria that we introduced when we moved from two-variable OLS to multiple OLS in Chapter 10 – "no perfect multicollinearity." The reason that we have failed to meet this is that, for two of the independent variables in our model, Male_i and Female_i, it is the case that

$$\text{Male}_i + \text{Female}_i = 1 \quad \forall\, i.$$

---

[1] In this survey, a respondent's family income was measured on a scale ranging from 1 to 24 according to which category of income ranges they chose as best describing their family's income during 1995.

[2] Most programs will throw one of the two variables out of the model and report the results from the resulting model along with an error message.

Table 11.1 Two models of the effects of gender and income on Hillary Clinton Thermometer scores

Independent variable	Model 1	Model 2
Male	—	−8.08***
		(1.50)
Female	8.08***	—
	(1.50)	
Income	−0.84***	−0.84***
	(0.12)	(0.12)
Intercept	61.18***	69.26***
	(2.22)	(1.92)
R^2	0.06	0.06
n	1542	1542

Notes: The dependent variable in both models is the respondent's thermometer score for Hillary Clinton.
Standard errors in parentheses.
Two-sided t-tests: ***$p < 0.01$; **$p < 0.05$; *$p < 0.10$.

In other words, our variables "Male" and "Female" are perfectly correlated: If we know a respondent's value on the "Male" variable, then we know their value on the "Female" variable with perfect certainty.

When this happens with dummy variables, we call this situation the **dummy-variable trap**. To avoid the dummy-variable trap, we have to omit one of our dummy variables. But we want to be able to compare the effects of being male with the effects of being female to test our hypothesis. How can we do this if we have to omit one of our two variables that measures gender? Before we answer this question, let's look at the results in Table 11.1 from the two different models in which we omit one of these two variables. We can learn a lot by looking at what is and what is not the same across these two models. In both models, the parameter estimate and standard error for income are identical. The R^2 statistic is also identical. The parameter estimate and the standard error for the intercept are different across the two models. The parameter estimate for male is −8.08, whereas that for female is 8.08, although the standard error for each of these parameter estimates is 0.12. If you're starting to think that all of these similarities cannot have happened by coincidence, you are correct. In fact, these two models are, mathematically speaking, the same model. All of the $\hat{Y}$ values and residuals for the individual cases are *exactly* the same. With income held constant, the estimated difference between being male and being female is 8.08. The sign on this parameter estimate switches from positive to negative when we go from Model 1 to Model 2 because we are phrasing the question differently across the two models:

- For Model 1: "What is the estimated difference for a female compared with a male?"
- For Model 2: "What is the estimated difference for a male compared with a female?"

So why are the intercepts different? Think back to our discussions in Chapters 9 and 10 about the interpretation of the intercept – it is the estimated value of the dependent variable when the independent variables are all equal to zero. In Model 1 this means the estimated value of the dependent variable for a low-income man. In Model 2 this means the estimated value of the dependent variable for a low-income woman. And the difference between these two values – you guessed it – is $61.18 - 69.26 = -8.08$!

What does the regression line from Model 1 or Model 2 look like? The answer is that it depends on the gender of the individual for which we are plotting the line, but that it does not depend on which of these two models we use. For men, where $\text{Female}_i = 0$ and $\text{Male}_i = 1$, the predicted values are calculated as follows:

Model 1 for Men:
$$\hat{Y}_i = 61.18 + (8.08 \times \text{Female}_i) - (0.84 \times \text{Income}_i)$$
$$\hat{Y}_i = 61.18 + (8.08 \times 0) - (0.84 \times \text{Income}_i)$$
$$\hat{Y}_i = 61.18 - (0.84 \times \text{Income}_i);$$

Model 2 for Men:
$$\hat{Y}_i = 69.26 - (8.08 \times \text{Male}_i) - (0.84 \times \text{Income}_i)$$
$$\hat{Y}_i = 69.26 - (8.08 \times 1) - (0.84 \times \text{Income}_i)$$
$$\hat{Y}_i = 61.18 - (0.84 \times \text{Income}_i).$$

So we can see that, for men, regardless of whether we use the results from Model 1 or Model 2, the formula for predicted values is the same. For women, where $\text{Female}_i = 1$ and $\text{Male}_i = 0$, the predicted values are calculated as follows:

Model 1 for Women:
$$\hat{Y}_i = 61.18 + (8.08 \times \text{Female}_i) - (0.84 \times \text{Income}_i)$$
$$\hat{Y}_i = 61.18 + (8.08 \times 1) - (0.84 \times \text{Income}_i)$$
$$\hat{Y}_i = 69.26 - (0.84 \times \text{Income}_i);$$

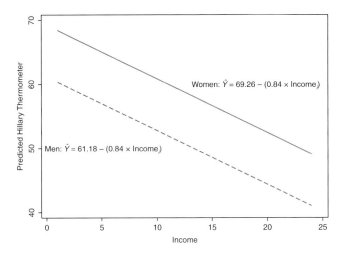

Figure 11.2 Regression lines from the model with a dummy variable for gender

Model 2 for Women:
$$\hat{Y}_i = 69.26 - (8.08 \times \text{Male}_i) - (0.84 \times \text{Income}_i)$$
$$\hat{Y}_i = 69.26 - (8.08 \times 0) - (0.84 \times \text{Income}_i)$$
$$\hat{Y}_i = 69.26 - (0.84 \times \text{Income}_i).$$

Again, the formula from Model 1 is the same as the formula from Model 2 for women. To illustrate these two sets of predictions, we have plotted them in Figure 11.2. Given that the two predictive formulae have the same slope, it is not surprising to see that the two lines in this figure are parallel to each other with the intercept difference determining the space between them.

11.2.2 Using Dummy Variables to Test Hypotheses about a Categorical Independent Variable with More Than Two Values

As you might imagine, when we have a categorical variable with more than two categories and we want to include it in an OLS model, things get more complicated. We'll keep with our running example of modeling Hillary Clinton Thermometer scores as a function of individuals' characteristics and opinions. In this section we work with a respondent's religious affiliation as an independent variable. The frequency of different responses to this item in the 1996 NES is displayed in Table 11.2.

Could we use the Religious Identification variable as it is in our regression models? That would be a bad idea. Remember, this is a categorical variable, in which the values of the variable are not ordered from lowest to highest. Indeed, there is no such thing as "lowest" or "highest" on

Table 11.2 Religious identification in the 1996 NES			
Assigned numeric value	Category	Frequency	Percent
0	Protestant	683	39.85
1	Catholic	346	20.19
2	Jewish	22	1.28
3	Other	153	8.93
4	None	510	29.75
	Totals	1714	100

this variable. So running a regression model with these data as they are would be meaningless. But beware: *Your statistics package does not know that this is a categorical variable.* It will be more than happy to estimate the regression and report parameter estimates to you, even though these estimates will be nonsensical.

In the previous section, in which we had a categorical variable (Gender) with only two possible values, we saw that, when we switched which value was represented by "1" and "0," the estimated parameter switched signs. This was the case because we were asking a different question. With a categorical independent variable that has more than two values, we have more than two possible questions that we can ask. Because using the variable as is is not an option, the best strategy for modeling the effects of such an independent variable is to include in our regression a dummy variable for each value of that independent variable *except one.*[3] The value of the independent variable for which we do not include a dummy variable is known as the **reference category**. This is the case because the parameter estimates for all of the dummy variables representing the other values of the independent variable are estimated with reference to that value of the independent variable. So let's say that we choose to estimate the following model:

$$\text{Hillary Thermometer}_i = \alpha + \beta_1 \text{Income}_i + \beta_2 \text{Protestant}_i + \beta_3 \text{Catholic}_i$$
$$+ \beta_4 \text{Jewish}_i + \beta_5 \text{Other}_i + u_i.$$

For this model we would be using "None" as our reference category for religious identification. This would mean that $\hat{\beta}_2$ would be the estimated effect of being Protestant *relative to* being nonreligious, and we

---

[3] If our theory was that only one category, such as Catholics, was different from all of the others, then we would collapse the remaining categories of the variable in question together and we would have a two-category independent variable. We should do this only if we have a theoretical justification for doing so.

Table 11.3 The same model of religion and income on Hillary Clinton Thermometer scores with different reference categories

Independent variable	Model 1	Model 2	Model 3	Model 4	Model 5
Income	−0.97***	−0.97***	−0.97***	−0.97***	−0.97***
	(0.12)	(0.12)	(0.12)	(0.12)	(0.12)
Protestant	−4.24*	−6.66*	−24.82***	−6.30**	—
	(1.77)	(2.68)	(6.70)	(2.02)	—
Catholic	2.07	−0.35	−18.51**	—	6.30**
	(2.12)	(2.93)	(6.80)	—	(2.02)
Jewish	20.58**	18.16**	—	18.51**	24.82***
	(6.73)	(7.02)	—	(6.80)	(6.70)
Other	2.42	—	−18.16**	0.35	6.66*
	(2.75)	—	(7.02)	(2.93)	(2.68)
None	—	−2.42	−20.58**	−2.07	4.24*
	—	(2.75)	(6.73)	(2.12)	(1.77)
Intercept	68.40***	70.83***	88.98***	70.47***	64.17***
	(2.19)	(2.88)	(6.83)	(2.53)	(2.10)
R^2	0.06	0.06	0.06	0.06	0.06
n	1542	1542	1542	1542	1542

Notes: The dependent variable in both models is the respondent's thermometer score for Hillary Clinton.
Standard errors in parentheses.
Two-sided t-tests: ***$p < 0.01$; **$p < 0.05$; *$p < 0.10$.

could use this value along with its standard error to test the hypothesis that this effect was statistically significant, controlling for the effects of income. The remaining parameter estimates ($\hat{\beta}_3$, $\hat{\beta}_4$, and $\hat{\beta}_5$) would all also be interpreted as the estimated effect of being in each of the remaining categories relative to "None." The value that we choose to use as our reference category does not matter, as long as we interpret our results appropriately. But we can use the choice of the reference category to focus on the relationships in which we are particularly interested. For each possible pair of categories of the independent variable, we can conduct a separate hypothesis test. The easiest way to get all of the p-values in which we are interested is to estimate the model multiple times with different reference categories. Table 11.3 displays a model of Hillary Clinton Thermometer scores with the five different choices of reference categories. It is worth emphasizing that this is *not* a table with five different models, but that this *is* a table with the same model displayed five different ways. From this table we can see that, when we control for the effects of income, some of the categories

Table 11.4 Model of bargaining duration

Independent variable	Parameter estimate
Ideological Range of the Government	2.57*
	(1.95)
Number of Parties in the Government	−15.44***
	(2.30)
Post-Election	5.87**
	(2.99)
Continuation Rule	−6.34**
	(3.34)
Intercept	19.63***
	(3.82)
R^2	0.62
n	203

Notes: The dependent variable is the number of days before each government was formed.

Standard errors in parentheses.

One-sided t-tests: ***$p < 0.01$; **$p < 0.05$; *$p < 0.10$.

of religious affiliation are statistically different from each other in their evaluations of Hillary Clinton whereas others are not. This raises an interesting question: Can we say that the effect of religious affiliation, controlling for income, is statistically significant? The answer is that it depends on which categories of religious affiliation we want to compare.

11.2.3 Using Dummy Variables to Test Hypotheses about Multiple Independent Variables

It is often the case that we will want to use multiple dummy independent variables in the same model. Consider the model presented in Table 11.4, which was estimated from data from a paper by Lanny Martin and Georg Vanberg (2003) on the length of time that it takes for coalition governments to form in Western Europe.[4] The dependent variable is the number of days that a government took to form. The model has two continuous independent variables ("Ideological Range of the Government" and

---

[4] The model that we present in Table 11.4 has been changed from what Martin and Vanberg present in their paper. This model contains fewer variables than the main model of interest in that paper. This model was also estimated using OLS regression whereas the models presented by the original authors were estimated as proportional hazard models. And, we have not reported the results for a technical variable (labeled "Number of Government Parties ∗ ln(T)" by the authors) from the original specification. All of these modifications were made to make this example more tractable.

Table 11.5 Two overlapping dummy variables in models by Martin and Vanberg		Continuation rule?	
		No (0)	Yes (1)
Post-	No (0)	61	25
Election?	Yes (1)	76	41

Note: Numbers in cells represent the number of cases.

"Number of Parties in the Government") measuring characteristics of the government that eventually formed and two dummy independent variables reflecting the circumstances under which bargaining took place. The variable "Post-Election" identifies governments that were formed in the immediate aftermath of an election while "Continuation Rule" identifies bargaining that took place in settings where the political parties from the outgoing government had the first opportunity to form a new government. As Table 11.5 indicates, all four possible combinations of these two dummy variables occurred in the sample of cases on which the model presented in Table 11.4 was estimated.

So, how do we interpret these results? It's actually not as hard as it might first appear. Remember from Chapter 10 that when we moved from a bivariate regression model to a multiple regression model, we had to interpret each parameter estimate as the estimated effect of a one-point increase in that particular independent variable on the dependent variable, *while controlling for the effects of all other independent variables in the model*. This has not changed. Instead, what is a little different from the examples that we have considered before is that we have two dummy independent variables that can vary independently of each other. So, when we interpret the estimated effect of each continuous independent variable, we interpret the parameter estimate as the estimated effect of a one-point increase in that particular independent variable on the dependent variable, while controlling for the effects of all other independent variables in the model, including the two dummy variables. And, when we interpret the estimated effect of each dummy independent variable, we interpret the parameter estimate as the estimated effect of that variable having a value of one versus zero on the dependent variable, while controlling for the effects of all other independent variables in the model, including the other dummy variable. For instance, the estimated effect of a one-unit increase in the Ideological Range of the Government, holding everything else constant, is a 2.57 day increase in the amount of bargaining time. And, the estimated effect of bargaining in the aftermath of an election (versus at a different time), holding everything else constant, is a 5.87 day increase in the amount of bargaining time.

11.3 TESTING INTERACTIVE HYPOTHESES WITH DUMMY VARIABLES

All of the OLS models that we have examined so far have been what we could call "additive models." To calculate the $\hat{Y}$ value for a particular case from an additive model, we simply multiply each independent variable value for that case by the appropriate parameter estimate and *add* these values together. In this section we explore some **interactive models**. Interactive models contain at least one independent variable that we create by multiplying together two or more independent variables. When we specify interactive models, we are testing theories about how the effects of one independent variable on our dependent variable may be contingent on the value of another independent variable. We will continue with our running example of modeling a respondent's thermometer score for Hillary Clinton. We begin with an additive model with the following specification:

$$\text{Hillary Thermometer}_i = \alpha + \beta_1 \text{Women's Movement Thermometer}_i$$
$$+ \beta_2 \text{Female}_i + u_i.$$

In this model we are testing theories that a respondent's feelings toward Hillary Clinton are a function of their feelings toward the women's movement and their own gender. This specification seems pretty reasonable, but we also want to test an additional theory that the effect of feelings toward the women's movement have a stronger effect on feelings toward Hillary Clinton among women than they do among men. Notice the difference in phrasing there. In essence, we want to test the hypothesis that the slope of the line representing the relationship between Women's Movement Thermometer and Hillary Clinton Thermometer is *steeper* for women than it is for men. To test this hypothesis, we need to create a new variable that is the product of the two independent variables in our model and include this new variable in our model:

Hillary Thermometer$_i$
$$= \alpha + \beta_1 \text{Women's Movement Thermometer}_i$$
$$+ \beta_2 \text{Female}_i + \beta_3 (\text{Women's Movement Thermometer}_i \times \text{Female}_i) + u_i.$$

By specifying our model as such, we have essentially created two different models for women and men. So we can rewrite our model as follows:

For Men (Female $= 0$):
$$\text{Hillary Thermometer}_i = \alpha + \beta_1 \text{Women's Movement Thermometer}_i + u_i;$$

For Women (Female $= 1$):

$$\text{Hillary Thermometer}_i = \alpha + \beta_1 \text{Women's Movement Thermometer}_i$$
$$+ (\beta_2 + \beta_3)(\text{Women's Movement Thermometer}_i)$$
$$+ u_i.$$

And we can rewrite the formula for women as:

For Women (Female $= 1$):

$$\text{Hillary Thermometer}_i = (\alpha + \beta_2) + (\beta_1 + \beta_3)$$
$$(\text{Women's Movement Thermometer}_i) + u_i.$$

What this all boils down to is that we are allowing our regression line to be different for men and women. For men, the intercept is α and the slope is β_1. For women, the intercept is $\alpha + \beta_2$ and the slope is $\beta_1 + \beta_3$. However, if $\beta_2 = 0$ and $\beta_3 = 0$, then the regression lines for men and women will be the same. Table 11.6 shows the results for our additive and interactive models of the effects of gender and feelings toward the women's movement on Hillary Clinton Thermometer scores. We can see from the interactive model that we can reject the null hypothesis that $\beta_2 = 0$ and the null hypothesis that $\beta_3 = 0$, so our regression lines for men and women are different. We can also see that the intercept for the line for women $(\alpha + \beta_2)$ is higher than the intercept for men (α). But, contrary to our expectations, the estimated effect of the Women's Movement Thermometer

Table 11.6 The effects of gender and feelings toward the women's movement on Hillary Clinton Thermometer scores

Independent variable	Additive model	Interactive model
Women's Movement Thermometer	0.68***	0.75***
	(0.03)	(0.05)
Female	7.13***	15.21***
	(1.37)	(4.19)
Women's Movement Thermometer × Female	—	−0.13**
		(0.06)
Intercept	5.98**	1.56
	(2.13)	(3.04)
R^2	0.27	0.27
n	1466	1466

Notes: The dependent variable in both models is the respondent's thermometer score for Hillary Clinton.
Standard errors in parentheses.
Two-sided t-tests: ***$p < 0.01$; **$p < 0.05$; *$p < 0.10$.

Figure 11.3 Regression lines from the interactive model

for men is greater than the effect of the Women's Movement Thermometer for women.

The best way to see the combined effect of all of the results from the interactive model in Table 11.6 is to look at them graphically in a figure such as Figure 11.3. From this figure we can see the regression lines for men and for women across the range of the independent variable. It is clear from this figure that, although women are generally more favorably inclined toward Hillary Clinton, this gender gap narrows when we compare those individuals who feel more positively toward the feminist movement.

11.4   OUTLIERS AND INFLUENTIAL CASES IN OLS

In Chapter 6 we advocated using descriptive statistics to identify outlier values for each continuous variable. In the context of a single variable, an outlier is an extreme value relative to the other values for that variable. But in the context of an OLS model, when we say that a single case is an outlier, we could mean several different things. For this reason, we prefer to use the term "influential" instead of "outlier" in the context of a regression model.

As we discussed in Chapter 6, we should always strive to know our data well. This means looking at individual variables one at a time before we estimate a regression with them and identifying univariate outliers. But just because a case is an outlier in the univariate sense does not necessarily imply that it will be an **influential case** in a regression. Nonetheless, we should look for outliers in the single-variable sense before we estimate our models and make sure that they are actual values and not values created by some type of data management mistake.

In the regression setting, individual cases can be influential in several different ways:

1. They can have unusual independent variable values. This is known as a case having large **leverage**. This can be the result of a single case having an unusual value for a single variable. A single case can also have large leverage because it has an unusual *combination* of values across two or more variables. There are a variety of different measures of leverage, but they all make calculations across the values of independent variables in order to identify individual cases that are particularly different.
2. They can have large residual values (usually we look at squared residuals to identify outliers of this variety).
3. They can have both large leverage and large residual values.

The relationship among these different concepts of influence for a single case in OLS is often summarized as

$$\text{influence}_i = \text{leverage}_i \times \text{residual}_i.$$

As this formula indicates, the influence of a particular case is determined by the combination of its leverage and residual values. There are a variety of different ways to measure these different factors. We explore a couple of them in the following sections with a controversial real-world example.

11.4.1 Identifying Influential Cases

One of the most famous cases of outliers and influential cases in political data comes from the 2000 US presidential election in Florida. In an attempt to measure the extent to which ballot irregularities may have influenced election results, a variety of models were estimated in which the raw vote numbers for candidates across different counties were the dependent variables of interest. These models were fairly unusual because the parameter estimates and other quantities that are most often the focus of our model interpretations were of little interest. Instead, these were models for which the most interesting quantities were the diagnostics of influential cases. As an example of such a model, we will work with the following:

$$\text{Buchanan}_i = \alpha + \beta \text{Gore}_i + u_i.$$

In this model the cases are individual counties in Florida, the dependent variable (Buchanan_i) is the number of votes in each Florida county for the independent candidate Patrick Buchanan, and the independent variable is the number of votes in each Florida county for the Democratic Party's nominee Al Gore (Gore_i). Such models are unusual in the sense that there is no claim of an underlying causal relationship between the

Table 11.7 Votes for Gore and Buchanan in Florida counties in the 2000 US presidential election

Independent variable	Parameter estimate
Votes for Gore	0.004***
	(0.0005)
Intercept	80.63*
	(46.4)
R^2	0.48
n	67

Notes: The dependent variable is the number of votes for Patrick Buchanan.
Standard errors in parentheses.
Two-sided t-tests: ***$p < 0.01$; **$p < 0.05$; *$p < 0.10$.

independent and dependent variables. Instead, the theory behind this type of model is that there should be a strong systematic relationship between the number of votes cast for Gore and those cast for Buchanan across the Florida counties.[5] There was a suspicion that the ballot structure used in some counties – especially the infamous "butterfly ballot" – was such that it confused some voters who intended to vote for Gore into voting for Buchanan. If this was the case, we should see these counties appearing as highly influential after we estimate our model.

We can see from Table 11.7 that there was indeed a statistically significant positive relationship between Gore and Buchanan votes, and that this simple model accounts for 48 percent of the variation in Buchanan votes across the Florida counties. But, as we said before, the more interesting inferences from this particular OLS model are about the influence of particular cases. Figure 11.4 presents a Stata lvr2plot (short for "leverage-versus-residual-squared plot") that displays Stata's measure of leverage on the vertical dimension and a normalized measure of the squared residuals on the horizontal dimension. The logic of this figure is that, as we move to the right of the vertical line through this figure, we are seeing cases with unusually large residual values, and that, as we move above the horizontal line through this figure, we are seeing cases with unusually large leverage values. Cases with both unusually large residual and leverage values are highly influential. From Figure 11.4 it is apparent that Pinellas,

---

[5] Most of the models of this sort make adjustments to the variables (for example, logging the values of both the independent and dependent variables) to account for possibilities of nonlinear relationships. In the present example we avoided doing this for the sake of simplicity.

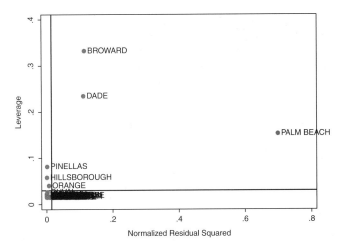

Figure 11.4 Stata lvr2plot for the model presented in Table 11.7

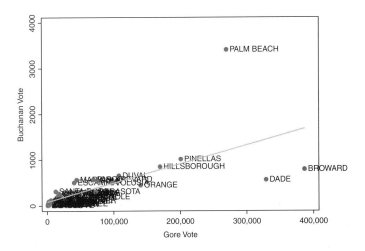

Figure 11.5 OLS line with scatter plot for Florida 2000

Hillsborough, and Orange counties had large leverage values but not particularly large squared residual values, whereas Dade, Broward, and Palm Beach counties were highly influential with both large leverage values and large squared residual values.

We can get a better idea of the correspondence between Figure 11.4 and Table 11.7 from Figure 11.5, in which we plot the OLS regression line through a scatter plot of the data. From this figure it is clear that Palm Beach was well above the regression line whereas Broward and Dade counties were well below the regression line. By any measure, these three cases were quite influential in our model.

A more specific method for detecting the influence of an individual case involves estimating our model with and without particular cases to

Table 11.8 The five largest (absolute-value) DFBETA scores for β from the model presented in Table 11.7	
County	DFBETA
Palm Beach	6.993
Broward	−2.514
Dade	−1.772
Orange	−0.109
Pinellas	0.085

see how much this changes specific parameter estimates. The resulting calculation is known as the **DFBETA score** (Belsley, Kuh, and Welsch, 1980). DFBETA scores are calculated as the difference in the parameter estimate without each case divided by the standard error of the original parameter estimate. Table 11.8 displays the five largest absolute values of DFBETA for the slope parameter (β) from the model presented in Table 11.7. Not surprisingly, we see that omitting Palm Beach, Broward, or Dade has the largest impact on our estimate of the slope parameter.

11.4.2 Dealing with Influential Cases

Now that we have discussed the identification of particularly influential cases on our models, we turn to the subject of what to do once we have identified such cases. The first thing to do when we identify a case with substantial influence is to double-check the values of all variables for such a case. We want to be certain that we have not "created" an influential case through some error in our data management procedures. Once we have corrected for any errors of data management and determined that we still have some particularly influential case(s), it is important that we report our findings about such cases along with our other findings. There are a variety of strategies for doing so. Table 11.9 shows five different models that reflect various approaches to reporting results with highly influential cases. In Model 1 we have the original results as reported in Table 11.7. In Model 2 we have added a dummy variable that identifies and isolates the effect of Palm Beach County. This approach is sometimes referred to as **dummying out** influential cases. We can see why this is called "dummying out" from the results in Model 3, which is the original model with the observation for Palm Beach County dropped from the analysis. The parameter estimates and standard errors for the intercept and slope parameters are identical from Models 2 and 3. The only differences are the model R^2 statistic, the number of cases, and the additional parameter estimate reported in Model 2 for the Palm Beach County dummy variable.[6]

---

[6] This parameter estimate was viewed by some as an estimate of how many votes the ballot irregularities cost Al Gore in Palm Beach County. But if we look at Model 4, where we include dummy variables for Broward and Dade counties, we can see the basis for an argument that in these two counties there is evidence of bias in the opposite direction.

Table 11.9 Votes for Gore and Buchanan in Florida counties in the 2000 US presidential election

Independent variable	Model 1	Model 2	Model 3	Model 4	Model 5
Gore	0.004***	0.003***	0.003***	0.005***	0.005***
	(0.0005)	(0.0002)	(0.0002)	(0.0003)	(0.0003)
Palm Beach dummy	—	2606.3***	—	2095.5***	—
		(150.4)		(110.6)	
Broward dummy	—	—	—	−1066.0***	—
				(131.5)	
Dade dummy	—	—	—	−1025.6***	—
				(120.6)	
Intercept	80.6*	110.8***	110.8***	59.0***	59.0***
	(46.4)	(19.7)	(19.7)	(13.8)	(13.8)
R^2	0.48	0.91	0.63	0.96	0.82
n	67	67	66	67	64

Notes: The dependent variable is the number of votes for Patrick Buchanan.
Standard errors in parentheses.
Two-sided t-tests: ***$p < 0.01$; **$p < 0.05$; *$p < 0.10$.

In Model 4 and Model 5, we see the results from dummying out the three most influential cases and then from dropping them out of the analysis.

Across all five of the models shown in Table 11.9, the slope parameter estimate remains positive and statistically significant. In most models, this would be the quantity in which we are most interested (testing hypotheses about the relationship between X and Y). Thus the relative robustness of this parameter across model specifications would be comforting. Regardless of the effects of highly influential cases, it is important first to know that they exist and, second, to report accurately what their influence is and what we have done about them.

11.5 MULTICOLLINEARITY

When we specify and estimate a multiple OLS model, what is the interpretation of each individual parameter estimate? It is our best guess of the causal impact of a one-unit increase in the relevant independent variable on the dependent variable, controlling for all of the other variables in the model. Another way of saying this is that we are looking at the impact of a one-unit increase in one independent variable on the dependent variable when we "hold all other variables constant." We know from Chapter 10 that a minimal mathematical property for estimating a multiple OLS model is that there is no perfect multicollinearity. Perfect multicollinearity, you will recall, occurs when one independent variable is an exact linear function of one or more other independent variables in a model.

In practice, perfect multicollinearity is usually the result of a small number of cases relative to the number of parameters we are estimating, limited independent variable values, or model misspecification. As we have noted, if there exists perfect multicollinearity, OLS parameters cannot be estimated. A much more common and vexing issue is **high multicollinearity**. As a result, when people refer to multicollinearity, they almost always mean "high multicollinearity." From here on, when we refer to "multicollinearity," we will mean "high, but less-than-perfect, multicollinearity." This means that two or more of the independent variables in the model are extremely highly correlated with one another.

11.5.1 How Does Multicollinearity Happen?

Multicollinearity is induced by a small number of degrees of freedom and/or high correlation between independent variables. Figure 11.6 provides a Venn diagram illustration that is useful for thinking about the effects of multicollinearity in the context of an OLS regression model. As you can see from this figure, X and Z are fairly highly correlated. Our regression model is

$$Y_i = \alpha + \beta_1 X_i + \beta_2 Z_i + u_i.$$

Looking at Figure 11.6, we can see that the R^2 from our regression model will be fairly high,

$$R^2 = \frac{f+d+b}{a+f+d+b}.$$

But we can also see from this figure that the areas for the estimation of our two slope parameters – area f for β_1 and area b for β_2 – are pretty small. Because of this, our standard errors for our slope parameters will tend to be fairly large, which makes discovering statistically significant relationships more difficult, and we will have difficulty making precise inferences about the impacts of both X and Z on Y. It is possible that because of this problem we would conclude neither X nor Z has much of an impact on Y. But clearly this is not the case. As we can see from the diagram, both X and Z *are* related to Y. The problem is that much of the covariation between X and Y and between Z and Y is also covariation

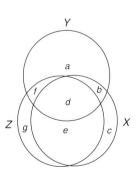

Figure 11.6 Venn diagram with multicollinearity

between X and Z. In other words, it is the size of area d that is causing us problems. We have precious little area in which to examine the effect of X on Y while holding Z constant, and likewise, there is precious little area in which to examine the effect of Z on Y while controlling for X.

It is worth emphasizing at this point that multicollinearity is not a statistical problem (examples of statistical problems include autocorrelation, bias, and heteroscedasticity). Rather, multicollinearity is a data problem. It is possible to have multicollinearity even when all of the assumptions of OLS from Chapter 9 are valid and all of the minimal mathematical requirements for OLS from Chapters 9 and 10 have been met. So, you might ask, what's the big deal about multicollinearity? To underscore the notion of multicollinearity as a data problem instead of a statistical problem, Christopher Achen (1982) has suggested that the word "multicollinearity" should be used interchangeably with **micronumerosity**. Imagine what would happen if we could double or triple the size of the diagram in Figure 11.6 without changing the relative sizes of any of the areas. As we expanded all of the areas, areas f and b would eventually become large enough for us to precisely estimate the relationships of interest.

11.5.2 Detecting Multicollinearity

It is very important to know when you have multicollinearity. In particular, it is important to distinguish situations in which estimates are statistically insignificant because the relationships just aren't there from situations in which estimates are statistically insignificant because of multicollinearity. The diagram in Figure 11.6 shows us one way in which we might be able to detect multicollinearity: If we have a high R^2 statistic, but none (or very few) of our parameter estimates is statistically significant, we should be suspicious of multicollinearity. We should also be suspicious of multicollinearity if we see that, when we add and remove independent variables from our model, the parameter estimates for other independent variables (and especially their standard errors) change substantially. If we estimated the model represented in Figure 11.6 with just one of the two independent variables, we would get a statistically significant relationship. But, as we know from the discussions in Chapter 10, this would be problematic. Presumably we have a theory about the relationship between each of these independent variables (X and Z) and our dependent variable (Y). So, although the estimates from a model with just X or just Z as the independent variable would help us to detect multicollinearity, they would suffer from bias. And, as we argued in Chapter 10, omitted-variables bias is a severe problem.

A more formal way to diagnose multicollinearity is to calculate the **variance inflation factor** (VIF) for each of our independent variables. This calculation is based on an **auxiliary regression model** in which one independent variable, which we will call X_j, is the dependent variable and all of the other independent variables are independent variables.[7] The R^2 statistic from this auxiliary model, R_j^2, is then used to calculate the VIF for variable j as follows:

$$\text{VIF}_j = \frac{1}{(1 - R_j^2)}.$$

Many statistical programs report the VIF and its inverse (1/VIF) by default. The inverse of the VIF is sometimes referred to as the tolerance index measure. The higher the VIF_j value, or the lower the tolerance index, the higher will be the estimated variance of X_j in our theoretically specified model. Another useful statistic to examine is the square root of the VIF. Why? Because the VIF is measured in terms of variance, but most of our hypothesis-testing inferences are made with standard errors. Thus the square root of the VIF provides a useful indicator of the impact the multicollinearity is going to have on hypothesis-testing inferences.

11.5.3   Multicollinearity: a Simulated Example

Thus far we have made a few scattered references to simulation. In this section we make use of simulation to better understand multicollinearity. Almost every statistical computer program has a set of tools for simulating data. When we use these tools, we have an advantage that we do not ever have with real-world data: we can *know* the underlying "population" characteristics (because we create them). When we know the population parameters for a regression model and draw sample data from this population, we gain insights into the ways in which statistical models work.

So, to simulate multicollinearity, we are going to create a population with the following characteristics:

1. Two variables X_{1i} and X_{2i} such that the correlation $r_{X_{1i},X_{2i}} = 0.9$.
2. A variable u_i randomly drawn from a normal distribution, centered around 0 with variance equal to 1 [$u_i \sim N(0, 1)$].
3. A variable Y_i such that $Y_i = 0.5 + 1X_{1i} + 1X_{2i} + u_i$.

---

[7] Students facing OLS diagnostic procedures are often surprised that the first thing that we do after we estimate our theoretically specified model of interest is to estimate a large set of atheoretical auxiliary models to test the properties of our main model. We will see that, although these auxiliary models lead to the same types of output that we get from our main model, we are often interested in only one particular part of the results from the auxiliary model. With our "main" model of interest, we have learned that we should include every variable that our theories tell us should be included and exclude all other variables. In auxiliary models, we do not follow this rule. Instead, we are running these models to test whether certain properties have or have not been met in our original model.

We can see from the description of our simulated population that we have met all of the OLS assumptions, but that we have a high correlation between our two independent variables. Now we will conduct a series of random draws (samples) from this population and look at the results from the following regression models:

$$\text{Model 1:} \quad Y_i = \alpha + \beta_1 X_{1i} + \beta_2 X_{2i} + u_i,$$
$$\text{Model 2:} \quad Y_i = \alpha + \beta_1 X_{1i} + u_i,$$
$$\text{Model 3:} \quad Y_i = \alpha + \beta_2 X_{2i} + u_i.$$

In each of these random draws, we increase the size of our sample starting with $n = 5$, then 10, and finally 25 cases. Results from models estimated with each sample of data are displayed in Table 11.10. In the first column of results ($n = 5$), we can see that both slope parameters are

Table 11.10 Random draws of increasing size from a population with substantial multicollinearity

Estimate	Sample: $n = 5$	Sample: $n = 10$	Sample: $n = 25$
Model 1:			
$\hat{\beta}_1$	0.546	0.882	1.012**
	(0.375)	(0.557)	(0.394)
$\hat{\beta}_2$	1.422*	1.450**	1.324***
	(0.375)	(0.557)	(0.394)
$\hat{\alpha}$	1.160**	0.912***	0.579***
	(0.146)	(0.230)	(0.168)
R^2	0.99	0.93	0.89
VIF_1	5.26	5.26	5.26
VIF_2	5.26	5.26	5.26
Model 2:			
$\hat{\beta}_1$	1.827**	2.187***	2.204***
	(0.382)	(0.319)	(0.207)
$\hat{\alpha}$	1.160**	0.912**	0.579***
	(0.342)	(0.302)	(0.202)
R^2	0.88	0.85	0.83
Model 3:			
$\hat{\beta}_2$	1.914***	2.244***	2.235***
	(0.192)	(0.264)	(0.192)
$\hat{\alpha}$	1.160***	0.912***	0.579***
	(0.171)	(0.251)	(0.188)
R^2	0.97	0.90	0.86

Notes: The dependent variable is $Y_i = 0.5 + 1X_{1i} + 1X_{2i} + u_i$.
Standard errors in parentheses.
Two-sided t-tests: ***$p < 0.01$; **$p < 0.05$; *$p < 0.10$.

positive, as would be expected, but that the parameter estimate for X_1 is statistically insignificant and the parameter estimate for X_2 is on the borderline of statistical significance. The VIF statistics for both variables are equal to 5.26, indicating that the variance for each parameter estimate is substantially inflated by multicollinearity. The model's intercept is statistically significant and positive, but pretty far from what we know to be the true population value for this parameter. In Models 2 and 3 we get statistically significant positive parameter estimates for each variable, but both of these estimated slopes are almost twice as high as what we know to be the true population parameters. The 95 percent confidence interval for $\hat{\beta}_2$ does not include the true population parameter. This is a clear case of omitted-variables bias. When we draw a sample of 10 cases, we get closer to the true population parameters with $\hat{\beta}_1$ and $\hat{\alpha}$ in Model 1. The VIF statistics remain the same because we have not changed the underlying relationship between X_1 and X_2. This increase in sample size does not help us with the omitted-variables bias in Models 2 and 3. In fact, we can now reject the true population slope parameter for both models with substantial confidence. In our third sample with 25 cases, Model 1 is now very close to our true population model, in the sense of both the parameter values and that all of these parameter estimates are statistically significant. In Models 2 and 3, the omitted-variables bias is even more pronounced.

The findings in this simulation exercise mirror more general findings in the theoretical literature on OLS models. *Adding more data will alleviate multicollinearity, but not omitted-variables bias.* We now turn to an example of multicollinearity with real-world data.

YOUR TURN: Imagining a different simulation

How would the output in Table 11.10 be different if $r_{X_{1i},X_{2i}} = -0.9$?

11.5.4   Multicollinearity: a Real-World Example

In this section, we estimate a model of the thermometer scores for US voters for George W. Bush in 2004. Our model specification is the following:

$$\text{Bush Thermometer}_i = \alpha + \beta_1 \text{Income}_i + \beta_2 \text{Ideology}_i + \beta_3 \text{Education}_i + \beta_4 \text{Party ID}_i + u_i.$$

Although we have distinct theories about the causal impact of each independent variable on people's feelings toward Bush, Table 11.11 indicates that some of these independent variables are substantially correlated with each other.

Table 11.11 Pairwise correlations between independent variables

	Bush Therm.	Income	Ideology	Education	Party ID
Bush Therm.	1.00	—	—	—	—
Income	0.09***	1.00	—	—	—
Ideology	0.56***	0.13***	1.00	—	—
Education	−0.07***	0.44***	−0.06*	1.00	—
Party ID	0.69***	0.15***	0.60***	0.06*	1.00

Notes: Cell entries are correlation coefficients.
Two-sided t-tests: ***$p < 0.01$; **$p < 0.05$; *$p < 0.10$.

Table 11.12 Model results from random draws of increasing size from the 2004 NES

Independent variable	Model 1	Model 2	Model 3
Income	0.77	0.72	0.11
	(0.90)	(0.51)	(0.15)
	{1.63}	{1.16}	{1.24}
Ideology	7.02	4.57*	4.26***
	(5.53)	(2.22)	(0.67)
	{3.50}	{1.78}	{1.58}
Education	−6.29	−2.50	−1.88***
	(3.32)	(1.83)	(0.55)
	{1.42}	{1.23}	{1.22}
Party ID	6.83	8.44***	10.00***
	(3.98)	(1.58)	(0.46)
	{3.05}	{1.70}	{1.56}
Intercept	21.92	12.03	13.73***
	(23.45)	(13.03)	(3.56)
R^2	0.71	0.56	0.57
n	20	74	821

Notes: The dependent variable is the respondent's thermometer score for George W. Bush.
Standard errors in parentheses; VIF statistics in braces.
Two-sided t-tests: ***$p < 0.01$; **$p < 0.05$; *$p < 0.10$.

In Table 11.12, we present estimates of our model using three different samples from the NES 2004 data. In Model 1, estimated with data from 20 randomly chosen respondents, we see that none of our independent variables are statistically significant despite the rather high R^2 statistic. The VIF statistics for Ideology and Party ID indicate that multicollinearity might be a problem. In Model 2, estimated with data from 74 randomly chosen respondents, Party ID is highly significant in the expected (positive) direction whereas Ideology is near the threshold of statistical significance. None of the VIF statistics for this model are stunningly high, though they are greater than 1.5 for Ideology, Education, and Party ID.[8] Finally, in Model 3, estimated with all 820 respondents for whom data on all of the variables were available, we see that Ideology, Party ID, and Education are all significant predictors of people's feelings toward Bush. The sample size is more than sufficient to overcome the VIF statistics for Party ID and Ideology. Of our independent variables, only Income remains statistically insignificant. Is this due to multicollinearity? After all, when we look at Table 11.11, we see that income has a highly significant positive correlation with Bush Thermometer scores. For the answer to this question, we need to go back to the lessons that we learned in Chapter 10: Once we control for the effects of Ideology, Party ID, and Education, the effect of income on people's feelings toward George W. Bush goes away.

11.5.5   Multicollinearity: What Should I Do?

In the introduction to this section on multicollinearity, we described it as a "common and vexing issue." The reason why multicollinearity is "vexing" is that there is no magical statistical cure for it. What is the best thing to do when you have multicollinearity? Easy (in theory): *collect more data.* But data are expensive to collect. If we had more data, we would use them and we wouldn't have hit this problem in the first place. So, if you do not have an easy way to increase your sample size, then multicollinearity ends up being something that you just have to live with. It is important to know that you have multicollinearity and to present your multicollinearity by reporting the results of VIF statistics or what happens to your model when you add and drop the "guilty" variables.

11.6   WRAPPING UP

The key to developing good models is having a good theory and then doing a lot of diagnostics to figure out what we have after estimating the model. What we've seen in this chapter is that there are additional (but not insurmountable!) obstacles to overcome when we consider that some of our theories involve noncontinuous independent variables. In the next chapter, we examine the research situations in which we encounter dummy dependent variables and a set of special circumstances that can arise when our data have been collected across time.

---

[8] When we work with real-world data, there tend to be many more changes as we move from sample to sample.

CONCEPTS INTRODUCED IN THIS CHAPTER

- auxiliary regression model – a regression model separate from the original theoretical model that is used to detect one or more statistical properties of the original model
- DFBETA score – a statistical measure for the calculation of the influence of an individual case on the value of a single parameter estimate
- dummying out – adding a dummy variable to a regression model to measure and isolate the effect of an influential observation
- dummy variable – a variable that takes on one of two values (usually one or zero)
- dummy-variable trap – perfect multicollinearity that results from the inclusion of dummy variables representing each possible value of a categorical variable
- high multicollinearity – in a multiple regression model, when two or more of the independent variables in the model are extremely highly correlated with one another, making it difficult to isolate the distinct effects of each variable
- influential case – in a regression model a case which has either a combination of large leverage and a large squared residual or a large DFBETA score
- interactive models – multiple regression models that contain at least one independent variable that we create by multiplying together two or more independent variables
- leverage – in a multiple regression model, the degree to which an individual case is unusual in terms of its value for a single independent variable, or its particular combination of values for two or more independent variables
- micronumerosity – a suggested synonym for multicollinearity
- reference category – in a multiple regression model, the value of a categorical independent variable for which we do not include a dummy variable
- variance inflation factor – a statistical measure to detect the contribution of each independent variable in a multiple regression model to overall multicollinearity

EXERCISES

1. Using the model presented in Table 11.4, how many days would you predict that it would take for a government to form if the government was made up of two different political parties with an ideological range of 2, if bargaining was taking place in the immediate aftermath of an election, and there was not a continuation rule? Show your work.

2. Using the model presented in Table 11.4, interpret the parameter estimate for the variable "Continuation Rule."

3. Using the model presented in Table 11.4, interpret the parameter estimate for the variable "Number of Parties in the Government."

4. Using the data set "nes2008.dta" (which is available on the textbook's web site at www.cambridge.org/fpsr), investigate two possible causes of a respondent's attitudes toward abortion (which you will, for the purposes of this exercise, need to treat as a continuous variable), using the respondent's gender and the respondent's level of education as your two key independent variables. First, construct an additive multiple regression model investigating the effects of gender and education on abortion attitudes. Next, construct an interactive multiple regression model that adds an interaction term for gender and education. Present the results of both models in a single table. Interpret, first, the additive regression model, and then interpret the interactive model. Does education have the same, a smaller, or larger effect on abortion attitudes for women than it does for men?

5. Using the data set "state_data.dta" (which is available on the textbook's web site at www.cambridge.org/fpsr), estimate Model C in Table 10.7. Test for influential observations in the model using a leverage versus squared residual plot. Write about what this diagnostic test tells you.

6. Test for influential observations in the model that you estimated for Exercise 5 using DFBETA scores. Write about what this diagnostic test tells you.

7. Based on what you found in Exercises 5 and 6, how would you adjust the original model?

8. Test for multicollinearity in the model that you estimated for Exercise 5. Write about what you have found.

12 Limited Dependent Variables and Time-Series Data

OVERVIEW

In this chapter we provide an introduction to two common extensions of multiple regression models. The first deals with cross-sectional models where the dependent variable is categorical rather than continuous. The second involves time-series models, where the variables of interest are measured repeatedly over time. Throughout the chapter, we use examples from a variety of substantive applications to illustrate the important issues that must be addressed in each research situation.

12.1 EXTENSIONS OF ORDINARY LEAST SQUARES

We have come a long way in the understanding and use of regression analysis in political science. We have learned, mathematically, where OLS coefficients come from; we have learned how to interpret those coefficients substantively; and we have learned how to use OLS to control for other possible causes of the dependent variable. In Chapter 11, we introduced so-called "dummy" variables – which, you will recall, are just categorical variables with two possible values – having used them as independent variables in our regression models. In this chapter, we extend this focus to research situations in which the dependent variable is a dummy variable. Such situations are common in political science, as many of the dependent variables that we find ourselves interested in – such as, whether or not an individual voted in a particular election, or whether or not two countries engaged in a dispute escalate the situation to open warfare – are dummy variables.

We also introduce some unique issues pertaining to using OLS to analyze time-series research questions. Recall that one of the major types of research design, the aptly named time-series observational study, involves data that are collected over time. The analysis of time-series data presents particular opportunities for political science researchers, but it also has a few unique pitfalls. In this chapter, we'll give you some tips about how to identify and avoid those pitfalls. We turn, first, to the analysis of so-called "dummy" dependent variables.

12.2 DUMMY DEPENDENT VARIABLES

Thus far, our discussion of dummy variables has been limited to situations in which the variable in question is one of the independent variables in our model. The obstacles in those models are relatively straightforward. Things get a bit more complicated, however, when our dependent variable is a dummy variable.

Certainly, many of the dependent variables of theoretical interest to political scientists are not continuous. Very often, this means that we need to move to a statistical model other than OLS if we want to get reasonable estimates for our hypothesis testing. One exception to this is the **linear probability model** (LPM). The LPM is an OLS model in which the dependent variable is a dummy variable. It is called a "probability" model because we can interpret the $\hat{Y}$ values as "predicted probabilities." But, as we will see, it is not without problems. Because of these problems, most political scientists do not use the LPM. We provide a brief discussion of the popular alternatives to the LPM and then conclude this section with a discussion of goodness-of-fit measures when the dependent variable is a dummy variable.

12.2.1 The Linear Probability Model

As an example of a dummy dependent variable, we use the choice that most US voters in the 2004 presidential election made between voting for the incumbent George W. Bush and his Democratic challenger John Kerry.[1] Our dependent variable, which we will call "Bush," is equal to one for respondents who reported voting for Bush and equal to zero for respondents who reported voting for Kerry. For our model we theorize that the decision to vote for Bush or Kerry is a function of an individual's

---

[1] There was only a handful of respondents to the NES who refused to reveal their vote to the interviewers or voted for a different candidate. But there were a large number of respondents who reported that they did not vote. By excluding all of these categories, we are defining the population about which we want to make inferences as those who voted for Kerry or Bush. Including respondents who voted for other candidates, refused to report their vote, or did not vote would amount to changing from a dichotomous categorical dependent variable to a multichotomous categorical dependent variable. The types of models used for this type of dependent variable are substantially more complicated, and are beyond the scope of this book.

Table 12.1 The effects of partisanship and performance evaluations on votes for Bush in 2004

Independent variable	Parameter estimate
Party Identification	0.09**
	(0.01)
Evaluation: War on Terror	0.08**
	(0.01)
Evaluation: Health of the Economy	0.08**
	(0.01)
Intercept	0.60**
	(0.01)
R^2	0.73
n	780

Notes: The dependent variable is equal to one if the respondent voted for Bush and equal to zero if they voted for Kerry.
Standard errors in parentheses.
Two-sided t-tests: ** $p < 0.01$; * $p < 0.05$.

partisan identification (ranging from -3 for strong Democrats, to 0 for Independents, to $+3$ for strong Republican identifiers) and their evaluation of the job that Bush did in handling the war on terror and the health of the economy (both of these evaluations range from $+2$ for "approve strongly" to -2 for "disapprove strongly"). The formula for this model is:

$$\text{Bush}_i = \alpha + \beta_1 \text{Party ID}_i + \beta_2 \text{War Evaluation}_i$$
$$+ \beta_3 \text{Economic Evaluation}_i + u_i.$$

Table 12.1 presents the OLS results from this model. We can see from the table that all of the parameter estimates are statistically significant in the expected (positive) direction. Not surprisingly, we see that people who identified with the Republican Party and who had more approving evaluations of the president's handling of the war and the economy were more likely to vote for him.

To examine how the interpretation of this model is different from that of a regular OLS model, let's calculate some individual $\hat{Y}$ values. We know from the estimates listed in Table 12.1 that the formula for $\hat{Y}$ is:

$$\hat{Y}_i = 0.6 + 0.09 \times \text{Party ID}_i + 0.08 \times \text{War Evaluation}_i$$
$$+ 0.08 \times \text{Economic Evaluation}_i.$$

For a respondent who reported being a pure Independent (Party ID $= 0$) with a somewhat approving evaluation of Bush's handling of the war on terror (War Evaluation = 1) and a somewhat disapproving evaluation of Bush's handling of the economy (Economic Evaluation = −1), we would calculate $\hat{Y}_i$ as follows:

$$\hat{Y}_i = 0.6 + (0.09 \times 0) + (0.08 \times 1) + (0.08 \times -1) = 0.6.$$

One way to interpret this predicted value is to think of it as a **predicted probability** that the dummy dependent variable is equal to one, or, in other words, the predicted probability of this respondent voting for Bush. Using the example for which we just calculated $\hat{Y}_i$, we would predict that such an individual would have a 0.6 probability (or 60 percent chance) of voting for Bush in 2004. As you can imagine, if we change the values of our three independent variables around, the predicted probability of the individual voting for Bush changes correspondingly. This means that the LPM is a special case of OLS for which we can think of the predicted values of the dependent variable as predicted probabilities. From here on, we represent predicted probabilities for a particular case as "$\hat{P}_i$" or "$\hat{P}(Y_i = 1)$" and we can summarize this special property of the LPM as $\hat{P}_i = \hat{P}(Y_i = 1) = \hat{Y}_i$.

YOUR TURN: Calculating predicted probabilities

Based on the above estimates, what is the probability that a strong Republican with a somewhat approving view of Bush's handling of the war, and a neutral view of Bush's handling of the economy, will cast a vote for Bush in 2004?

One of the problems with the LPM comes when we arrive at extreme values of the predicted probabilities. Consider, for instance, a respondent who reported being a strong Republican (Party ID = 3) with a strongly approving evaluation of Bush's handling of the war on terror (War Evaluation = 2) and a strongly approving evaluation of Bush's handling of the economy (Economic Evaluation = 2). For this individual, we would calculate $\hat{P}_i$ as follows:

$$\hat{P}_i = \hat{Y}_i = 0.6 + (0.09 \times 3) + (0.08 \times 2) + (0.08 \times 2) = 1.19.$$

This means that we would predict that such an individual would have a 119 percent chance of voting for Bush in 2004. To be sure, if we went to the other extremes for the values of our independent variables, it would be similarly possible to obtain a predicted probability of less than zero. Such predicted probabilities are, of course, nonsensical because probabilities cannot be smaller than zero or greater than one. So one of the problems with the LPM is that it can produce such values. In the greater scheme of things, though, this problem is not so severe, as we can make sensible interpretations of predicted values higher than one or lower than zero – these are cases for which we are very confident that probability is close to one (for $\hat{P}_i > 1$) or close to zero (for $\hat{P}_i < 0$).

To the extent that the LPM has potentially more serious problems, they come in two forms: heteroscedasticity and functional form. We discussed heteroscedasticity in Chapter 9 when we noted that, any time that we estimate an OLS model, we assume that there is homoscedasticity (or equal error variance). We can see that this assumption is particularly problematic with the LPM because the values of the dependent variable are all equal to zero or one, but the $\hat{Y}$ or predicted values range anywhere between zero and one (or even beyond these values). This means that the errors (or residual values) will tend to be largest for cases for which the predicted value is close to 0.5. Any nonuniform pattern of model error variance such as this is called heteroscedasticity, which means that the estimated standard errors may be too high or too low. We care about this because standard errors that are too high or too low will have bad effects on our hypothesis testing, and thus ultimately on our conclusions about the presence or absence of causal relationships.

The problem of functional form is related to the assumption of parametric linearity that we also discussed in Chapter 9. In the context of the LPM, this assumption amounts to saying that the impact of a one-unit increase in an independent variable X is equal to the corresponding parameter estimate $\hat{\beta}$ regardless of the value of X or any other independent variable. This assumption may be particularly problematic for LPMs because the effect of a change in an independent variable may be greater for cases that would otherwise be at 0.5 than for those cases for which the predicted probability would otherwise be close to zero or one. Obviously the extent of both of these problems will vary across different models.

For these reasons, the typical political science solution to having a dummy dependent variable is to avoid using the LPM. Most applications that you will come across in political science research will use a **binomial logit** (BNL) or **binomial probit** (BNP) model instead of the LPM for models in which the dependent variable is a dummy variable. BNL and BNP models are similar to regression models in many ways, but they involve an additional step in interpreting them. In the next section we provide a brief overview of these types of models.

12.2.2 Binomial Logit and Binomial Probit

In cases in which their dependent variable is dichotomous, most political scientists use a BNL or a BNP model instead of an LPM. In this section we provide a brief introduction to these two models, using the same example that we used for our LPM in the previous section. To understand these models, let's first rewrite our LPM from our preceding example in terms of a probability statement:

$$P_i = P(Y_i = 1) = \alpha + \beta_1 \times \text{Party ID}_i + \beta_2 \times \text{War Evaluation}_i$$
$$+ \beta_3 \times \text{Economic Evaluation}_i + u_i.$$

This is just a way of expressing the probability part of the LPM in a formula in which "$P(Y_i = 1)$" translates to "the probability that Y_i is equal to one," which in the case of our running example is the probability that the individual cast a vote for Bush. We then further collapse this to

$$P_i = P(Y_i = 1) = \alpha + \beta_1 X_{1i} + \beta_2 X_{2i} + \beta_3 X_{3i} + u_i,$$

and yet further to

$$P_i = P(Y_i = 1) = X_i \beta + u_i,$$

where we define $X_i \beta$ as the systematic component of Y such that $X_i \beta = \alpha + \beta_1 X_{1i} + \beta_2 X_{2i} + \beta_3 X_{3i}$.[2] The term u_i continues to represent the stochastic or random component of Y. So if we think about our predicted probability for a given case, we can write this as:

$$\hat{Y}_i = \hat{P}_i = \hat{P}(Y_i = 1) = X_i \hat{\beta} = \hat{\alpha} + \hat{\beta}_1 X_{1i} + \hat{\beta}_2 X_{2i} + \hat{\beta}_3 X_{3i}.$$

A BNL model with the same variables would be written as:

$$P_i = P(Y_i = 1) = \Lambda(\alpha + \beta_1 X_{1i} + \beta_2 X_{2i} + \beta_3 X_{3i} + u_i) = \Lambda(X_i \beta + u_i).$$

The predicted probabilities from this model would be written as:

$$\hat{P}_i = \hat{P}(Y_i = 1) = \Lambda(\hat{\alpha} + \hat{\beta}_1 X_{1i} + \hat{\beta}_2 X_{2i} + \hat{\beta}_3 X_{3i} = \Lambda(X_i \hat{\beta}).$$

A BNP with the same variables would be written as:

$$P_i = P(Y_i = 1) = \Phi(\alpha + \beta_1 X_{1i} + \beta_2 X_{2i} + \beta_3 X_{3i} + u_i) = \Phi(X_i \beta + u_i).$$

The predicted probabilities from this model would be written as:

$$\hat{P}_i = \hat{P}(Y_i = 1) = \Phi(\hat{\alpha} + \hat{\beta}_1 X_{1i} + \hat{\beta}_2 X_{2i} + \hat{\beta}_3 X_{3i} = \Phi(X_i \hat{\beta}).$$

The difference between the BNL model and the LPM is the Λ, and the difference between the BNP model and the LPM is the Φ. The Λ and Φ are known as **link functions**. A link function *links* the linear component of a logit or probit model, $X_i \hat{\beta}$, to the quantity in which we are interested, the predicted probability that the dummy dependent variable equals one, $\hat{P}(Y_i = 1)$ or $\hat{P}_i$. A major result of using these link functions is that the relationship between our independent and dependent variables is no

---

[2] This shorthand comes from matrix algebra. Although matrix algebra is a very useful tool in statistics, it is not needed to master the material in this text.

Table 12.2 The effects of partisanship and performance evaluations on votes for Bush in 2004: three different types of models

	LPM	BNL	BNP
Party Identification	0.09**	0.82**	0.45**
	(0.01)	(0.09)	(0.04)
Evaluation: War on Terror	0.08**	0.60**	0.32**
	(0.01)	(0.09)	(0.05)
Evaluation: Health of the Economy	0.08**	0.59**	0.32**
	(0.01)	(0.10)	(0.06)
Intercept	0.60**	1.11**	0.58**
	(0.01)	(0.20)	(0.10)

Notes: The dependent variable is equal to one if the respondent voted for Bush and equal to zero if they voted for Kerry.
Standard errors in parentheses.
Two-sided significance tests: **$p < 0.01$; *$p < 0.05$.

longer assumed to be linear. In the case of a logit model, the link function, abbreviated as Λ, uses the cumulative logistic distribution function (and thus the name "logit") to link the linear component to the probability that $Y_i = 1$. In the case of the probit function, the link function abbreviated as Φ uses the cumulative normal distribution function to link the linear component to the predicted probability that $Y_i = 1$. Appendices C (for the BNL) and D (for the BNP) provide tables for converting $X_i\hat{\beta}$ values into predicted probabilities.

The best way to understand how the LPM, BNL, and BNP work similarly to and differently from each other is to look at them all with the same model and data. An example of this is presented in Table 12.2. From this table it is apparent that across the three models the parameter estimate for each independent variable has the same sign and significance level. But it is also apparent that the magnitudes of these parameter estimates are different across the three models. This is mainly due to the difference of link functions. To better illustrate the differences between the three models presented in Table 12.2, we plotted the predicted probabilities from them in Figure 12.1. These predicted probabilities are for an individual who strongly approved of the Bush administration's handling of the war on terror but who strongly disapproved of the Bush administration's handling of the economy.[3] The horizontal axis in this figure is this individual's

[3] These were the modal answers to the two evaluative questions that were included in the model presented in Table 12.2. It is a fairly common practice to illustrate the estimated impact of a variable of interest from this type of model by holding all other variables constant at their mean or modal values and then varying that one variable to see how the predicted probabilities change.

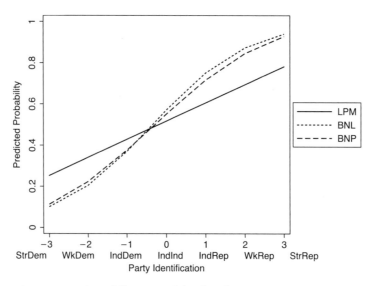

Figure 12.1 Three different models of Bush vote

party identification, ranging from strong Democratic Party identifiers on the left end to strong Republican Party identifiers on the right end. The vertical axis is the predicted probability of voting for Bush. We can see from Figure 12.1 that the three models make very similar predictions. The main differences come as we move away from a predicted probability of 0.5.

The LPM line has, by definition, a constant slope across the entire range of X. The BNL and BNP lines of predicted probabilities change their slope such that they slope more and more gently as we move farther from predicted probabilities of 0.5. The differences between the BNL and BNP lines are trivial. This means that the effect of a movement in Party Identification on the predicted probability is constant for the LPM. But for the BNL and BNP, the effect of a movement in Party Identification *depends* on the value of the other variables in the model. It is important to realize that the differences between the LPM and the other two types of model are by construction instead of some novel finding. In other words, our choice of model determines the shape of our predicted probability line.

12.2.3   Goodness-of-Fit with Dummy Dependent Variables

Although we can calculate an R^2 statistic when we estimate a linear probability model, R^2 doesn't quite capture what we are doing when we want to assess the fit of such a model. What we are trying to assess is the ability of our model to separate our cases into those in which $Y = 1$ and those in which $Y = 0$. So it is helpful to think about this in terms of a 2×2 table of model-based expectations and actual values. To figure out the

Table 12.3 Classification table from LPM of the effects of partisanship and performance evaluations on votes for Bush in 2004

	Model-based expectations	
Actual vote	**Bush**	**Kerry**
Bush	361	36
Kerry	28	355

Notes: Cell entries are the number of cases. Predictions are based on a cutoff of $\hat{Y} > 0.5$.

model's expected values, we need to choose a cutoff point at which we interpret the model as predicting that $Y = 1$. An obvious value to use for this cutoff point is $\hat{Y} > 0.5$. Table 12.3 shows the results of this in what we call a **classification table**. Classification tables compare model-based expectations with actual values of the dependent variable.

In this table, we can see the differences between the LPM's predictions and the actual votes reported by survey respondents to the 2004 NES. One fairly straightforward measure of the fit of this model is to look at the percentage of cases that were correctly classified through use of the model. So if we add up the cases correctly classified and divide by the total number of cases we get:

$$\text{correctly classified LPM}_{0.5} = \frac{361 + 355}{780} = \frac{716}{780} = 0.918.$$

So our LPM managed to correctly classify 0.918 or 91.8 percent of the respondents and to erroneously classify the remaining 0.082, or 8.2 percent.

Although this might seem like a pretty high classification rate, we don't really know what we should be comparing it with. One option is to compare our model's classification rate with the classification rate for a naive model (NM) that predicts that all cases will be in the modal category. In this case, the NM would predict that all respondents voted for Bush. So, if we calculate the correctly classified cases for the NM we get:

$$\text{correctly classified NM} = \frac{361 + 36}{780} = \frac{397}{780} = 0.509.$$

This means that the NM correctly classified 0.509, or 50.9 percent, of the respondents and erroneously classified the remaining 0.491, or 49.1 percent.

Turning now to the business of comparing the performance of our model with that of the NM, we can calculate the **proportionate reduction**

of error when we move from the NM to our LPM with party identification and two performance evaluations as independent variables. The percentage erroneously classified in the naive model was 49.1 and the percentage erroneously classified in our LPM was 8.2. So we have reduced the error proportion by $49.1 - 8.2 = 40.9$. If we now divide this by the total error percentage of the naive model, we get $40.9/49.1 = 0.833$. This means that we have a proportionate reduction of error equal to 0.833. Another way of saying this is that, when we moved from the NM to our LPM, we reduced the classification errors by 83.3 percent.

12.3   BEING CAREFUL WITH TIME SERIES

In recent years there has been a massive proliferation of valuable time-series data in political science. Although this growth has led to exciting new research opportunities, it has also been the source of a fair amount of controversy. Swirling at the center of this controversy is the danger of spurious regressions that are due to trends in time-series data.[4] As we will see, a failure to recognize this problem can lead to mistakes about inferring causality. In the remainder of this section we first introduce time-series notation, discuss the problems of spurious regressions, and then discuss the trade-offs involved with two possible solutions: the lagged dependent variable and the differenced dependent variable.

12.3.1   Time-Series Notation

In Chapter 4 we introduced the concept of a time-series observational study. Although we have seen some time-series data (such as the Ray Fair data set used in Chapters 8–10), we have not been using the mathematical notation specific to time-series data. Instead, we have been using a generic notation in which the subscript i represents an individual case. In time-series notation, individual cases are represented with the subscript t, and the numeric value of t represents the temporal order in which the cases occurred, and this ordering is very likely to matter.[5] Consider the following OLS population model written in the notation that we have worked with thus far:

$$Y_i = \alpha + \beta_1 X_{1i} + \beta_2 X_{2i} + u_i.$$

---

[4] The word "trends" has both formal and informal definitions. Informally, of course, a "trend" is simply a recent pattern in data. ("What's the recent trend in the president's approval rating?") But the problem of trends in time series arise from a different use of the word, and more or less connote the degree of memory in a time series. We will elaborate on this below.

[5] In cross-sectional data sets, it is almost always the case that the ordering of the cases is irrelevant to the analyses being conducted.

If the data of interest were time-series data, we would rewrite this model as:

$$Y_t = \alpha + \beta_1 X_{1t} + \beta_2 X_{2t} + u_t.$$

In most political science applications, time-series data occur at regular intervals. Common intervals for political science data are weeks, months, quarters, and years. In fact, these time intervals are important enough that they are usually front-and-center in the description of a data set. For instance, the data presented in Figure 2.2 would be described as a "Monthly time series of presidential popularity."

Using this notation, we talk about the observations in the order in which they came. As such, it is often useful to talk about values of variables relative to their **lagged values** or **lead values**. Both lagged and lead values are expressions of values relative to a current time, which we call time t. A lagged value of a variable is the value of the variable from a previous time period. For instance, a lagged value from one period previous to the current time is referenced as being from time $t-1$. A lead value of a variable is the value of the variable from a future time period. For instance, a lead value from one period into the future from the current time is referenced as being from time $t + 1$. Note that we would not want to specify a model with a leading value for an independent variable because this would amount to a theory that the future value of the independent variable exerted a causal influence on the past.

12.3.2 Memory and Lags in Time-Series Analysis

You might be wondering what, aside from changing a subscript from an i to a t, is so different about time-series modeling. We would like to bring special attention to one particular feature of time-series analysis that sets it apart from modeling cross-sectional data.

Consider the following simple model of presidential popularity, and assume that the data are in monthly form:

$$\text{Popularity}_t = \alpha + \beta_1 \text{Economy}_t + \beta_2 \text{Peace}_t + u_t,$$

where Economy and Peace refer to some measures of the health of the national economy and international peace, respectively. Now look at what the model assumes, quite explicitly. A president's popularity in any given month t is a function of that month's economy and that month's level of international peace (plus some random error term), *and nothing else, at any points in time.* What about last month's economic shocks, or the war that ended three months ago? They are nowhere to be found in this equation, which means quite literally that they can have no effect on a president's popularity ratings in this month. Every month – according to this model – the public starts from scratch evaluating the president, as if to say, on the first of the month: "Okay, let's just forget about last month. Instead, let's check this month's economic data, and also this month's international conflicts, and render a verdict on whether the president is doing a good job or not." There is no memory from month to month whatsoever. Every independent variable has an immediate impact, and that impact lasts exactly one month, after which the effect immediately dies out entirely.

This is preposterous, of course. The public does not erase its collective memory every month. Shifts in independent variables from many months in the past can have lingering effects into current evaluations of the president. In most cases, we imagine that the effects of shifts in independent variables eventually die out over a period of time, as new events become more salient in the minds of the public, and, indeed, some collective "forgetting" occurs. But surely this does not happen in a single month.

And let's be clear what the problems are with a model like the preceding simple model of approval. If we are convinced that at least some past values of the economy still have effects today, and if at least some past values of international peace still have effects today, but we instead estimate only the contemporary effects (from period t), then we have committed omitted-variables bias – which, as we have emphasized over the last two chapters, is one of the most serious mistakes a social scientist can make. Failing to account for how past values of our independent variables might affect current values of our dependent variable is a serious issue in time-series observational studies, and nothing quite like this issue exists in the cross-sectional world. In time-series analysis, even if we know that Y is caused by X and Z, we still have to worry about how many past lags of X and Z might affect Y.

The clever reader might have a ready response to such a situation: Specify additional lags of our independent variables in our regression models:

$$\text{Popularity}_t = \alpha + \beta_1 \text{Economy}_t + \beta_2 \text{Economy}_{t-1} + \beta_3 \text{Economy}_{t-2}$$
$$+ \beta_4 \text{Economy}_{t-3} + \beta_5 \text{Peace}_t + \beta_6 \text{Peace}_{t-1} + \beta_7 \text{Peace}_{t-2}$$
$$+ \beta_8 \text{Peace}_{t-3} + u_t.$$

This is, indeed, one possible solution to the question of how to incorporate the lingering effects of the past on the present. But the model is getting a bit unwieldy, with lots of parameters to estimate. More important, though, it leaves several questions unanswered:

1. How many lags of the independent variables should we include in our model? We have included lags from period t through $t-3$ in the preceding specification, but how do we know that this is the correct choice?

From the outset of the book, we have emphasized that you should have *theoretical* reasons for including variables in your statistical models. But what theory tells with any specificity that we should include three, four, or six periods' worth of lags of our independent variables in our models?

2. If we do include several lags of all of our independent variables in our models, we will almost surely induce multicollinearity into them. That is, X_t, X_{t-1}, and X_{t-2} are likely to be highly correlated with one another. (Such is the nature of time series.) Those models, then, would have all of the problems associated with high multicollinearity that we identified in Chapter 11 – in particular, large standard errors and the adverse consequences on hypothesis testing.

Before showing two alternatives to saturating our models with lots of lags of our independent variables, we need to confront a different problem in time-series analysis. Later in this chapter, we will see an example of real-world research into the causes of presidential approval that deals with this problem.

12.3.3 Trends and the Spurious Regression Problem

When discussing presidential popularity data, it's easy to see how a time series might have a "memory" – by which we mean that the current values of a series seem to be highly dependent on its past values.[6] Some series have memories of their pasts that are sufficiently long to induce statistical problems. In particular, we mention one, called the **spurious regression problem**.[7]

By way of example, consider the following facts: In the United States after World War II, golf became an increasingly popular sport. As its popularity grew, perhaps predictably the number of golf courses grew to accommodate the demand for places to play. That growth continued steadily into the early twenty-first century. We can think of the number of golf courses in the United States as a time series, of course, presumably one on an annual metric. Over the same period of time, divorce rates in the United States grew and grew. Whereas divorce was formerly an uncommon practice, today it is commonplace in US society. We can think of family structure

---

[6] In any time series representing some form of public opinion, the word "memory" is a particularly apt term, though its use applies to all other time series as well.

[7] The problem of spurious regressions was something that economists like John Maynard Keynes worried about long before it had been demonstrated by Granger and Newbold (1974) using simulated data. Their main source of concern was the existence of general trends in a variable over time.

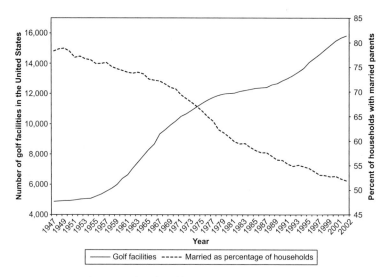

Figure 12.2 The growth of golf and the demise of marriage in the United States, 1947–2002

as a time series, too – in this case, the percentage of households in which a married couple is present.[8]

And both of these time series – likely for different reasons – have long memories. In the case of golf courses, the number of courses in year t obviously depends heavily on the number of courses in the previous year. In the case of divorce rates, the dependence on the past presumably stems from the lingering, multiperiod influence of the social forces that lead to divorce in the first place. Both the number of golf facilities in the United States and the percentage of families in which a married couple is present are shown in Figure 12.2.[9] And it's clear that, consistent with our description, both variables have trends. In the case of golf facilities, that trend is upward; for marriage, the trend is down.

What's the problem here? Any time that one time series with a long memory is placed in a regression model with another series that also has a long memory, it can lead to falsely finding evidence of a causal connection between the two variables. This is known as the "spurious regression problem." If we take the demise of marriage as our dependent variable and use golf facilities as our independent variable, we would surely see that these two variables are related, statistically. In substantive terms, we might be tempted to jump to the conclusion that the growth of golf in the United States has *caused* the breakdown of the nuclear family. We show the results of that regression in Table 12.4. The dependent variable

---

[8] For the purposes of this illustration, we are obscuring the difference between divorce and unmarried cohabitation.
[9] The National Golf Foundation kindly gave us the data on golf facilities. Data on family structure are from the Current Population Reports from the United States Census Bureau.

there is the percentage of households with a married couple, and the independent variable is the number of golf courses (in thousands). The results are exactly as feared. For every thousand golf facilities built in the United States, there are 2.53 percent fewer families with a married couple present. The R^2 statistic is quite high, suggesting that roughly 93 percent of the variance in divorce rates is explained by the growth of the golf industry.

We're quite sure that some of you – presumably nongolfers – are nodding your heads and thinking, "But maybe golf *does* cause divorce rates to rise! Does the phrase 'golf widow' ring a bell?" But here's the problem with trending variables, and why it's such a potentially nasty problem in the social sciences. We could substitute *any* variable with a trend in it and come to the same "conclusion." To prove the point, let's take another example. Instead of examining the growth of golf as the culprit that caused the demise of the nuclear family, let's look at a different kind of growth – economic growth. In the postwar United States, GDP has grown steadily, with few interruptions in its upward trajectory. Figure 12.3 shows GDP, in annual terms, along with the now-familiar time series of the decline in marriage.

Table 12.4 Golf and the demise of marriage in the United States, 1947–2002	
Variable	Coefficient (std. error)
Golf facilities	−2.53* (0.09)
Constant	91.36* (1.00)
N	56
R^2	0.93
*$p < 0.05$.	

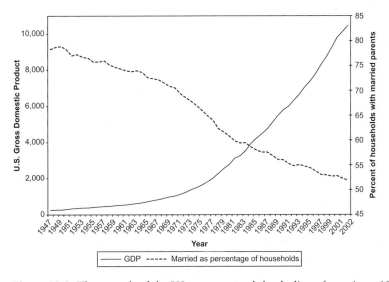

Figure 12.3 The growth of the US economy and the decline of marriage, 1947–2002

Obviously, GDP is a long-memoried series, with a sharp upward trend, in which current values of the series depend extremely heavily on past values.

> **YOUR TURN: Economic growth and the US family**
>
> Interpret the coefficient for GDP in Table 12.5, as well as the other information in the table. Do you think that you should conclude, on the basis of this table, that economic growth is detrimental to the stability of the US family?

The spurious regression problem has some bite here, as well. Using Marriage as our dependent variable and GDP as our independent variable, the regression results in Table 12.5 show a strong, negative, and statistically significant relationship between the two. This is not occurring because higher rates of economic output have led to the destruction of the US family. It is occurring because both variables have trends in them, and a regression involving two variables with trends – even if they are not truly associated – will produce spurious evidence of a relationship.

> **YOUR TURN: What other factors can we blame for the demise of the US family?**
>
> Try to think of another variable – like golf course construction, or GDP – that just goes up (or down) over a long period of time. Can you invent a causal "story" (that is almost certainly false) about how that variable might have "caused" the decline in two-parent households in the United States?

The two issues just mentioned – how to deal with lagged effects in a time series, and whether or not the spurious regression problem is relevant – are tractable ones. Moreover, new solutions to these issues arise as the study of time-series analysis becomes more sophisticated. We subsequently present two potential solutions to both problems.

12.3.4   The Differenced Dependent Variable

One way to avoid the problems of spurious regressions is to use a **differenced dependent variable**. We calculate a differenced (or, equivalently, "first differenced") variable by subtracting the first lag of the variable (Y_{t-1}) from the current value Y_t. The resulting time series is typically represented as $\Delta Y_t = Y_t - Y_{t-1}$.

In fact, when time series have long memories, taking first differences of both

Table 12.5 GDP and the demise of marriage in the United States, 1947–2002

Variable	Coefficient (std. error)
GDP (in trillions)	−2.71*
	(0.16)
Constant	74.00*
	(0.69)
N	56
R^2	0.84

*$p < 0.05$.

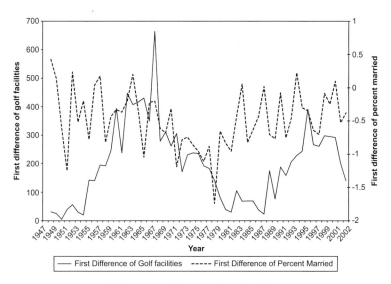

Figure 12.4 First differences of the number of golf courses and percentage of married families in the United States, 1947–2002

independent and dependent variables can be done. In effect, instead of Y_t representing the *levels* of a variable, ΔY_t represents the period-to-period *changes* in the level of the variable. For many (but not all) variables with such long memories, taking first differences will eliminate the visual pattern of a variable that just seems to keep going up (or down).

Figure 12.4 presents the first differences of the number of golf courses in the United States, as well as the first differences of the US annual married percentage. You will notice, of course, that the time series in these figures look drastically different from their counterparts in levels from Figure 12.2. In fact, the visual "evidence" of an association between the two variables that appeared in Figure 12.2 has now vanished. The misleading culprit? Trends in both time series.

Because, in these cases, taking first differences of the series removes the long memories from the series, these transformed time series will not be subject to the spurious regression problem. But we caution against thoughtless differencing of time series. In particular, taking first differences of time series can eliminate some (true) evidence of an association between time series in certain circumstances.

We recommend that, wherever possible, you use theoretical reasons either to difference a time series or to analyze it in levels. In effect, you should ask yourself if your theory about a causal connection between X and Y makes more sense in levels or in first differences. For example, if you are analyzing budgetary data from a government agency, does your theory specify particular things about the sheer amount of agency spending (in which case, you would analyze the data in levels), or does it specify particular things about what causes budgets to shift from year to year (in which case, you would analyze the data in first differences)?

It is also worth noting that taking first differences of your time series does not directly address the issue of the number of lags of independent variables to include in your models. For that, we turn to the lagged-dependent-variable specification.

12.3.5   The Lagged Dependent Variable

Consider for a moment a simple two-variable system with our familiar variables Y and X, except where, to allow for the possibility that previous lags of X might affect current levels of Y, we include a large number of lags of X in our model:

$$Y_t = \alpha + \beta_0 X_t + \beta_1 X_{t-1} + \cdots + \beta_k X_{t-k} + u_t.$$

This model is known as a **distributed lag model**. Notice the slight shift in notation here, in which we are subscripting our β coefficients by the number of periods that that variable is lagged from the current value; hence, the β for X_t is β_0 (because $t - 0 = t$). Under such a setup, the **cumulative impact** β of X on Y is:

$$\beta = \beta_0 + \beta_1 + \beta_2 + \cdots + \beta_k = \sum_{i=0}^{k} \beta_i.$$

It is worth emphasizing that we are interested in that cumulative impact of X on Y, not merely the **instantaneous effect** of X_t on Y_t represented by the coefficient β_0.

But how can we capture the effects of X on Y without estimating such a cumbersome model like the preceding one? We have noted that a model like this would surely suffer from multicollinearity.

If we are willing to assume that the effect of X on Y is greatest initially and decays geometrically each period (eventually, after enough periods, becoming effectively zero), then a few steps of algebra would yield the following model that is mathematically identical to the preceding one.[10] That model looks like:

$$Y_t = \lambda Y_{t-1} + \alpha + \beta_0 X_t + v_t.$$

This is known as the **Koyck transformation**, and is commonly referred to as the **lagged-dependent-variable model**, for reasons we hope are obvious. Compare the Koyck transformation with the preceding equivalent

---

[10] We realize that the model does not *look* mathematically identical, but it is. For ease of presentation, we skip the algebra necessary to demonstrate the equivalence.

distributed lag model. Both have the same dependent variable, Y_t. Both have a variable representing the immediate impact of X_t on Y_t. But whereas the distributed lag model also has a slew of coefficients for variables representing all of the lags of 1 through k of X on Y_t, the lagged-dependent-variable model instead contains a single variable and coefficient, λY_{t-1}. Because, as we said, the two setups are equivalent, then this means that the lagged dependent variable does *not* represent how Y_{t-1} somehow causes Y_t, but instead Y_{t-1} is a stand-in for the cumulative effects of all past lags of X (that is, lags 1 through k) on Y_t. We achieve all of that through estimating a single coefficient instead of a very large number of them.

The coefficient λ, then, represents the ways in which past values of X affect current values of Y, which nicely solves the problem outlined at the start of this section. Normally, the values of λ will range between 0 and 1.[11] You can readily see that if $\lambda = 0$ then there is literally no effect of past values of X on Y_t. Such values are uncommon in practice. As λ gets larger, that indicates that the effects of past lags of X on Y_t persist longer and longer into the future.

In these models, the cumulative effect of X on Y is conveniently described as:

$$\beta = \frac{\beta_0}{1 - \lambda}.$$

Examining the formula, we easily see that, when $\lambda = 0$, the denominator is equal to 1 and the cumulative impact is exactly equal to the instantaneous impact. There is no lagged effect at all. When $\lambda = 1$, however, we run into problems; the denominator equals 0, so the quotient is undefined. But as λ approaches 1, you can see that the cumulative effect grows. Thus, as the values of the coefficient on the lagged dependent variable move from 0 toward 1, the cumulative impact of changes in X on Y grows.

This brief foray into time-series analysis obviously just scratches the surface. When reading research that uses time-series techniques, or especially when embarking on your own time-series analysis, it is important to be aware of both the issues of how the effects of shifts in independent variables can persist over several time periods, and also of the potential pitfalls of long-memoried trends. We turn now to a prominent example from the literature on US public opinion that uses time-series analysis.

12.4 EXAMPLE: THE ECONOMY AND PRESIDENTIAL POPULARITY

All of you, we suspect, are familiar with **presidential popularity** (or presidential approval) polls. Presidential popularity, in fact, is one of the great

---

[11] In fact, values close to 1, and especially those greater than 1, indicate that there are problems with the model, most likely related to trends in the data.

Figure 12.5 A simple causal model of the relationship between the economy and presidential popularity

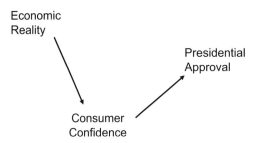

Figure 12.6 A revised model of presidential popularity

resources that presidents have at their disposal; they use approval as leverage in bargaining situations. It is not easy, after all, to say "no" to a popular president. In contrast, unpopular presidents are often not influential presidents. Hence all presidents care about their approval ratings.

But why do approval ratings fluctuate, in both the short term and the long term? What systematic forces cause presidents to be popular or unpopular over time? Since the early 1970s, the reigning conventional wisdom held that *economic reality* – usually measured by inflation and unemployment rates – drove approval ratings up and down. When the economy was doing well – that is, when inflation and unemployment were both low – the president enjoyed high approval ratings; and when the economy was performing poorly, the opposite was true.[12] That conventional wisdom is represented graphically in Figure 12.5. Considerable amounts of research over many years supported that wisdom.

In the early 1990s, however, a group of three political scientists questioned the traditional understanding of approval dynamics, suggesting that it was not actual *economic reality* that influenced approval ratings, but the public's perceptions of the economy – which we usually call "consumer confidence" (see MacKuen, Erikson, and Stimson, 1992). Their logic was that it doesn't matter for a president's approval ratings if inflation and unemployment are low if people don't *perceive* the economy to be doing well. Their revised causal model is presented in Figure 12.6.

---

[12] It has always been the case that scholars have recognized other systematic causes of presidential approval ratings, including scandals, international crises, and battle fatalities. We focus, in this example, exclusively on the economy for simplicity of presentation.

	A	B
Table 12.6 Excerpts from MacKuen, Erikson, and Stimson's (1992) table on the relationship between the economy and presidential popularity		
$Approval_{t-1}$	0.87*	0.82*
	(0.04)	(0.04)
Inflation	−0.39*	−0.17
	(0.13)	(0.13)
Change in Unemployment	−1.51*	0.62
	(0.74)	(0.91)
Consumer Confidence	—	0.21*
	—	(0.05)
R^2	0.93	0.94
N	126	117

Notes: Other variables were estimated as a part of the regression model but were excluded from this table for ease of presentation. Standard errors are in parentheses.
*$p < 0.05$.

What these researchers needed to do, then, was to test the conventional wisdom about an established relationship between an independent variable (X) and a dependent variable (Y) by controlling for a new variable (Z) based on their theoretical expectations. By use of quarterly survey data from 1954:2 through 1988:2, this is what they did. Table 12.6 re-creates a portion of MacKuen, Erikson, and Stimson's table 2. In column A, we see a confirmation of the conventional wisdom. (Can you think why the authors might include a column in their tables like this?) You should think of this column of results as testing the causal model in Figure 12.5. The coefficient for the inflation rate, −0.39, indicates that, for every one-point increase in the inflation rate, presidential approval will immediately fall by 0.39 points, on average, controlling for the effects of unemployment (and other variables in their model, which we do not show). According to the table, the ratio of the coefficient to the standard error places this effect easily past the threshold of statistical significance.

YOUR TURN: Connecting a causal theory to data in a table

Carefully examine Figures 12.5 and 12.6, and try to connect the causal ideas conveyed in those figures to the different regression models presented in Table 12.6. Can you see the correspondence?

Similarly, column A presents the results for the effects of changes in the unemployment rate on presidential approval. The slope of -1.51 indicates that, for every one-point increase in the unemployment rate, presidential approval falls by 1.51 points, on average, controlling for the effects of inflation (and other variables that we do not show). This parameter estimate is also statistically significant.

Because of our focus in this chapter on some of the basics of time-series analysis, notice also the presence of a lagged dependent variable in the model, labeled Approval$_{t-1}$. Recalling our earlier discussion, we find that the coefficient of 0.87, which is statistically significant, indicates that 87 percent of the effects of a shift in one of the independent variables persists into the following period. Thus the effects of shifts in X do not die out instantly; rather, a large portion of those effects persist into the future.[13] What this means is that, for example, the coefficient for Inflation of -0.39 represents only the *immediate* effects of Inflation, not the *cumulative* effects of Inflation. The cumulative effect for Inflation, as we learned earlier, is equal to the immediate impact divided by one minus the coefficient for the lagged dependent variable, or,

$$\beta = \frac{\beta_0}{1 - \lambda} = \frac{-0.39}{1 - 0.87} = -3.0.$$

The immediate impact of -0.39, then, considerably understates the total impact of a shift in the Inflation rate, which, because of the strong dynamics in the model – the value of the lagged dependent variable, 0.87, is a lot closer to 1 than it is to 0 – is considerably more impressive in substantive terms. A one-point shift in the Inflation rate eventually costs a president 3.0 points of approval.

In short, the first column of data in Table 12.6 provides some preliminary confirmation for the conventional wisdom. But the results in column A do not control for the effects of Consumer Confidence. The results from when MacKuen, Erikson, and Stimson did control for Consumer Confidence are provided in column B of Table 12.6. Notice first that Consumer Confidence has a coefficient of 0.21. That is, for every one-point increase in Consumer Confidence, we expect to see an immediate increase in presidential approval of 0.21 points, *controlling for the effects of Inflation and Unemployment*. This effect is statistically significant.[14]

---

[13] Indeed, in the second quarter, 0.87^2 of the effect of a shift in X at time t remains, and 0.87^3 remains in the third period, and so forth.

[14] Again, notice that the cumulative effect of a one-point shift in Consumer Confidence will be larger, because of the strong dynamics in the model represented by the lagged value of the dependent variable.

Notice also, however, what happens to the coefficients for Inflation and Unemployment. Comparing the estimated effects in column A with those in column B reveals some substantial differences. When there was no control for Consumer Confidence in column A, it appeared that Inflation and Unemployment had modestly strong and statistically significant effects. But in column B, the coefficients change because of the control for Consumer Confidence. The effect of Inflation shrinks from −0.39 to −0.17, which reflects the control for Consumer Confidence. The effect is not close to being statistically significant. We can no longer reject the null hypothesis that there is no relationship between Inflation and presidential approval.

The same thing happens to the effect for the Change in Unemployment rate. In column B, when Consumer Confidence is controlled for, the effect for the Change in Unemployment changes from −1.51 to 0.62, a substantial reduction in magnitude, but also a change in the *direction* of the relationship. No matter, because the coefficient is no longer statistically significant, which means we cannot reject the null hypothesis that it is truly zero.

The second column of Table 12.6, then, is consistent with Figure 12.6, which shows no direct connection between economic reality and presidential approval. There is, however, a direct connection between consumer confidence and approval ratings. In this case, introducing a new variable (Consumer Confidence) produced very different findings about a concept (Economic Reality) that scholars had thought for decades exerted a direct causal influence on approval.

12.5   WRAPPING UP

In this chapter, we discussed two commonly encountered research situations – dummy dependent variables and data collected across time. We have provided an introductory presentation of the problems associated with each of these situations and some of the approaches commonly taken by researchers. It is important that you realize two things at this point: First, for both dummy variables and time-series data, there are potential pitfalls to ignoring the unique nature of the data and simply modeling the relationships with standard OLS that was introduced to you in Chapters 9 and 10. In both cases, statistical problems are likely to arise with the estimated coefficients and standard errors, making standard hypothesis testing potentially misleading. To avoid these problems, we have introduced some straightforward approaches that help you get things right. Second, bear in mind that these two topics are quite complex. Dealing with categorical dependent variables and dealing with time series data are subjects of extensive and growing literatures; our treatment here is, of necessity, at the introductory level. Our goal has been to alert you to the key pitfalls of failing to account for the nature of the data, and the first steps that most analysts would take to getting it right.

CONCEPTS INTRODUCED IN THIS CHAPTER

- binomial logit (BNL) – a model of a dummy dependent variable that uses the logistic distribution to convert predicted values into predicted probabilities
- binomial probit (BNP) – a model of a dummy dependent variable that uses the cumulative normal distribution to convert predicted values into predicted probabilities
- classification table – tables that compare model-based expectations with actual values of the dependent variable
- cumulative impact – in a lagged-dependent-variable model, the impact of a one-unit increase in an independent variable at all times t and after
- differenced (or "first differenced") dependent variable – a transformation of the dependent variable in which the lagged value is subtracted from the current value
- distributed lag model – a time-series model in which the cumulative impact of an independent variable is measured by including many lags of that variable
- instantaneous effect – in a lagged-dependent-variable model, the impact of a one-unit increase in an independent variable at time t
- Koyck transformation – a theoretical justification of the lagged-dependent-variable model
- lagged-dependent-variable model – a time-series model in which the lagged value of the dependent variable is included as an independent variable in the model
- lagged values – in a time series, values of a variable that occur before the current time period
- lead values – in a time series, values of a variable that occur after the current time period
- linear probability model (LPM) – an OLS model in which the dependent variable is a dummy variable
- link functions – functions that convert the linear component of a nonlinear model to a quantity of interest
- predicted probability – in models with a dummy dependent variable, the expected value of the dependent variable conditioned on the values of the independent variable(s)

- presidential popularity (or approval) – the degree to which members of the mass public approve or disapprove of the way a president is performing in their job as president
- proportionate reduction of error – a calculation used to assess the usefulness of a model by comparing its predictive accuracy with that of a naive model that always predicts the modal category of the dependent variable
- spurious regression problem – a situation in which long-lasting trends in variables produce false evidence of a statistical relationship between those variables when none truly exists

EXERCISES

1. Imagine a respondent who reported being a strong Republican (Party ID = 3) with a strongly disapproving evaluation of Bush's handling of the war on terror (War Evaluation = −2) and a strongly disapproving evaluation of Bush's handling of the health of the economy (Economic Evaluation = −2). Using the results from the linear probability model (LPM) in Table 12.2, calculate the predicted probability of this individual voting for Bush. Show all of your work.

2. Using the binomial logit model (BNL) in Table 12.2, calculate the predicted probability of the individual described in Exercise 1 voting for Bush. Show all of your work.

3. Using the binomial probit model (BNP) in Table 12.2, calculate the predicted probability of the individual described in Exercise 1 voting for Bush. Show all of your work.

4. Table 12.7 is the classification table from a binomial probit model (BNP) in which the dependent variable was a dummy variable equal to one if the respondent reported voting for Obama and equal to zero if the respondent reported voting for McCain. The independent variables in this model were measures of party identification and respondents' expectations about economic and foreign policy performances with each of the two major party candidates

Table 12.7 Classification table from a BNP of the effects of partisanship and prospective expectations on votes for Obama in 2008

Actual vote	Model-based expectations	
	Obama	McCain
Obama	1575	233
McCain	180	1201

Notes: Cell entries are the number of cases.
Predictions are based on a cutoff of $\hat{Y} > 0.5$.

as the president. Calculate the percentage of respondents classified correctly by this model. Show all of your work.

5. Using Table 12.7, calculate the percentage of respondents that would be correctly classified by a naive model that predicts that all respondents choose the modal category of the dependent variable. Show all of your work.

6. Using the calculations that you made in Exercises 4 and 5, calculate the proportionate reduction of error when we move from the naive model (NM) to the BNP model. Show all of your work.

7. For column B in Table 12.6, calculate the long-run effects of a ten-point shift in consumer confidence on a president's approval ratings. Show all of your work.

8. Find and read the article "Recapturing the Falklands: Models of Conservative Popularity, 1979–83" (Clarke, Mishler, and Whiteley, 1990). What is the key dependent variable in their model? From what you've learned in this chapter, does that variable appear to have long-term trends in it that could pose problems in their analysis? Do the authors of the article adequately describe how they dealt with this issue? Explain your answer to each of these questions.

9. Collect a time series from a government source (such as https://www.usa.gov/statistics), produce a graph of that series, and examine it for evidence of long-memory trends. Write about what you think is going on in this series. Turn in the graph with your answer.

10. Create a first difference of the series you used in Exercise 9. Produce a graph of the differenced series. What is the substantive interpretation of this new series, and how is that different from the original series?

Critical Values of Chi-Squared

df	Level of significance				
	0.10	0.05	0.025	0.01	0.001
1	2.706	3.841	5.024	6.635	10.828
2	4.605	5.991	7.378	9.210	13.816
3	6.251	7.815	9.348	11.345	16.266
4	7.779	9.488	11.143	13.277	18.467
5	9.236	11.070	12.833	15.086	20.515
6	10.645	12.592	14.449	16.812	22.458
7	12.017	14.067	16.013	18.475	24.322
8	13.362	15.507	17.535	20.090	26.125
9	14.684	16.919	19.023	21.666	27.877
10	15.987	18.307	20.483	23.209	29.588
11	17.275	19.675	21.920	24.725	31.264
12	18.549	21.026	23.337	26.217	32.910
13	19.812	22.362	24.736	27.688	34.528
14	21.064	23.685	26.119	29.141	36.123
15	22.307	24.996	27.488	30.578	37.697
20	28.412	31.410	34.170	37.566	45.315
25	34.382	37.652	40.646	44.314	52.620
30	40.256	43.773	46.979	50.892	59.703
35	46.059	49.802	53.203	57.342	66.619
40	51.805	55.758	59.342	63.691	73.402
50	63.167	67.505	71.420	76.154	86.661
60	74.397	79.082	83.298	88.379	99.607
70	85.527	90.531	95.023	100.425	112.317
75	91.061	96.217	100.839	106.393	118.599
80	96.578	101.879	106.629	112.329	124.839
90	107.565	113.145	118.136	124.116	137.208
100	118.498	124.342	129.561	135.807	149.449

Critical Values of t

df	Level of significance					
	0.10	0.05	0.025	0.01	0.005	0.001
1	3.078	6.314	12.706	31.821	63.657	318.313
2	1.886	2.920	4.303	6.965	9.925	22.327
3	1.638	2.353	3.182	4.541	5.841	10.215
4	1.533	2.132	2.776	3.747	4.604	7.173
5	1.476	2.015	2.571	3.365	4.032	5.893
6	1.440	1.943	2.447	3.143	3.707	5.208
7	1.415	1.895	2.365	2.998	3.499	4.782
8	1.397	1.860	2.306	2.896	3.355	4.499
9	1.383	1.833	2.262	2.821	3.250	4.296
10	1.372	1.812	2.228	2.764	3.169	4.143
11	1.363	1.796	2.201	2.718	3.106	4.024
12	1.356	1.782	2.179	2.681	3.055	3.929
13	1.350	1.771	2.160	2.650	3.012	3.852
14	1.345	1.761	2.145	2.624	2.977	3.787
15	1.341	1.753	2.131	2.602	2.947	3.733
20	1.325	1.725	2.086	2.528	2.845	3.552
25	1.316	1.708	2.060	2.485	2.787	3.450
30	1.310	1.697	2.042	2.457	2.750	3.385
40	1.303	1.684	2.021	2.423	2.704	3.307
50	1.299	1.676	2.009	2.403	2.678	3.261
60	1.296	1.671	2.000	2.390	2.660	3.232
70	1.294	1.667	1.994	2.381	2.648	3.211
75	1.293	1.665	1.992	2.377	2.643	3.202
80	1.292	1.664	1.990	2.374	2.639	3.195
90	1.291	1.662	1.987	2.368	2.632	3.183
100	1.290	1.660	1.984	2.364	2.626	3.174
∞	1.282	1.645	1.960	2.326	2.576	3.090

The Λ Link Function for Binomial Logit Models

$X_i\hat{\beta}$	Translating negative $X_i\hat{\beta}$ values into predicted probabilities $(\hat{P}_i)$									
	−0.00	−0.01	−0.02	−0.03	−0.04	−0.05	−0.06	−0.07	−0.08	−0.09
−4.5	0.0110	0.0109	0.0108	0.0107	0.0106	0.0105	0.0104	0.0103	0.0102	0.0101
−4.0	0.0180	0.0178	0.0176	0.0175	0.0173	0.0171	0.0170	0.0168	0.0166	0.0165
−3.5	0.0293	0.0290	0.0287	0.0285	0.0282	0.0279	0.0277	0.0274	0.0271	0.0269
−3.0	0.0474	0.0470	0.0465	0.0461	0.0457	0.0452	0.0448	0.0444	0.0439	0.0435
−2.5	0.0759	0.0752	0.0745	0.0738	0.0731	0.0724	0.0718	0.0711	0.0704	0.0698
−2.0	0.1192	0.1182	0.1171	0.1161	0.1151	0.1141	0.1130	0.1120	0.1111	0.1101
−1.9	0.1301	0.1290	0.1279	0.1268	0.1256	0.1246	0.1235	0.1224	0.1213	0.1203
−1.8	0.1419	0.1406	0.1394	0.1382	0.1371	0.1359	0.1347	0.1335	0.1324	0.1312
−1.7	0.1545	0.1532	0.1519	0.1506	0.1493	0.1480	0.1468	0.1455	0.1443	0.1431
−1.6	0.1680	0.1666	0.1652	0.1638	0.1625	0.1611	0.1598	0.1584	0.1571	0.1558
−1.5	0.1824	0.1809	0.1795	0.1780	0.1765	0.1751	0.1736	0.1722	0.1708	0.1694
−1.4	0.1978	0.1962	0.1947	0.1931	0.1915	0.1900	0.1885	0.1869	0.1854	0.1839
−1.3	0.2142	0.2125	0.2108	0.2092	0.2075	0.2059	0.2042	0.2026	0.2010	0.1994
−1.2	0.2315	0.2297	0.2279	0.2262	0.2244	0.2227	0.2210	0.2193	0.2176	0.2159
−1.1	0.2497	0.2479	0.2460	0.2442	0.2423	0.2405	0.2387	0.2369	0.2351	0.2333
−1.0	0.2689	0.2670	0.2650	0.2631	0.2611	0.2592	0.2573	0.2554	0.2535	0.2516
−0.9	0.2891	0.2870	0.2850	0.2829	0.2809	0.2789	0.2769	0.2749	0.2729	0.2709
−0.8	0.3100	0.3079	0.3058	0.3036	0.3015	0.2994	0.2973	0.2953	0.2932	0.2911
−0.7	0.3318	0.3296	0.3274	0.3252	0.3230	0.3208	0.3186	0.3165	0.3143	0.3112
−0.6	0.3543	0.3521	0.3498	0.3475	0.3452	0.3430	0.3407	0.3385	0.3363	0.3340
−0.5	0.3775	0.3752	0.3729	0.3705	0.3682	0.3659	0.3635	0.3612	0.3589	0.3566
−0.4	0.4013	0.3989	0.3965	0.3941	0.3917	0.3894	0.3870	0.3846	0.3823	0.3799
−0.3	0.4256	0.4231	0.4207	0.4182	0.4158	0.4134	0.4110	0.4085	0.4061	0.4037
−0.2	0.4502	0.4477	0.4452	0.4428	0.4403	0.4378	0.4354	0.4329	0.4305	0.4280
−0.1	0.4750	0.4725	0.4700	0.4675	0.4651	0.4626	0.4601	0.4576	0.4551	0.4526
−0.0	0.5000	0.4975	0.4950	0.4925	0.4900	0.4875	0.4850	0.4825	0.4800	0.4775

(continued)

Appendix C (*continued*)

	Translating negative $X_i\hat{\beta}$ values into predicted probabilities ($\hat{P}_i$)									
$X_i\hat{\beta}$	+0.00	+0.01	+0.02	+0.03	+0.04	+0.05	+0.06	+0.07	+0.08	+0.09
+0.0	0.5000	0.5025	0.5050	0.5075	0.5100	0.5125	0.5150	0.5175	0.5200	0.5225
+0.1	0.5250	0.5275	0.5300	0.5325	0.5349	0.5374	0.5399	0.5424	0.5449	0.5474
+0.2	0.5498	0.5523	0.5548	0.5572	0.5597	0.5622	0.5646	0.5671	0.5695	0.5720
+0.3	0.5744	0.5769	0.5793	0.5818	0.5842	0.5866	0.5890	0.5915	0.5939	0.5963
+0.4	0.5987	0.6011	0.6035	0.6059	0.6083	0.6106	0.6130	0.6154	0.6177	0.6201
+0.5	0.6225	0.6248	0.6271	0.6295	0.6318	0.6341	0.6365	0.6388	0.6411	0.6434
+0.6	0.6457	0.6479	0.6502	0.6525	0.6548	0.6570	0.6593	0.6615	0.6637	0.6660
+0.7	0.6682	0.6704	0.6726	0.6748	0.6770	0.6792	0.6814	0.6835	0.6857	0.6878
+0.8	0.6900	0.6921	0.6942	0.6964	0.6985	0.7006	0.7027	0.7047	0.7068	0.7089
+0.9	0.7109	0.7130	0.7150	0.7171	0.7191	0.7211	0.7231	0.7251	0.7271	0.7291
+1.0	0.7311	0.7330	0.7350	0.7369	0.7389	0.7408	0.7427	0.7446	0.7465	0.7484
+1.1	0.7503	0.7521	0.7540	0.7558	0.7577	0.7595	0.7613	0.7631	0.7649	0.7667
+1.2	0.7685	0.7703	0.7721	0.7738	0.7756	0.7773	0.7790	0.7807	0.7824	0.7841
+1.3	0.7858	0.7875	0.7892	0.7908	0.7925	0.7941	0.7958	0.7974	0.7990	0.8006
+1.4	0.8022	0.8038	0.8053	0.8069	0.8085	0.8100	0.8115	0.8131	0.8146	0.8161
+1.5	0.8176	0.8191	0.8205	0.8220	0.8235	0.8249	0.8264	0.8278	0.8292	0.8306
+1.6	0.8320	0.8334	0.8348	0.8362	0.8375	0.8389	0.8402	0.8416	0.8429	0.8442
+1.7	0.8455	0.8468	0.8481	0.8494	0.8507	0.8520	0.8532	0.8545	0.8557	0.8569
+1.8	0.8581	0.8594	0.8606	0.8618	0.8629	0.8641	0.8653	0.8665	0.8676	0.8688
+1.9	0.8699	0.8710	0.8721	0.8732	0.8744	0.8754	0.8765	0.8776	0.8787	0.8797
+2.0	0.8808	0.8818	0.8829	0.8839	0.8849	0.8859	0.8870	0.8880	0.8889	0.8899
+2.5	0.9241	0.9248	0.9255	0.9262	0.9269	0.9276	0.9282	0.9289	0.9296	0.9302
+3.0	0.9526	0.9530	0.9535	0.9539	0.9543	0.9548	0.9552	0.9556	0.9561	0.9565
+3.5	0.9707	0.9710	0.9713	0.9715	0.9718	0.9721	0.9723	0.9726	0.9729	0.9731
+4.0	0.9820	0.9822	0.9824	0.9825	0.9827	0.9829	0.9830	0.9832	0.9834	0.9835
+4.5	0.9890	0.9891	0.9892	0.9893	0.9894	0.9895	0.9896	0.9897	0.9898	0.9899

The Φ Link Function for Binomial Probit Models

$X_i\hat{\beta}$	Translating negative $X_i\hat{\beta}$ values into predicted probabilities ($\hat{P}_i$)									
$X_i\hat{\beta}$	−0.00	−0.01	−0.02	−0.03	−0.04	−0.05	−0.06	−0.07	−0.08	−0.09
−3.4	0.0003	0.0003	0.0003	0.0003	0.0003	0.0003	0.0003	0.0003	0.0003	0.0002
−3.0	0.0013	0.0013	0.0013	0.0012	0.0012	0.0011	0.0011	0.0011	0.0010	0.0010
−2.5	0.0062	0.0060	0.0059	0.0057	0.0055	0.0054	0.0052	0.0051	0.0049	0.0048
−2.0	0.0228	0.0222	0.0217	0.0212	0.0207	0.0202	0.0197	0.0192	0.0188	0.0183
−1.9	0.0287	0.0281	0.0274	0.0268	0.0262	0.0256	0.0250	0.0244	0.0239	0.0233
−1.8	0.0359	0.0351	0.0344	0.0336	0.0329	0.0322	0.0314	0.0307	0.0301	0.0294
−1.7	0.0446	0.0436	0.0427	0.0418	0.0409	0.0401	0.0392	0.0384	0.0375	0.0367
−1.6	0.0548	0.0537	0.0526	0.0516	0.0505	0.0495	0.0485	0.0475	0.0465	0.0455
−1.5	0.0668	0.0655	0.0643	0.0630	0.0618	0.0606	0.0594	0.0582	0.0571	0.0559
−1.4	0.0808	0.0793	0.0778	0.0764	0.0749	0.0735	0.0721	0.0708	0.0694	0.0681
−1.3	0.0968	0.0951	0.0934	0.0918	0.0901	0.0885	0.0869	0.0853	0.0838	0.0823
−1.2	0.1151	0.1131	0.1112	0.1093	0.1075	0.1056	0.1038	0.1020	0.1003	0.0985
−1.1	0.1357	0.1335	0.1314	0.1292	0.1271	0.1251	0.1230	0.1210	0.1190	0.1170
−1.0	0.1587	0.1562	0.1539	0.1515	0.1492	0.1469	0.1446	0.1423	0.1401	0.1379
−0.9	0.1841	0.1814	0.1788	0.1762	0.1736	0.1711	0.1685	0.1660	0.1635	0.1611
−0.8	0.2119	0.2090	0.2061	0.2033	0.2005	0.1977	0.1949	0.1922	0.1894	0.1867
−0.7	0.2420	0.2389	0.2358	0.2327	0.2296	0.2266	0.2236	0.2206	0.2177	0.2148
−0.6	0.2743	0.2709	0.2676	0.2643	0.2611	0.2578	0.2546	0.2514	0.2483	0.2451
−0.5	0.3085	0.3050	0.3015	0.2981	0.2946	0.2912	0.2877	0.2843	0.2810	0.2776
−0.4	0.3446	0.3409	0.3372	0.3336	0.3300	0.3264	0.3228	0.3192	0.3156	0.3121
−0.3	0.3821	0.3783	0.3745	0.3707	0.3669	0.3632	0.3594	0.3557	0.3520	0.3483
−0.2	0.4207	0.4168	0.4129	0.4090	0.4052	0.4013	0.3974	0.3936	0.3897	0.3859
−0.1	0.4602	0.4562	0.4522	0.4483	0.4443	0.4404	0.4364	0.4325	0.4286	0.4247
−0.0	0.5000	0.4960	0.4920	0.4880	0.4840	0.4801	0.4761	0.4721	0.4681	0.4641

(*continued*)

Appendix D (*continued*)

$X_i\hat{\beta}$	+0.00	+0.01	+0.02	+0.03	+0.04	+0.05	+0.06	+0.07	+0.08	+0.09
	Translating negative $X_i\hat{\beta}$ values into predicted probabilities ($\hat{P}_i$)									
+0.0	0.5000	0.5040	0.5080	0.5120	0.5160	0.5199	0.5239	0.5279	0.5319	0.5359
+0.1	0.5398	0.5438	0.5478	0.5517	0.5557	0.5596	0.5636	0.5675	0.5714	0.5753
+0.2	0.5793	0.5832	0.5871	0.5910	0.5948	0.5987	0.6026	0.6064	0.6103	0.6141
+0.3	0.6179	0.6217	0.6255	0.6293	0.6331	0.6368	0.6406	0.6443	0.6480	0.6517
+0.4	0.6554	0.6591	0.6628	0.6664	0.6700	0.6736	0.6772	0.6808	0.6844	0.6879
+0.5	0.6915	0.6950	0.6985	0.7019	0.7054	0.7088	0.7123	0.7157	0.7190	0.7224
+0.6	0.7257	0.7291	0.7324	0.7357	0.7389	0.7422	0.7454	0.7486	0.7517	0.7549
+0.7	0.7580	0.7611	0.7642	0.7673	0.7704	0.7734	0.7764	0.7794	0.7823	0.7852
+0.8	0.7881	0.7910	0.7939	0.7967	0.7995	0.8023	0.8051	0.8078	0.8106	0.8133
+0.9	0.8159	0.8186	0.8212	0.8238	0.8264	0.8289	0.8315	0.8340	0.8365	0.8389
+1.0	0.8413	0.8438	0.8461	0.8485	0.8508	0.8531	0.8554	0.8577	0.8599	0.8621
+1.1	0.8643	0.8665	0.8686	0.8708	0.8729	0.8749	0.8770	0.8790	0.8810	0.8830
+1.2	0.8849	0.8869	0.8888	0.8907	0.8925	0.8944	0.8962	0.8980	0.8997	0.9015
+1.3	0.9032	0.9049	0.9066	0.9082	0.9099	0.9115	0.9131	0.9147	0.9162	0.9177
+1.4	0.9192	0.9207	0.9222	0.9236	0.9251	0.9265	0.9279	0.9292	0.9306	0.9319
+1.5	0.9332	0.9345	0.9357	0.9370	0.9382	0.9394	0.9406	0.9418	0.9429	0.9441
+1.6	0.9452	0.9463	0.9474	0.9484	0.9495	0.9505	0.9515	0.9525	0.9535	0.9545
+1.7	0.9554	0.9564	0.9573	0.9582	0.9591	0.9599	0.9608	0.9616	0.9625	0.9633
+1.8	0.9641	0.9649	0.9656	0.9664	0.9671	0.9678	0.9686	0.9693	0.9699	0.9706
+1.9	0.9713	0.9719	0.9726	0.9732	0.9738	0.9744	0.9750	0.9756	0.9761	0.9767
+2.0	0.9772	0.9778	0.9783	0.9788	0.9793	0.9798	0.9803	0.9808	0.9812	0.9817
+2.5	0.9938	0.9940	0.9941	0.9943	0.9945	0.9946	0.9948	0.9949	0.9951	0.9952
+3.0	0.9987	0.9987	0.9987	0.9988	0.9988	0.9989	0.9989	0.9989	0.9990	0.9990
+3.4	0.9997	0.9997	0.9997	0.9997	0.9997	0.9997	0.9997	0.9997	0.9997	0.9998

Bibliography

Achen, Christopher H. 1982. *Interpreting and Using Regression.* Sage University Paper Series on Quantitative Applications in the Social Sciences, vol. 29. Beverly Hills, CA: Sage Publications.

Ansolabehere, Stephen, and Shanto Iyengar. 1997. *Going Negative.* New York: Simon and Schuster.

APA. 2013. *Diagnostic and Statistical Manual of Mental Disorders.* 5th edn (DSM-5). Washington, DC: American Psychiatric Publishing.

Arceneaux, Kevin, Martin Johnson, and Chad Murphy. 2012. "Polarized Political Communication, Oppositional Media Hostility, and Selective Exposure." *Journal of Politics* 74:174–186.

Arrow, Kenneth. 1990. *Social Choice and Individual Values.* 2nd edn. New York: Wiley. [1st edn 1951]

Axelrod, Robert. 1986. "An Evolutionary Approach to Norms." *American Political Science Review* 80:1095–1111.

Bachrach, Peter, and Morton S. Baratz. 1962. "Two Faces of Power." *American Political Science Review* 56:947–952.

Barabas, Jason, and Jennifer Jerit. 2010. "Are Survey Experiments Externally Valid?" *American Political Science Review* 104:226–242.

Beck, Nathaniel, and Jonathan N. Katz. 1995. "What to Do (and Not to Do) with Time-Series Cross-Section Data." *American Political Science Review* 89: 634–647.

Belsley, David A., Edwin Kuh, and Roy E. Welsch. 1980. *Regression Diagnostics: Identifying Influential Data and Sources of Collinearity.* New York: Wiley.

Brady, Henry E. 2002. "Models of Causal Inference: Going Beyond the Neyman–Rubin–Holland Theory." Paper presented at the Annual Meeting of the Political Methodology Society, Seattle, WA.

Brady, Henry E. 2004. "Introduction." *Perspectives on Politics* 2:295–300.

Broockman, David E., and Daniel M. Butler. 2017. "The Causal Effects of Elite Position-Taking on Voter Attitudes: Field Experiments with Elite Communication." *American Journal of Political Science* 61:208–221.

Cameron, David R. 1978. "The Expansion of the Public Economy: a Comparative Analysis." *American Political Science Review* 72:1243–1261.

Campbell, Donald T., and Julian C. Stanley. 1963. *Experimental and Quasi-Experimental Designs for Research.* Chicago: Rand McNally.

Clarke, Harold D., William Mishler, and Paul Whiteley. 1990. "Recapturing the Falklands: Models of Conservative Popularity, 1979–83." *British Journal of Political Science* 20:63–81.

Converse, Philip E. 1964. "The Nature of Belief Systems in Mass Publics." In *Ideology and Discontent*, ed. David E. Apter. New York: Free Press of Glencoe, pp. 206–261.

Copernicus, Nicolaus. 2004. *On the Revolutions of Heavenly Spheres*. Philadelphia: Running Press Book Publishers. [Translation of 1543 book in Latin]

Currie, Janet, and Duncan Thomas. 1995. "Does Head Start Make a Difference?" *American Economic Review* 85:341–364.

Dahl, Robert A. 1971. *Polyarchy: Participation and Opposition*. New Haven: Yale University Press.

Danziger, Sheldon, and Peter Gottschalk. 1983. "The Measurement of Poverty: Implications for Antipoverty Policy." *American Behavioral Scientist* 26:739–756.

Deutsch, Karl W. 1961. "Social Mobilization and Political Development." *American Political Science Review* 55:493–514.

Dixon, William, and Bruce Moon. 1993. "Political Similarity and American Foreign Trade Patterns." *Political Research Quarterly* 46:5–25.

Doyle, Michael W. 1986. "Liberalism and World Politics." *American Political Science Review* 80:1151–1169.

Druckman, James N. 2001. "The Implications of Framing Effects for Citizen Competence." *Political Behavior* 23(3):225–256.

Duflo, Esther, Michael Kremer, and Jonathan Robinson. 2011. "Nudging Farmers to Use Fertilizer: Theory and Experimental Evidence from Kenya." *American Economic Review* 101:2350–2390.

Edmonds, David, and John Eidinow. 2003. *Wittgenstein's Poker: The Story of a Ten-Minute Argument Between Two Great Philosophers*. New York: Harper Perennial.

Elkins, Zachary. 2000. "Gradations of Democracy? Empirical Tests of Alternative Conceptualizations." *American Journal of Political Science* 44: 293–300.

Fenno, Richard F. 1973. *Congressmen in Committees*. Boston: Little, Brown.

Fiorina, Morris P. 1989. *Congress: Keystone to the Washington Establishment*. 2nd edn. New Haven: Yale University Press.

Geer, John G. 2006. *In Defense of Negativity: Attack Ads in Presidential Campaigns*. Chicago: University of Chicago Press.

Gibson, James L. 1992. "Alternative Measures of Political Tolerance: Must Tolerance Be 'Least-Liked'?" *American Journal of Political Science* 36:560–577.

Gibson, James L., Gregory A. Caldeira, and Vanessa A. Baird. 1998. "On the Legitimacy of National High Courts." *American Political Science Review* 92(2):343–358.

Gilbert, Susan. 2005. "Married with Problems? Therapy May Not Help." *New York Times*, April 19, 2005.

Gowa, Joanne. 1989. "Bipolarity, Multipolarity, and Free Trade." *American Political Science Review* 83:1245–1256.

Gowa, Joanne, and Edward D. Mansfield. 1993. "Power Politics and International Trade." *American Political Science Review* 87:408–420.

Granger, Clive W. J., and Paul Newbold. 1974. "Spurious Regressions in Econometrics." *Journal of Econometrics* 2(2):111–120.

Green, Donald P., and Ian Shapiro. 1994. *Pathologies of Rational Choice Theory: a Critique of Applications in Political Science*. New Haven: Yale University Press.

Hibbs, Douglas A. Jr. 1977. "Political Parties and Macroeconomic Policy." *American Political Science Review* 71:1467–1487.

Inglehart, Ronald. 1971. "The Silent Revolution in Europe: Intergenerational Change in Post-Industrial Societies." *American Political Science Review* 65:991–1017.

Inglehart, Ronald. 1988. "The Renaissance of Political Culture." *American Political Science Review* 82:1203–1230.

Iyengar, Shanto, and Donald R. Kinder. 2010. *News that Matters: Television and American Opinion*. 2nd edn. Chicago: University of Chicago Press.

King, Gary. 1986. "How Not to Lie with Statistics: Avoiding Common Mistakes in Quantitative Political Science." *American Journal of Political Science* 30: 666–687.

Kramer, Gerald H. 1971. "Short-Term Fluctuations in U.S. Voting Behavior, 1896–1964." *American Political Science Review* 65:131–143.

Kuhn, Thomas S. 1962. *The Structure of Scientific Revolutions*. Chicago: University of Chicago Press.

Lauderdale, Benjamin E., and Alexander Herzog. 2016. "Measuring Political Positions from Legislative Speech." *Political Analysis* 24:374–394.

Lazarsfeld, Paul F., Bernard R. Berelson, and Hazel Gaudet. 1948. *The People's Choice: How the Voter Makes Up His Mind in a Presidential Campaign*. 1st edn. New York: Columbia University Press.

Levendusky, Matthew S. 2009. *The Partisan Sort: How Liberals Became Democrats and Conservatives Became Republicans*. Chicago: University of Chicago Press.

Lewis-Beck, Michael S. 1997. "Who's the Chef? Economic Voting under a Dual Executive." *European Journal of Political Research* 31:315–325.

Lindquist, Stefanie A., and Frank B. Cross. 2009. *Measuring Judicial Activism*. Oxford: Oxford University Press.

Lipset, Seymour Martin. 1959. "Some Social Requisites of Democracy: Economic Development and Political Legitimacy." *American Political Science Review* 53:69–105.

Lithwick, Dahlia. 2004. "Activist, Schmactivist." *New York Times*, August 15, 2004.

Luskin, Robert C. 1987. "Measuring Political Sophistication." *American Journal of Political Science* 31:856–899.

MacKuen, Michael B., Robert S. Erikson, and James A. Stimson. 1992. "Peasants or Bankers? The American Electorate and the U.S. Economy." *American Political Science Review* 86(3):597–611.

Maoz, Zeev, and Bruce Russett. 1993. "Normative and Structural Causes of Democratic Peace, 1946–1986." *American Political Science Review* 87: 624–638.

March, James G., and Johan P. Olsen. 1984. "The New Institutionalism: Organizational Factors in Political Life." *American Political Science Review* 78: 734–749.

Martin, Lanny W., and Georg Vanberg. 2003. "Wasting Time? The Impact of Ideology and Size on Delay in Coalition Formation." *British Journal of Political Science* 33:323–344.

Mathews, Jay. 2000. "Scores Improve for D.C. Pupils with Vouchers." *Washington Post*, August 28, 2000, A1.

Mayhew, David R. 1974. *Congress: the Electoral Connection*. New Haven: Yale University Press.

McClosky, Herbert. 1964. "Consensus and Ideology in American Politics." *American Political Science Review* 58:361–382.

Milgram, Stanley. 1974. *Obedience to Authority: an Experimental View*. New York: Harper and Row.

Miller, Arthur H. 1974. "Political Issues and Trust in Government: 1964–1970." *American Political Science Review* 68:951–972.

Miller, Warren E., and Donald W. Stokes. 1963. "Constituency Influence in Congress." *American Political Science Review* 57:45–56.

Morrow, James D., Randolph M. Siverson, and Tressa E. Tabares. 1998. "The Political Determinants of International Trade: the Major Powers, 1907–1990." *American Political Science Review* 92:649–661.

Morton, Rebecca B., and Kenneth C. Williams. 2010. *Experimental Political Science and the Study of Causality: from Nature to the Lab*. New York: Cambridge University Press.

Mueller, John. 1973. *War, Presidents and Public Opinion*. New York: Wiley.

Munck, Gerardo L., and Jay Verkuilen. 2002. "Conceptualizing and Measuring Democracy: Evaluating Alternative Indices." *Comparative Political Studies* 35:5–34.

Niemi, Richard G., and M. Kent Jennings. 1974. *The Political Character of Adolescence: the Influence of Families and Schools*. Princeton: Princeton University Press.

Palmer, Harvey D., Guy D. Whitten, and Laron K. Williams. 2013. "Who Should be Chef? The Dynamics of Valence Evaluations across Income Groups during Economic Crises." *Electoral Studies* 32(3):425–431.

Pearl, Judea. 2000. *Causality: Models, Reasoning, and Inference*. New York: Cambridge University Press.

Piazza, Thomas, Paul M. Sniderman, and Philip E. Tetlock. 1990. "Analysis of the Dynamics of Political Reasoning: a General-Purpose Computer-Assisted Methodology." *Political Analysis* 1:99–120.

Pollins, Brian M. 1989. "Does Trade Still Follow the Flag?" *American Political Science Review* 83:465–480.

Polsby, Nelson W. 1968. "The Institutionalization of the U.S. House of Representatives." *American Political Science Review* 62:144–168.

Poole, Keith T., and Howard Rosenthal. 1997. *Congress: a Political-Economic History of Roll Call Voting*. New York: Oxford University Press.

Posner, Daniel N. 2004. "The Political Salience of Cultural Difference: Why Chewas and Tumbukas Are Allies in Zambia and Adversaries in Malawi." *American Political Science Review* 98:529–545.

Powell, G. Bingham Jr., and Guy D. Whitten. 1993. "A Cross-National Analysis of Economic Voting: Taking Account of the Political Context." *American Journal of Political Science* 37:391–414.

Putnam, Robert P. 1995. "Tuning In, Tuning Out: The Strange Disappearance of Social Capital in America." *PS: Political Science & Politics* 28(4):664–683.

Putnam, Robert P. 2000. *Bowling Alone*. New York: Simon & Schuster.

Richards, Diana, T. Clifton Morgan, Rick Wilson, Valerie L. Schwebach, and Garry D. Young. 1993. "Good Times, Bad Times and the Diversionary Use of Force: a Tale of Some Not So Free Agents." *Journal of Conflict Resolution* 37:504–535.

Riker, William H. 1982. *Liberalism Against Populism: a Confrontation Between the Theory of Democracy and the Theory of Social Choice*. San Francisco: W. H. Freeman.

Riker, William H., and Peter C. Ordeshook. 1968. "A Theory of the Calculus of Voting." *American Political Science Review* 62:25–42.

Rogers, James R. 2006. "A Primer on Game Theory." In *Institutional Games and the U.S. Supreme Court*, eds James R. Rogers, Roy B. Flemming, and Jon R. Bond. Charlottesville: University of Virginia Press.

Rubin, Donald. 1974. "Estimating Causal Effects of Treatments in Randomized and Nonrandomized Studies." *Journal of Educational Psychology* 66:688–701.

Salmon, Wesley C. 1993. "Probabilistic Causality." In *Causation*, eds Ernest Sosa, and Michael Tooley. Oxford: Oxford University Press, chapter 8, pp. 137–153.

Shapley, L. S., and Martin Shubik. 1954. "A Method for Evaluating the Distribution of Power in a Committee System." *American Political Science Review* 48:787–792.

Sherman, Lawrence W., and Richard A. Berk. 1984. "The Specific Deterrent Effects of Arrest for Domestic Assault." *American Sociological Review* 49:261–272.

Sigelman, Lee. 2006. "Top Twenty Commentaries." *American Political Science Review* 100(3):667–687.

Skidmore, Thomas E. 2009. *Brazil: Five Centuries of Change*. 2nd edn. Oxford, UK: Oxford University Press.

Sniderman, Paul M., and Thomas Piazza. 1993. *The Scar of Race*. Cambridge, MA: Harvard University Press.

Stouffer, Samuel C. 1955. *Communism, Conformity, and Civil Liberties*. New York: Doubleday.

Sullivan, John L., James Piereson, and George E. Marcus. 1979. "An Alternative Conceptualization of Political Tolerance: Illusory Increases 1950s–1970s." *American Political Science Review* 73:781–794.

Tijms, Henk. 2004. *Understanding Probability: Chance Rules in Everyday Life*. Cambridge: Cambridge University Press.

Tufte, Edward R. 1975. "Determinants of the Outcomes of Midterm Congressional Elections." *American Political Science Review* 69:812–826.

Verba, Sidney, Kay Lehman Schlozman, Henry Brady, and Norman H. Nie. 1993. "Race, Ethnicity and Political Resources: Participation in the United States." *British Journal of Political Science* 23:453–497.

Walker, Jack L. 1969. "The Diffusion of Innovations among the American States." *American Political Science Review* 63:880–899.

Wattenberg, Martin P., and Craig Leonard Brians. 1999. "Negative Campaign Advertising: Demobilizer or Mobilizer?" *American Political Science Review* 94:891–899.

Weatherford, M. Stephen. 1992. "Measuring Political Legitimacy." *American Political Science Review* 86:149–166.

Index